THE GENERAL
AND
THE JAGUAR

ALSO BY EILEEN WELSOME

The Plutonium Files:
America's Secret Medical Experiments in the Cold War

THE GENERAL
AND
THE JAGUAR

PERSHING'S HUNT
FOR PANCHO VILLA

A TRUE STORY OF
REVOLUTION AND REVENGE

EILEEN WELSOME

Little, Brown and Company

NEW YORK • BOSTON

Little, Brown and Company
Hachette Book Group USA
1271 Avenue of the Americas, New York, NY 10020
Visit our Web site at www.HachetteBookGroupUSA.com

First Edition: June 2006

Graphic illustrations and maps by Julie Hutchinson

Frontispiece photographs courtesy of Robert Bouilly, Richard Dean, Gloria Roach, Columbus Historical Society Museum, National Archives, Sullivan Museum and History Center at Norwich University, and the University of Nebraska's Gallery of the Open Frontier, an Internet site.

Library of Congress Cataloging-in-Publication Data

Welsome, Eileen.
    The general and the jaguar : Pershing's hunt for Pancho Villa : a true story of revolution and revenge / Eileen Welsome.
        p. cm.
    Includes bibliographical references and index.
    ISBN-10: 0-316-71599-9 (hardcover)
    ISBN-13: 978-0-316-71599-7 (hardcover)
        1. Mexican-American Border Region — History — 20th century.
2. Mexico — History — Revolution, 1910–1920. 3. United States.
Army — History — Punitive Expedition into Mexico, 1916.
4. Pershing, John J. (John Joseph), 1860–1948. 5. Villa, Pancho,
1878–1923. 6. Columbus (N.M.) — History — 20th century. I. Title.
F1234.W375 2006
972.08'16 — dc22

                                                        2005030513

            10 9 8 7 6 5 4 3 2 1

                    Q-MART

            Book designed by Brooke Koven

            Printed in the United States of America

For Libby, Racheal, Courtney, and
in memory of Jay

Contents

Prologue   1

Part I: The Attack

1. *A Microbe Challenges an Elephant*   13
2. *A Diverting Brute*   31
3. *Veracruz*   42
4. *Downhill*   49
5. *Tell President Wilson to Save You*   62
6. *Only One Chance to Die*   71
7. *Rumors, Warnings, and Telegrams*   81
8. *Villa Is Coming Tonight, for Sure*   97
9. *The Fiddler Plays*   108
10. *Very Unnatural Deaths*   136

Part II: The Hunt

11. *To the End of the Furrow*   155
12. *Sunburn, Frostbite, and Blisters*   173
13. *Pershing's Indigestion*   197
14. *No One to Seek For*   225

Part III: Revenge and Revival

15. *Gasoline Baths and Confessions*   237
16. *Jerked to Jesus*   249
17. *A Ripe Pear*   260
18. *A Terrible Blunder*   270
19. *Whore Dust and a Rabid Dog*   287
20. *An Old Colonel*   299
21. *A Reborn Town*   304
22. *Victims or Bandits?*   311
23. *Death Comes for the Horsemen*   318

Acknowledgments   336
Casualties of the Columbus Raid   338
Chronology   340
Notes   341
Selected Bibliography   387
Index   394

Maps

The Raid   109
Punitive Expedition Campaign Route   156
Parral Skirmish   198
Carrizal   271

I can whip Carranza and his entire army, but it is asking a great deal to whip the United States also, but I suppose I can do that, too.

— PANCHO VILLA, *on the eve of the battle of Agua Prieta, October 31, 1915*

THE
ATTACK
COLUMBUS, N.M.
March 9, 1916

PANCHO VILLA
AND HIS TROOPS

Dorados [80 soldiers]

Nicolás
Fernández
[60 soldiers]

Francisco
Beltrán
[125 soldiers]

Pablo
López
[100 soldiers]

Candelario
Cervantes
[80 soldiers]

República Mexicana
EJÉRCITO CONVENCIONISTA

Not shown:
Juan Pedrosa
[40 soldiers]

THE PUNITIVE EXPEDITION

MARCH 1916-
FEBRUARY 1917

GEN. JOHN PERSHING
AND KEY OFFICERS

1st Lt. George Patton
Aide

Col. George Dodd
7th Cavalry

Maj. Frank Tompkins
13th Cavalry

Lt. Col. Henry Allen
11th Cavalry

Capt. Benjamin Foulois
1st Aero Squadron

Maj. Robert Howze
11th Cavalry

Prologue

WHEN THE SOLDIERS saw the yellow lights of the ranch house, they were seized with hunger.

Sometimes they lived for two or three days on a handful of parched corn, and the thought of well-cooked beef and hot green chiles stimulated their dormant hunger pangs. Still, they did not dare spur their tired mounts past the erect back of the colonel and continued to follow him down the hill.

The troops traveled mostly at night, wrapped in their serapes and sunk deep into their saddles, the clink of bridles and the occasional ping of a horseshoe the only sounds on the trail. By restricting their movements to darkness, the soldiers were able to evade the watchful eyes of their enemies, but the cold marches had sapped their strength. Once the sun rose and fell upon their faces, the men slipped into jittery, colorless dreams on the backs of their moving animals. The heat soon brought its own misery: the chafe of rotting clothes and the unbearable itch of unwashed bodies. They were tortured by lice, by mysterious rashes, by abscesses and pimples that covered their buttocks, their groins, their backs. Some were scarred by smallpox, others with poorly healed wounds. They had grown listless and numb, except for the buzz of anger deep in their brains. The ponies and mules suffered, too. White worms bored into their withers and their backs were covered with sores that oozed and spread each evening when the blankets were removed. The little animals did not cling to life and often died with a quick sigh, collapsing under their riders along the frigid mountain passes or in the alkali dust of the desert. While their bodies were still warm, they were butchered and their meat strapped onto the saddles.

Picking their way down the slope, the soldiers leaned back on their mounts to lessen the strain on the front legs of the ponies. Gray *palomas* whirred up in front of their faces and all around them were loose, treacherous rocks and the thorny pull of cactus and mesquite. With dusk came a penetrating cold, but it was early spring and a blue light still lingered in the sky. Mountains curled along the horizon, fields lay waiting for crops, and crows exploded from thickening branches of cottonwood trees, their ragged cries accentuating the stillness of the land.

Drawing near the ranch house, the soldiers could see a young woman, her soft, brown hair tucked up in a dust cap, moving back and forth in the window. They smelled animals dozing in their straw stalls, a tank of drip water, and food; something hot and bubbling on the stove — beans probably, seasoned with a few hunks of last winter's pork, and cornbread or biscuits in the oven. Once again, hunger gripped them.

Colonel Nicolás Fernández dismounted from his horse and walked across the courtyard, passing a small adobe dwelling where the hired help lived, and headed for the main house. He was six feet tall and thin, with fine, almost delicate features and deep-set, gray eyes inherited from German ancestors who had settled in Mexico in the seventeenth century. He wore a khaki uniform, leather leggings that came up over the knees, and on the front of his battered hat was a bronze insignia the size of a silver dollar with the word *Dorado* inscribed in the middle. Though his clothing was dirty and his face hollow with fatigue, he was a commanding presence. He stamped the dust from his boots and knocked.

Maud Wright touched her hand to her cap and jerked open the

door, staring fearlessly at the cloaked visitor. Beyond the colonel, in the courtyard, she counted a dozen soldiers, their dead eyes trained on her. More soldiers were pouring like dark water down the hill. She saw a rind of blue sky, a few faint stars, and no sign of her husband, Ed, or his young friend, Frank Hayden. The two men had left for the nearby town of Pearson earlier that afternoon to buy supplies and she expected them back momentarily. A small tingle of fear ran down her backbone, but she stepped forward and welcomed the officer.

Speaking in courteous, mellifluous tones, he introduced himself and asked her if she would be willing to sell him food.

Puedo comprar comida para mis soldados?

No tengo muchísimo. Pero se doy lo que puedo.

Maud had only enough food for herself, her husband, and the hired family, but said she would give him what she could. The colonel smiled tightly and swept past her into the warm kitchen. He glanced at her son, Johnnie, who was almost two, and already spoke a few Spanish and English words. When Fernández had satisfied himself that no one else was present, he relaxed and grew more talkative. He said that he and his troops were Carrancistas and were hunting the bandit Pancho Villa.

Maud nodded noncommittally. Their small ranch was located in the state of Chihuahua, about a hundred miles south of the New Mexico border. She and Ed had been living in Mexico off and on since 1910, when the Mexican Revolution first began, and knew that their long-term survival depended on their ability to remain neutral and friendly to all sides. In 1913 they had been driven out of the country with more than a thousand other foreigners, but had returned the following year. They had rebuilt their modest herd of cattle and horses and moved back to the ranch in February 1916, just a few weeks earlier, thinking the worst was over.

It was easy to think that way. After years of civil war, the Mexican countryside was bleak and empty. Fields lay fallow and small shops and stores had been looted so often that the shelves were bare. There was no food, no medicine, no clothing. Curtains, carpets, and even the green cloth that covered pool tables had been ripped up and fashioned into clothing. When that was gone, the people had covered themselves with corn sheaves and string. Thousands were dying from *tifus* — typhus. Starvation was claiming an even greater number of lives. "It was the custom," remembered Martin Lyons, a mining engineer, "to pick up little children and people sleeping in doorways and shake them to see if they were dead or alive and many times they were dead."

Bandits of all kinds roamed the countryside, robbing both foreigners and the native born. They extracted "loans" from mine owners and lumber-mill operators and kidnapped wealthy landowners and held them for ransom. Villa's troops were invariably blamed for the depredations, yet the people in the villages and towns knew that the Constitutionalist troops commanded by Venustiano Carranza, the self-proclaimed *primer jefe*, or "first chief" of Mexico, were equally adept at plundering. Even before villagers could recognize approaching horsemen, they hid their few valuables, and men of fighting age took to the hills to keep from being forcibly pressed into service by one side or the other.

Maud was worried; the cattle and horses they had brought to the ranch represented years of hard work, and she found herself growing angry as she wondered whether Fernández planned to take their livestock. Just twenty-seven years old, she was tall and carried herself with an easy, unconscious strength. Her calico dress, soft and shapeless from many washings, hid her long horsewoman's legs and the fullness that had come with the birth of her first child. To the soldiers outside, she must have seemed lovely, with gray eyes and a smile that unfolded slowly and filled her face with happiness. She spoke Spanish fluently, but with an Alabama accent that slowed the quick, tripping syllables.

Maud served the colonel the food she had prepared for her family. While he was eating, Ed and Frank Hayden rode up in the yard leading two pack mules. The two men nodded in a friendly way to the soldiers as they nonchalantly pulled the saddles off their horses and carried them into the house. As soon as they had gone, the troops tore open the packages on the pack mules, looking for food, clothing, money.

Maud introduced the two men to the colonel. Fernández nodded and continued to eat. When he was finished, he rose from the table and announced that he had to feed his horse and asked Ed to show him where the grain was kept. The two men went outside together, and a few moments later Hayden, who was twenty-five and from a wealthy New Orleans family, stood up and followed them.

After they left, soldiers poured into the house, bringing with them the ripe, fruity smell of their unwashed bodies. Johnnie began to whimper. The soldiers ordered Maud to open her storeroom, where she kept a small stock of canned vegetables, flour, beans, corn, salt, and molasses. The men longed to dip their fingers into the molasses but knew one mouthful surreptitiously taken could mean a summary execution before a firing squad or a slow, gagging death at the end of a rope.

The troops loaded up the goods and carried them outside. Maud snatched up her baby and followed them out just in time to see her husband and his friend being led away. They were sitting on one of the pack mules and their hands were tied. She ran to her husband's side.

"They're going to kill you," she said.

He looked down at his young wife. "It's cold out here," he said. "Take the baby and go back inside."

Ed had loved Maud from the moment they met, eight years earlier, in Oklahoma. Her parents had moved to New Mexico to keep them apart, but he was an adventurous, determined man, and followed them there. Fifteen years older than Maud and an Englishman by birth, Ed had arrived in the United States by stowing aboard a ship. One day, they decided to elope and traveled by horseback and then by stagecoach to El Paso, Texas, where they were married on January 10, 1910, before a justice of the peace. The next day they crossed the international bridge and entered the glittering promise of Mexico.

Maud returned to the house, watching in fascinated horror as the soldiers moved from the kitchen to the bedroom area, ripping the linens from her bed, stuffing hairbrushes and combs and mirrors down their shirts. She was too agitated to remain inside and when she went out again, Fernández ordered her to leave the child with the wife of the hired man, and swing up behind him. When she resisted, he told her that he would kill her. Reluctantly, she mounted one of her own horses. Then, softening his tone, Fernández explained that his troops were not Carrancistas at all.

Somos soldados de la División del Norte, he said with slow pride.

The Division of the North was the army of peasants, small farmers, cowboys, and unemployed miners who had flocked to Pancho Villa's side during the revolution. The army had swelled to more than fifty thousand men at its zenith. But Villa had suffered a string of military defeats the previous year and had also fallen out of favor with the United States. Surrounded suddenly by the unmistakable odor of failure, lacking the money to feed and clothe his army or to buy ammunition or arms, he had watched in mounting fury as his soldiers deserted him. Now the celebrated División del Norte had dwindled to a few hundred soldiers and a fiercely loyal cadre of bodyguards known as the Dorados, or "Golden Ones." These were Villa's handpicked men, soldiers who were bronzed and hardened by war and were willing to lay down their lives for their commander. Among this loyal group of men, the U.S. Army would later write, Nicolás Fernández was one of the most devoted.

Before the revolution, Fernández had been the administrator of several sprawling haciendas belonging to Luis Terrazas, Chihuahua's wealthiest citizen and the owner of upwards of fifteen million acres of land. His grandfather's brother had governed Chihuahua in the 1880s. By virtue of his family ties and occupation, he was a solid member of the upper class, wrote one historian, adding, "It's not easy to understand why he took part in the revolution, and even less easy to explain why he joined Villa's forces." Whatever his motives, Fernández's loyalty to General Villa was so strong that U.S. Army officials would note that he "preferred death to separation from his chief." Like Villa, he was a harsh disciplinarian and shunned both tobacco and alcohol.

Fernández picked up his reins and looked back at Maud. Seeing her distress, he reassured her that he only wanted the two American men to help guide the troops out of the heavily patrolled Carrancista territory. Then they would be freed.

It was the evening of March 1, 1916.

IN THE BLUE-BLACK darkness, the steaming breath of the men and the dust from the horses' hooves swirled together, blotting out the nearby landmarks and the distant stars. Maud groped for a rolled, dirty serape she had found on the back of her saddle. Though the serape was worn and offered scant protection from the cold night air, she untied it and drew it down around her shoulders. She breathed in the scent of her horse and watched the jostling troops, hoping to see the pack mule carrying her husband and Frank Hayden. They would be easy to distinguish from the soldiers, many of whom were small and slender as young boys and sat the choppy trot of their mounts with a supple ease.

At daybreak, they reached Cave Valley, a mile-long canyon some thirty miles north of the ranch with steep, heavily forested walls and a stream that meandered along its shadowy bottom. There, they rendezvoused with two to three thousand other Villistas who were camped on either side of the stream, their ponies staked randomly around smoky campfires. The animals stood in motionless dejection, too exhausted even to nibble at the weeds.

Through the smoke, Maud suddenly saw her husband and Frank Hayden. They were still bound and sitting astride one of the mules. She edged her horse closer so they could talk.

Her husband told her that they had been taken to Pancho Villa. "He says he's not going to kill us," Ed said.

"I'm not so sure," she responded, looking bleakly around her.

In the brief moment they were together, they tried to come up with an escape plan but their wits failed them. All they could agree upon was that whoever was freed first would return to the ranch for their little boy.

A guard named Castillo was assigned to Maud and together they rode parallel to and east of the main body of soldiers. From her position she could see the entire column. Her husband and Frank Hayden were in the rear. She waved to them and then turned to ask Castillo a question. When she glanced back again, she saw the two Americans being escorted around a hill by several soldiers. They were visible one moment and the next they were gone. The same soldiers soon rejoined the column without the two captives and Maud felt certain her husband and her friend had been killed. A huge grief began to rise up within her but she pushed it back down. What she needed to survive was not the softness of grief but the hardness that comes from rage.

The column marched in crazy, drunken loops, traveling east, then west, but always north, toward the border. The soldiers wore faded serapes and floppy sombreros plucked from the heads of their deceased compañeros on the battlefield. They were armed with German-made Mausers, Winchester rifles, and old shotguns and pistols, and carried their ammunition in tremendous bandoliers that crisscrossed their chests or in feed bags attached to their saddles. Several pack mules stumbled along at the rear of the column, their backs weighed down with badly rusted machine guns, sacks of corn, jerked beef, and grain for the horses.

That evening they made their first prolonged stop at a small ranch whose owners long ago had fled the turbulent countryside. Maud's body ached with pain and her brain was clogged with fear. Her thoughts had slowed and drifted through her head with no urgency at all. A new guard named Juan Ramón Ruiz, who spoke perfect English, was assigned to look after her. With a chivalry that seemed out of place, he threatened to report any man who swore in her presence. Maud dismounted stiffly, kneading the tight muscles at the small of her back as she looked around. The mountains wavered in the blue air, weightless as dropped silk, and light slanted through the chamisa and sage. She listened to the watery sounds of nesting quail and experienced an acute sense of dislocation. Her husband had been murdered. She had been kidnapped. She worried that she would never again see her son. So how could the outer world still be so tranquil and beautiful?

Her reverie was broken by the sound of cattle being driven into camp. As the herd boiled toward them, the soldiers leaped to their feet and formed a human corral around the animals. When the last cow was driven into their midst, the corral was closed and an officer barked a sharp command. Dozens of lassos sizzled through the air and the cows suddenly found themselves entangled by five or six different ropes. As they struggled to break free of the snares, a small man holding a long-bladed knife appeared at the far end of the corral. He skipped through the churning dust, pausing in front of each animal long enough to run his blade beneath its throat. Some of the cows squealed in surprise and dropped to their knees immediately; others seemed not to know that they had been fatally wounded and continued to pitch and buck, flinging gouts of wet crimson from their gaping throats, until finally they, too, subsided in dreamy bewilderment. Into the squirming knot of bleeding bodies waded soldiers with their own dull knives. Many of the cows not yet dead kicked out desperately at their assailants. Soon enough, though, they lay unmoving on the ground and the men deftly skinned the carcasses and scooped their hands into the warm bellies to fish out the organs. They rammed the chunks onto sharpened sticks and held them out briefly over the campfires. Too hungry to wait for the meat to cook properly, they gobbled it down while it was still raw. After they finished, they returned to the carcasses once more, fingering out the flesh from the cavernous heads and the heavy thighbones and roasting it over the fires.

Maud was stunned by the hunger. She had been slipping into a kind of stupor, but the ferocity of the killing, the squeals of the terrified animals, and the iron smell of blood brought her back to the present. A soldier tossed her a black flour tortilla and a piece of meat. The meat was burned on the outside, raw and bloody on the inside. Maud held it in her hands, feeling the fire's warmth, but could not put it in her mouth. She ate the tortilla and tied the meat onto the back of her saddle.

On the second or third day of the march, she saw Pancho Villa for the first time. He was wearing a small round hat and riding a mule. When he passed Maud, he bowed in her direction, smiled tightly, and rode on. He was much larger than the other soldiers, with heavy slabs of muscle padding his shoulders and a thick, retracted neck that absorbed the gait of the mule and left his massive head motionless, pointed into the wind like a ship's prow. Although Villa chose the mule, he could have ridden any one of his own horses, which carried no food, weapons, or men and pranced alongside the plodding column with coltish happiness. Each night, his horses were fed, curried, and brushed and their hooves inspected for small stones. These animals had one function only: to carry Villa into battle.

Those battles consisted of little more than skirmishes now. Villa had once been hailed in the United States as the "Man of the Hour," but by the time Maud saw him, much of his grandeur and prestige had vanished. Everything had been lost. His amigo, Rodolfo Fierro, a man of "sinister beauty" who killed men just to watch death well up in their eyes, was dead himself, drowned in quicksand, and his most trusted general, Felipe Ángeles, melancholy, incorruptible, and brilliant, had left for Texas, where he was trying to eke out a living on a small ranch. Other high-ranking officers from Villa's army had also fled to the United States or gone over to Carranza's side. Villa had let some of them go with his blessing, but others he had killed himself. He could tolerate almost anything but betrayal.

Maud had lived in Mexico long enough to have heard the many stories recounting Villa's military victories, his courage, his appeal to women. The peasants who thronged to his side had many names for him: *gorra gacha* — slouch hat; *el centauro del norte* — the centaur of the north; *el jaguar indomado* — the untamed jaguar; *la fiera* — the wild beast. Maud sensed immediately the crouching, unpredictable energy from which the latter names were drawn. She had four brothers and could swing an ax, handle a crosscut saw, and drive a team of mules as well as any man. But she found herself afraid of this man, this Pancho Villa. The desultory banter among the troops ceased as he rode by and she realized that his men feared him, too.

Maud worked the leather reins between her fingers, squeezing and releasing the pressure until she felt the animal drop its head and come onto the bit. The horse, at least, was under her control. The column rode on.

PART I
THE ATTACK

→>1<←

A Microbe Challenges
an Elephant

FOR THIRTY YEARS, Porfirio Díaz had been Mexico's benefactor and father, his grizzled head as timeless as the volcanoes that ringed Mexico City. At the age of eighty he had a mountainous nose, a mustache that rushed from its base like two white rivers, and mahogany skin that was still taut and smooth. He had been a firebrand and rebel himself once, sweeping the old guard from power during a revolution that he had stoked and organized in Brownsville, Texas. From roughly 1876 until 1911, Díaz had ruled Mexico, using his federal troops and rural police force to crush rebellions and strengthening his base of support by creating alliances with the elite. He had a realistic, albeit cynical, view of his countrymen and maintained control over his clamorous subjects by using both *pan y palo* — bread and bludgeon.

By the end of Díaz's reign, Mexico had a population of fifteen million. The majority were mestizo — individuals of mixed blood — but one-third were of pure Indian stock. Chihuahua and Sonora, two of the northern states that lay along the U.S. border, were home to the Tarahumara and the Yaquis. The Cora, Huichol, and Tarascans lived along the Pacific coast and in the hills and valleys west of Mexico City. The Mazahua, Nahuatl, and Otomí had settled in the central highlands. The Gulf state of Veracruz was home to the Huastec and Totonac. The Zapotecs, Mixes, Zoque, Huave, and Mixtec, Tzeltal, Tojolabal, Chontal, and Tzotzil lived in the southern states of Oaxaca and Chiapas. And in the Yucatán peninsula, remnants of the ancient Maya had survived.

In 1521, Hernán Cortés conquered Tenochtitlán, the great center of the Aztec civilization and the site of what was to become Mexico City. For the next three centuries, Mexico lived under Spain's rule, which could be harsh, benign, or indifferent, depending upon the financial needs of the mother country and the temperament of the monarch who happened to be in power at the time. When Mexico finally gained its independence, in 1821, political chaos, internal revolts, and repeated clashes with foreign powers ensued. Texas was lost in 1836 to English-speaking colonizers who had been encouraged by Spain to settle the far reaches of its empire. A decade later, following a war with the United States, Mexico lost another huge chunk of territory to its hungry neighbor — millions of acres that one day would become New Mexico, Arizona, California, Nevada, Utah, as well as parts of Colorado and Wyoming.

Exhausted and humiliated, struggling under a huge debt load, Mexico found itself in 1863 once again under the yoke of a European power. This time it was France and Napoleon III, who installed Ferdinand Maximilian von Hapsburg and his wife, Carlota, as emperor and empress of Mexico. The monarchy survived less than five years, defeated by an army led by Benito Juárez, a Zapotec Indian. Afterward, Maximilian was executed, Carlota went insane, the republic was restored, and Juárez was elected president. Juárez died of a heart attack in 1872, after winning a new term in office, and was succeeded by Sebastián Lerdo de Tejada. Four years later, Porfirio Díaz toppled Lerdo from power and began a thirty-year authoritarian regime known as the Porfiriato.

In order to bring Mexico into the twentieth century, Díaz had opened the doors of his country to foreign investors and through them came the Guggenheims, Hearsts, and Rockefellers, Standard

Oil and Phelps Dodge, and hundreds of other, smaller land specula-
tors, wildcatters, miners, ranchers, and farmers. The Americans
built railroads and sank mine shafts, the Spaniards opened small
retail shops, and the French established factories and banks. Vast
cattle ranches emerged along the northern tier of states, and huge
farms devoted to single crops such as sugar, cacao, coffee, and rubber were carved from the tropical lowlands. For his efforts, Díaz
garnered admiration from industrialists, politicians, and even great
literary figures, such as Leo Tolstoy.

His popularity was greatest in Mexico City, where wealthy
foreigners and daughters and wives of native hacendados lived
in walled compounds fragrant with roses, bougainvillea, and hibis-
cus. The melancholy cries of tamale women and scissors grinders
dropped like birdsong into the somnolent quiet of late afternoons,
and in the distant recesses of the lovely old homes, legions of cooks
and nannies and cleaning girls worked soundlessly, faceless and
nameless to the lady of the house. With its colonial languor and lin-
gering Victorian mannerisms, Mexico City seemed like a metropo-
lis enclosed in a shining glass bubble, drifting in its own time.
Wearing Paris gowns, London-made tuxedos, or hand-sewn lace,
the wealthy shuttled to luncheons and teas and dinner parties in
horse-drawn carriages and chauffeur-driven cars. They went horseback riding in Chapultepec Park, organized group outings to the
floating gardens of Xochimilco, and in the evenings flocked to the
opera.

Pouring through their salon windows was a golden sunlight
that made everything seem like a dream. So dreaming, the wealthy
foreigners and their Mexican friends failed to see the horrors in
their midst: the women crouching behind the waiting carriages
picking undigested corn kernels from horse manure; the press
gangs who snatched husbands and sons and young girls off the
street, the men destined for the army and the women for gunpowder factories; the tubercular Indians who clogged the charity wards
and were fodder for medical experiments; the political victims of
the firing squads, who spun on their heels in the liquid light, the
bullets turning them round and round until they collapsed in front
of adobe walls stained dark with old blood.

The modernization and prosperity that Díaz had presided over caused grave dislocation among the country's peasants, factory workers, and even Mexico's elite ruling class. By the time the Mexican Revolution erupted, foreigners controlled most of the country's vast natural resources, its railroads and businesses. "By 1910," writes historian John Mason Hart in a penetrating economic analysis of the revolution, "American real estate holdings totaled over 100 million acres and encompassed much of the nation's most valuable mining, agricultural and timber properties." By contrast, he notes, 90 percent of the Mexican campesino population was landless.

Henry Lane Wilson, the U.S. ambassador to Mexico, lived at the epicenter of the elegant Mexico City society. He was a lawyer by training, patrician in appearance, suave in manners but contemptuous of anyone who questioned Díaz's efforts. Wilson was always immaculately dressed, wearing a silk tie, jeweled stickpin, and a little derby hat that seemed to accentuate his small head. Dangling from a ribbon around his neck was his pince-nez, which he often left perched upon his nose.

Wilson believed that foreign investment had transformed Mexico from a desert to a paradise, and if those investors made handsome profits, well, what was wrong with that? In a congressional hearing held in 1920, after ten years of civil war had left Mexico exhausted and empty, he laid out the reasons for the fratricide with an airy matter-of-factness: "Practically all of the railways belonged to foreigners; practically all of the mines. Practically all of the banks and all of the factories were owned by the French. A very considerable part of the soil of Mexico, probably over a third, was in the hands of foreign-born elements, and practically all the public utilities were in the hands of Americans or British. Naturally this foreign ownership excited hostility, which was not lessened by the circumstance that these interests, or whatever they may have been, had been honestly acquired."

In fact, many of the great haciendas and single-crop estates had been cobbled together from communal lands that had been illegally seized from small farmers and villagers. The peons on the great estates worked in conditions that were as hopeless and cruel as any found in the pre–Civil War South. (The politically connected governor of Sonora, for example, had a torture chamber on the premises for the Yaqui Indians who labored for him.) The peons were often paid in scrip that had to be redeemed at the company stores — the hated *tiendas de rayas* — and when they died, their debts were passed on to their children. An American representative sent to Mexico in 1913 by President Wilson was deeply shocked by what he found:

> I saw this remarkable situation in the twentieth century of men being scattered through the corn fields in little groups of 8 or 10, accompanied by a driver, a cacique, an Indian from the coast, a great big burly fellow with a couple of revolvers strapped to a belt and a blacksnake that would measure eight or ten feet, right after the group that were digging and then at the farther end of the row a man with a sawed off shotgun. These men were put out in the morning, worked under these overseers in that manner, and locked up at night in a large shed with shelves to sleep on. Each had a blanket. They were slaves to all intents and purposes.

In the state of Chihuahua alone, which was the birthplace of the Mexican Revolution, U.S. investors owned more than fifteen million acres. As settlers poured in and put up fences on these lands, resentment increased and led to attacks on foreign-owned properties during the peak years of the revolution. "The attacks were frequently led by local small landowners and other men of note, who usually called themselves Villistas and Zapatistas but who were in fact outside any organized authority," Hart writes.

When disputes emerged between foreign owners and Mexican citizens, Díaz and his circle of government officials — more often than not board members of the biggest companies and handsomely remunerated — sided with the foreigners. In the years leading up to the revolution, a violent strike broke out at a Rockefeller-controlled copper mine and an even bloodier revolt occurred at a textile factory in Veracruz. The growing militancy of factory workers and miners, the resentment among farmers and peasants, and the inability of Mexico's elite to compete with the foreign companies that had gained control of their country created alliances between classes and cultures. Drought, crop failures, mine closures, growing unemployment, and a 50 percent decline in the purchasing power of the peso further contributed to the growing dissatisfaction with the Díaz regime. Thus, when an ineffectual-looking man named Francisco Madero in 1908 called for reform, his call was met with a surprising amount of support.

With the bland features of an accountant, a high-pitched, quavering voice, and a diminutive frame, Madero seemed an unlikely figure to spearhead the violent revolt. In Mexico City, the wealthy tittered behind his back, referring to him as "loco Franco." His grandfather likened his campaign to a "microbe's challenge to an elephant," and his brother, Gustavo, would famously remark, "In a family of clever men, the only fool was President."

The Maderos ranked among the twelve richest families in Mexico and represented "the cream of the enterprising, northern Mexican landed elite," writes Alan Knight, the author of a multivolume history of the revolution. They owned cotton and rubber plantations, mines and lumber mills, textile factories and distilleries. Madero, who had studied in Paris and at the University of California in Berkeley, may have been considered an impractical, dreamy-eyed mystic, but in reality he was an enterprising and resourceful businessman who before the age of thirty had acquired a fortune that was independent of his family's great wealth.

Ambassador Wilson had only contempt for Madero and made no effort to camouflage it when he testified before a congressional hearing investigating losses suffered by U.S. citizens and companies during the revolution: "When Madero first attracted my attention he was engaged in the business of making incendiary speeches, usually of very little intellectual merit, before audiences in remote parts of Mexico. These meetings were usually interrupted by the soldiers, and generally Madero was put in jail, his release following some days afterwards. He never appealed to popular sympathy in Mexico. He was a practically unknown person in public affairs who appeared at the psychological moment." While conceding that

Madero was a man of "absolute personal honesty" and "of excellent morals," Wilson also considered him to be mentally unsound: "Madero was incoherent and illogical in speech, physically in a state of continual contortion, unable to elucidate clearly any opinion which he entertained, easily impressed by fakers and international confidence men." And if all that weren't damning enough, Wilson also reported that Madero believed in the "spectral appearance" of deceased people. "Upon one occasion, he said to me, 'George Washington is sitting right there beside you, listening to every word that you say.'"

Madero was an adherent of Spiritualism, a religious doctrine popular in the nineteenth century whose followers believed that the dead could be contacted. Acting as a "writing medium," Madero channeled the thoughts of Benito Juárez, a prince from the Bhagavad Gita, and his own dead brother. He purified himself by eliminating meat, alcohol, and tobacco from his diet, and eventually came to believe that his mission in life was to free his beloved *patria* from "oppression, slavery and fanaticism."

Madero was convinced Mexico's woes could be traced to a single phenomenon: the concentration of power in the hands of one man. In 1909, he gained national recognition with the publication of an influential book in which he argued that the president of Mexico should be allowed to remain in office for only one term. The following year, he began actively campaigning for president as a member of the Antireelectionist Party. Contrary to what Ambassador Wilson believed, the Mexican people adored Madero and dubbed him the "Apostle of Democracy." In Veracruz, where Díaz's troops had brutally suppressed a labor strike, he told cheering crowds, "You do not want bread, you want only freedom, because freedom will allow you to win that bread."

Porfirio Díaz, like Madero's own family, did not take Madero's bid for the presidency seriously. But when he saw the crowds that Madero was drawing, he threw him in jail. Through the intercession of his family, Madero was released and fled to San Antonio, Texas. There, in the dampness of a boardinghouse, he worked out the details of his revolutionary platform, proclaimed himself as provisional president, and called upon the Mexican people to overthrow the aged dictator. If the revolution were to succeed, Madero knew he would need courageous men to fight the entrenched federal army. One evening, probably in the late summer or early fall of 1910, Abraham González, a close friend of Madero's, went to a darkened house in Chihuahua City to meet with a young man of dubious background who called himself Francisco Villa.

AT FIRST GLANCE, Villa may have struck González as just another member of the lower classes. He was about thirty-two years old at the time, five feet ten inches tall, thick through the middle, with a full head of kinky black hair and a bristly mustache. His eyes were his most memorable feature and were capable of expressing both a childlike innocence and a predator's unblinking cruelty. "His mouth hangs open, and if he isn't smiling, he's looking gentle. All except for his eyes, which are never still and full of energy and brutality," wrote the journalist John Reed, whose articles would make Pancho Villa into an international hero. Carlos Husk, an American physician who worked for a mining company in Mexico and had observed Villa's behavior for many years, had a similar impression: "He has the most remarkable pair of prominent brown eyes I have ever seen. They seem to look through you; he talks with them and all of his expressions are heralded and dominated by them first, and when in anger, or trying to impress some particular point, they seem to burn and spit out sparks and flashes of fire between the hard-drawn, narrowed and nearly closed lids."

Villa's life was such a deeply fused mix of fanciful stories, myths, and half-truths that even during his lifetime biographers and writers had a difficult time trying to decipher the facts of his upbringing. Most historians agree he was born in 1878 on a hacienda in Durango to sharecropper parents and was baptized with the name Doroteo Arango. In his memoirs, which tend to portray him as a heroic figure, Villa says that he came home from the fields to find the hacienda owner, Agustín López Negrete, in his house and his sister, Martina, in tears and clinging to his mother. "My mother wept but spoke firmly, 'Leave my house, Señor. Have you no shame?' I went to my cousin Romualdo Franco's for the pistol I kept there and returned and fired at Don Agustín and hit him three times."

Following the shooting, Villa fled into the sierra, where he eventually joined up with a group of bandits, changed his name to Francisco Villa, and committed a number of crimes. For more than fifteen years he lived an outlaw's life, always on the run, sleeping on the hard ground, a hunted coyote — a fate he once told a friend he would not wish on his worst enemy. But Mexico was on the verge of vast upheaval and the visit from Abraham González would propel him into history as one of the best-known revolutionary leaders of the twentieth century.

Villa would become an idol in his country and the hero of leftists and radicals throughout the world, but the fame would leave him curiously untouched. He was nearly always disheveled looking, as if he had just risen from a nap, and had no use for pomp or show of any kind. When he was not on a military campaign, he was most often seen in a tan, shapeless sweater and the small-brimmed Stetson that he wore pushed back on the crown of his head. Sitting hunched over a newspaper, muttering the words under his breath, Villa seemed like an ordinary man, even a simple one, and such is what he often professed to be to journalists. But, in reality, he was extremely complex and his volatile personality was largely forged in the crucible of humiliation he had endured as a youth. In Porfirio Díaz's class-conscious society, there was no place for smart, ambitious, and penniless boys, and the degradation and shame that Villa and his family endured had created a great, smoldering rage in him. A mocking question, the slightest whiff of condescension, could ignite the fire.

The Spaniards, he believed, had exploited and enslaved the Mexican people; the Chinese were leeches who sent their profits back to China instead of investing in Mexico; and the Catholic priests were simply corrupt. "I believe in God but not in religion," Villa once confided to a magazine journalist. "I have recognized the priests as hypocrites ever since when I was twenty I took part in a drunken orgy with a priest and two women he had ruined. They are all frauds, the priests, and their cloth, which is supposed to be a protection, they use to entice the innocent."

He loved canned asparagus and soda pop and sweets of all kinds, especially peanut brittle, which made his brown, ruined teeth flare with pain. He enjoyed ribald jokes, scratched his feet in public, loved to dance, and shunned intoxicating liquors — a fact that had endeared him to President Woodrow Wilson's venerable secretary of state, William Jennings Bryan, who had had the temerity to serve grape juice at a social function and had earned the undying contempt of the diplomatic corps. Villa suffered from rheumatism caused by years of sleeping on the cold, hard ground and his muscles had been shortened by years of horseback riding, which gave him a shallow stride halfway between a shuffle and a glide. But he was a superb horseman, full of energy and possessing a genuine charisma, and on the battlefield, amid the dust and smoke, his galloping figure would so inspire his men that they would hurl themselves willingly into the withering machine-gun fire of their enemies. He was also a man who kept his word and never forgot a favor.

WRAPPED IN HIS serape, the yellow lantern light flickering, Abraham González described to Villa the inequities that had befallen the people of Mexico. González hardly seemed a revolutionary figure himself. Tall, portly, bespectacled, he was the impoverished son of a wealthy family and had the air of a bumbling but gentle college professor. The transition to violent revolutionary had been an arduous one and González was convinced that his life would be short. *"Yo muero en la raya"* — "I will die on the firing line," he often told friends. His voice was absent of the condescension that Villa was keenly attuned to and by the time he was finished talking, Villa was no longer a bandit but a committed revolutionary:

There I learned one night how my long struggle with the exploiters, the persecutors, the seducers, could be of benefit to others who were persecuted and humiliated as I had been.

There I felt the anxiety and hate built up in my soul during years of struggle and suffering change into the belief that the evil could be ended, and this strengthened my determination to relieve our hardships at the price of life and blood if necessary. I understood without explanation — for nobody explains anything to the poor — how our country, which until then had been for me no more than fields, ravines, and mountains to hide in, could become the inspiration for our best actions and the object of our finest sentiments.

From his exile in the United States, Madero instructed his followers to begin the uprising on November 20, 1910. The initial revolts, small and relatively mild, occurred in small villages and towns of Chihuahua. Eventually the rebellion spread throughout the country. In February of 1911, Madero returned to Mexico from Texas to take charge of the revolution himself. In one of his first armed confrontations, at the town of Casas Grandes, which is about one hundred miles south of the New Mexico border, Madero was soundly defeated, but his followers had witnessed his indomitable courage and their devotion to him grew. He set up his provisional headquarters at Hacienda de Bustillos, west of Chihuahua City, and summoned Villa to a meeting.

Villa was deeply impressed by Madero and maintained affection and loyalty toward him for the rest of his life. "I thought to myself, 'Here is one rich man who fights for the people. He is a little fellow, but he has a great soul. If all the rich and powerful in Mexico were like him, there would be no struggle and no suffering, for all of us would be doing our duty. And what else is there for the rich to do if not to relieve the poor of their misery?'"

On April 7, 1911, Madero and his boisterous army of *insurrectos* began marching toward Ciudad Juárez — a railway hub, port of entry, and conduit for contraband flowing to and from the United States. As the army approached the border town, it swelled with new recruits. Pancho Villa led a column of five hundred soldiers. Pascual Orozco, another revolutionary leader, led a second column of equal strength. "Maderito," as Villa would fondly call him, brought up the rear with fifteen hundred horsemen. With its crowded saloons, gambling dens, and brothels, Juárez was considered one of the most wicked — and exciting — cities in North America. Martín Luis Guzmán, a Mexican writer who participated in the revolution and later wrote a brilliant book describing that period, observed that going from the United States to Juárez was

> one of the greatest sacrifices, not to say humiliations, that human geography had imposed on the sons of Mexico traveling on that part of the border. . . . Streetcars clanged by. People and shapes resembling people crowded the streets. Occasionally above the mass of noise in Spanish — spoken with the soft accent of the north — phrases of cowboy English exploded. The hellish music of the automatic pianos went on incessantly. Everything smelled of mud and whisky. Up and down the streets, rubbing against us, walked cheap prostitutes, ugly and unhappy if they were Mexican; ugly and brazen if they were Yankees; and all this intermingled with the racket and noise of the gambling machines that came from the saloons and taverns.

The *insurrectos* surrounded Juárez on three sides. Instead of pressing forward and attacking the city, the gentle Madero, at the urging of his family, implemented a cease-fire while he tried to negotiate a peaceful settlement with the Díaz government. During the interlude, young boys from El Paso crossed the swaying bridges and sold sardines, cookies, candy, pop, and Washington State canned salmon to the revolutionaries. Similarly, *insurrectos* crossed into El Paso and outfitted themselves with khaki campaign uniforms, underwear, and shoes. "It was estimated some five hundred men outfitted themselves in one day," Mardee Belding de Wetter, an El Paso writer, noted. A Mexican restaurant opened to standing-room-only crowds on San Antonio Street in downtown El Paso and some of the profits were set aside to pay for Red Cross doctors and nurses who would be treating the *insurrectos*.

As the cease-fire continued into its third week, Madero's troops grew restless and their revolutionary fervor began to fade. Some soldiers slipped away in the darkness to return home to their families. In an effort to prevent further demoralization, Pancho Villa and Pascual Orozco decided to attack Juárez without Madero's express approval, figuring that he would join the assault when he saw that their side was winning.

An advance group of about forty men started into Juárez. When a sentry spotted the invaders and fired at them, the battle began. To shield themselves from bullets, the *insurrectos* hacked their way house to house toward the center of the city, blowing out the adobe walls with bombs made from tin cans and gunpowder. Carrying rifles, pistols, machetes, and dull swords, they moved silently down the narrow alleys and unguarded side streets. Crouching behind the cover of buildings and doorways, they would spend a few hours firing at the federal troops and then drift back to the rear for food and a few hours of rest before returning once more to the fighting. Across the river in El Paso, hundreds of spectators flocked to rooftops and the tops of boxcars to observe the battle. The exploding shrapnel was a "beautiful sight," remembered one local judge. Five observers were killed by stray bullets and another twelve wounded, but the casualties did not dampen the crowd's enthusiasm. In the battles to come, enterprising capitalists sold reserved seats on the top of buildings for a dollar a chair and views for twenty-five cents. (If the fight did not materialize, refunds were promised.)

Madero did try to stop the fighting, sending out a white flag and even going so far as to ask the federal commander to order his own men to stop shooting, but when the federal troops obliged, the *insurrectos* kept firing and the opposition had no choice but to pick up their guns again. After several days of heavy casualties on both sides, the federal army surrendered on May 10, 1911.

Afterward Villa went to a local bakery and instructed the baker to begin making bread. At four o'clock in the morning, he returned and gathered up the loaves and first distributed them to the federal prisoners and then took what was left to his own men.

While the victors broke bread with their enemies, an unruly mob in Mexico City halted under the windows of an apartment in the National Palace where Porfirio Díaz lay suffering from a badly ulcerated tooth. "Death to Díaz!" they screamed. The aging dictator, who had created modern Mexico, knew his time had come.

With the help of a loyal general named Victoriano Huerta, he was smuggled out of the city with his family and taken to Veracruz, from where he left for Europe.

MADERO WAS SWORN IN as the new president in the fall of 1911. On the day that he made his triumphant entry into Mexico City, Ambassador Wilson sent a telegram to the State Department in which he predicted continued uprisings and the eventual overthrow of the newly elected leader. "The revolution never ceased," he would say later. "The revolution begun against Díaz continued without any interruption whatever through the time of Madero." Indeed, the flames of rebellion Madero had helped stoke were nearly impossible to quench and fighting broke out again throughout the country. One of the gravest threats came from Emiliano Zapata, a committed revolutionary in Morelos, a small state south of Mexico City. In other parts of the country, frustrated peasants also took land, looted homes, and murdered the wealthy hacendados who had so oppressed them.

In Mexico City, the wives and daughters of those hacendados sipped tea and ate jelly sandwiches and spoke in nervous whispers of the unrest. One lovely woman was forced to flee her plantation when the peons revolted: "They were all right until they suddenly threatened to kill all of us and set fire to the house. My husband frightened them thoroughly with his Mauser pistol. I think he killed one or two. But of course I couldn't stay there."

Madero made many tactical errors as he attempted to restore order. He demobilized the revolutionary troops that had brought him to power, including Villa and his men, yet left the federal army in place. Similarly, he did not purge his administration of the Díaz loyalists. By the end of 1912, writes Hart,

> the Madero government had entered a state of deep crisis. The president could not satisfy the aspirations of the campesino and industrial working classes without betraying himself and his closest associates. He lost the support of the leftist intellectuals

who were at the forefront of the ideological debate with Díaz. He failed to maintain law and order in the countryside and city and therefore could satisfy neither the investors, the industrial elite, nor the great landowners. His open investment policy and reassurances to foreign investors were blunted by his inability to protect their properties from attack. The army officer corps remained hostile toward what it regarded as his upstart and weak leadership.

But perhaps one of his worst decisions was to use Victoriano Huerta, a ruthless holdover from the Díaz regime, to quell the dissent. Then in his late fifties, Huerta was a Huichol Indian born in an adobe hut in the state of Jalisco, located on the Pacific coast. He was a handsome man, with a hard body and hard face, and hands that were soft as kitten paws. Huerta seemed destined for a life of poverty, but in a twist of fate an army general passing through his village hired him as an assistant. With the general as his mentor, Huerta was eventually able to enroll in the prestigious Colegio Militar and embark upon a military career. Among his countrymen, Huerta developed the reputation of a "bloodthirsty animal," but to the foreign diplomats he seemed a gallant and tragically misunderstood figure. A heavy drinker, he favored pulque in his youth, but switched to brandy as his career flourished and his tastes grew more refined. He showed no signs of dissipation from alcohol and friends noticed that the more he drank the clearer his brain seemed to become. "To even his intimates, Huerta was always a silent man," the *New York Times* wrote:

He seldom spoke, and his face was always expressionless, with thin lips tightly drawn together, and his cold, black penetrating eyes looking straight ahead. He was said to have an indomitable will, great strength, fixity of resolve, absolute ignorance of fear and utter mercilessness. There was always the same look in his face, whether he was watching his fighting cocks, himself facing death on the battle line, in the Hall of Congress, or at the El Globo tea rooms in Mexico City, where he was wont to drink large quantities of cognac, during his social talks with members of his Cabinet, who, however, always drank tea.

Madero had an uneasy relationship with Huerta and twice had him removed from command positions. But on Sunday, February 9, 1913, when several army generals launched a coup in Mexico City, he accepted Huerta's help in putting down the rebellion. Thus the inexperienced and naive president unwittingly delivered himself and his vice president, José María Pino Suárez, into the arms of their executioner. During this period, known as the *Decena Trágica,* or Tragic Ten Days, the avenues of Mexico City grew thick with dust and smoke as a rebel army led by dissident generals fought Huerta's troops. Newspapers closed their doors as artillery fire destroyed the beautiful turn-of-the century buildings and elegant homes. Trolleys and buses ground to a halt, mobs roamed the city. Soon the air filled with the stench of decaying human corpses and the bloating bodies of horses caught in the cross fire.

During an apparent lull in the artillery attacks, two U.S. citizens, Josephine Griffith and Minnie Holmes, who lived in a boardinghouse on Calle Ayuntamiento, crept upstairs from the basement to make lunch. "My mother had just entered the kitchen where there was a horrible explosion in front of us, not more than twenty feet from where we sat," remembered Josephine's son, Percy Griffith. His mother's left leg had been so shattered by the blast that her clothing was littered with small pieces of bone. When she awoke, her son gave her sips of whiskey to blunt her pain and then ran out into the street to look for a doctor. Eventually he was able to locate members of the Red Cross, who put the woman on a stretcher and made their way through the streets to a hospital, their white flag ignored as artillery shells exploded around them. When they reached the hospital, they learned no doctor was available. "We waited for probably half an hour when several men finally volunteered to search for a doctor. They brought in a Mexican doctor. I asked him immediately to amputate the leg if that would help save my mother's life. He said he would amputate the leg if it were possible, but that lack of proper assistance would make the task difficult and dangerous as well. My mother called to me several times in moments of consciousness, each time asking me to kill her." Mrs. Griffith survived the amputation only to go into heart failure soon afterward and die about four o'clock that afternoon. When Percy returned to the boardinghouse, he was told the other woman had died, too.

Ambassador Wilson, in a state of high excitement over the bloodshed, asked President William Howard Taft for the authority to help negotiate a peace between the warring factions. Taft refused, unwilling to intervene in Mexico's internal affairs. Still not content to sit on the sidelines, the American ambassador then urged the ministers of Great Britain, Germany, and Spain to request Madero's resignation. "Mr. Wilson, nervous, pale, and with exotic gestures, told us for the hundredth time that Madero was crazy, a fool, a lunatic who could and should be declared incompetent to sit in office. This situation in the capital is intolerable. 'I will put in order [*sic*],' he told us, hitting the table," the Spanish minister said.

Huerta was eager to see Madero's government fall and his purported defense of the capital was merely an effort to maintain the status quo while pressure built for Madero's resignation. Madero's brother, Gustavo, increasingly convinced of Huerta's malevolent intentions, arrested him at gunpoint on February 17. Madero had Huerta brought before him and questioned him closely. After Huerta convinced him of his loyalty, Madero gave the general back his gun and chastised his brother for his impulsive behavior.

But Gustavo, who would be savagely murdered, was correct in his suspicions; a mere twenty-four hours later, Madero and his vice president were arrested. The little president took the detention in stride but Pino Suárez was bewildered and hurt. Once in custody, they agreed to resign under protest — "*Protestamos lo necesario*" — after their military captors promised that they and their families would be allowed to leave the country. The promise of safe passage was also extended to Felipe Ángeles, an army general who had refused to support the coup and was arrested at the same time as Madero and his vice president. The resignations led to a swift series of events that culminated with Huerta being sworn in as the provisional president. Ambassador Wilson, by all accounts a coconspirator in the coup, sent a telegram to Washington, exulting, "A wicked despotism has fallen."

On the evening of February 22, 1913, while Huerta was drinking with his cronies, the two deposed leaders were taken under guard from the National Palace and driven in separate cars to the penitentiary. The vehicles halted and a harsh voice cursed Madero and ordered him from the car. A bullet was fired into the back of his neck and he fell dead to the sidewalk. His vice president, who had an extra moment or two to consider his fate, was dispatched with the same efficiency. The bodies were wrapped in rough gray serapes and taken inside and the two cars were riddled with bullets. Huerta then proclaimed to the world that the two men were killed while allegedly trying to escape, a type of political assassination that was prevalent in the Díaz era and known as the *ley fuga*, or literally, the fugitive law. Several days later, Abraham González, just appointed governor of Chihuahua, was also murdered. The man he had recruited, Pancho Villa, remained at large.

With the assassination of Francisco Madero, the first, relatively bloodless phase of the revolution was over. Mexico was now poised to embark on a second phase that would be longer and much more violent.

✦ 2 ✦

A Diverting Brute

VICTORIANO HUERTA often studied the newspaper photos of President Wilson while nursing a brandy at one of Mexico City's bustling cafés. With his gray hair, colorless skin, and long coat flapping over his knees, the American president seemed to personify wintry El Norte. Huerta had dubbed Wilson the "Puritan of the North," a nickname that captured the physical appearance of the newly inaugurated president, as well as something of his zealous character and religious background. (Wilson's father had, in fact, been a Presbyterian minister in Augusta, Georgia, during the Civil War.) Soon the Mexico City newspapers embellished upon the nickname, referring to Wilson as the "Wicked Puritan with Sorry Horse Teeth." The sobriquet was no more complimentary in the Spanish.

Wilson was sworn into office two weeks after Francisco Madero and his vice president were murdered and was deeply affected by the assassinations. In Madero, he saw a like-minded reformer and detested Huerta for his alleged role in the killings. Still, Wilson was not blind to the usurper's cunning charm and at times confessed to having a grudging admiration for him. "Our friend Huerta is a diverting brute! He is always so perfectly in character; so false, so sly, so full of bravado (the bravado of ignorance, chiefly) and yet so courageous, too, and determined — such a mixture of weak and strong, of ridiculous and respectable! One moment you long for his blood, and the next you find yourself entertaining a sneaking admiration for his nerve. He will not let go till he pulls the whole house down with him. . . . What an indomitable fighter he is for his own hand!"

Wilson was determined to help the Mexican people rid themselves of the new despot and stubbornly refused to recognize Huerta as the president of Mexico. "I will not recognize a government of butchers," he fumed. Sixteen nations had done otherwise, including Great Britain, whose Royal Navy was receiving most of its oil from Mexico. Numerous business leaders in the United States, who had substantial investments in Mexico, were also in favor of recognizing Huerta's government, as was Ambassador Wilson, who sent harried telegrams to Secretary of State William Jennings Bryan and to President Wilson, outlining all the reasons why Huerta should be recognized. "By hesitating too long," he wrote, "we might contribute to the weakening and possible demolition of the present Government and re-invoke movements of disorder and anarchy." The U.S. president believed the ambassador had played an "evil part" in the assassination, and within a few short months he was recalled from his post.

Absent the diplomat, the relations between the Mexican government and the United States devolved to the chargé d'affaires at the U.S. embassy in Mexico City and presidential representatives. By now — superficially at least — Huerta had succeeded in remaking himself as a gentleman. He wore a frock coat, top hat, and spectacles thick as aquarium glass behind which his two eyes swam warily. He was married to a handsome, graceful woman, doted on his eleven children, and gave oddly appealing speeches: *"Yo soy indio"* — "I am an Indian," he declared to a group of Englishmen. "My people are young compared to your Anglo-Saxon race, but in our veins there are the same red corpuscles as in yours." In another speech, he asserted that Theodore Roosevelt was "the Zapata" of the United States.

Huerta preferred his small bungalow to the marble and tapestried salons of the National Palace and frequently conducted the affairs of state from the backseat of his automobile or a table at the Café Colon. Breakfast often consisted of a raw egg and a glass of claret followed by a shot of brandy. Mexico City's urbane diplomats joked that the only "foreigners" Huerta really valued were Hennessy and Martell.

Although far more experienced and ruthless than Madero, Huerta had an equally difficult time subduing the various insurgency movements. The threat was most serious in the northern tier of states, where several revolutionary leaders, including Venustiano Carranza and Pancho Villa, were amassing support. To increase the size of his federal army, Huerta's press-gangs began kidnapping every able-bodied man they could find. Residents were snatched on their way to the market, to the post office, and as they were leaving the hospital. "After the bullfight on Sunday," wrote Edith O'Shaughnessy, wife of the American chargé d'affaires, "seven hundred unfortunates were seized, doubtless never to see their families again. . . . At a big fire a few days ago nearly a thousand were taken, many women among them, who are put to work in the powder mills. A friend told me this morning that the father, mother, two brothers, and the sister of one of her servants were taken last week. They scarcely dare, any of them, to go out after dark. Posting a letter may mean, literally going to the cannon's mouth."

John Lind, the former governor of Minnesota, was one of President Wilson's handpicked representatives to Mexico. He was completely devoid of diplomatic experience and could not speak Spanish. With the help of interpreters, Lind presented the Huerta government with a Wilson-drafted settlement that called for an immediate cessation to fighting, the holding of early and free elections (in which Huerta would refrain from becoming a candidate), and the willingness of all factions to abide by the results.

Huerta, naturally, rejected the settlement. Lind was told to resubmit the offer and add something extra to the pot: the U.S. government, he was instructed to say, would use its influence with American bankers to make a loan to the new government if free and open elections (without Huerta) were held. This proposal, considered by many to be little more than a bribe, was also icily rejected.

President Wilson then went before Congress and described his failed mission. He reaffirmed his good intentions and said there was nothing more he could do for the Mexican people but "await the time of their awakening to the actual facts. We cannot thrust our good offices upon them. We can afford to exercise the self restraint of a great nation." His position in the future would be one of "watchful waiting."

Huerta then announced his plan to hold an election on October 26, 1913. The news buoyed Wilson and his aides, who believed the canny dictator had been converted to the principles of democracy after all. But the hope was dashed when Huerta dissolved Mexico's Constitution and what remained of the duly elected congress and proceeded to invalidate the election results, saying the returns were too small to reflect the will of the people. Huerta then announced that he would remain in office until the rebel elements were pacified.

In response, the State Department distributed a circular to governments throughout the world, laying out in blunt terms the new U.S. position toward Mexico: "The present policy of the United States is to isolate General Huerta entirely; to cut him off from foreign sympathy and aid and domestic credit, whether moral or material, and to force him out."

In keeping with that philosophy, the United States used its influence to get a loan to Mexico from a consortium of international bankers pared down from 150 to 50 million dollars. U.S. warships were sent to Mexico, where they idled within view of the coastlines — purportedly to help citizens who were fleeing the country, but clearly meant to intimidate the Huerta regime. And to further weaken the government, Wilson decided to lift the embargo on munitions that had been put in place by President Taft's administration. Soon guns and weapons began flowing to rebel troops across the border. Wrote Secretary of State Bryan, "Settlement by civil war carried to its bitter conclusion is a terrible thing, but it must come now whether we wish it or not."

The move dismayed the foreign diplomats in Mexico City. But

Pancho Villa was thrilled: "I think President Wilson is the most just man in the world. All Mexicans will love him now, and we will look on the United States as our greatest friend, because it has done us justice."

VILLA HAD RETURNED to private life after Madero had been sworn into office, opening four prosperous butcher shops in Chihuahua City. At one point, President Madero had called upon him to help the then loyal Victoriano Huerta in stamping out local revolts and Villa had responded with alacrity, rounding up his old troops and placing himself under Huerta's command. But Huerta had treated Villa with contempt, referring to him sarcastically as *el general honorario*. Villa, in turn, began referring to Huerta as *el borrachito* — the little drunkard. "Not once in all the times I spoke with him was he altogether sober," Villa said in his memoirs, "for he drank morning, afternoon, and night."

One morning, raging with fever, Villa had been summoned to Huerta's headquarters, placed under arrest for taking a horse, and escorted to an adobe wall where a firing squad awaited him. At the last minute he received a reprieve from Madero and was sent to prison instead. There he languished for months, improving his reading skills and writing long beseeching letters to Madero in which he begged him for help. Finally, six weeks before Madero was assassinated, Villa disguised himself as a lawyer and escaped from prison. He walked out the front gate, wearing a black overcoat and dark glasses and carrying a handkerchief in front of his face.

He made his way to El Paso, where he took up residence at the Hotel Roma, checking in under the name Doroteo Arango. He kept a box of homing pigeons in his room, telling people that he had a very delicate stomach and had to live on squab, but in reality used the birds to send messages to friends in Chihuahua. He rode around town on a motorcycle and went to the Emporium, a Greek-owned bar and club where Mexican expatriates congregated, and to the Elite Confectionery, where he bought ice cream and peanut brittle and strawberry pop. "He had fallen back into obscurity, wore a bowler hat — no better sign there is of abdication from romantic dreams — and his career seemed over. But the fates were to give him another chance, and he was the man to take that chance," observed James Hopper, a correspondent for *Collier's*, who wrote many insightful pieces about the Mexican Revolution and the border.

When Villa learned that Huerta had assassinated his beloved "Maderito," he vowed to topple him. On March 6, 1913, two weeks after the assassinations, Villa and eight companions splashed across the Rio Grande on horseback, carrying rifles and ammunition, two pounds of sugar, coffee, and a pound of salt. As Villa made his way south, he recruited men and collected horses and arms to rebuild his army. Within eight months, the entire state of Chihuahua would be under his control and the uneducated Villa — who had learned how to sign his name from a store clerk and copied it over and over in the sand until he got the elaborate curves and flourishes just right — would find himself building schools, printing money, enacting price controls on bread, meat, and milk, and putting his peon army to work cleaning the streets and operating the local power plant.

In the early months of his campaign, Villa used guerrilla tactics to weaken Huerta's army, mounting surprise attacks in the middle of the night and then melting back into the countryside. As his fame spread, other rebel leaders joined his army, anxious to save themselves from annihilation and convinced that cooperation was the only way to defeat Huerta. Huerta dispatched his sharpshooters to kill Villa, but no one seemed to be able to hit him. Oblivious to the danger, Villa rode up and down behind his artillery guns, shouting out directions: *"Mas derecho! Poco mas izquierda!"* — "More to the right! A little more to the left!"

By late September of 1913, the División del Norte had a troop strength of six to eight thousand men and Villa was ready to lay siege to the city of Torreón, an important source of supplies and a communications hub located in north-central Mexico. Attacking at night, the Villistas captured the federal army's artillery and took command of the outlying hills. After a few days, Torreón weakened and fell.

Villa imposed a rigid discipline upon his troops and began strategizing for his next battle. He set his sights on Ciudad Chihuahua, the state capital, some 250 miles south of El Paso. On November 5, the Villistas launched their attack. This time the entrenched federal army fought hard, and successfully repelled Villa's soldiers. After a five-day siege, the rebel forces withdrew.

Villa then executed a dazzling maneuver that would propel him onto the world stage. Capturing a supply train, he loaded his troops onto it and proceeded north toward the city of Juárez. Pretending to be the colonel in charge of the captured train, he sent a message to the federal commander in Juárez informing him that the engine had broken down and asking him to send another engine and five cars. After receiving them, Villa wired another message to Juárez: "Wires cut between here and Chihuahua. Large force of rebels approaching from south. What shall I do?" The commander in Juárez instructed him to return and he obeyed, confirming his whereabouts at every stop along the way. Military authorities in Juárez, thinking Villa's men were still laying siege to Chihuahua, enjoyed a leisurely dinner and entertainment. At one o'clock on the morning of November 15, 1913, Villa's troops rolled into the city and routed the surprised federal troops with a minimum of bloodshed. Villa immediately shut down the saloons, swept up the silver from the gambling tables, ordered his men to shoot any looters, and made plans to go to a cockfight, one of his favorite pastimes.

The capture of Juárez was condemned as "shameful" by Mexico City's upper class, who still believed war was a gentlemanly pursuit to be conducted only in daylight hours. But the U.S. Army generals who sat on the American side of the border watching the revolution were delighted. The War Department's chief of staff, Brigadier General Hugh Scott, a bluff old Indian fighter with a walrus mustache and a bad case of lumbago, wrote, "The taking of Juárez by Villa was a beautiful piece of strategy. . . . Altogether he is the strongest character yet developed in Mexico in the present Revolution, and may yet develop into a ruler, although he is said to have no ambition to be president of Mexico, on account of his conviction of lack of sufficient education."

Scott, who prided himself on educating "primitive people,"

quickly developed a rapport with Villa, whom he hoped to enroll one day in military school in Leavenworth. Villa was a great sinner, Scott often said, but he also had been greatly sinned against.

"Civilized people look upon you as a tiger or a wolf," Scott once told him.

"Me?" Villa exclaimed.

"Yes, you."

"How is that?"

"Why, from the way you kill wounded and unarmed prisoners."

Scott gave Villa a booklet on the rules of engagement, a treatise that amused him no end, wrote journalist John Reed. "It seems to me a funny thing to make rules about war. It's not a game," Villa mused.

Villa was a strong and ruthless leader. Disobedience brought swift and merciless justice. One correspondent watched in amazement as he stepped onto the balcony of his office and calmly shot one of his soldiers, who was wasting ammunition by firing his gun into the air. As was the custom on both sides, Villa promptly executed captives but his economical way of doing so horrified the civilized world: he would line up his prisoners three or four deep and dispatch them with one bullet through the head. Once he had bent men to his will, however, he treated them with a lofty generosity. He paid his troops whenever possible and took care of their widows if they were killed.

As Villa's movement grew, representatives from Venustiano Carranza approached him and asked him to join with them in the fight to topple Huerta. Villa initially scoffed at Carranza's overtures, pointing out that Carranza had no military victories to speak of. But Villa, acutely aware of his own lack of education and political experience and cognizant of the fact that he needed help to finish off Huerta, eventually decided to ally himself with Carranza.

The two insurgent leaders came from very different backgrounds. Carranza was a former governor and hacendado from Coahuila, a state that lay east of Chihuahua and south of Texas. Texas had once been part of Coahuila, and Carranza, a voracious reader of history and highly nationalistic, still resented the loss. He wore tinted glasses, a black frock coat, and a long white beard, which he combed with his fingers while talking. "Above all, he is white, pure white," observed writer Vicente Blasco Ibáñez. "His Spanish ancestors came from the Basque Provinces and from the Basques he inherited the vigorous health and the silent tenacity of that race." He was tall and well muscled for his age, but his grandfatherly appearance was marred by a red-veined, bulbous nose. Two decades older than Villa, Carranza was a shrewd and opportunistic politician who gave lip service to the revolutionary cause and the slain Madero, but remained fixed upon his own political agenda. Edith O'Shaughnessy, the wife of the U.S. diplomat, had observed Carranza's movement with dismay. "Those who have watched Carranza's long career, say that a quiet, tireless sleepless greed has been his motive force through life, and his strange lack of friendliness to Washington is accompanied by the fact that he really hates foreigners, any and all, who prosper in Mexico."

Villa used long trains to transport his soldiers from city to city. On top of the boxcars rode pigs, chickens, children, and *soldaderas* — wives, daughters, and even grandmothers who served as helpmates and nurses and fellow fighters. His pride and joy was his hospital train, which consisted of forty enameled boxcars staffed with Mexican and U.S. physicians and supplied with the latest surgical appliances. With its bright blue crosses and the words *Servicio Sanitario* stenciled on the sides, the hospital train followed Villa's troops into battle and transported the most severely wounded back to hospitals in the cities. He had a boxcar for correspondents, a boxcar for moving-picture men, a boxcar for his cannons and extra railroad ties, and a caboose, which he used for his headquarters. Painted gray and decorated with chintz window curtains, the caboose was big enough for a couple of bunks and a partitioned area for his cook. In the early days, Villa would sit in his caboose in his blue underwear while as many as fifteen generals lounged at his feet to argue and plot strategy for their next campaign. Hanging on the walls above them were pictures of Villa on one of his frothing horses; the querulous Don Venustiano; and Rodolfo Fierro, Villa's handsome and ruthless friend, who was christened *el carnicero* — the butcher — after he had made a sport of shooting three hundred prisoners as they tried to escape over a corral wall.

If Fierro represented the dark side of Pancho Villa's nature, then the aristocratic and exquisitely mannered Felipe Ángeles represented the good. Ángeles, the army general who had been detained along with Madero and his vice president, had been educated at the Colegio Militar and excelled at mathematics and artillery science. He was in the federal army when the revolution broke out and offered to fight against the revolutionaries. But he soon became personal friends with Madero during the latter's brief presidency. After Madero was killed, Ángeles joined Don Venustiano's counterrevolution. Disgusted by Carranza's opulent lifestyle and the preening sycophants who surrounded him, Ángeles eventually aligned himself with Pancho Villa's División del Norte. Villa revered Ángeles's intellectual and military capabilities and his rigorous honesty. While he considered himself far too ignorant and uneducated to govern a turbulent country like Mexico, Villa often thought Ángeles could be the next president.

Writer and revolutionary Martín Luis Guzmán met Villa for the first time in Juárez, in a poorly lit room off a muddy side street. Surrounded by his Dorados, Villa was resting on a cot in a back room, fully clothed, wearing his hat, coat, pistols, and ammunition belts. Guzmán studied Villa closely and afterward recorded the strange, unsettled emotions that he felt: "We came fleeing from Victoriano Huerta, the traitor, the assassin, and this same vital impulse, with everything that was good and generous in it, flung us into the arms of Pancho Villa, who had more of a jaguar about him than a man. A jaguar tamed, for the moment, for our work, or for what we believed was our work; a jaguar whose back we stroked with trembling hand, fearful that at any moment a paw might strike out at us."

But if Villa was a jaguar, then he was a jaguar with rapidly developing political instincts. From the beginning, he went out of his way to accommodate U.S. investments and property in Mexico. He knew that he needed to maintain good relations with the United States in order to sell the crops and cattle from the confiscated estates of the *ricos* — the wealthy — across the border and to purchase the armaments and supplies vital to his army. And, despite the rabid nationalism of his countrymen, he also understood intuitively that the ultimate victor in the revolution would need the recognition and support of the U.S. government to survive.

When his soldiers entered Torreón, for example, the residents girded themselves for the looting that inevitably accompanied the occupying forces. But to everyone's surprise, Villa issued strict orders against looting and executed those who disobeyed. George Carothers, a rotund ex-grocer and businessman who eventually was assigned to Villa as a special State Department agent, remembered: "By 11 o'clock at night the city was very quiet and guards stationed on every street corner. The next morning at daylight I sent a communication to General Villa asking protection for Americans and their property, and within an hour a squad of twenty-five men and an officer appeared with a letter from Villa stating that he sent these men to guard American property and that they would take orders from me as to where to be stationed." Such protections played extremely well in Washington.

As the rebel armies gained strength, Victoriano Huerta's hold on Mexico began to weaken. But the United States was not the only country that was monitoring the Mexican civil war; Germany, too, had been studying the anarchy, and rather than trying to bring about a peaceful resolution, saw the strife as an opportunity. ("Whenever war occurs in any part of the world, we in Germany sit down and make a plan," historian Barbara Tuchman quotes Kaiser Wilhelm as saying.) The German ambassador to Mexico offered to supply Huerta with munitions provided Huerta would cut off oil to Great Britain if war in Europe broke out. Huerta agreed and three ships were loaded with arms and began chugging toward Veracruz. It would prove to be an extremely risky move — one that would lead to a full-scale invasion.

❧ 3 ❧

VERACRUZ

THE MORNING OF APRIL 9, 1914, dawned calm in Tampico, a malodorous and malaria-ridden port on the Gulf coast bristling with smokestacks and tank farms and refineries belonging to the world's largest oil companies. Although the city had been the scene of sporadic fighting between the federal troops and rebels, everything appeared quiet as Ensign Charles Copp and crew members from the warship *USS Dolphin* rowed toward the shore, the only sound the flutter of two American flags hanging from the front and rear of the boat.

Upon reaching shore, the sailors tied up, retrieved supplies from a warehouse, returned to the dock, and began loading them into the boat. Suddenly a squad of federal soldiers surrounded them and placed them under arrest for being in a military zone. When a higher-ranking Huertista officer learned of the capture, he was dismayed, and instructed that the Americans be escorted at once back to the landing. Their release soon followed, along with profuse apologies for the incident.

The matter might have ended there, but the irascible American admiral Henry T. Mayo, whose eyes appeared to have been crushed into a permanent squint by the weight of his huge forehead, was infuriated. Two of his sailors had been ordered from a boat flying the American flag, which under international law was considered roughly equal to abducting them from the territory of a sovereign nation. Mayo demanded a formal apology, severe punishment for the officer who committed the "hostile act," and a twenty-one-gun salute to the American flag. Afterward, he said, the U.S. ship would return the salute.

In a matter of hours, the situation escalated into an international crisis. President Wilson interpreted the event as another example of Huerta's contempt for the United States. Claiming it was not an "isolated case," he asked Congress for approval to use armed force to "obtain from General Huerta and his adherents the fullest recognition of the rights and dignity of the United States." Desperate to avoid a showdown, Huerta mulled over ways that he could comply with the U.S. demand and still hold on to his pride and his presidency. After nearly two weeks. Huerta finally capitulated and agreed to salute the U.S. flag provided the United States signed a protocol promising to salute the Mexican flag in return. But Secretary of State Bryan refused, saying that "it might be construed as recognition of the Huerta government."

The stalemate grew more complicated when the United States learned that the *Ypiranga,* a ship carrying weapons and millions of rounds of ammunition for Huerta, was on its way to Veracruz.

VERACRUZ, WRITES Martín Luis Guzmán, was a city periodically swept by "impotence, humiliation, and tragedy." During its four-hundred-year history, it had been sacked by buccaneers, bombarded by foreign powers, and had suffered through periodic bouts of cholera and yellow fever and malaria. In 1519, it had served as the launching point for Hernán Cortés. In 1847, U.S. General Winfield Scott waded ashore with his troops, killed thousands of civilians, then marched on to Mexico City. And in 1864, the French arrived, intent upon establishing a monarchy. Through it all, Veracruz had survived, and by 1914 the population had grown to roughly forty thousand. Located on the Gulf coast, south of

Tampico and about two hundred miles east of Mexico City, Veracruz seemed picturesque, with its glowing pastel houses, green
wooden balconies, and graceful, colonial-style buildings. Coconut
palms waved in the salty air and the great, snowy peak of Cit-
laltépetl, fifty miles inland, offered a shimmering vision to those
below of something dreamed about on hot summer days: cool air
and free ice. Each evening an excellent brass band played in Plaza
Constitución and the soothing, sweet sound of mandolins and gui-
tars spilled from open windows. Surrounding the plaza were the
Municipal Palace, the Parochial Church, and the Hotel Diligen-
cias. Flower girls, picture postcard sellers, and young bootblacks
threaded their way among diners and the coffee drinkers who sat at
tables beneath the shaded porticoes.

But Veracruz's charm was quickly lost on foreign visitors, especially those from the soap-crazed land of the Great Puritan, who
minced through the streets, swatting flies and holding their breath.
"Veracruz was filthy, foul smelling and incredibly ill kept," writes
author Jack Sweetman. "Waste disposal was left entirely to the
zopilotes, the great, black vultures by which Veracruz was overrun.
Protected by a municipal ordinance imposing a fine of five pesos on
anyone doing a zopilote harm, they flocked along the seawall,
perched on the cupolas of the Municipal Palace and vied with
packs of mongrel dogs at the refuse heaps which littered the city."
Near the entrance to the harbor was the lugubrious Castillo San
Juan de Ulúa, a decaying edifice built by Cortés's troops that was
still being used to house prisoners, most of whom had merely tried
to escape conscription. Edith O'Shaughnessy had walked the parapets in her black Jeanne Hallé hobble skirt and a black tulle hat.
"Peering down in the darkness, thirty feet or so of any one of these,
there would be, at first, no sound, only a horrible indescribable
stench mingling with the salt air. But as we threw boxes of cigarettes into the foul blackness there came vague, human groans and
rumbling noises, and we could see, in the blackness, human hands
upstretched or the gleam of an eye. If above, in that strong norther,
we could scarcely stand the stench that arose, what must it have
been in the depths below?"

Rear Admiral Frank F. Fletcher, a trim Annapolis graduate with melancholia-tinged eyes, commanded the U.S. naval forces at Veracruz. He was a humane and cultivated man, who, unlike his predecessors, wanted to avoid bloodshed and prevent the lovely old town from being bombarded into rubble. As he studied Veracruz through his binoculars, he noticed dirty white waves racing toward the shore and the sky filling with clouds. Far out in the harbor, buoys began to clang. A storm was blowing in. Fletcher realized that if he was going to take the customhouse, he would have to do it quickly. The plan, transmitted to Fletcher from Washington, was to take control of the town and prevent the munitions from reaching Huerta's troops. At eleven o'clock, eight hundred heavily armed U.S. marines and sailors began rowing toward the shore. The Veracruzaños, unaware that anything was amiss, went about their late-morning chores. Donkeys laden with milk jars clip-clopped through the cobblestoned streets, *tortilleras* fired up their braziers, and the café-goers turned the sea-damp pages of their newspapers.

General Gustavo Maass, the military commander of Veracruz, wired Mexico City for instructions on how to handle the invasion and then hurried to the military barracks where two infantry battalions were stationed. Maass suspected that his superiors in Mexico City would order him to withdraw after putting up a respectable fight, so he dispatched a small contingent of soldiers in the direction of the harbor, freed some captives being held at a local prison, and armed the militia. As he suspected, orders soon came for him to fall back to a village ten miles inland and he obeyed, leaving the volunteers, prisoners, and a small contingent of soldiers to defend the city.

The Veracruzaños distributed themselves through the town with no plan other than to kill as many of the foreigners as they could. Armed with Mausers and machine guns and ancient dueling pistols, they climbed up onto the roofs and took up positions around the plaza. Silently, they watched as American sailors and marines disembarked and advanced slowly, passing by cantinas and pulquerias. The marines were dressed in floppy hats and khakis and the sailors had dyed their navy whites with coffee grounds so that they would make less conspicuous targets.

The marines were to take the railroad station, the cable office,

and the ice plant. The sailors were charged with securing the telegraph office, post office, and the Hotel Terminal, where they would
set up a semaphore on the roof to communicate with Admiral
Fletcher. A young naval officer named George Lowry was given the
plum assignment of capturing the customhouse. As he and a small
contingent of men advanced across the broad promenade toward
the building, the warmth seemed to have gone out of the air and an
eerie silence reigned. Then a sniper's bullet whizzed through the air.
All at once, gunfire roared from parapets and rooftops, windows,
doors and alleys. One sailor was shot in the head and toppled
over dead. Several others were wounded and fell to the pavement,
writhing and screaming in agony. Lowry and his men raced for
cover, dragging their injured and bleeding comrades with them.
They broke a window on the side of the customhouse and heaved
themselves inside. Fletcher, monitoring the battle from the deck of
one of the battleships, heard the small-arms fire and sent four hundred additional men ashore. Over the next two days, another three
thousand men would be ordered into the city.

The U.S. forces fought block by block, house to house, basement
to rooftop. One Veracruzaño sat on his balcony and calmly read
his newspaper, periodically stopping midsentence to shoot at the
passing Americans. Other residents fired at the passing troops from
their basements. Both sides fought with extraordinary bravery.

In the midst of all this, the *Ypiranga* arrived. An American officer boarded the ship and explained that the customhouse had been
seized to prevent the ship's huge cache of arms from reaching the
Huerta government. The German captain agreed to remain in the
outer harbor and then he quietly set sail for another Mexican port,
where he unloaded more than a thousand crates of munitions.
Ironically, the munitions had been purchased from the Remington
Arms Company in the United States and then routed through
Hamburg to escape the embargo, since lifted.

The fighting in Veracruz continued for nearly two days. By the
time the U.S. forces gained control of the town, 126 Mexicans lay
dead and another 195 wounded. The Americans also suffered significant losses: 17 marines or sailors were killed and 63 wounded.
In Washington, members of the press corps noticed that President

Wilson appeared to become almost physically ill as reports of the carnage rolled in.

Carranza condemned the invasion as an attack upon Mexico's sovereignty. But Villa reassured George Carothers that he wasn't going to let Huerta draw him into the conflict. "As far as he was concerned," Carothers reported, "we could keep Veracruz. . . . He said that no drunkard, meaning Huerta, was going to draw him into war with his friend." To his followers, Villa gave a more practical and less obsequious explanation: "It is Huerta's bull that is being gored."

Losing a million pesos a day in revenue, his army demoralized by losses, Victoriano Huerta finally resigned his post in July of 1914 and departed for Europe, arriving just in time to witness the outbreak of World War I. The resignation may have saved both his dignity and his neck. "By precipitating a conflict with the United States," wrote one observer, "he retires with a shred of honor; beaten by the Constitutionalists, he would have been disgraced definitely, if not hanged with the same finality."

But Huerta's departure did not bring peace to Mexico or the stability that President Wilson had hoped for. The relationship between Villa and Carranza was unraveling quickly and on September 23, 1914, Villa publicly repudiated Carranza. In an effort to avoid more bloodshed, 150 revolutionary leaders from throughout Mexico held a convention beginning in October of 1914 in Aguascalientes, a small city located in the center of the country known for its hot springs and beautiful textiles. The participants included Villistas, Carrancistas, and a third block of revolutionaries who favored neither side, but were intent upon their own agendas.

At the urging of Felipe Ángeles, Emiliano Zapata, who controlled the state of Morelos, located south of Mexico City, sent twenty-six representatives to the convention. Land was at the heart of Zapata's rebellion. The residents of his village, Anenecuilco, had grievances that went back to 1607, when they received a land grant from the Spanish viceroy. The owners of a nearby hacienda immediately seized the property, and the villagers had been fighting to get it back ever since. At the outbreak of the revolution, Zapata had issued his Plan de Ayala, which had three major points: restitution for villages and citizens whose property and water had been illegally seized; expropriation of one-third of the disputed lands accompanied by compensation to current owners; and finally, seizure of the remaining two-thirds for "war indemnities" if the owners failed to cooperate.

Although Zapata was wary of making alliances with other revolutionary leaders, he was partial to Villa because Villa had also shown himself to be in favor of land reform, confiscating huge estates in northern Mexico and promising to divide the land between villagers and his soldiers when the revolution was over. The convention delegates overwhelmingly adopted the Plan de Ayala — a move that Zapata undoubtedly found gratifying — but the primary focus remained on preventing a new civil war. After numerous debates and emotional speeches, the delegates concluded that the only way to restore peace to Mexico was to have both Villa and Carranza resign. Villa agreed and took the idea one step further: Why not have both him and Carranza shot?

Carranza, however, was not amenable to the idea of resigning or being shot. After more wrangling, the leaders of the revolutionary convention, which according to the Mexican Constitution represented the legitimate government at that time, declared Carranza in rebellion and named Villa as commander in chief.

So began the most deadly phase of the revolution. "As in the history of most revolutions, the bloodiest phase of the Mexican Revolution occurred not when revolutionaries were fighting the old regime but when they began to fight one another," observes historian Friedrich Katz. "In 1913–1914, when they fought against the federal army, revolutionary volunteers confronted mostly unwilling, forcibly impressed conscripts. This time volunteer would fight mostly against volunteer."

Carranza's Constitutionalist forces and Villa's Conventionalist army began fighting each other with a savagery that had not been seen on the North American continent since the Civil War. Chief among the killers would be Pancho Villa himself.

⟶4⟵

DOWNHILL

As COMMANDER IN CHIEF of the armed forces, Villa's first task was to march south and take control of Mexico City. Carrancista soldiers garrisoned in nearby towns fled before his troops and crowds showered them with flowers. Battle hardened and confident, enjoying an almost fanatical loyalty from his men, Villa was at the peak of his power and the División del Norte had an aura of invincibility that was demoralizing to opposing forces. In keeping with his stature, Villa upgraded the private train from which he directed his battles, one boxcar serving as his office, sitting room, and bedroom; a second containing barbershop, bath, and a player piano; a third reserved for siestas; and a fourth his dining room, staffed by dark-eyed beauties.

On December 2, 1914, in the village of Xochimilco on the outskirts of Mexico City, he met with Emiliano Zapata. Although the two revolutionaries had exchanged correspondence and knew a lot about each other, it was the first time they had actually had a face-to-face meeting.

"Sr. General Zapata, today I realize my dream of meeting the chief of the great Revolution of the South," said Villa.

"And I now realize that same dream regarding the chief of the Northern Division," Zapata responded.

Their joint public appearance sent a strong message to the rest of the country, as well as the international community, that the Villistas and Zapatistas — not the Carrancistas — represented the will of the Mexican people and would triumph in the new civil war. Followed by adoring crowds, the two adjourned to a nearby school for a conference. "For a half-hour, they sat in an embarrassed silence, occasionally broken by some insignificant remark, like two country sweethearts," a U.S. representative later wrote. In an effort to lighten the atmosphere, Zapata called for a bottle of cognac. Reluctantly, Villa took a few swigs, turning red faced and spluttering from the liquor.

Several days later, they rode through the streets of Mexico City to the National Palace, two splendid figures on horseback, sitting relaxed in their saddles, right hands casually holding the reins. Zapata wore tight-fitting charro pants, a short jacket, a scarf, and a huge sombrero that shaded his perpetual scowl. Villa was dressed up, too, his bulk squeezed into a military tunic, his huge head topped by a visored cap. In addition to their superb horsemanship, the two charismatic leaders had many things in common: a keen intelligence, a genuine concern for the poor, suspicious natures that bordered on paranoia, and fierce hatred of the Carrancistas. They are "men who have always slept on soft pillows," Villa sneered. "How could they ever be friends of the people who have spent their lives with nothing but suffering?" Zapata agreed. "Those cabrones, as soon as they see a little chance, well, they want to take advantage of it and line their pockets!"

When Villa and Carranza parted ways, the Villistas and Zapatistas, along with other generals friendly to their cause, controlled most of the country, including the northern states adjacent to the U.S. border and the central highlands, as well as scattered enclaves along the Gulf coast and the Pacific Ocean. The Carrancistas controlled less territory, but the land they did control provided them with more valuable resources. Carranza's forces, for example, occupied the oil-producing region of Tampico, which had been relatively untouched by revolution and was generating far more revenue than the agricultural regions that Villa depended upon to finance his army. Carranza had also inherited the huge cache of weaponry left behind in Veracruz when the U.S. forces pulled out in November of 1914, which included millions of rounds of ammunition, rifles, pistols, machine guns, barbed wire, and explosives. Perhaps most important of all, Carranza had Álvaro Obregón on his side. A former chickpea farmer, Obregón is viewed by many historians as the most talented military general to emerge in the revolution. He was blessed with a photographic memory, had some schooling, and was modest in appearance. Martín Luis Guzmán believed Obregón's unpretentious demeanor only camouflaged an immense conceit and sense of his own importance. "His ideas, his beliefs, his feelings were intended like those of the theater, for the public. They lacked all roots and conviction." Obregón was no fool, however, and unlike the semiliterate Villa, took the time to study the lessons being learned in the trenches of Europe and apply them to the bloody civil war that raged on beneath the hot Mexican sun.

Following the historic meeting between Villa and Zapata in Mexico City, Felipe Ángeles had urged Villa, together with Zapata's Liberating Army of the South, to capture Veracruz, where Carranza had his headquarters. Villa disagreed, pointing out that his home base in the north was being threatened and that other cities were also in danger of being overrun by the Carrancistas. Responded Ángeles, "I understand you, my General; but those lesser dangers will disappear when the great danger that Carranza represents has passed. These other chiefs are like hats hanging on a rack; the rack is Carranza, and the best use of our forces is not to pick off the hats one by one but to topple the rack, because then all the hats will fall." Though Villa valued Ángeles's advice, he ignored it this time and sent troops to Guadalajara, Saltillo, and Monterrey. The Carrancistas were vanquished in all three cities. Although the victories were of little strategic importance, Villa's sense of invincibility grew.

Álvaro Obregón, meanwhile, was busily reorganizing his army. He drilled his troops, recruited new soldiers from the nascent labor movement, and pondered his opponent's crude military tactics. In

April of 1915, Obregón was ready to launch a major offensive and he loaded his army onto a train and began chugging toward the town of Celaya. Located about 130 miles northwest of Mexico City, Celaya was surrounded by green fields that were irrigated by a network of ditches and canals. Obregón, who happened to have a German adviser on his military team, immediately saw how the waterways could be used to erect a formidable defense against his reliably hotheaded rival. He unrolled barbed wire in front of the ditches and placed nests of deadly machine guns and cannons behind them. Then, with his combined forces of six thousand cavalry and five thousand infantry, he sat back and waited for *el jaguar* to enter the deadly web.

Villa's network of spies had informed him of the buildup of troops in Celaya, and true to Obregón's prediction, he wanted to rush there immediately and give the "little banty rooster" the thrashing of his life. But Felipe Ángeles had more respect for Obregón's military skills and urged Villa to avoid a direct battle. He suggested that Villa instead taunt Obregón, leading him away from his supply base before launching his own ground attack. Villa argued that a defensive posture would tarnish "the prestige of my troops and my own reputation would suffer in the eyes of the enemy. . . . When have I not gone out to fight him, shattering him with my momentum, putting him to rout?"

On April 6, Obregón's advance guard accidentally ran into a much larger contingent of Villistas and Obregón himself steamed out in an armored train to rescue them. The following morning, the full-fledged battle began. Sitting astride a horse, Villa ordered his cavalry and infantry and artillerymen to assemble along a line about three miles in length. Once his troops were in position, Villa sent in the first wave, shining and gold-colored in the sun. As Obregón's machine guns and artillery fire cut them to pieces, another wave rose up through the haze and rode out to be butchered. At dusk, the Villistas halted their assault. Obregón's artillerymen kept up their bombardment through the night and Villa watched the shells exploding in the darkness, marveling at the wasteful use of ammunition. He slept little, frequently interrupted by generals who came to him, voicing their fears about their own dwindling arsenal. He tried to comfort them, saying, "The city will fall under the fury of our first assault, and if not then, under the second."

The following morning brought even bloodier fighting. Obregón's Yaqui riflemen, well hidden in dugouts, picked off Villa's infantry and cavalry. Villa's artillerymen lobbed shell after shell into the enemy camp. The shells hit their targets but they were so poorly constructed that they did little damage. Nevertheless, Obregón's center began to weaken and Villa ordered his men to charge in "one great onslaught." As they raced across the fields, Villa noticed that the ground had been inundated with water, which had probably been piped in from the drainage ditches. While his soldiers floundered through the water, Obregón's cavalry engulfed the Villistas in a brilliant pincer movement. Villa's right flank weakened and broke, then the center, and finally the left. Villa rode out onto the field and drove back the enemy long enough for his troops to rescue most of their cannons and begin an orderly withdrawal. "We abandoned our dead; we collected our arms; we gathered our wounded and carried them to the trains of my health service, where they were taken aboard and sent to my hospitals in the north."

Another general might have surrendered, but Villa still had enormous energy and confidence. Over the next few days the two opposing forces swelled in strength. By the time the second titanic battle of Celaya began, a week later, there were perhaps fifteen thousand men in Obregón's camp and twenty thousand in Villa's.

The battle began at noon on the thirteenth of April and continued all day and throughout the night, which brought heavy rain. Villa did not alter his suicidal strategy at all. "Our attacks were thin and weak, but a single instant of weakness at a single point in the enemy line might give us a chance," he said later. Once again, his artillery shells, made in his shops in Chihuahua and lacking the proper mix of chemicals, inflicted little damage. Then an eerie replay of the first Celaya battle occurred: Obregón's line once again began to weaken; Villa's infantrymen charged, and Obregón's cavalry — six thousand horsemen who had remained hidden for two days in a mesquite thicket — enveloped their flanks. The once-mighty Villistas threw down their guns and began to run for their lives.

In the two battles, approximately three thousand of Villa's men were killed and six thousand were taken as prisoners. He also lost a thousand horses, five thousand rifles, and thirty-two cannons. But the bitterest blow of all came in the milling confusion afterward. Smiling pleasantly and glowing with success, the apple-cheeked Obregón asked the captured Villista officers, clad in the same muddy clothes as their troops, to come forward. Some 120 brave men stepped forth and were promptly executed.

Distraught by the carnage, on June 2, 1915, President Wilson sent a lengthy public letter to Mexico City in which he urged the revolutionary factions to settle their differences. "I feel it to be my duty to tell them that, if they can not accommodate their differences and unite for this great purpose within a very short time, this Government will be constrained to decide what means should be employed by the United States in order to help Mexico save herself and serve her people."

Wilson's appeal fell on deaf ears. Villa and Obregón were locked in a death struggle and neither intended to stop until the other was destroyed. The two armies lumbered north. Near the town of León, northwest of Celaya, Obregón played the defense again, ordering his troops into a protective square and preparing for more suicidal attacks. This time Villa heeded the advice of Felipe Ángeles to "outpatience" Obregón and fought more defensively himself, ordering his infantry to dig in along the edge of a wide, level plain. The battle stretched over forty days. During one of the skirmishes, an artillery shell struck a tower where Obregón and his generals were observing the battlefield and blew off Obregón's right arm. Obregón reached for his pistol to shoot himself but an aide had removed the bullets while cleaning his gun the day before and he was rushed to an emergency hospital. ("It was a very efficient staff that I had," he would later joke. "When I regained consciousness I found they had already amassed my watch and pocketbook.")

Finally Villa could tolerate the stalemate no longer and sent one of his officers to attack a fortified hill. "Standing on a rocky pinnacle, cursing and blaspheming, he saw his lieutenant defeated — and then nothing could hold him," wrote James Hopper, the *Col-*

lier's correspondent. Villa gathered up his cavalry and charged. Once again, he was soundly defeated.

The two opposing armies staggered on in a northwesterly direction, facing off against each other for the third time in Aguascalientes. By then, Obregón had recovered somewhat from his injury and he again opted for a defensive posture. This time, his supply lines were overextended and Villa was confident that he could defeat his nemesis with ease. Villa reverted to his old guerrilla tactics, ordering his cavalry to circle behind Obregón's men in order to divert some of his forces and disrupt his communication and supply lines. Obregón, knowing he was in danger of being cut off, ordered his soldiers to mount an attack, and they routed Villa's men so unexpectedly that the Villistas left pots of "bubbling stew" on the battlefield.

With the third defeat, Villa vented his fearsome rage on the army he had nurtured and loved, spewing out bitterness. "Oh, yes," he would say, "but those fellows are not what they used to be. They run now if you but shake a bell!" And victory did not lessen Obregón's vindictiveness. From the dusty green trees that lined the plaza in Aguascalientes, he hanged more than eighty musicians from Villa's glorious band — guitarists, trombonists, drummers, and trumpet players. "And such was the instantaneous fall of the man who had climbed so fast and so high," Hopper reported. "The rest is simply a vertiginous slide downhill. The shattered remnants of Villa's army fled north, on foot, on horses, on mules, along the railroad track, soldiers, camp followers, men, women, and children all mixed up."

VILLA DECIDED TO MARCH to Sonora to recuperate and rebuild his forces. There, his agents could slip over the border to buy needed arms and ammunition and he could avail himself of the rich haciendas that had been relatively untouched by the revolution. One of his tasks would be to take Agua Prieta, the town of "dark water," which is located across the border from Douglas, Arizona. Once fortified with the garrison's arms and supplies, Villa planned to move south and attack Hermosillo, the capital of Sonora.

Before departing, he went to Juárez to raise funds for his troops. There, a reporter for the *El Paso Morning Times* happened to interview him and Villa spoke frankly of his terrible defeats: "I am thoroughly exhausted. My physical powers have been taxed to the limit. The last month has been the most fatiguing of my life, but I have never doubted the justice of our cause." He continued:

I am here in Juárez, but this is as far as I shall go — north! Mexico is my country. I shall not run away from it. Here I have lived and here I have fought. Here I shall fight and here I shall live. Here maybe I shall die, and that probably soon, but I am content. They may kill me in battle; they may murder me on the highway; they may assassinate me while asleep in my bed, but the cause I have fought for 22 years will live. It is the cause of liberty; the cause of human freedom; the cause of justice — long delayed and long denied to my suffering countrymen.

Soon after the interview, Villa left the civilized comforts of Juárez and began the arduous march across the Sierra Madre. It took his men twenty-five days to get through the mountains with their horses, forty-two cannons, and pack mules. Men and horses perished when they lost their footing on the narrow passes and plunged headlong into the deep canyons. Especially treacherous was the Cañón del Púlpito, a name taken from a towering rock shaped like a church pulpit.

When the Villistas had exited the mountains and were toiling toward Agua Prieta, Villa learned that President Wilson had recognized Venustiano Carranza as the de facto leader of Mexico. To Villa, who had professed himself a friend of the Americans early on, Wilson's decision was an unthinkable betrayal.

FOR WILSON, the decision had as much to do with the deteriorating geopolitical conditions as it did with Villa. In Berlin, the German high command had continued to watch with interest the tension between the United States and Mexico, hoping against hope that war might break out between the two countries. Such a conflict, they theorized, would slow the U.S. supplies going to Great Britain and discourage the United States from entering the European war. An even more delicious scenario involved manipulating Japan, which had allied itself with Great Britain, into joining Mexico in a war against the United States, thereby diverting resources from that potential enemy as well.

The Germans had hoped to use Victoriano Huerta as their catalyst and had offered to supply him with arms and money to return to Mexico, regain control of the country, and attack the United States. Huerta accepted the German offer and arrived in New York City on April 13, 1915, almost a year to the day after the Veracruz invasion. Two months later, he boarded a train for the border and was arrested a few miles west of El Paso. By then, Huerta was extremely ill from cirrhosis of the liver, and was eventually allowed to spend his remaining days with family members, who were now living in El Paso. He died on January 13, 1916, his bed facing his convulsed country and his parlor filled with old generals who wept openly and smoked corn-husk cigarettes. Thousands attended his funeral, where he lay in a coffin covered with flowers, wearing his full-dress uniform. Worried about further German attempts to destabilize Mexico, the United States decided to recognize the bellicose Carranza. The War Department's chief of staff, Hugh Scott, had gotten wind of the administration's plan and did everything he could to stop it. "The recognition of Carranza had the effect of solidifying the power of the man who had rewarded us with kicks on every occasion and of making an outlaw of the man who had helped us." But the American decision was a pragmatic one. Carranza had the upper hand, Villa's fortunes were in decline, and stability in Mexico mattered most.

The United States had even gone beyond simply recognizing Carranza as Mexico's legitimate leader. The government allowed Carranza's troops to travel by train through the border states of Texas, New Mexico, and Arizona to reinforce Agua Prieta. On the thirty-first of October, as the yellow plume of dust signaling the advance guard of Villa's army appeared on the horizon, three infantry brigades consisting of five thousand Carrancistas arrived in the little town.

Agua Prieta sits on a small rise with its north side running along the U.S. border. Anticipating Villa's arrival, the Carrancistas had dug trenches along the remaining three sides of the town and covered each sector with barbed wire and land mines constructed from dynamite. Stocked with ammunition, food, and water, the Carrancistas waited confidently. Many of these soldiers were veterans of Celaya and had no doubts they could again defeat Villa. General Plutarco Elías Calles, a tough Carrancista officer who was in charge of defending Agua Prieta and someday would become president of Mexico, estimated on the eve of the battle that even if he were to lose a thousand men, Villa's casualties could easily be five or six times as high. "An enemy weakened in those proportions would have to withdraw, a prey to terror," he said.

En route to Agua Prieta, Villa learned that the little town had been reinforced with additional Carrancista troops. Still, he vowed to press on with the attack. "This is the way the United States repays me for the treatment and protection I have given foreigners in Mexico. Hereafter I don't give a —— what happens to foreigners in Mexico or in my territory," he told reporters. "I can whip Carranza and his entire army, but it is asking a great deal to whip the United States also, but I suppose I can do that, too."

Alarmed by the size of the foreign armies massing on its southern flank, the U.S. Army had stationed hundreds of troops in seven-foot-deep trenches on the other side of the border at Douglas, Arizona. One of those soldiers was a young recruit named Chant Branham, who remembered watching the Villistas pouring out of the mountains: "Finally the hour came, a high broken dust indicating horse cavalry coming through the Pass. . . . This continued two to three hours, then a solid stream of low heavy dust appeared indicating infantry, which continued throughout the night and part of next day."

Villa himself, accompanied by four officers, rode up to the border fence separating the United States from Mexico.

"Do you expect to take Agua Prieta today?" a U.S. Army officer asked him.

"Sure, Mike," Villa responded, smiling broadly.

Reverting to Spanish, Villa then asked if the U.S. troops planned to help Calles and was told the United States would remain neutral. Villa was strongly warned not to fire into U.S. territory. The Mexican leader said he had no intention of doing so and rode back to his troops.

At 1:37 on the afternoon of November 1, the battle began. Villa's artillery pounded the Carrancista trenches and the enemy answered with its own well-placed shells. Despite the efforts of the two Mexican armies, shell fragments and machine-gun bullets crossed into the United States, killing and wounding soldiers and civilians.

By about six thirty that evening, the Villistas were within a mile of Calles's fortified trenches. When darkness fell, Villa hurled his troops at the barricades. As his soldiers crawled on their bellies through the minefields and barbed-wire fences, powerful searchlights illuminated the battlefield. Villa watched helplessly as machine-gun and rifle fire poured down on the wriggling forms, killing the men where they lay. The searchlights, which had undoubtedly come from the United States, marked a third betrayal by the Wilson administration.

When morning came, the silence reminded the young Branham of a huge factory mill shutting down. "It was horrifying to look over the battlefield of dead bodies, they were thick as flies on a sticky paper." Villa's medical corps retrieved 376 wounded. Another 223 soldiers lay dead on the battlefield.

Villa's agents crossed the border and purchased emergency medical supplies that spoke sadly of casualties: twenty pounds of cotton, twenty yards of gauze, ten pounds of peroxide, iodine, painkillers, quinine caps, carbolic soap, alcohol, chloroform, zinc oxide, and syringes. From other stores, they purchased forty quilts and four tons of hay, and picked up five thousand undershirts, underpants, and shirts that had been sent by special express from El Paso.

On November 3, the remains of Villa's army withdrew and began moving west, toward the border town of Naco, where Villa hoped to rest and procure food and water for his famished troops. Members of Calles's cavalry rode out to harass the retreating forces but were driven back by small-arms fire and machine guns. Villa decided to split his forces, leaving roughly five thousand men to protect his rear while he moved south to take the city of Hermosillo. Upon arriving in that city, he once again launched suicidal assaults against well-fortified positions and destroyed what was left of his army.

Filled with a rage that bordered on dementia, Villa and his remaining followers eventually turned back east toward home. As they approached the remote mountain settlement of San Pedro de la Cueva, the villagers fired upon the soldiers, thinking they were marauders, and killed several Villistas. Despite their profuse apologies, Villa subsequently ordered every able-bodied man in the village executed. Seventy-seven villagers were killed, including Father Andrés Abelino Flores, who had gone to Villa begging for mercy. Villa had twice warned the priest to go away and when he returned for the third time, he pulled out his own pistol and shot him in the head.

Back in Douglas, Arizona, the U.S. troops were ordered to remain for another two weeks on the off chance that Villa might return. While they waited, Branham watched the preparation for the great funeral pyres. Corpses were picked up by donkey carts and dumped into numerous piles. Brush and debris were placed on top and barrels of oil and kerosene were poured over the mounds. More wood was added. Finally, he wrote, "they got all the human heaps to burning."

The odor wafted over the U.S. troops, and officers sent repeated requests to their superiors, begging for permission to withdraw. At last, the orders came, and the U.S. soldiers slipped away, leaving Agua Prieta and its sister city of Douglas to deal with the bones and ashes.

VILLA WAS CONVINCED that Venustiano Carranza had cut a deal with the Americans that would make Mexico little more than a protectorate. On the evening of December 21, in Chihuahua City, Villa delivered a public address in which he claimed that Don Venustiano had sold the Mexican people into bondage and that the Americans would soon invade their beloved homeland. Villa also was convinced that Carranza, in exchange for a loan of five hundred million dollars, had agreed to cede Magdalena Bay, located on the Baja peninsula, to the United States for a term of ninety-nine years, had also given the United States a financial stake in Mexico's rich oil fields and railroads, and had offered the Americans a voice in the appointment of two top ministers of the federal government.

The following day, Villa went by train to Hacienda de Bustillos for a meeting of his most trusted advisers. (The surroundings must have held bittersweet memories for him; this was the hacienda where he had first met the little fellow — Francisco Madero.) The gathering, which became known as the Conference of Twenty-seven Generals, was called in order to decide whether the struggle should continue. Villa listened to the debate only a short time and then he announced that the generals could do whatever they wanted but that he — General Villa — would never seek amnesty from his hated rival. He then left in a carriage for the town of Rubio, taking with him a mistress and the wife of Colonel Nicolás Fernández. Over Christmas, Villa recuperated and reflected upon his defeats. On January 8, 1916, he penned a lengthy letter to Emiliano Zapata, whose troops for the most part had remained in their home state of Morelos, suggesting that the Zapatistas march north and join him in his fight against the Americans. "We decided not to fire a bullet more against the Mexicans, our brothers," he wrote, "and to prepare and organize ourselves to attack the Americans in their own dens and make them know that Mexico is a land for the free and tomb for thrones, crowns and traitors." Whether Zapata joined him or not, Villa had found his new target.

⊶5⊷

TELL PRESIDENT WILSON
TO SAVE YOU

AS MAUD WRIGHT and the column of guerrilla fighters struggled north, moving with the ungainly shamble of an arthritic animal, Pancho Villa may have thought longingly of his once great army and noisy troop trains. Temperatures still plunged below freezing at night and daytime brought a hot spring sun. Villa had lived as a hunted coyote for so long that he knew how to read the land. Water, for example, lent a certain heft to the air, infused the distant scrub with a tender greenness. The soldiers rested mostly in the afternoons, for three or four hours, and then pushed on in the zigzagging pattern that was designed to confuse anyone who might be observing them. Seen from above by the *zopilotes* — the buzzards — the column resembled a palsied black scrawl being written across the brown parchment of earth.

Villa lived in fear of assassins. He ate only after one of his trusted lieutenants had first sampled his plate of food and each night went out in the desert to sleep, returning the next morning from a direction opposite that from which he had left. Defeat and disgrace had only made him more wary and he drew closer to the dwindling cadre of officers who had not deserted him. They included Candelario Cervantes, wiry, dark eyed, and ruthless; Pablo and Martín López, two brothers who had fought at Villa's side since the beginning of the revolution; Francisco Beltrán, once known as *el general de los yaquis,* who, at the age of fifty, was one of Villa's oldest generals; and Juan Pedrosa, a cheerful and outgoing general from Sonora.

Though Villa's officers had lost none of their revolutionary zeal, the same could not be said for the rank and file. Many of the men were veterans of Villa's earlier campaigns who had returned home exhausted and thoroughly sickened by war. But Villa had succeeded in getting them to rejoin him after issuing orders such as the following:

> *I hereby order the immediate mobilization of all soldiers resid-*
> *ing in the districts of Namiquipa and Cruces who have had pre-*
> *vious service in the Conventional Army, and their assignment*
> *to the detachment in command of Colonel Candelario Cer-*
> *vantes. Those who fail to join said detachment shall be shot.*
> *Those who conceal themselves and are not found, the families*
> *of these shall pay the penalty.*
>
> *Francisco Villa*

Forced conscription, or the *leva,* was something that Díaz and Huerta had relied upon to fill their armies and rid the countryside of troublemakers, and the threat demonstrated Villa's dwindling popularity. The conscripts were nothing like the enthusiastic volunteers who had once filled the ranks of the División del Norte. With no money for wages, Villa's henchmen used a deadly discipline to keep the troops from bolting. Stragglers were brutally beaten with the flats of swords and deserters run down in the brush and shot.

One day, when the column was lashed with a cold rain, the Villistas took refuge in the burned-out adobe huts and buildings that once marked the outskirts of a flourishing farm. The next morning, they wrung out their clothes and laid them in the sun to dry. In the rain-washed air, Pablo López, thirty-five, tall and angular, bearing little resemblance to his brother, Martín, who was three years older, could see for many miles and may have let his animal wariness slacken momentarily. At the time he was the target of an intense manhunt.

ON SATURDAY, JANUARY 8, 1916, the day that Pancho Villa penned his letter to Emiliano Zapata seeking an alliance, eighteen workers were on their way to reopen a silver mine in Cusihuíriachic, a small town roughly a hundred miles southwest of Chihuahua City. The mine had been closed because of the civil unrest, but General Obregón had been in El Paso for a banquet on December 30 and had urged U.S. businessmen to return to Mexico. "I want you to come down into our territory and open your business enterprises. I give you my word that you will be given full protection. Our government is in complete control of every important center in Chihuahua. Nothing will happen to you because the Villistas are whipped. Villa is a thing of the past."

Charles Rea Watson, a well-built man of forty-eight with a ruddy complexion and a stubby red mustache, was the general manager of the mining operation. Despite Obregón's assurances, he had decided to personally investigate whether it was safe to return, making several trips to Chihuahua City to meet with military authorities. Satisfied, he had obtained safe-conduct passports for the eighteen members of his party, which guaranteed their protection by Carrancista forces and instructed Mexican officials to cooperate with them. On the eve of their departure, he also offered to pay Carrancista troops to escort the group to the mine but was assured that the state of Chihuahua was peaceful and soldiers would not be needed.

The train chugged south to Chihuahua City. The miners disembarked and made their way to the Robinson House, where they spent the rest of the weekend. At about ten o'clock on Monday morning, the tenth of January, they boarded a train that would take them to the mining facility. Some of the passengers began playing cards, using a suitcase as a table, while others dozed or read. In addition to Watson's party, there were a number of Mexicans on the train who were returning to Cusi. They included Elena G. de López, whose husband worked for the mining company; Pedro

Chacón, formerly an officer in Villa's army, who had accepted amnesty from the Carranza government; and Cesar Sala, an Italian by birth and naturalized Mexican citizen, who had gone to Chihuahua City to buy goods for his store, which had been looted the previous month by Villistas. Also traveling with the Watson party was Thomas Holmes, a cheerful young American from Keene, New Hampshire, who wore a jaunty straw hat and had decided to accompany the party in order to check on his own mining enterprises.

At about one o'clock that afternoon, the train pulled into the little station of Santa Isabel, located forty miles west of Chihuahua City. While it was idling, two armed men rode up, looked inside, and then rode away. After refueling, the train continued toward Cusi and had gone perhaps five miles when it encountered a railroad car lying diagonally across the tracks. Thomas Holmes peered out the window to see what was going on. Tom Evans, twenty-nine, a member of the mining party, took his gold watch from his vest and slipped it inside his underwear, and then stood and looked over Holmes's shoulder. Evans thought a train that had preceded them must have jumped the tracks and the two men decided to get off and investigate. Several other passengers followed them to the rear platform.

The men had gone perhaps ten feet when they heard gunfire. The train had halted inside a narrow railroad cut. To the right of the tracks was a river and to the left was a steep embankment. Holmes glanced back over his shoulder and saw twelve to fifteen Mexican soldiers standing on the bank above the train, firing down on them. "How many others were there I could not say, as my view was obstructed by the train," Holmes said. "At this time I saw Mr. Watson just leaping off of the rear steps of the train. He landed right at the entrance of this cut on the river side and ran directly away from the train and at right angles from the train towards the river."

Watson did not get far. One of the Mexican passengers, José María Sánchez, ran to a window, where he saw some of the soldiers dropping to their knees to improve their aim. Watson fell after running about a hundred yards. "He got up, limping, but went on a short distance farther, when he threw up his arms and fell forward, his body rolling down the bank into the river," Sánchez recalled.

Holmes and the other men scattered as the attackers poured down gunfire on the train. The passengers inside dropped to the floor to protect themselves from the flying glass and bullets. When someone screamed that there were women and children inside, the firing gradually stopped. Suddenly Pablo López and about thirty soldiers appeared in the doorway of the passenger car. Cesar Sala, the Italian, was just rising to his feet when López struck him in the face with his revolver. *"Abajo, gringo!"* he snarled. Sala responded that he was not a gringo, but a naturalized Mexican citizen. López then ordered him to sit down and be quiet.

Then he pointed his Mauser at Pedro Chacón, the ex-Villista and former military commander of Cusihuíriachic when Villa had controlled the state. *"Está aquí, traidor?"* — "You here, traitor?"

Chacón protested that he was no traitor. "The reason I got my amnesty was that Villa had turned us loose."

"We will arrange this later," responded López, motioning him to get out of the car.

Two of the attackers pulled Elena G. de López up from her seat to take her outside with the other Americans, but when she protested that both she and her husband were Mexican citizens, López ordered the men to release her. To other Mexican passengers, he hollered, "If you want to see some fun, watch us kill these gringos. *Vámanos, muchachos!*"

As López swaggered through the passenger car, he taunted the Americans. "He was cursing the Americans who were in the car, the President of the United States, and Carranza, and was telling the Americans in effect, in Spanish, 'Tell Wilson to come and save you, and tell Carranza to give you protection. Now is the time to come here and protect you,' and at the same time using vulgar expressions and curse words of the President of the United States, of the Americans, and of Carranza," Cesar Sala wrote in a sworn affidavit. He continued:

> I heard López order the Americans to remove their clothing and get out of the car. Young Maurice Anderson, barefooted and in

his underclothes, passed me from behind, going up the aisle of the car, and getting off the car at the front door, stepping off to the right hand side toward the river. He was followed by Mc-Hatton and an old man (whose name I did not know), who was bleeding from the side of his face, whom I remember in particular. They also had removed their clothes. After that I heard the report of guns on the right hand side of the train. I inquired of the Mexicans sitting across the aisle, who could see out of the window, what was being done, and they told me they were killing the Americans. Becoming more frightened, I kept quiet.

The soldiers lined up the members of the Watson party on the right side of the railroad tracks just a few feet from the train. Recalled another Mexican passenger, "Two soldiers using Mausers were told by Colonel López to kill the Americans. One of them went up to the first foreigner and shot him, and as he died the second one fired his Mauser at the second foreigner, standing in line. A general confusion began when the first two were killed, but the two men ran along the line, taking turns shooting the Americans. Some of the foreigners attempted to break away, but they were forced back by the soldiers until the entire line had been killed. Only two men did the executing. The others stood around cheering and crying, 'Viva Villa.'"

Within a few minutes, added José María Sánchez, "The Americans lay on the ground, gasping and writhing in the sand and cinders. The suffering of the Americans seemed to drive the bandits into a frenzy. 'Viva Villa!' they cried and 'Death to the gringos!' Colonel López ordered the 'mercy shot' given to those who were still alive, and the soldiers placed the ends of their rifles at their victims' heads and fired, putting the wounded out of misery."

López and his men moved on to the express car, where they smashed the locks on suitcases and trunks and took what valuables they could find. They seized eleven small sacks of Mexican silver, valued at approximately 6,518 pesos, and filled their saddlebags with coffee beans. López ordered the frightened crew to take the train back to Chihuahua City and then he and his soldiers made their way to a small town, where they went to sleep.

The assailants had inadvertently left one American eyewitness alive: Thomas Holmes. When Holmes had leaped from the train with Watson, he had tripped and rolled into the bushes. "I lay there perfectly quiet and looked around and could see the Mexicans shooting in the direction in which Watson was running when I last saw him. I could see that they were not shooting at me and thinking they believed me already dead I took a chance and crawled into some darker bushes. I crawled through the bushes until I reached the bank of the stream and made my way to a point probably one hundred yards from the train. There I lay under the bank for half an hour and heard the shooting as they were evidently finishing the Americans, shots by ones, twos and threes."

Thirteen bodies lay in a heap next to the railroad tracks. Five more bodies, including Watson's, lay between the tracks and the river. Dozens of spent cartridges littered the ground, evidence that the soldiers had continued pumping bullets into their victims long after they were dead. Young Maurice Anderson was lying on top of the pile, with his arms up before him as if endeavoring to protect his face. Other bodies had been bayoneted repeatedly or mutilated, genitals crushed, eyes gouged out, and heads twisted around from the original position in which they fell. Nearly all the victims were stripped of their possessions — right down to the buttons on their clothing. Only Charles Watson, who was still lying in the river, remained clothed. He was wearing a threadbare khaki suit so old it was later speculated that even the soldiers didn't want it.

News of the murders caused an uproar in the United States. U.S. Army officials would write that Villa was far from the scene and could not have had advance knowledge of the whereabouts of the train carrying the American miners. Yet, there was no doubt in the press or among the public that he had ordered the atrocity and many people, civilians and politicians alike, wanted President Wilson to send troops into Mexico to capture the marauders. But the Carrancistas reassured the administration that the de facto government would bring the culprits to justice and Wilson decided to let Carranza's government handle it, believing that intervention by the United States would only bolster Pancho Villa's popularity and destabilize the fledgling government.

In Chihuahua City, the bodies were placed in pine coffins, which were then draped with black cloth and affixed with small identification cards, and loaded onto a train bound for El Paso. Several dogs that had accompanied the miners and remained at the massacre site also rode in the train. The local newspapers were filled with the grisly details of the murders, and churches and funeral parlors overflowed with grieving relatives and outraged friends. In Juárez, General Gabriel Gavira and the Mexican consul, Andrés García, a thin, harassed-looking man who was well liked by reporters, had an urgent discussion about the matter. An El Paso nurse, who could speak Spanish fluently, overheard the conversation:

"Why did you not send an escort with the train, as you told me you were going to do?" asked García.

"I did not have the men to send, and it was not needed from here to Chihuahua, but I ordered General Gonzáles to give them an escort from Chihuahua to Cusi."

"Why did not General Gonzáles give them the escort?"

"He said he did not have men enough, and, in the second place, he advised me that the train did not need an escort, as there was no danger, as that portion of the country had been rid of the Villistas."

Andrés García sighed. "We will wait and see the consequences of this stupidity."

On the evening of January 13, 1916, a riot broke out in downtown El Paso when two U.S. soldiers knocked two Mexicans from the sidewalk at San Antonio and Broadway Streets. Generalized fighting erupted in the streets and saloons. A National Guard unit hurried to the police station to guard a jail where twenty-three Villista generals and politicians loyal to Villa were imprisoned. Several companies of soldiers from nearby Fort Bliss were sent to the business district to help maintain order. Instead of quelling the uprising, though, some joined it. Wrote a local reporter, "It was estimated that not less than 25 Mexicans were beaten up and assaulted by the soldier mobs and many of these came or were brought to the police emergency hospital for treatment, though the majority were hastened to their homes by friends."

The reports of the beatings quickly made their way to Juárez, where Mexican soldiers became so enraged that they began agitating to cross the river and go to the defense of their brothers. Fortunately, El Paso officials were able to disperse the rioters with a water hose. Nineteen men were arrested and many more taken briefly into custody. Soon the only sounds in downtown El Paso were the coyote yelps of the peanut sellers and the sulfurous thump of moving-picture men lighting their fuses.

⟶6⟵

ONLY ONE CHANCE
TO DIE

TO MAUD WRIGHT, the desert sometimes seemed like a choppy sea and the jagged, blue mountains like waves caught in the moment of turning. The effect was heightened by the voices of the soldiers, which were muffled and indistinct, as if the sounds were traveling across a large body of water. She let the voices spill over her, too exhausted to grab the words from the air and break them into English.

Each morning she awoke expecting to be killed by the end of the day. Unable to withstand the strain any longer, she finally asked Colonel Fernández why they didn't just go ahead and do it. Unmoved by Maud's terror, Fernández regarded her impassively. Then he shrugged and said that Villa hoped that she would die from the rigors of the march. "He intends for you to die a terrible death."

But the rank-and-file soldiers displayed an unexpected delicacy toward her, finding her shelter in the ruins of an abandoned adobe hut where she could rub a little cool water on her burning thighs and caked cheeks. Impressed by her stoicism, they began calling her the queen of the Villistas. Many of the soldiers, she realized, were mere boys and she grew less afraid.

The alkali dust rose from the horses' hooves and covered her in white powder. At night, when she lowered her lids over her scorched eyes, she thought of her dim, clean rooms; the drowsing baby and her husband, blinking as he crossed the threshold, momentarily blind. Not given to introspection or self-pity, Maud had thrived in Mexico. She had filled her kitchen vases with the wildflowers that grew along the irrigation ditches and had seen the drenched reds that burst once a year from the palms of the cactus plants, and the moon, bigger than what she remembered from childhood, lofting up over the wrinkled hills.

One night she crept past her guards and tried to escape on one of Villa's horses, but the horse pranced uneasily and before she could untie it, a guard awakened and demanded to know what she was trying to do. "Untangling the horse," she replied. He shoved her back inside, and from that moment on she was watched around the clock.

Maud pushed her heels down in the stirrups to brace her body against the painful trot of her flat-footed horse, ate the unsalted mule meat and tortilla scraps that were tossed her way, and watched as the soldiers around her began developing the classic symptoms of dehydration. Their tongues became thick in their mouths and their eyes grew red. Even Villa's watchful eyes flared with red, as if he had swallowed a piece of the sun. For the first time she noticed couriers coming and going from their camp, which meant that Villa was in communication with the outside world. And when the column stopped to rest or graze the horses, she saw Villa and his officers huddling together in animated conferences. As the mental fog began to lift, she listened to the Spanish conversations and with a shock realized the purpose of the march: Villa was going to attack Columbus, New Mexico, a flyspeck of a town located just three miles north of the border.

It was the second time Villa had led his guerrilla band in the direction of the United States. In late January, after the Santa Isabel massacre, he had planned to attack U.S. settlements in the Big Bend area of Texas. "I shall hold none of you after that adventure and I assure you that you will not regret participating in this last expedition with me," he promised his troops. But his column suffered from so many desertions that he decided to turn back and rebuild his forces. On the return trip, he held up a train bound for Juárez and allowed his soldiers to take as much loot as they could carry. One of the passengers was a former Villista general named Porfirio Ornelas, who had accepted Carranza's offer of amnesty. Villa killed him instantly. "I might have let the fool live," he said later, "but he did deserve punishment for his ingratitude toward me."

ON SUNDAY, MARCH 5, the column of Villistas ransacked another ranch and took a second American hostage: an African-American named Edwin "Bunk" Spencer. They "feasted" on molasses and corn they had taken from the ranch and then continued on their way. As they drew closer to the border they grew more secretive and restricted their movements almost entirely to nighttime. Soon they were traveling across a high flat plateau that tipped north like a tray. As shooting stars sped across the oceanic darkness, the soldiers talked softly about Pancho Villa. Many were convinced that he wore an invisible suit of armor that kept bullets from piercing his body. To Maud, though, he seemed almost shell-shocked, his forehead creased in a permanent frown, his mouth hanging open, and his eyes fixed on some invisible point in the distance. She tried to talk with him repeatedly, but he always waved her away, telling her to speak to one of his subordinates.

The following day, Monday, March 6, couriers arrived in camp with news of a dreadful fire that had occurred that morning in the El Paso city jail. Sixteen men had been killed outright and another nineteen had been badly burned in the blaze, according to initial reports. Villa grew crazed with rage, thinking the fire had been intentionally set and that some of his closest supporters had perished. In fact, the El Paso newspapers reported that the fire had been accidentally started while the inmates were undergoing their weekly delousing procedure. Some prisoners were just stepping from their vinegar and coal oil baths, others were still dipping their clothing in gasoline, and many had already put back on their gasoline-soaked garments and had been locked back into their cells. All the prisoners had been warned against smoking or striking a match, but a young man named H. M. Cross, who had been arrested that morning for trying to steal a baseball glove, had apparently not been given the instructions and started to light a cigarette. Instantly the gassy air exploded into flames. The prisoners who were still wet from their baths or who had put back on their gasoline-soaked clothes died horribly. Others who were locked in cells on the upper level suffocated. A lucky few managed to escape.

Forty-three people were in the jail at the time of the fire. Nearly two dozen former generals and politicians who had supported Villa had been rounded up and jailed two months earlier, at the time of the train massacre, but the initial newspaper stories make no mention of any Villistas among the prisoners and it's not clear whether any, or all, of these men were still in jail when the fire broke out. Nevertheless, the incident only bolstered Villa's determination to attack Columbus; he vowed that upon arriving, he would make "torches" of every man, woman, and child.

But two more days of hard riding still lay ahead of them and Villa's officers struggled to keep the conscripts from bolting. When darkness fell that night, five soldiers slipped away and Candelario Cervantes was dispatched to hunt them down. He returned to the camp several hours later with their horses, saddles, guns, and ammunition, which were divided among the remaining marchers. The deserters, presumably, were lying dead somewhere in the brush. It was not surprising that Villa would assign Cervantes the task. He was a fanatically loyal and resourceful fighter who had come to Villa's attention early in the revolution when he scared off a contingent of federal troops by making them think that wood stacked on the backs of mules was artillery guns. He had a square face, a fleshy nose, and a left eye slightly larger than the right, which gave him an unpredictable and volatile air. The volatility was further enhanced by his hands, clenching and unclenching at his sides, at rest only when he was holding his beautiful sword.

Cervantes commanded the eighty-member advance guard, the most cohesive and disciplined detachment in the column. Most of his troops came from Namiquipa, one of the oldest towns in Mexico, whose proud and independent inhabitants had been fighting off Indian attacks for hundreds of years and whose residents had been among the first to take up arms against Díaz. Cervantes ruled his men with an iron will and they lived in dread of him and simultaneously felt indebted to him for past kindness. He was the father of two children and appears to have been a prosperous man — a photograph obtained by the U.S. Army shows him wearing a handsome suit and a Texas-style Stetson. "Cervantes' control over them was perfect," army intelligence officers wrote, adding, "Villa appeared to repose greater confidence in Cervantes than in any other leader."

On Tuesday morning, March 7, the column saw a wavering green that signified a stand of cottonwood trees. With its broad, shiny leaves and great, outstretched limbs, the cottonwood was the most beloved of all trees in the desert and a sure sign that water was near. The soldiers sprinted forward, eager to feel the wet mud between their *dedos del pie*. They had reached the Boca Grande River and the grassy plains of the Palomas Land and Cattle Company, a vast ranch encompassing two and a half million acres that sprawled along the international border below the states of Texas, New Mexico, and Arizona.

To the uninitiated, the Palomas ranch seemed like a desiccated wasteland of hills and arroyos flayed unceasingly by wind and light. In fact, the ranch was quite fertile and capable of sustaining large herds of horses and cattle. Black grama, crowfoot grama, white grama, and salt grass provided the animals with both sustenance and salt. The Boca Grande River meandered along its southern boundary, springs bubbled from the ground, and more than 150 earthen reservoirs had been constructed to supplement the water supply in the dry seasons.

Owned largely by U.S. investor Edwin Marshall, the Palomas Land and Cattle Company had become a frequent target during the revolution. Cattle and horses were often stolen and the ranch cowboys were killed or held for ransom. Villa, as usual, was blamed for the crimes, but a ranch official at the time identified at least three other bands who preyed upon the vast spread. "I know that in the fall of 1914 and the spring of 1915, the Palomas Land and Cattle

Company, in order to salvage their cattle, drove approximately 40,000 head across the international boundary line," rancher Walter P. Birchfield recalled in a 1936 affidavit. The ranch owners were in the process of rounding up their remaining livestock when the column of Villistas arrived.

HENRY ARTHUR MCKINNEY, the thirty-three-year-old range foreman, spotted the Mexican troops as they were unsaddling their horses and making coffee. McKinney was an amiable, good-natured man who had lived in Mexico for many years and was not unduly alarmed by the troops' presence. Before the revolution, Pancho Villa had often stopped at his ranch to visit the vaqueros who worked for him, and whenever Villa saw McKinney's little sister, Pearl, he tried to stroke her bright red hair. "To me he was repulsive, big and burly and dirty looking," Pearl recalled. "I didn't want him to touch me. I learned later that it is an Indian superstition that anyone having red hair is related to the sun god, and to touch such hair brings good luck."

The McKinneys had deep roots in the Southwest, particularly in Texas, where a town had been named after the family. One ancestor, Colin McKinney, had been a signer of the Texas Declaration of Independence; another, Robert McKinney, had died at the Alamo; and a third, Thomas L. McKinney, was with Pat Garrett when he killed Billy the Kid.

Like so many others, McKinney had been forced to abandon his ranch in Mexico as the civil war dragged on. He and his wife, Mamie, were trying to reestablish themselves on a homestead claim near Hachita, a border town thirty miles west of Columbus, New Mexico. They had no children, but Arthur was a kind and indulgent husband and they were happily married. To bring in extra money, he had hired on as a foreman at the Palomas at a salary of $125 a month. On the eve of his departure for Mexico, Mamie had been terribly worried for his safety and he had gently reassured her, pulling out three letters of safe-conduct he had received from the Mexican government, including a letter from General Obregón himself.

McKinney was well liked by his men and particularly valued by his employer because of his ability to speak Spanish. He was tall and slender, and might have been handsome but for his front teeth, which one of his associates cryptically described as "peculiar." He was dressed like a gentleman that morning, wearing a yellow shirt and red sweater, gray trousers and matching vest, white Stetson, boots and chaps.

McKinney decided to ride down and talk to the soldiers. A companion, Antonio Múñez, begged him not to go. If the soldiers were Villistas, Múñez cautioned, they would undoubtedly kill them. "I told him this several times but finally he turned to me and said, 'Well, I'm going to talk to them; are you such a coward that you don't want to go with me?' "

Antonio Múñez shook his head in a mixture of shame and embarrassment. The truth was, he would rather be a coward than dead, and he watched with a fatalistic detachment as the dapper-looking McKinney loped down into the camp.

When McKinney reached the soldiers, he pulled out his papers and showed them to the highest-ranking officer present, who happened to be Colonel Nicolás Fernández. The colonel glanced at the documents, then handed them back. As McKinney put the papers back into his shirt pocket, Fernández demanded to know the location of the cattle and the number of cowboys on the roundup. McKinney answered in his forthright, honest way and was startled when Fernández then refused to let him return to his men. Fernández held out his hands in a graceful, apologetic gesture and reassured him that he would be detained for only a short while, until the other ranch hands were rounded up.

Múñez, meanwhile, turned his horse and rode off to warn the other cowboys. He soon caught up with William Nye Corbett, Juan Favela, and several others who were driving a herd of cattle down the river. Corbett, about twenty-seven years old, tall and slender like his boss, wanted to join McKinney immediately. But Favela, who owned a small working ranch adjacent to the huge Palomas spread, thought they should be more cautious. As the cowboys were debating what to do, Fernández's men rode up the hill toward them. Corbett trotted down to meet them with his hands up in the air. Antonio Múñez and Juan Favela kicked their horses into a gallop and headed for the border.

At the Villista camp, a young "towheaded soldier" seemed to take great glee in the capture of Arthur McKinney and William Corbett. He immediately rode to Villa's headquarters and informed him that they had taken two more prisoners. Villa instructed his orderly to bring a horse and galloped over to take a look at the two Americans. His friendship with McKinney, it seemed, had been very superficial. He took a few sips of coffee and tossed the cup onto the ground. *Maten a los hombres!* he growled.

With the pronouncement of the death sentence, the mood in the camp became inexplicably festive. In shock — or disbelief — McKinney took off his boots, chaps, and hat and gave them to his executioners. A noose was thrown over the branches of a cottonwood tree and he was positioned beneath it on his horse. He laughed and joked and shook hands as the rope was pulled down around his neck and tightened. Then a sharp, stinging slap was delivered to the horse's rump and the animal bolted, leaving McKinney dangling in the air. Corbett, demonstrating the same cavalier attitude, was hanged next.

While McKinney and Corbett were being killed, the Mexican cowboys who worked for the Palomas Land and Cattle Company remained locked up in a room at the ranch house. James O'Neal, who was thirty-four years old and ranch cook, was with them. O'Neal had drifted into Columbus in February looking for work. A restaurant owner, A. A. Keeler, had agreed to hire him for a dollar a day plus room and board, but the day before he was to begin his new job, Arthur McKinney came in looking for a camp cook. The restaurant owner knew O'Neal preferred ranch work and introduced him to McKinney. The two hit it off and O'Neal joined the outfit with a starting salary of thirty dollars a month.

O'Neal may well have been the American that Maud saw murdered as the soldiers resumed their northward march. He was standing in the middle of the road, gesticulating frantically, when the riders swarmed over him. The horsemen grabbed him by his hair and playfully tossed him back and forth between them. When he fell to the ground, they forced their horses over his body. The animals shied wildly and jumped sideways, for it is not in their nature to trample a human being, but the Villistas raked their mounts with spurs. Somehow, the man managed to grab the saddle strings of one of the riders and swing up behind him. The soldier he now sat behind was Candelario Cervantes. Cervantes motioned his troops to get out of the way, then he raised his pistol and shot the man through the neck. The bullet exited under his right arm and he fell from the horse. Unbelievably, he managed to get back on his feet and began to run. But the soldiers quickly overtook him and trampled him until he was dead. Later, O'Neal's mutilated body would be found toward the river.

In keeping with his vow not to waste one more bullet on his own countrymen, Pancho Villa did not kill any of the Mexican cowboys. Instead, they were told of the impending attack on Columbus and ordered to accompany the column. If any of the cowboys escaped, they were warned, everyone left behind would be killed.

THE COLUMN CONTINUED its northward march, with some of the soldiers now wearing the clothes of the dead men. As the troops struck out across the flat prairie, the wind began to rise and brown gritty clouds obscured the horizon. The sulfurous, buffeting air was almost too much to endure and sandy tears leaked from the eyes of man and beast. The soldiers drew their hats down and their serapes up over their faces. The little ponies plodded on: Right back leg. Right front leg. Left back leg. Left front leg. Four beats to a walk, an immeasurable number of beats to go.

At last, the men reached a deep arroyo, where a halt was ordered. The pummeled troops slid to the ground, the wind still keening in their ears. The ponies wrapped their tails over their exposed flanks to wait out the storm. The dust collected in their ears and noses, between their eyelashes, and sifted down through their loosening winter hair to the tender skin where the saddles were laid.

The Mexican troops were now close enough to see Columbus through their binoculars. Pancho Villa, Candelario Cervantes, Nicolás Fernández, and a fourth officer named Carmen Ortiz remounted their horses and rode off in the direction of a hill where they could better observe the town. When they returned, several of the resting soldiers overheard their excited voices. Villa apparently had a change of heart. He pointed out that the cavalry regiment garrisoned at Columbus seemed large, and he saw no need to sacrifice the lives of their men for such an "unimportant town." But Cervantes maintained the army post was staffed by not more than fifty men and that two hours of fighting should bring victory. "A heated discussion continued for about two hours," states an army report, which was written after the attack and based upon interviews with prisoners. "Finally Villa being pressed for a decision, consented to attack and issued orders that the attack on Columbus, N.M. would be undertaken on the following morning."

It was Wednesday, March 8, 1916.

⇥ 7 ⇤

Rumors, Warnings, and Telegrams

COLUMBUS, NEW MEXICO, not only was an "unimportant town," but also was exceedingly ugly. Not a single tree existed in the small settlement, nor was there any grass to keep the parched earth from being scoured by the spring windstorms. The western-style stores and blistered houses seemed no more substantial than a mirage. They leaned against each other, coated with dust, seemingly ready for abandonment almost as soon as they were built. When the turmoil of spring had exhausted itself, a white, sizzling ball appeared in the sky and poured down a heat that immobilized everything. The stunned emptiness rolled away to the four horizons, relieved only by broken-backed cactus, brambles of mesquite and sage, and the three cone-shaped mountains northwest of town known as the Tres Hermanas.

The town had been founded in the 1890s by Colonel Andrew O. Bailey, a one-armed Civil War veteran. Bailey wanted to name the settlement Columbia, after the 1893 Columbian Exposition, which commemorated the four-hundredth anniversary of Christopher Columbus's discovery of the New World, but it was rejected by the U.S. Post Office because so many others had requested the same name. So he settled upon Columbus, taken from Columbus, Ohio, where he had once lived. The town grew slowly, with the first settlers drawn by free land and reports of ample underground water.

In 1912, James Dean, a distinguished-looking man with a neatly trimmed beard, arrived in Columbus from Artesia, another sunbaked New Mexico town. He was fifty-eight years old at the time and had suffered unbelievable hardship moving his family and household goods to Columbus. Although it was only three hundred miles, the trip took nine days in his 1910 touring car. There were no gas stations, no restaurants, no hotels, and only a few "made" roads. He had to stop often to repair the car himself and relied on the kindness of strangers and their teams of horses to pull him through mud and vast stretches of deep sand. Compounding his misery was a poorly capped tooth that had ulcerated and caused him great pain. In a letter to his wife, Eleanor, he talked of crossing the Rio Grande, where he had gotten stuck in a hole and had to dig his way out: "It was awful hot & I got hot and my drinking water got as hot as dish water. It made me sick, vomited & diarrhea." He drove for another five hours, through prairie grass and around the mud holes and sand bogs and arroyos. That evening, a family who lived nearby brought him a dinner of bread and pork roast and coffee and he found himself sick again in the night. The next morning, after receiving more coffee and food from neighbors, he continued on his way. "Did not get stuck in the sand but it was heavy pulling. Had to stop every ½ hour and let the engine cool." When he finally reached Columbus and had recuperated from the ordeal, he began work on his property, sinking a well and putting up the wild hay that grew on his land. Eventually he opened a grocery store and bought several additional lots.

Other settlers, equally tough and independent, soon followed. Archibald Frost opened a store that specialized in hardware, furniture, arms and ammunition. His wife, Mary Alice, was a mail-order bride, blue eyed, freckled, and petite. Archibald could hardly believe his good fortune, and fifteen months later they were celebrating the arrival of their first son. John and Susan Moore, a childless couple who had found each other in middle age, operated a dry-goods store. And Charlie Miller, an eccentric fellow, though greatly admired, ran the drugstore. "He had come to the Mimbres Valley as a tubercular, got a herd of goats and lived in the open until he regained his health, then resumed his vocation of druggist," recalled Roy E. Stivison, a medical doctor who served as the school principal.

The newcomers did what they could to improve Columbus, building churches, schools, and houses and planting rosebushes and fruit trees in the sand. They established a chamber of commerce, a newspaper, and a literary club. (*Monuments of Egypt* was being read in 1912, with special attention devoted to a chapter on Queen Hatasu.) They organized masked balls and waltz contests, and held outdoor tea parties under tall yuccas. Those who stuck around long enough often came to appreciate the disinfecting power of bright sunshine and the stunning transformation that occurred in the blue slices of dawn and dusk, when the air grew intoxicating and infused with a subtle perfume that seemed to seep from the earth itself.

The arrival of the U.S. cavalry and the town's proximity to Mexico brought a faint veneer of prosperity to Columbus. Eventually there was enough business to support three hotels, a bank, drugstore, livery stable, two restaurants, and several general stores. Automobiles, or "machines," as they were often called, were just coming into use and a few enterprising owners rented them out for twenty-five cents per mile "or more according to the character of the roads" and charged one dollar per hour for "standing time." By 1916, the population had swelled to roughly thirteen hundred civilians and soldiers and Columbus had managed to acquire an aura that, if not exactly gay, had a restrained liveliness.

The settlement was divided into four quadrants by a dirt road, which ran in a north–south direction from the town of Deming to the Mexican border, and the El Paso and Southwestern Railroad tracks, which bisected the town in an east–west direction. The commercial businesses and the residences were on the north side of the railroad tracks and Camp Furlong, with its barracks, cook-shacks, stables, and other miscellaneous buildings, was on the south side. Most of the military officers lived in small clapboard homes in the northeast or northwest quadrants. The home of Captain Rudolph E. Smyser was typical of the officers' quarters: Smyser and his wife and two children lived in a three-room house. The living room, which was converted at night to a bedroom for one of the boys, was furnished with a cane chair and a cheap couch. Behind the living room was a bedroom, which held a brass bed for the adults and an army cot on which the other boy slept. The kitchen, which also doubled as the dining room, had a wood-stove for cooking and heating. An orderly, or "striker," lived in a tent opposite the kitchen and made a few extra bucks each week cleaning Captain Smyser's boots and saddle and currying his horse.

For the most part, a feeling of friendship and goodwill existed between the townspeople and the soldiers in the army camp. The military families sent their children to the public school and the officers and privates alike attended church services in town. "Many an evening my young wife and I spent in camp watching the flag come down at retreat and the officer of the day inspect the guard for nightly border patrol. Every morning we were wakened by the bugle's reveille and at night went to sleep to the melancholy sound of taps," Roy Stivison recalled.

AT THE COMMERCIAL HOTEL, the guests listened in awe to the banging shutters and the shrieking wind, which sounded like something sinister and alive trying to get in. The unceasing din made the Methodists, who were in town for a Sunday school convention, think of God's wrath, but the natives may have been reminded of El Delgado, the skinny, dark-eyed witch who was said to live at the base of the Tres Hermanas. The guests waited for something — a blizzard or a downpour — to douse the violent clamor, but the air contained no hint of moisture at all, only dust, which came through the cracks in the door and the windows. It was the color of an ancient seabed, of bleached fossils returning to sand.

In the Southwest, where wood was scarce, many dwellings were built from adobe bricks made of mud, stones, and hay. But William and Laura Ritchie had been determined to build the Commercial Hotel from the proper materials. So they had torn down their grocery store and house in Porterville, Texas, and shipped the wooden planks to Columbus, on the train that was often filled with inebriated salesmen and became known as the Drunkard's Special. They built a ramshackle two-story building with the recycled wood and when it was completed, they sold the entire structure to Sam Ravel, a local merchant, and rented back the second story for fifty dollars a month. Located just north of the train depot, the hotel consisted of twenty-two rooms, a guest parlor, and a long porch facing the street. William Ritchie, fifty-seven, had been ill in recent weeks and much of the work had fallen to Laura. She was of Dutch ancestry, a short, plump woman who enjoyed an occasional glass of beer and wore dark shapeless dresses and old-fashioned black shoes. In one of the few photographs of her, she resembles a boxer — legs planted far apart, head flung back, hands closed into fists. Yet the aggressive posture could not conceal the kindness that emanated from her open face. The Ritchies lived in the hotel, along with their three girls, Edna, Blanche, and Myrtle, and a canary, which twittered brightly in its cage, oblivious to the tumult outside.

After the hotel was completed, Laura had managed to furnish it with amenities that made it one of the most popular places in town. Curtains framed the windows, rugs covered the floors, and kerosene lamps filled the small cramped rooms with soft yellow light. Each room was furnished with a washbasin and pitcher, slop jar, bureau, and bed. A hand-cranked Victrola, a piano, and an organ stood in the parlor. On the porch were eighteen rocking chairs. If the guests were hungry, they had only to walk downstairs to a restaurant owned by Sam Ravel. Also located on the first floor was a warehouse owned by Ravel, where two hundred cases of oil and gasoline, twenty cases of axle grease, and rock salt, coffee, flour, and other foodstuffs were stored.

The Ritchies had many guests staying with them. The best room in the house, located at the top of the stairs and overlooking the street, had gone to Rachel and John Walton Walker, who had come to town for the Methodist convention. Both were Sunday school teachers from Playas, New Mexico, a tiny community sixty-three miles west of Columbus. The Walkers had been married for less than a month and the trip to Columbus was also their honeymoon.

They had much to celebrate. John Walton Walker, thirty-nine, was on his way to becoming a prosperous rancher and contractor. A native of Louisiana, he had been lured to the harsh climate of southern New Mexico by the Homestead Act, which awarded settlers 160 acres of free land after they had built a home and farmed the property for five years. His wife, Rachel, was two decades younger, a pretty woman who liked to ride horses and hike in the mountains. John was a good man, she wrote, "steady and moderate, and at all times hard-working and frugal, at no time given to intemperance in drinking or excesses of any kind." The inclement weather gave the Walkers an excuse to linger beneath the extra quilt that Mrs. Ritchie had provided them and at the end of the day, they hurried back to their narrow bed.

Laura Ritchie was delighted to have the honeymooners as guests. She, too, had been looking forward to the Methodist convention. Her daughter Edna was to play the piano and her youngest daughter, Blanche, was to sing during the evening festivities. Laura had made Blanche a new dress out of frothy pink material and bought her a pair of patent-leather slippers for the occasion.

Another guest staying at the hotel was Dr. Harry Hart, a thirty-three-year-old veterinarian who had come to Columbus to inspect a shipment of cattle. He normally stayed at the two-story Hoover Hotel, which advertised rooms for twenty-five cents, fifty cents, or a dollar — "and WORTH IT!" — but for some reason, he had decided to break routine and checked into the Commercial Hotel. A native of Columbus, Ohio, Hart was the son of a well-known ice cream manufacturer and had attended Ohio State University from 1904 to 1906. In addition to his veterinary duties, Hart was allegedly moonlighting as a "secret agent" for the State Department. He knew both Carranza and Villa personally and had stated publicly that he hoped Carranza would be the victor in Mexico's civil war. Hart was a sober and serious-looking man, with thinning hair and unlined skin. His only concession to vanity was the beautiful diamond and ruby ring that he wore on his right hand, which he had received from a Mexican refugee in exchange for a hundred-dollar loan.

José Pereyra, twenty-five, who worked for the Mexican consul in El Paso, also was staying at the Commercial Hotel. Several days earlier, Pereyra and H. N. Gray, who worked for the Mexican consulate's secret service, were returning from Mexico when the car in which they were riding turned over. Gray had dislocated his shoulder in the accident and been unable to go to Columbus, where he had been assigned to keep an eye on border activities, and Pereyra had volunteered to go instead. Clad in a gray suit, a white shirt, expensive shoes, and a new Stetson, which had his name punched in the hatband, Gray was hardly undercover.

A number of guests lived in the hotel year-round, including Steven Birchfield, a withered cattleman whom the three Ritchie girls loved dearly and referred to as "Uncle," and Sam Ravel, who lived in room 13. Ravel had emigrated to the United States from Russia in 1905 to avoid being drafted into the Russian army. His first stop was El Paso, where he worked in a pawnshop with two of his uncles and learned to speak English. When he had enough money, he sent for his younger brother, Louis, and got him a job working as a clerk at the Don Bernardo Hotel in Las Cruces, New Mexico. Eventually he bought another ticket for Arthur, the youngest of the three Ravel brothers, who crossed the Atlantic Ocean alone in steerage class with his aunt and uncle's silver taped to his legs. When the Mexican Revolution began, Sam Ravel moved to Columbus and opened up a general store that catered to the locals, as well as to the military troops south of the border. He advertised aggressively and kept the store open until ten o'clock at night. Since there was little to do in the evenings, the store was always filled with "kibbichers," Arthur recalled.

Sam Ravel was pugnacious and hot tempered and had a stormy, little-understood relationship with the Villistas. In July of 1914, he had been held prisoner for four days by "a bunch of Villa's men" in Palomas, the little settlement across the border from Columbus. The reasons for Ravel's imprisonment are unknown but in one letter he notes that he had delivered $771.25 worth of "merchandise" to one of Villa's colonels and had not been paid. He was released after he contacted the powerful New Mexico senator Albert Fall, but continued to complain bitterly of his detention.

The man who had ordered Sam Ravel's arrest happened to be Captain Leoncio Figueroa, another permanent guest at the Commercial Hotel and a dashing figure whom the young Blanche Ritchie would remember as having a constant stream of visitors to his room. In a letter to the state attorney general, Ravel complained about Figueroa: "He still continues to threaten me, and talks to all the citizens in a very unpleasant way about me, as he seems to do anything he pleases." Two years earlier, Figueroa and another Villa agent who lived at the hotel had sued the Columbus constable, T. A. Hulsey, for forcibly entering their rooms and examining their private papers without authority. The outcome of the lawsuit is unknown.

FROM A WINDOW of his drafty headquarters south of the railroad tracks, Colonel Herbert Slocum, commander of the Thirteenth Cavalry, could see the horse patrols crow-hopping down the dirt streets. The wind made the horses spookier than usual and the animals jumped sideways when huge tumbleweeds spun toward them. But they were cavalry horses, big boned and well fed, and each morning they were saddled up and spurred out into the thrashing air. The patrols clattered along the crumbling rocks that comprised the international boundary between the United States and Mexico.

Slocum had been a handsome man in his youth, but the long years of campaigning had left his skin deeply weathered. Back East, he had kept his mustache waxed and trimmed, but now it was an unwashed mass of gray bristles that smelled of cigar smoke and his own body. Just a month shy of his sixty-first birthday, Slocum was beginning to think about retirement and his return to the East Coast. He missed the changing seasons, the pleasure of all-day rain, the luxury and abandon of growing things. Thanks to the generosity of his extremely wealthy and powerful aunt, he had more than enough money to live comfortably for the rest of his life. But he had been in the cavalry for forty years and wanted to remain in the service until he reached the mandatory retirement age of sixty-four. Despite the remote postings, the physical hardships, the utter lack of cultural activities, Slocum knew that he would greatly miss the

U.S. cavalry. "Chivalry, courtesy, hospitality and consideration were characteristics of that old army," one aged general reminisced.

Slocum was a direct descendant of Myles Standish, one of the original members of Plymouth Colony, and a town bearing the name of Slocum exists today in Rhode Island. The Slocums were a prosperous, well-educated clan but their financial position radically changed in 1869 after Herbert's schoolteacher aunt, Margaret Olivia Slocum, married Russell Sage, a secretive and ruthless Wall Street financier. When Sage died, he left Margaret Olivia his entire fortune, which was valued at approximately seventy-five million dollars.

Mrs. Russell Sage, as his aunt preferred to be called, believed strongly in helping others. She established the Russell Sage Foundation, which was dedicated to the "improvement of social and living conditions in the United States," and founded Russell Sage College in upstate New York to train young women entering the field of social reform. Mrs. Sage distributed the rest of the fortune among family members, with eight million dollars going to her brother Joseph Jermain Slocum — Colonel Slocum's father. Joseph Jermain, in turn, passed some of the money on to his son.

Like his aunt, Colonel Slocum was generous and gave away more than what he earned each month in army pay. Even then, he had enough left over to hire house servants and provide monthly disbursements to his two sons. Wealth gave Colonel Slocum a special status even among the well-connected cavalry officers, yet he remained humble about his great fortune. He was a considerate husband, a thoughtful father, and had a soldier's belief in duty and honor, which he sought to instill in his children: "Be constant on the job; do more than you are expected to do, and do it well. Get to the office, on the job, early, and stay late; get there before the time required, so that you may always be known to be a man on hand. Do all that which is placed before you to do to the very limit of your ability. But in doing all of these things do them without antagonizing those with whom you are associated for fear that jealousies may be aroused, which are sometimes injurious."

Slocum's long, thoughtful letters were prompted perhaps by knowledge of his own youthful follies. He had entered West Point in 1872, where he proved to be a lackluster student, ranking near the bottom of his class in most subjects. He also received a large number of demerits each year, which were given for various infractions. In 1876, the year he was to graduate, he was found deficient and discharged from the academy. The discharge did not seem to have any serious consequences for his military career and that summer he was made a second lieutenant in the Twenty-fifth Infantry. A month later he transferred to the Seventh Cavalry, which had suffered many casualties at Little Bighorn but was still stationed on the frontier.

Slocum was at Fort Beaufort in the Dakotas when Sitting Bull, who had fled to Canada after the Bighorn battle, decided to surrender. "His rag tail outfit were bunched together on the prairie in front of the C.O. quarters and came forward and laid down their guns. Of course they did not have any modern or very serviceable guns, naturally, these had been left behind (for cash) with their late friends in Canada but we took what they had and searched their travois and the Red River Carts, old and dilapidated." As Slocum was putting away their guns, an Indian named Lone Wolf pulled his own weapon from the pile and gave it to him as a gift.

Slocum participated in the military campaigns against the Sioux, Nez Percé, Cheyenne, and Apache. He went on to fight in the Spanish-American War and in the Philippines before returning to the United States. He was promoted to colonel in 1913 and soon thereafter was appointed commander of the Thirteenth Cavalry.

Despite his less than stellar performance at West Point, Slocum had made many good friends at the military academy, and by 1916 some of those friends had risen to the highest ranks of the War Department. They included Hugh Scott, chief of staff, and Tasker Bliss, assistant chief of staff, both promoted to major generals the previous year, and Ernest Garlington, the inspector general of the army and a brigadier general. But to the farmers and shopkeepers in Columbus, Slocum often appeared high-handed and pompous and frequently referred to Mexicans and Mexican-Americans in derogatory terms. He was not alone; a pernicious racism existed in the army and in the civilian community toward all minorities. In routine dispatches and even official reports, rank-and-file soldiers and officers alike regularly referred to Hispanics as "greasers," "chile peppers," "half breeds" and "spics."

Sitting on Slocum's desk was a pile of yellow telegrams, all of which claimed to have solid information on Villa's whereabouts. Like other military commanders along the border, Slocum knew Villa personally. "The old scoundrel and I had become very good friends," he once told a military officer in an affectionate, rueful tone. Slocum had been in Arizona when Villa had suffered the devastating defeat at Agua Prieta and afterward threatened to lay siege to Douglas. He had not followed through with the threat and Slocum judged an attack on the United States even less likely now, especially given the fact that Villa's army had dwindled to perhaps a twentieth of its original size. Besides, he thought (unwittingly echoing the same sentiments that Pancho Villa himself had expressed), what glory was there in attacking such an insignificant outpost as Columbus?

DESPITE PANCHO VILLA'S efforts to keep his whereabouts secret, both U.S. and Mexican officials were tracking his movements with a good degree of accuracy. His motives, though, remained obscure and contradictory. The man responsible for much of the confusion was undoubtedly George Seese, an ambitious, thirty-three-year-old reporter for the Associated Press, who had been in touch with Villa's agents since the time of the train massacre. Villa was purportedly anxious to prove himself innocent of that crime and Seese had offered to personally escort Villa to Washington so he could make his case. Villa had allegedly agreed — provided he could be promised safe-conduct — but Seese's supervisor in New York had quashed the scheme on March 2. (It's unlikely Villa ever actually intended to cross the border peacefully but he may have deliberately encouraged Seese in order to confuse both Carrancista and U.S. authorities).

The first to suggest Villa was planning something serious was Zach Cobb, the U.S. Customs official in El Paso, a sparrowlike man with hair that was parted in the middle and plastered to either side of his skull. A staunch Democrat, perennial political candidate, and lawyer by training, Cobb was from an old Georgia family whose members had served in both national and local politics for decades. His grandfather had lost his family plantation during General Sherman's march to the sea and as a consequence, writes his biographer, Cobb was passionate about the need to protect private property. In 1901 he had moved to El Paso, and quickly ingratiated himself with the powerful men who ran the city. In the run-up to the 1912 presidential election, Cobb had stumped tirelessly for Woodrow Wilson and had been rewarded for his effort with the coveted job of customs collector. He got a second job working as an intelligence agent for the State Department through his friend George Carothers, the special agent assigned to Villa, who suggested that his reports be filtered through Cobb. He worked tirelessly to crush Pancho Villa and in the fall of 1915 had largely succeeded in blocking the exportation of coal needed for Villa's troop trains, as well as the importation of Mexican beef, which Villa depended upon to raise cash for his army.

Cobb had good connections in El Paso and Juárez and in March of 1916 these sources paid off. He sent six telegrams to the State Department, his sense of urgency increasing as his information grew more accurate. On March 3, he sent his first telegram: "Villa left Pacheco Point, near Madera, on Wednesday, March 1 with 300 men headed toward Columbus New Mexico. He is reported west of Casas Grandes today. There is reason to believe that he intends to cross to the United States and hopes to proceed to Washington. Please consider this possibility and the necessity of instructions to us on the border." The State Department forwarded the message the following day to Hugh Scott in the War Department. From there, it was relayed to General Frederick Funston in San Antonio, who commanded the Southern Department, which had jurisdiction over all the cavalry posts along the border. Funston, in turn, passed the information along to Colonel Slocum. During the ensuing days, Cobb sent five more messages to the State Department. At least three of those messages were forwarded to the War Department:

- **March 6:** "My March 3, 2 p.m. seems confirmed.
  Commanding General Gavira in Juárez announced to reporters

this morning that Villa was proceeding to the border and that he had asked the American military authorities to be on the lookout for him. My tip is that he is due tonight or tomorrow. I have instructed deputy at Columbus to rush any information."

- **March 7 (8:00 p.m.):** "Deputy Columbus phones report that Villa with estimated four hundred men is on river southwest of Columbus, fifteen miles west and fifty odd miles south, where they stopped round up of cattle by employees of Palomas Land and Cattle Co., all of which employees except one are reported to have hastened to American side."

- **March 8 (12:00 noon):** "Villa party captured and holds fourteen employees of Palomas Land and Cattle Company, thirteen Mexicans and one American named McKinney. Villa camped at point stated, and apparently unafraid. He is reported to have three hundred and fifty men and eight hundred saddled horses in good condition. His purpose is indefinite. He could take the part of Palomas, which has a Carranza garrison of about forty men all of who are prepared to cross to the American side if Villa appears. I suspect that Villa is in communication with agencies of himself and others on this side."

In addition to Cobb's warnings, General John Pershing, stationed at Fort Bliss in El Paso, had also received at least three reports of Villa's whereabouts from Gabriel Gavira, the Carrancista general in Juárez. Six days before the raid, Gavira's secret service agents had learned that Villa was not coming to the border to make a case in his own defense for the Santa Isabel train massacre but to "commit some act of violence" that would force the United States to intervene in Mexico. Gavira had passed the information along to Pershing, who, however, was singularly unimpressed. "The General replied that he had heard similar stories so many times before that he was inclined to take them all with a grain of salt. All of the army officers stationed at Columbus felt as did General Pershing. For years, we of the border patrol, had heard many rumors, which had never materialized," wrote Major Frank Tompkins, who was stationed in Columbus at the time.

Pershing received a second report from General Gavira on March 6 stating that Villa had been seen one mile south of Palomas on the previous evening. He passed the information along to Funston in San Antonio, who once again relayed the information to Colonel Slocum in Columbus. And on March 7, Pershing received a third report indicating that "Villa, with 500 men southwest of Palomas, had raided the ranches of the Palomas Land and Cattle Company; that the Mexican consul stated that his information was that Villa was near Boca Grande, and that one of the stockholders of the company reported that his information was that Villa was about fifty miles southwest of Palomas going south."

Other military officers stationed along the border were also picking up the disquieting reports. Colonel George Dodd, who was based in Douglas and was Slocum's direct supervisor, had also sent a telegram to Funston reporting Villa's appearance on the Palomas ranch and the capture of horses and the foreman. And finally, George Carothers, on March 8, had dashed off a telegram to State Department officials in Washington saying that Villa was supposed to be at a ranch about twenty-five miles south of the border, and headed west into Sonora.

The knowledge of Villa's whereabouts was not confined to a handful of officials within the War Department or the State Department. Newspapers in El Paso and in Mexico were filled with front-page stories about Villa's approach to the border and speculation about his motives. Some of these stories were picked up and carried in newspapers such as the *Chicago Tribune, New York Herald Tribune, New York Times,* and *Washington Post.* Thus, virtually every member of Wilson's cabinet and even the president himself could have read of Villa's movements simply by opening their morning newspaper. The *New York Tribune* even reported that Villa was depending on his friendship with General Scott to secure favorable terms for political asylum and planned to confer with army officials near Columbus.

Colonel Slocum had the unenviable task of trying to make sense of the conflicting reports. Was Villa in Palomas? Or was he sixty-five miles away? Was he coming to the border on a peaceful mission or a violent one? Was he moving west into Sonora as George Carothers had reported? Or south as General Gavira had reported? Army scouts could have cleared up the mystery but Slocum was barred from sending troops across the border. Still, he did what he could to chase down the rumors, checking frequently with civilian authorities and questioning the "supposedly friendly" Mexicans in town.

On Tuesday, March 7, Slocum received strong confirmation of Villa's whereabouts from two eyewitnesses: Juan Favela and Antonio Múñez, the two cowboys who had narrowly escaped being caught by Villa's men on the Boca Grande River. When Nicolás Fernández's troops surged up the hill after them, they had eluded the soldiers in a canyon. Juan had urged Antonio to remain behind and watch the soldiers through his field glasses in order to ascertain the direction in which they were headed. Meanwhile, he said, he would race ahead and warn the cavalry. At about eleven o'clock on Tuesday morning, Favela had reached Gibson's Line Ranch, fourteen miles southwest of Columbus. Exhausted and perspiring, he told a young lieutenant of the morning's events. The lieutenant advised him to take the information on to Slocum. "I came on to Columbus and notified Colonel Slocum about 4 o'clock in the afternoon of that day," said Favela.

Múñez — who hadn't hung around for too much longer — also reached Columbus on Tuesday and went to Slocum to report what he had seen. Slocum hit upon the idea of sending Antonio back into Mexico to spy on Villa, persuading him with the promise of twenty dollars.

Slocum's troops patrolled a strip of border sixty-five miles long. Most of their work was concentrated west of Columbus, the thinking being that it would be the most likely point of incursion since to the east there was almost no water, which was necessary for horses and men. At the Border Gate, three miles south of town, were 2 officers and 65 men of Troop G under the command of Captain Jens. E. Stedje. Another 165 men and 7 officers under the command of Major Elmer Lindsley were at Gibson's Line Ranch. On the evening of March 7, Slocum also ordered an officer's patrol from the Border Gate to go to Moody's Ranch, which was located between these two outposts. These soldiers were to scout in both directions, meeting up with the other patrols. His troops thus deployed, Slocum was confident that his old friend Pancho Villa couldn't slip through.

➤➤8◅◅

VILLA IS COMING TONIGHT,
FOR SURE

ON WEDNESDAY, MARCH 8, while the people of Columbus went about their business, Pancho Villa's spies drifted through town, scoping out the layout of Camp Furlong, the location of the stores, and the homes where the officers lived.

Milton and Bessie James hurried to the depot as soon as they heard the whistle announcing the afternoon train from El Paso. The train was Columbus's lifeline to the outside world and stopped at the little wooden depot three times a day, dropping off passengers, mail, and household goods. The couple chatted happily as they awaited the arrival of Milton's stepsister, Myrtle Wright Lassiter, who was going to spend a few days with them. Milton, thirty-one, was an engineer and pumpman for the El Paso and Southwestern Railroad. Bessie was just nineteen and studying to be a telegraph operator. They had been married for less than two years and were full of plans for their future.

When Myrtle arrived, they greeted one another happily and then walked back to Milton and Bessie's home, a wooden, three-room house that they had begun to fill with the first proud possessions of their new life together. Myrtle, who had just celebrated her twenty-seventh birthday the day before, was glad to see her step-brother married. He had not had an easy upbringing; his father had died several months before he was born and his mother passed away soon after giving birth. Myrtle's parents had taken him in and raised him as one of their own. While he was never formally adopted, the two were as affectionate and close as any siblings could be.

The James house was crowded; Bessie's little sister, Ethel, was also staying with them while she attended the new brick elementary school. When she came home that afternoon, she may have re-marked about how empty the classrooms were; only a handful of the Spanish-speaking children who attended the school had shown up for classes. It was an ominous sign.

While Milton and Bessie James chatted with their houseguests, Susan Moore, a lovely woman who wore her dark hair in a loose pile on top of her head, sat in the rear of her husband's dry-goods store doing her lacework. Nothing had prepared the former New Yorker for Columbus's windstorms, which often began as an inno-cent but robust breeze on a cloudless blue morning and blotted out the sun by noon. Sometimes, when she listened to the shrieking wind, she caught herself thinking that she had inadvertently com-mitted some terrible offense. Why else would the Lord have plunged her, still living, into this hell on earth? But it was Susan herself who had brought this about when she rekindled her romance with John Moore, appearing in El Paso in 1912 and inviting him to visit her there. They had not seen each other in eighteen years. They were both middle-aged, single — and alone. Soon they had married.

The couple owned a little spread called Mooreview, which lay southwest of Columbus and about a mile and a half from the bor-der. Their house was constructed from adobe bricks, with porches on the north and west sides and another off the kitchen. The walls were plastered, the woodwork gleaming, and a handsome fireplace in the center of the house provided warmth and light. "Altogether one of the finest houses in the valley," a local booster gushed. Susan had a taste for beautiful, impractical things and anything French. She had brought with her to Columbus silk petticoats, silk gloves, silk hose, beaded evening slippers, a hand-painted chiffon waist dress (not yet sewed up), French gowns, French blouses, French corsets, French underwear, and a feather fan made in Paris. Sadly, there was no place to wear her pretty things and everything lay packed away.

The Moores planted rosebushes and nearly twenty acres of fruit trees around their house. But the eternity of land and sky, which pressed in upon Susan from every window, was more than she could handle and she spent most days in the store with her husband. She kept a glass of cold water at her side. The desert, she had discovered, created a thirst that was both physical and psychological. On Wednesday, every customer who came into the store spoke of nothing but Villa:

> These reports caused some of the people, especially the women, much anxiety. Others seemed to put no faith in the rumors. I was one of the anxious ones. Probably the most anxious one, owing to the fact that I was not very well acquainted with the ways along the border, having recently come from New York City; and also owing to the fact that I was daily horrified by the detailed newspaper accounts of the unbelievable outrages which occurred at frequent intervals along the border and in Mexico. Seeing these reports worried me. Mr. Moore made an effort to keep the papers from me and then asked me to not read these accounts. I did not for a time.

Remote and formal in her demeanor, Susan Moore had made few friends in Columbus and came to relish the diversion of her Spanish lessons. Just that day, in the middle of her lesson, the young instructor had asked her if she was afraid of Pancho Villa.

"Señora Moore, no tiene miedo de Villa?"

"No, y usted?"

"No, no tengo miedo pero mi madre y mi hermano tienen mucho miedo."

Toward four o'clock, an expensively dressed man entered the store. When Susan Moore got up to wait on him, a "cold chill" swept over her. "He was a small man, with dark eyes, black mustache, he had on one of these high class Mexican hats, and I

thought to myself: 'He must be a lieutenant in the Mexican army.'"
In her schoolbook Spanish, she asked:

Buenas tardes. En qué puedo servirle?

Quiero comprar unos pantalones.

While Mrs. Moore looked for pants in his size, she could feel his eyes following her. Later, she would say, "I did not look at him any more until I handed him the change, and I took a good look at him again because I thought if it was ever necessary to know him again I would recognize him, and he smiled, and took his change, and I could feel his eyes on me the whole time."

For the next two hours she debated whether they should spend the night in the back room of the store or return home to Mooreview. "I decided it would be better to go out there because if they did come in they would raid the stores and hotels, and I thought he would hardly come out of his way for just one family."

They went home between six and seven o'clock. On the way, they stopped at the house of Earl Moore, one of her husband's cousins.

"Earl," said Susan, "you want to look out, they say Villa is coming tonight for sure."

He laughed, saying, "That would tickle me to death."

WHILE THE MOORES were going home, Laura Ritchie and her family were on their way to the closing night's festivities at the Methodist convention. Mrs. Ritchie's garter had come loose in the street and she stopped to fix it. Thinking she would be helpful, her daughter Blanche turned on the flashlight and Mrs. Ritchie scolded her harshly, afraid that someone might see her. Her husband laughed, though, and the anger she felt evaporated.

On their way to church, they had all stopped to admire the sleek Ford touring car parked in front of the hotel. The automobile belonged to engineer Charles DeWitt Miller, who had checked in about five o'clock that afternoon. Miller was only thirty years old, but was rapidly developing a reputation as one of the West's water experts. He was a soft-looking man, with pale cheeks and dark hair, whose mild demeanor hid an aggressive business sense. At that time, he was working with two separate groups of developers on the purchase of two large parcels of land, one totaling twenty-six thousand acres and a second, irrigable tract that encompassed approximately thirty thousand acres. He was to receive a commission of fifty cents per acre when the deals were finalized.

Miller had been traveling for three days and was tired from the jarring, unpaved roads. On Monday, he had bundled his wife, Ruth, and their two little girls, ages two and four, into the new car and driven to Rincon, New Mexico, sixty-five miles north of Columbus, where they spent the night with Ruth's sister. The following morning, Charles left his wife and children in Rincon so they could continue their visit and motored on to Las Cruces. He had lunch with his brother, a cashier at a local bank, then got back in his car and drove south to Deming. He spent Tuesday night in Deming and the following day he continued his inspection of property around Columbus. When he arrived at the Commercial Hotel on Wednesday evening, Edna Ritchie was playing the piano in the parlor. "That sounds like home," he remarked to Laura as he signed the guest register. He took his bags to room 3, returned to the parlor, and sang a few songs with Edna. Then he dashed off a postcard to his wife and strolled over to the post office to mail it.

The performances of the Ritchie girls went beautifully. The family stayed for refreshments and walked back to the hotel. Blanche took off her pink frock and her black patent-leather shoes and laid them on a chair. Edna covered the little canary. Mr. Ritchie retired to bed while Laura puttered about the hotel, putting away the punch bowl that she had provided for the Methodist reception, picking up the newspapers in the parlor, blowing out the lamps.

In their room overlooking the street, the honeymooners, Rachel and John Walker, were packing their suitcases. They were checking out the following morning and were eager to return home; they had heard the ugly rumor that two of their friends, Arthur McKinney and William Corbett, had been killed by Pancho Villa's men and the news had deeply shaken the Walkers.

"Can they get their bodies brought across the border for burial?" Rachel had asked the man who brought them the news.

"Too risky," he responded.

"Well," said her husband, "when Villa gets me, I hope he finishes me north of the border."

Rachel hushed him. The idea was too horrifying to contemplate.

The other hotel guests — Harry Hart, the veterinarian; José Pereyra, the well-mannered young man from the Mexican consulate; and the wily old cattleman, Uncle Birchfield — were in their rooms. Sam Ravel's room was dark; he had gone to the dentist in El Paso and had not yet returned. Captain Leoncio Figueroa, his enemy, was also out for the evening. The hotel seemed unnaturally silent without Figueroa's booming laughter.

HERBERT SLOCUM stayed late at his headquarters on Wednesday night, still poring over the telegrams and reported sightings of Pancho Villa. Another employee of the Palomas ranch, J. L. Fonville, forty, had independently come across the tracks of Villa's soldiers. He followed the tracks and spotted the Villistas on the Boca Grande River. He immediately wired the information to the ranch's agent in Columbus.

Around 5:00 p.m., Sam Ravel's brother Louis, twenty-seven, had crossed the border to Palomas to pick up some telegrams and discovered the entire town in pandemonium. The telegraph lines were out of commission and officials in Palomas were anxious to get messages to the Mexican consul in El Paso and Carranza's military men. Villa was very close, they wrote in the telegrams, begging for instructions on what to do. As Ravel was returning to Columbus, he glanced back across the flat plain that dipped down into Mexico and saw a huge amount of dust "as might be caused by a large body of men." He continued on to the local telegraph office, where he proceeded to send the telegrams. While there, he bumped into Captain George Williams, Slocum's adjutant. Louis shared the contents of the telegrams with the captain and also told him of the large cloud of dust he had seen. "Captain Williams said that men would be sent out to investigate and ascertain with regards to these facts."

It was already dark by the time Antonio Múñez returned to

Gibson's Line Ranch from his "spying" mission south of the border. Major Elmer Lindsley drove him in a Ford car fourteen miles back to Columbus so he could give Colonel Slocum his report. Slocum spoke Spanish poorly and Antonio's English was equally lacking so Major Lindsley acted as interpreter. Also present was Captain Williams. Later, Antonio would tell Marcus Marshall, the son of the owner of the sprawling Palomas Land and Cattle Company, "I reported that night, Wednesday, that Villa with about 500 or 700 men was on the Boca Grande River and was headed this way." But Slocum would inform investigators for the U.S. Army that he had been given exactly the opposite information: Antonio, he said, told him that Villa and his main body had turned off to the southeast and were moving away from Columbus. A smaller group of a hundred soldiers had split off from the main body and were heading for Palomas but these soldiers, too, had turned south away from the border, he added.

There are several possible explanations for the differences. Antonio's information may have been garbled in translation. Another possibility is that Villa, who was extremely canny, deliberately turned south away from the border with the express purpose of deceiving any observers and then doubled back under cover of darkness. Or, someone was lying. But who? Major Lindsley would later confirm Slocum's account in his own sworn statement of what transpired, but he also said that Antonio was questioned very carefully and was "too scared to be lying."

After Antonio left, Slocum went to the Border Gate and tried to elicit information from the Carrancista soldiers on the other side. "I found everyone on the Mexican side more or less terrified and not willing to go very far to the south and find out what could be learned of Villa. They told me that one of their men had the day before, or night before, I have forgotten, been out in the hills, heard some voices, this frightened him and he had returned to the gate."

Slocum again went over the disposition of his troops: a total of 270 soldiers and officers were stationed at various points along the border, leaving 341 men and 12 officers in Camp Furlong. Of these, 79 were noncombatants, which meant that there was a fighting force of 274 men in Columbus. Sending more soldiers to the border would mean fewer men in the camp and Slocum decided to leave the troops where they were.

Three sentinels and a watchman were assigned to guard Camp Furlong. One sentinel was posted at the guard tent, where the regiment's machine guns and ammunition were locked up; a second was posted near the stables; and a third was stationed in the vicinity of the headquarters building near the northwest corner of the camp. The watchman patrolled an area that included the stables, band barracks, hospital, and haystacks. In addition to this regular guard, one noncommissioned officer and three soldiers made an inspection of the town and camp every evening.

Slocum did not increase the number of sentinels assigned to the camp, nor did he dispatch additional guards to look after the town. The troops remaining in camp were also not ordered on alert. The reason for this was simple: despite the telegrams, the three eyewitness accounts of the Palomas ranch hands, and the excited report of Louis Ravel, Slocum still didn't believe that Pancho Villa would attack an armed military encampment. And he had said as much to George Carothers, the State Department agent. Carothers had planned to come out to Columbus on the midday train but hadn't been able to reach Slocum until that evening. He had obtained new information, apparently, and no longer thought that Villa was moving away from the border. "I told him that I knew Villa was very close to Columbus; that I didn't know what he was doing there, but my information was very positive. . . ."

Slocum's response?

"He ridiculed the idea," Carothers would later say. "He said that his information was that Villa was 65 or 70 miles away, and I told him I knew different."

As darkness fell, Slocum put on his canvas jacket and his battered cavalry hat. Exiting the headquarters building, he nodded to Fred Griffin, a nineteen-year-old sentry from Cottondale, Alabama, who had caused his parents much grief two years earlier when he had enlisted in the army without their knowledge.

The wind had finally died down and the land had the brushed look of stiff corduroy. Here and there, among the clumps of sage, were the small modest houses belonging to the officers and the townspeople. Looking to the northeast, Slocum could just make out the lights of his own home. Relief washed over him.

AT HIS SMALL HOME on the Mexican side of the border, Juan Favela, the other Mexican cowboy who had escaped capture on the Boca Grande River, sat under the stars with his young wife, Petra. He was discouraged by the brush-off that he had received from Colonel Slocum. As he told his wife what had transpired, she became convinced that Villa would attack their place on his way to Columbus. They also had family who lived in Columbus and needed to be protected. "It does not matter if the Colonel does not believe you, my Juan. We have loved ones there. Your mother, who is alone. We must go now."

She pulled him to his feet and they got into their Star sedan and drove through the sand hills back to Columbus. Eight months pregnant, Petra held a lantern out the window so they could see where they were going. The mesquite and creosote bushes exuded a tangy scent, but in the blackness beyond the swinging lantern light, Juan sensed something malevolent. "The air was bad," he would later say.

At the Border Gate, Juan told the officer in charge that Villa was coming. He was brushed off once more, but vowed to try to talk to Slocum again in the morning. Their sedan lurched over the railroad tracks, past the train station, and rolled into town.

At ten o'clock, Susan Moore opened her kitchen door and stepped out into the yard. The night was awash in starlight, and the uneasy restlessness that had plagued her all day evaporated. The Moores slept on a sleeping porch facing the small town. Before she went to sleep, Susan placed her navy blue coat on a chair. On a second chair, she placed her clothes in the order in which she would put them on. "Mr. Moore, being very tired, went to sleep in a short time. I studied about the rumored raid about an hour. Finally I decided the night was too clear for it and went to sleep."

At fifteen minutes before midnight, E. A. Van Camp, one of the fastest press telegraphers in the United States, stepped down from the westbound train from El Paso. He walked quickly through the empty streets to a small out-of-the-way hotel, where his friend, George Seese, the Associated Press reporter, was staying. Seese, duly chastised by his bureau chief in New York, was still covering the Pancho Villa story. Earlier in the week, he had slipped away from his hard-drinking newspaper buddies back in El Paso and made his way to Columbus. Accompanying him was a charming new wife, whom he had married in Deming only eleven days earlier. (Her newlywed bliss would be shattered when she learned the flamboyant newspaperman had another wife and four children back in Los Angeles.)

Also getting off the midnight train were John P. Lucas and Horace Stringfellow Jr., both West Point graduates and second lieutenants who had been in El Paso at a polo tournament. The tournament had ended earlier that afternoon and they decided to catch the train back to Columbus. The El Paso papers had been filled with stories about Villa and the two young officers, Stringfellow would later write, "were hoping to get in the aftermath of some raid on a border ranch, although of course we could not even have imagined an attack on Columbus itself."

First Lieutenant James Castleman, the officer of the day, had greeted Lucas and Stringfellow as they stepped down from the train. Castleman was relaxed and mentioned nothing to them about Villa. As Lieutenant Lucas walked to the house where he lived, the unredeemed ugliness of Columbus once again assaulted his senses: "A cluster of adobe houses, a hotel, a few stores and streets knee deep in sand combined with the cactus, mesquite and rattle snakes of the surrounding desert were enough to present a picture horrible to the eyes. . . ."

Lucas commanded the Machine Gun Troop, a relatively new unit in the U.S. cavalry, which, in the case of the Thirteenth Regiment, consisted of misfits and troublemakers and outcasts that no one else wanted. Lucas had taken them all under his wing. He knew they were brave men and could think of no better soldiers to have at his side during a fight.

Upon arriving at the small house he shared with Second Lieutenant Clarence C. Benson, who was on patrol along the border, Lucas picked up his revolver and noticed that it was empty. Though the hour was late and he was exhausted, he proceeded to move the boxes that were piled up in front of their trunk room in order to get at his extra ammunition. He sat down on his cot and pushed the bullets into the chamber, wondering why he was going to the extra trouble. The night was calm and still and he had seen nothing out of the ordinary to alarm him. After reloading his weapon, he lay down on his hard bed and fell immediately into a deep sleep.

Castleman returned to his shack, which was on the east side of the road that ran south into Mexico. Knowing that he would have to make another inspection at four o'clock, he continued reading deep into the night. Soon his was the only light burning in the unbroken darkness.

✦ 9 ✦

The Fiddler Plays

As Susan Moore was drifting off to sleep, the Mexican soldiers were being kicked awake by their *jefes*. They rose instantly, blinking back the dreams and the fatigue-induced hallucinations that danced at the corners of their vision. In silence, they ate their tortillas and fetched the ponies. The little animals opened their mouths docilely as the metal bits were shoved between their teeth and the girth straps tightened. No mediating layer of moisture existed between the troops and the night sky and the air was very cold. The soldiers stamped their feet and shook the numbness from their hands. Most had no idea where they were going, but the knowledge of an impending battle had spread among them. Some sang mournful songs; others developed mysterious flus and stomachaches. The devout murmured prayers to the Virgin of Guadalupe and the soldiers who were resigned to their fate composed farewell messages for their families. Only the half-witted fiddler, Juan Alarconcon, seemed himself. He longed to put his bow to his fiddle in the shining dark and strike up an inspiring rendition of "La Cucaracha," the División del Norte's old battle song, but was told that he would be shot if he did so.

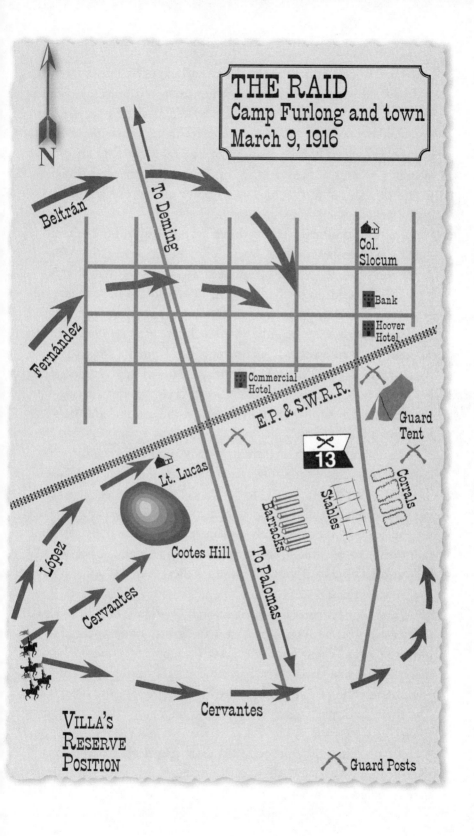

N

THE RAID
Camp Furlong and town
March 9, 1916

Beltrán

To Deming

Col.
Slocum

Bank

Hoover
Hotel

Fernández

Commercial
Hotel

E.P. & S.W.R.R.

Guard
Tent

López

Lt. Lucas

13

Corrals

Cervantes

Cootes Hill

Barracks

Stables

To Palomas

Cervantes

VILLA'S
RESERVE
POSITION

Guard Posts

Maud noticed that Pancho Villa had changed into a uniform and was riding a spirited paint stallion that had been taken from the Palomas ranch. Earlier that day, Nicolás Fernández had approached her with a rifle. Maud felt certain her time had come, but instead of killing her, he wanted her to take the rifle and use it against her countrymen. Maud refused, saying the first thing she would do was shoot him and every other officer. He laughed, saying he believed her, and walked away.

Whatever doubts Villa may have harbored about the attack, he didn't share them with the rank and file. Bunk Spencer, the African-American hostage, would later tell newspaper reporters that Villa gave a demented, rage-filled speech. "He told the men that 'gringos' were to blame for the conditions in Mexico, and abused Americans with every profane word he knew because the Carranza soldiers were allowed to go through the United States to reach Agua Prieta, where Villa was defeated. He didn't talk very long, but before he got through, the men were crying and swearing and shrieking. Several of them got down on the ground and beat the earth with their hands."

The column began marching slowly across the country in a northerly direction, retaining the same formation that they had on the long journey up from Mexico. Two small groups of soldiers were positioned at different points near the border to cover Villa's retreat, leaving approximately 450 men in the main body. At some point prior to the attack, fences had been cut along the border and the railroad's right-of-way to facilitate the Mexicans' escape from the United States.

When they reached the international boundary line, about two miles west of Columbus, Maud saw five lights. Two appeared to be moving toward each other and greatly frightened some of the soldiers, who considered them bad omens. They soon realized they were merely the headlights of trains moving in opposite directions. The three stationary lights were fires to help guide their entry into town.

Crossing the border, they rode north up a deep arroyo that hid them from anyone who might be watching. Near a railroad bridge that spanned the arroyo, they paused for a few minutes while a train passed by. "We were finally so close to the tracks that when the train passed, we were able to see the passengers in the coaches," Maud remembered.

They then resumed their slow, stealthy march eastward across the flat open country until they reached a point roughly a mile and a quarter west of a small rounded knoll known as Cootes Hill. It was the only hill of any size in the Columbus area and allowed them to prepare for the attack undetected. It was now about three o'clock on the morning of March 9, Villa's favorite time for attack. He and his officers reviewed the troops and picked out the men who would participate and those who would be left behind to hold the horses. As usual, they were short of ammunition, so the horse holders were ordered to turn their bullets over to the selected raiders. (The Mexican troops were notoriously bad shots; few had marksmanship training or knew how to use the sights on their rifles.)

The plan called for a three-pronged assault, with the Mexican troops converging on Camp Furlong and the town simultaneously from the west, north, and east. The right wing, composed of Candelario Cervantes's troops and half of Villa's personal escort, would occupy the knoll and continue forward into the military encampment. Some of these soldiers were to swing counterclockwise around the military post and take the horses stabled on the east side of the camp. Pablo López and his men would make up the center wing and use the railroad tracks to guide them into the town. The left wing, commanded by Nicolás Fernández and Francisco Beltrán, was to circle around the town and come down from the north and northwest.

In one of the last orders of business, Villa announced that Colonel Nicolás Fernández had been promoted to general. Then he gave the order for the men to dismount and advance on foot.

Vámonos, amigos!

Viva Villa!

Viva México!

Matemos a los gringos!

Hundreds of armed soldiers streamed through bushes toward town. Soon the percussive explosions of the Mexicans' Mausers alternated with the pop-pop of the cavalry troopers' Springfield rifles. The high-pitched Mexican bugles dueled with the lower-pitched cavalry bugles, which were frantically rallying the American soldiers to arms. From somewhere near the top of the knoll came the first ghostly strains of "La Cucaracha." And a few blocks to the northeast, Colonel Slocum bolted up in his bed. "My God, we are attacked!"

LIEUTENANT LUCAS was awakened by the creak of leather and crept to the window, where he saw men riding toward the military camp. He recognized the intruders as Villistas by the hats they were wearing and judged that he was completely surrounded. Lucas grabbed up his pistol, thankful now that he had taken the time to load it, and positioned himself in the middle of the room, where he would have ample view of the door. He was sure he would be killed but if that was to be his fate, he figured that he would take a few of the Mexicans with him.

Before they had time to enter Lieutenant Lucas's house, Fred Griffin, the young sentry posted in front of headquarters, spotted the invaders. He was standing perhaps 250 feet east of Lucas's house and called for them to halt. The Mexicans charged toward Griffin, firing. Shot in the stomach, chest, and arm, Griffin managed to squeeze off a few rounds, killing two or three raiders before he collapsed. The diversion saved Lucas's life, enabling him to get out of his house. He dashed past the headquarters building, where Griffin lay dying, and ran to the barracks, where he told the acting first sergeant to turn out his men and have them meet him at the guard tent, where the machine guns were kept. On his way to the tent, an armed Mexican suddenly appeared in front of him. Both men fired. When the smoke and noise died away, it was Lucas — one of the poorest shots in the regiment — who was still standing.

When he reached the guard tent, Lucas saw another young sentry sprawled across the door. He stepped over the soldier and fumbled in the dark to open the cabinet where the French-made Benét-Mercié machine guns were kept. The guns were in great demand on the black market because Mexican troops would pay as much as five or six hundred dollars apiece for them. One had disappeared from the Thirteenth Cavalry's arsenal a few years earlier, and as a consequence they were always kept under lock and key. Weighing only thirty pounds, they were easy to carry, but difficult to feed in the darkness. Lucas and several of his men grabbed one anyway and set it up near the stables. Lucas fed the clip of bullets into the metal slot while a corporal acted as gunner. Almost immediately, the weapon seized up. Lucas and his men swore violently, picked up the gun, and raced toward the hospital, where they hoped to repair the weapon behind the building's bulletproof adobe walls.

While Lucas was getting his machine guns and troops deployed, Lieutenant Castleman was running toward the barracks to rouse his men. It just so happened that the soldiers had recently been drilled in what to do in the event of a surprise attack and were already falling in. With about twenty-five men from Troop F, Castleman proceeded north toward the town, where his first priority was to check on his wife and make sure she was safe. As they advanced, the Mexicans poured heavy gunfire on them and the bright yellow flashes lit up the terrain with a surreal beauty. The Americans dropped to the ground and returned fire. "On account of the darkness," wrote a young sergeant named Michael Fody, "it was impossible to distinguish anyone, and for a moment I was under the impression that we were being fired on by our own regiment, who had preceded us to the scene. The feeling was indescribable and when I heard Mexican voices opposite us you can imagine my relief."

Incredibly, none of Castleman's men were hit in the fusillade and they stood and began making their way north again. As they were crossing the railroad tracks, Private Jesse P. Taylor was shot in the leg. Fody told him to lie down and be quiet, promising that they would pick him up later. Ten yards farther, another private tripped, setting off his gun and giving himself a nosebleed, as well as alerting the attackers to their location. More gunfire rained down on them. Castleman's men again dropped to the ground and returned the volley. When the onslaught lessened, they stood and advanced. "We made about four stands in about five hundred yards," remembered Fody. "Private Thomas Butler was hit during the second stand but would not give up and went on with us until he was hit five distinct times, the last one proving fatal."

Whether it was a deliberate part of Villa's strategy or not, the regiment's officers, who lived in the northwest and northeast quadrants, were now cut off from the camp by the hundreds of Villistas moving toward town. The officers were faced with a difficult choice: staying with their loved ones or trying to make it through the enemy lines to the camp, where their men were fighting alone. Each officer solved the dilemma differently.

Herbert Slocum decided he had to first get his wife to safety, and led her through the darkness to the adobe shack of their laundress. "The bullets were falling like rain," Mary Slocum recalled. "We were so bewildered, Col. Slocum, even Herbert was. It seemed as if we were dreaming."

In the northwest quadrant, Major Frank Tompkins, his wife, Alice, and two female houseguests grabbed mattresses off the beds and threw them in front of the door. "Our greatest fear, though unexpressed until later, was that they would set fire to the house and shoot us as we ran out," Alice Tompkins said. Captain Smyser and his family, who lived to the southeast of the Tompkins family, concluded that their house wasn't safe and slipped outside and hid in an outhouse. Soon they decided the outhouse wasn't safe either and crept farther into the brush. Lieutenant William McCain decided to make a dash for the army camp and set off with his wife, small daughter, and orderly. On the way, they ran into Captain George Williams, who lived just a few blocks south of Colonel Slocum and had apparently decided to make a counterclockwise loop around the north side of the town in hopes of reaching the camp.

By now, other raiders were converging on Columbus from the east. Harry Davidson and his buddy, R. L. Carlin, both members of the Texas National Guard who happened to be in Columbus that morning, were sitting on a platform on the south side of the icehouse waiting for the train to El Paso when they heard Spanish voices. "We sat up and in the moonlight saw three Mexicans on horseback coming toward us. They were armed. We did not have a chance to get away. I said to Davidson, 'It's up to us to take 'em as they are' and we sailed into them," Carlin remembered.

It was an extremely reckless strategy since neither was armed. Harry Davidson was killed instantly when a bullet bored into his head. Carlin, now realizing the insanity of their decision, took off running. "The three men followed me, firing. I ran down the railroad track, zigzagging. Then I got into a ditch and made for the north across the field, crawling on my hands and knees whenever I got far enough ahead for it to be safe. The bushes were not high enough to give me much protection." The Mexicans chased him for about three miles and then turned and galloped back toward the corrals and stables, where their companions were already rounding up the horses. Frank T. Kindvall, a farrier, rushed from his tent to protect the animals. It was a noble but suicidal move. "When we picked him up later," said one of his friends, "it was hard to recognize him for he had been shot several times and rode over." Another stable guard, though, caught one of the intruders and beat his "brains out with a baseball bat."

WHILE THE FIGHT RAGED in the army camp, one group of Mexican soldiers advanced to the bank, a second to the train station, a third toward the Commercial Hotel. In the first minutes of the battle, the Mexican invaders were able to go about their looting in a leisurely way, halting occasionally to remove their rotting clothes and don the shirts and pants that they were stealing. Eventually they accumulated so much loot that they commandeered at least one buggy and several mules to cart off things they couldn't carry. From J. L. Walker's place, they hauled off saddles, bridles, spurs, bed blankets, saddle covers, razors, pistols, revolvers and gun scabbards, ammunition, shirts and socks. From the home of W. R. Page, they took a gray coat with a pair of gold spectacles in the upper pocket; a pair of "very fine quality" gray trousers; one pair of ladies' shoes, tan, size five, A–; one black velvet hat trimmed in white ribbon; a gray cloth skirt; another pair of ladies' shoes, these size six; sheets, pillowcases, napkins, handkerchiefs, socks, and men's underwear. From Harry Casey, the jeweler, they took rings, lockets, chains, buttons, and gents' cuff links; packages of rubies, sapphires, and emeralds; nine boxes of chocolates and one jar of chewing gum.

One detachment of Mexican soldiers was charged with finding Sam Ravel, the storekeeper the Villistas had imprisoned in Palomas. ("We did not go to Columbus to kill women and children as it has been said," Juan Muñoz, one of the Villistas, told a Mexican author years later. "We went to Columbus to take Sam Ravel and burn his properties for the robbery and treason which he committed. *Ésa es la verdad.*")

Ravel's youngest brother, Arthur, just sixteen, was asleep when the soldiers burst through the door of the house where Ravel was believed to be staying. *"No me maten!"* — "Don't kill me!" he screamed. They marched the boy to the family store, which was a block away. Louis Ravel, the middle brother, was asleep in the store and scurried into the back room and hid under a pile of hides. The intruders smashed in the windows, broke open the display cases, and took clothing, boots, shoes, hats, cigars, and candy. They instructed Arthur to open the safe. *Abre la caja!* they shouted. But Arthur didn't know the combination, and in frustration, they grabbed him by either arm and escorted him down the street toward the Commercial Hotel, where they hoped to find Sam Ravel. Near the hotel entrance, Arthur saw other armed Mexicans milling about. Candelario Cervantes was the officer in charge. He shouted, *"No molesten a las mujeres, pero maten a todos los gringos!"* — "Don't harm the women, but kill all the men!"

The invaders hammered on the door. Laura Ritchie, who had seen a guest off on the 2:45 a.m. train, was the first to recognize that the hotel was under attack. She heard the sound of breaking glass, wood splintering, staccato bursts of Spanish, and a volley of shots that sounded like a handful of rocks being thrown at the hotel.

Moving with the slowness of dreamers, the Ritchies donned what clothes they could find and gathered up their three daughters. They stumbled into the hallway and encountered the frightened faces of their guests: Rachel and John Walker, Charles DeWitt Miller, Harry Hart, Uncle Birchfield, and José Pereyra. The guests, too, moved slowly, their limbs numb and their heads so clogged with sleep that they could not yet grasp what was going on. Who were all these half-dressed strangers? Why were they milling about in this narrow hallway? And what was that noise down below?

William Ritchie tried to calm them, his wife remembered, "telling them what he thought it was, of course, they were all strangers at the hotel, he tried to tell them the best he could, he thought it was an attack on the town, all this time this shooting was going on, I can not tell you how it sounded. I cannot explain the noise, then after that they called 'Viva México' and we all ran out to the front of the hotel, the lobby, to see what we could see."

Since the hotel was on the second story of the building, there was no way to escape except by the front or back exits, which were blocked now by the Mexican troops. Several of the men had guns, but William Ritchie was afraid the raiders might set the building on fire if they used them. Instead, he dashed downstairs and bolted the front door, hoping that they would be safe until the American soldiers arrived. But a few moments later, the door burst open and the raiders thundered up the stairs.

The sight of the soldiers only increased the feeling among the guests that they were dreaming. The Villistas were unlike any humans they had ever seen: sun blackened and unshaved, smelling of horse sweat and smoke, pants held up with twined horsehair, sandals and shoes made from untanned cowhide. At the end of their rifles were bayonets and perhaps it was their dull points that prodded the hotel occupants into wakefulness.

Señor Pereyra stepped in front of the women and begged the Villistas not to shoot, saying that they were all Mexicans. *No disparen, por favor! Somos méxicanos aqui!* The soldiers dragged each of the women into the light and asked in disbelief, *Es ésta una méxicana?*

In their harsh voices, so absent of the courtesy of the Spanish language, the attackers demanded money and jewelry. Uncle Birchfield, the wily old cattleman, scolded them: *Cállate! Cállate!* — Quiet! Quiet! he said, as he began writing checks.

William Ritchie gave the intruders his watch and fifty dollars. His wife struggled to remove her rings, but the Mexicans grew impatient. One tore the locket from her neck. Another struck her hand with the butt of his pistol, a third clubbed her in the side. While the guests were being robbed, other raiders were smashing trunks and valises and pawing through clothes. Blanche Ritchie watched in horror as a dirty soldier stuffed her pink dress and black patent-leather shoes down his shirt. The troops fired their weapons into the bureaus and beds and demanded to know where Sam Ravel was. *Dónde está Sam Ravel?* they shouted. Laura Ritchie was dragged down the hall and ordered to unlock Sam Ravel's room. But luck was with the inhabitant of room 13; he was still in El Paso.

The light in the corridor was a queasy yellow. With each tic of fear that the guests displayed, the Mexicans found their own cruelty increasing. Using Arthur Ravel as interpreter, the Mexican soldiers asked the male guests to go downstairs to meet their commander.

Charles DeWitt Miller, wearing one laced boot, a brown wool shirt, and khaki pants, descended the stairs. He may have thought of his two little girls, ages two and four, who would one day watch the snow fall on the Sandia Mountains and wear flowered chiffon gowns to college dances, and his wife, Ruth, who would cry bitterly when she received his postcard. Miller stepped into the street.

"*Éste es gringo — mátalo!*" the officer commanded. As the Mexicans raised their rifles, Miller bolted toward his low-slung touring car and managed to jump in and slam the door. When he tried to start the engine, a bullet sped through the door and pierced his body. He slumped across the seat.

Harry Hart, the veterinarian, was second down the stairs. He was wearing pin-striped trousers and his ruby and diamond ring, which the invaders had somehow overlooked. The Mexican soldiers waved their guns in his face and told him to run. As Harry Hart began to run, no different from the cattle he had inspected that day, the commander ordered his troops to kill him. Shots rang out and Hart fell motionless in the street.

John Walton Walker, contractor, rancher, and hay farmer, was next. His young wife, Rachel, was determined not to let him go and clung to him on the stairs. A Mexican soldier dug his fingers into her arm and yanked her back up the steps. As John Walker turned to look up at his wife, a gunshot blast to the chest sent him reeling out the door.

"They have killed him!" Rachel screamed. She continued to scream, only adding to the terror and confusion of the remaining hotel guests. She grabbed the hand of Mrs. Ritchie's eldest daughter, Myrtle, and said, "Come with me. I must go and see if I can find my husband." They went out on the upper porch of the balcony and looked down, where she saw John's body lying in an immense pool of blood.

"There he is! There he is!" Rachel yelled, her voice filled with hysteria. She called to her husband but knew intuitively that he was already dead. With some effort, Myrtle managed to drag her back into the hotel, afraid that Rachel was going to "jump from the porch to her husband's body."

Now it was time for William Ritchie, white-haired and dignified, with the thin red skin of a very old man, to begin his descent to the firing squad. As he slowly raised his hands into the air, he may have thought that it was his own restless nature, urging him forever onward, that had brought him to this moment. Ritchie had taken to heart Horace Greeley's advice and had moved his family farther and farther west. By sea, they had journeyed to New Orleans. By rail to McKinney, Texas. By rail again to Porterville, Texas, a town that would dry up and leave no trace of its existence, and finally to Columbus. Not until William Ritchie had built the hotel and five rental houses was he able to rest, and begin to appreciate the joys of a settled life.

To the Mexicans, he said, "I cannot go and leave the women and children to protect themselves." But his protestations fell on deaf ears. "They put their hands on him," remembered his wife, "and forced him down there; they told him he would have to go and he found out he had to go, and they took him down, and my daughter put her hand out and says, 'Don't go, daddy; don't go.' He says, 'I will be back in a minute.'" At the foot of the stairs, the Mausers roared.

In the brief pause that followed, the Villistas heard the growing battle in the direction of the army camp. The machine-gun fire — *el tableteo de una ametralladora* — especially caught their attention, and they decided to withdraw from the hotel, taking José Pereyra and Arthur Ravel with them. Some of the Villistas marched the Ravel boy toward the Columbus State Bank. *"No lo matamos todavía"* — "We're not going to kill you yet," one growled to Arthur. They walked past William Ritchie's bleeding body. "He said, 'Humph,' just like that," Arthur remembered. The Mexicans gave him no notice.

NOT FAR FROM the Commercial Hotel, Milton and Bessie James and their two houseguests cowered in the darkness, listening to the rat-tat-tat of rifle shots alternating with the long, rolling thunder of the machine guns. When a bullet shattered a lamp, they became convinced the wooden walls would not adequately protect them and decided to make a dash for the Hoover Hotel, which was three hundred feet away and made of thick adobe bricks. They flung open the door and began to run. On the far left was the little girl, Ethel, then came Bessie, then Milton, and finally his stepsister, Myrtle Wright Lassiter. They held hands, clasping one another, as if the physical bond would protect them from the swarm of bullets that lifted the dirt at their feet.

They sprinted toward the adobe hotel, ghost colored and floating like a ship in the first glimmer of morning. Coming toward them down Broadway Street was a crowd of Mexican soldiers. The troops raised their rifles and screamed, *"Viva Villa!" "Viva México!"*

Milton was hit once, then a second time. He began to fall, folding himself around a fiery redness that had materialized somewhere below his waist. On his left, he saw Bessie, leaping into the air, her eyes round as those of a caught fish. On his right, Myrtle staggered against some invisible current and then was sucked under. Only the little girl, Ethel, made it safely through the hotel door.

Ethel told Will Hoover, the big-bellied man who owned the hotel and who also happened to be mayor of Columbus, that the Mexican soldiers had killed her sister. William Hoover and his mother, Sarah, crept down the hall to the office. Cautiously they looked out the window and saw their dear neighbor, Bessie, groaning in the sand. William Hoover was very frightened, but he took a deep breath, opened the door, and dragged Bessie back into the hallway. His mother stood by with a blanket, begging God to spare them. They could see the Mexicans in the street firing indiscriminately at the windows and doors. "Why they did not shoot into the hall, was God's answer to my earnest prayer," Sarah Hoover later wrote.

Bessie's skirts were soaked with blood. She had been shot twice, once in the abdomen and once through the chest. With William and Sarah Hoover crouched over her, the young woman murmured, "I am safe," and died.

Will Hoover and his mother returned to her room, where the rest of the family lay on the floor. It was the safest room in the hotel because the raiders couldn't shoot directly in. Charlie Miller, the druggist, lived in one of the upstairs rooms. During a seeming lull in the fighting, he grabbed up his keys and decided to check on his business. As he opened the hotel door, wrote Sarah Hoover, "They shot him and he fell back dead in our office."

In a tiny house next to the Hoover Hotel, Susan Parks, a nineteen-year-old telephone operator, cowered with her baby daughter, Gwen. When she peeped out the window, she saw a Mexican officer giving orders:

> A bugler stood beside him and a little farther off was a drummer. The man in the uniform was Villa. I am absolutely certain of it. He was dressed in a brigadier's uniform with a cap on in front of which was a medallioned Mexican eagle worked in gold braid with a black background. I have seen so many pictures of the man that there is no possibility of mistake. His beard was about two inches long. If I had not been sure of recognizing him by his features, the proof would have been in the way the Mexicans came dashing up to him every minute or so for orders.

Villa's exact position during the raid has been a matter of controversy for decades. Some Mexicans who were captured said that he remained at the rear, directing the fight. Others argue that he was superstitious about dying on U.S. soil and hovered just on the other side of the international border. But Maud Wright insisted that Villa was mounted on horseback and entered Columbus with his officers.

Mrs. Parks grabbed up her little baby girl and crept to the switchboard. When she lit a match to see the instruments, bullets shattered the window, covering them with glass and splinters. On her hands and knees, she crawled back across the room and put the baby under the bed and then returned to the switchboard and began dialing the number for the U.S. Army at Fort Bliss.

ALL OVER COLUMBUS, in the wooden houses that rose tentatively from the desert floor, the residents were making life-and-death decisions. Should they flee? Should they stay? Would the marauders burn them alive?

Archibald Frost and his wife, Mary Alice, lived in a modest home behind their furniture store with their four-month-old son. Archibald thought the best place to hide might be the store basement. "I realized by the bullets flying around it was an attack of some kind, and I thought possibly that we had time to get into the store and get in the cellar." He grabbed his pistol and his wife held their infant son. Together they crept around to the front of the store. "We had to pass through what seemed to me was machine gun fire. The bullets sang as they came through the air. And there seemed to be many of them in the air at the same time," Archibald later said. He unlocked the door and Mary Alice dashed inside with the baby. Archibald returned to the porch and looked in the direction of the gunfire. "It was to the west and southwest of me and there were so many guns firing that it caused a halo for a space of about a block, the light of the flashes from the rifles. Previously to that I had heard a bugle, it must have been a Mexican bugle, for its call was different from any bugle call I had ever heard, and was beautiful to listen to."

As Frost started across the porch, a bullet slammed into his right shoulder and knocked him to the ground. On his hands and knees now, he crawled into the store as bullets shattered the windows behind him. Once inside, Frost realized that the cellar might not be a safe place after all because the raiders could set the store on fire and roast them alive. Then he remembered his new Dodge Brothers touring car parked in a garage behind the store. "I whispered to my wife that I thought we had better get into the car there, and get started and beat it; she did not know I was even wounded at that time, so we walked out the back door and I managed some way to unlock the garage in the night."

Frost's car turned over readily enough. He released the brake, threw the machine into reverse, and started to manually push the automobile out of the garage. "Usually I give her one shove that sends her clear to the middle of the road." This time, though, the car rolled back inside. He gave the car another shove and the vehicle hit the door. On his third attempt, he saw a Villista standing across the road. The soldier shot at Frost and Frost returned the gunfire. "This Mexican soldier continued to fire at us during the time the car was being backed down on him, stopped for gear shifting, and started forward again, except such times as he dodged back of our car to avoid being fired upon himself, when he seemed to be having things too much of his own way."

As they raced down the dirt street, other raiders fired on them. A second bullet tore through Frost's left arm, ricocheting off the bone before exiting. He kept his foot on the gas and gunned the car north toward Deming. He was bleeding heavily and soon grew so weak that he asked Mary Alice to take the wheel. She had never driven a car before and hit a bump with such force that her infant son was catapulted from the backseat to the front seat. Fortunately, he was unharmed. Only after they were in Deming did they examine the automobile and realize how miraculous their escape had been. Multiple bullets had pierced the metal behind the driver's seat. Another bullet, clearly meant for his wife, had ripped through the leather cushion on the passenger side and struck the windshield. Frost's clothing was soaked with blood. The front seat, side of the car, and its running board were also covered with blood. Marveling at their close escape, Archibald suddenly remembered something else: it was his thirty-fifth birthday.

James Dean and his wife, Eleanor, and their son, Edwin, twenty-three years old, lived north of the business district. When they heard the gunfire, James thought it was only the cavalry staging a mock battle. "If you have good sense, you will go to bed and get your rest," he told his wife and son. Eleanor and Edwin dressed anyway. Edwin loaded a rifle and left it at the head of his parents' bed and started down to the grocery store to get more guns and ammunition. Eleanor wanted to go to the home of their neighbor, R. W. Elliot, whose house was made of adobe. James told her to go ahead and that he would join her later. "So I went & he came but would not go in the house. We all tried to get him in but he wanted to watch. He would go over to the house & look around and then come back."

As James paced back and forth, the attack on the small town intensified. The Mexicans set fire to the Lemmon and Romney general merchandise store and the flames soon leaped to the dry wood of the Commercial Hotel. James decided to go downtown and help put out the fires. "Mr. Dean, you can't do that. Come back here. They'll kill you!" screamed a neighbor. But he would not be deterred and disappeared into the night. Eleanor grew frantic with worry. She went home, built a fire, made coffee, and waited for her husband and son to return. "I knew there would be lots of wounded & they would need water & made coffee, so that any who needed it could be refreshed. I took some over to the others and drank a cup myself. . . ."

The Commercial Hotel began to burn rapidly, the fire stoked by the kerosene and gasoline stored in Ravel's warehouse on the ground floor. Upstairs, Rachel Walker and Laura Ritchie and her three daughters ran from window to window looking for help. Laura Ritchie kept wondering where the U.S. cavalry was. "I wondered why — the soldiers had always been good to us — I wondered why they had not come to us; I wondered why somebody did not come to our assistance after our building had caught on fire."

Suddenly up the back stairs came Juan Favela, the modest and gentle cowboy-rancher who had tried so hard to warn Colonel Slocum of the impending attack. "The hotel was afire. At that time my daughter, Edna, appeared at the back door; she darted back again and she said, 'Oh, mamma, there is Juan Favela at the bottom of the stairs.' She recognized Juan Favela's voice, and he says, 'Edna, come to me, I will take care of you.' So we all went down." Joining them was Uncle Birchfield.

Favela led the group down the stairs and across the alley toward an adobe hut that had already been ransacked. Edna suddenly remembered her canary and broke free and ran back up the stairs to retrieve the bird. But the cage was smashed and the canary already dead. Then she ran down the front steps to look for her father and saw his body lying in the street. "So it was Edna who brought back the sad news that our father, our wonderful, gentle, gay and lighthearted father was dead," Blanche would later write.

Rachel Walker, irrational after seeing her husband's body, remembered a man holding her, telling her she must get out, that the hotel was burning, and that she must not go down the front stairs as they were burning, too. Two men lowered her from a rear window with a blanket. When she was about half a block from the army post, an American soldier ran out from their lines and carried her to the post hospital, where she spent the remainder of the night, begging someone to go for her husband's body.

One man did not escape with the others and his remains would be found in the rubble the following day. William Ritchie had registered him and Laura thought he was a soldier. "Any more than that, I do not know," she said.

FROM ABOUT 4:30 TO 5:45 A.M., the battle raged. Horses stampeded through the streets and small groups of men could be seen fighting in the lurid light cast by the burning buildings. In the army camp, the cooks engaged in fierce, hand-to-hand combat with attackers who sought shelter near the adobe cookshacks. One group of Mexicans broke down a door only to find the cooks waiting for them with pots of boiling water and kitchen axes. A second group was dislodged from their hiding space by the shotgun pellets that the cooks used to hunt game. A third was raked by machine-gun fire.

Corporal Paul Simon, twenty-six, who played in the regiment's marching band, was killed when a bullet crashed through the flimsy walls of the barracks. John C. Nievergelt, fifty, another member of the band, was shepherding his wife and daughter from their home to the camp when he was fatally wounded. Sergeant Mark Dobbs, twenty-four, one of Lucas's machine gunners, was shot through the liver but remained at his post until he died from loss of blood.

Lieutenant Castleman and his troopers set up a skirmish line, with the Hoover Hotel on their left flank and the Columbus State Bank on their right. Nearby was Castleman's own house, where many of the officers' wives had taken cover. Using the light from the fires, they aimed their rifles down Broadway, methodically picking off the invaders. Lieutenant Lucas had three of the machine guns aiming north into the town from various points along the railroad tracks and a fourth trained on the corrals. Thirty riflemen were deployed along the railroad tracks facing the town. South of the railroad tracks, in a deep ditch that ran parallel to the Deming road, crouched Lieutenant Horace Stringfellow and his men.

An army account of the raid noted that Herbert Slocum managed to join his troops "about dawn," which is consistent with what several eyewitnesses remembered. Louis Ravel, who had been hiding beneath the pile of hides, escaped out the back door of the store and ran into Slocum in front of the colonel's house. Slocum asked the young man what was going on and Ravel told him "that the town had been attacked by Mexicans and was then in possession of the Mexicans, and that part of the town was burning. . . ."

Edwin Dean, who had wound up at the intersection where Castleman and his troopers were having good success at methodically picking off Villistas, saw Slocum coming down the street from the direction of his house. Castleman reassured Slocum that everything was under control and urged him to go home. "Everything is all right, Colonel, you had better go back. You can not do anything here." Slocum "stood around and talked a little bit and then went back north," Dean added.

Eventually Colonel Slocum made his way to the small knoll south of the railroad tracks, which the Villistas had used as a cover and landmark to coordinate their attack. Also converging on the hill were Lieutenant Stringfellow and Captain Smyser and Major Tompkins and some sixty other armed soldiers. Remembered Stringfellow: "Colonel Slocum had been shot at. He had a bullet hole transversely through the barrel of his revolver and began walking up and down the firing line on top of the hill with me at his side until I persuaded him not to risk his life so freely."

Villa and his men had fallen back a thousand yards west of the knoll. Their identities were difficult to make out in the dawn light and Colonel Slocum ordered his men to momentarily hold their fire, thinking the soldiers might actually be their own cavalry troops coming from Gibson's Line Ranch. Said Stringfellow, "Not having field glasses I had to take a chance, opened fire and then stopped to listen to the bullets. The Villistas went into action beautifully, dismounted as one and their return fire clipped the top of the hill but there was no 'crack' of the Springfields. These were Mexicans."

MAUD WRIGHT was one of the first to realize that the battle was turning against the Mexican troops. A bullet struck the ground in front of her horse, another grazed its mane. "They began to bring the wounded back to the horseholders. They were placed on their blankets side by side where they lay groaning and crying. Many of them died right there," she remembered.

Villa, she continued, "had been in the thick of the fight, for many times I heard his stallion squeal from some particularly noisy section of town." At some point, she said, the stallion was shot out from under him and one of his soldiers dashed back and got a replacement horse. Before retreating, Villa galloped up and down among the disorganized and frightened soldiers, slashing from right to left with his sword, trying to make them stand and fight. A few did kneel and fire their rifles at the Americans, then began a fairly orderly retreat toward the border. Maud and her horse were swept up with them. Bunk Spencer, the other hostage, made his escape by lying flat on the ground, somehow managing to avoid being trampled.

One of the retreating Mexicans stumbled into Lieutenant William McCain's party, which included his wife and young daughter.

McCain raised his shotgun and fired. The Mexican fell to the ground, moaning, but still very much alive. McCain suddenly remembered that the gun was filled only with bird shot. He and Captain George Williams did not want to fire the gun again for fear of alerting other Mexicans so McCain tried to choke him, but the wounded man fought back ferociously and the little girl began to cry. Mrs. McCain tried to hush her and then handed her husband a pocketknife. "Slit his throat," she whispered. McCain took the knife and hacked at the man's throat but the blade was too dull. Finally, he tossed the knife away, and with his family looking on he picked up the shotgun and bludgeoned the Mexican to death.

Pablo López, who had directed the Santa Isabel train massacre, had been severely wounded near the Columbus train depot. A bullet had struck him in the middle of the chest, at the exact point where his bandoliers crisscrossed his body. The heavy leather straps kept the bullet from penetrating his chest but the impact knocked him from his horse: "As I was sitting on the ground, another came and went clean through both of my legs, from left to right, while still another broke the loading lever of my rifle. I thought it was time to go. A stray horse, also wounded, was standing by, and I crawled to it and dragged myself on it. Having lots of clips for my automatic, I kept emptying my pistol to protect my retreat. My comrades were riding southward, too."

As the Mexicans withdrew, they continued to hear gunfire. *"Por buen rato pelearon americanos contra americanos"* — "For a time Americans were fighting Americans," remembered Juan Muñoz. "They didn't realize that we were retiring and they followed with thick fire; but not against us, it was against the people of the village, the ones who were already organized and had begun to fight."

The Villistas galloped toward the border, passing Mooreview, where John and Susan Moore lived. "We rode past the ranch and I once again saw Villa," recalled Maud. "He threw away an empty cartridge belt and pulled out his revolver and emptied it in the general direction of the soldiers. When those shots were gone he took off his hat and waved it defiantly at all of them. I sincerely believe he was unafraid and almost willing to fight the whole U.S. Army by himself."

Once they crossed the international line, Villa rode back to Maud. Sweat streamed down his horse's flanks and the animal's dark eyes rolled, the whites grown wide with fear. He held his reins lightly while the horse plunged up and down.

Quieres regresar a los Estados Unidos?

Sí, por favor.

Bueno. Puedes irse. Te quedas con el caballo y la silla.

Maud did not argue. She took her horse and saddle and turned back toward Columbus. Her horse had been badly spooked by the gunfire and the smell of blood and kept trying to rejoin the horses that were fleeing in the opposite direction. Finally she dismounted and began leading the mare through the brush. "When I would pass Villistas, many of them would tell me good-bye and shake my hand, saying they were sorry that they had treated me badly. They actually acted as though I was their best friend."

She had not gone far when she heard a voice begging in Spanish for water. It was Castillo, one of her guards, who had taunted her on the long northward march by telling her she probably would not be alive the next day. He had been badly wounded and her first impulse was to kill him. Instead, she took his saddle, which was much better than hers, and put it on top of her own. "I was sorely tempted to impale him on a sword, but instead asked him what he thought of the American soldiers now. He turned his head and I walked away, leaving him to die."

She reached a small compound and went into the corral, watered her horse and drank deeply herself, and then walked toward the house. John Moore was lying dead in a pool of blood at the edge of the porch. She heard a faint noise and followed the sound out behind the house, where she came upon Susan Moore.

JOHN AND SUSAN MOORE had been sound asleep on their porch, buried under their heavy auto robe, when the attack began. Susan, the first to hear the gunfire, was so afraid for a moment that she couldn't speak.

"Wake up. Look. Villa has come and is burning the town," she finally whispered.

John Moore raised himself up on his elbows. Although they were several miles away, the orange flames were plainly visible against the black horizon. "You are right. We had better get dressed."

Susan was already slipping on her clothes, grateful that she had taken the time to arrange them so carefully the night before. They tiptoed around the house and drew down the shades. Her husband returned to a pantry window, which faced the town. Susan stood next to him. Quietly, John said, "If I were in your place, I would not stand there. Someone might see you or you might be hit by a bullet."

Susan moved back into the shadows and began walking from room to room, her eyes lighting upon the small beautiful things that she had brought with her to Columbus — the hand-painted vase, her linen table runner, the fancy bedroom clock that she had bought at Macy's.

Imperceptibly, the sky lightened and the dirt road alongside their house began to grow visible. A dark shape clattered by. A few moments later, another passed.

She looked at her husband. "Maybe we had better go to the mesquite bushes and hide."

He shook his head, telling her they had nothing to fear, that they had always treated their Mexican customers fairly.

Soon the road was filled with retreating Villistas. One group turned into the Moore's yard and watered their horses at the tub of drip water. "Again I looked towards town and saw the road and open space covered with stumbling, wounded, dirty, ragged men. Some of these men were afoot, some on horseback, clinging desperately to the necks of their horses."

An officer wearing a cape coat and sitting astride a white horse ordered several of his men to check out a neighbor's home to the north of them. It was Candelario Cervantes and *los namiqui-penses* — the men from Namiquipa. He nodded toward the Moore home. The soldiers climbed up onto their front porch. One used the butt of his rifle to break the glass on a bedroom window. Mr. Moore told his wife to go into the dining room. Then he went to the front door and opened it.

"Sabe usted dónde se puede haber escondido Ravel?" — "Do you know where Ravel is hiding?" Cervantes asked.

"No soy el guardián de Ravel," John responded.

"Muy bien," said Cervantes.

Then his soldiers fell upon John.

"They raised their hands and struck him. They raised their sabers and knives and stabbed and slashed him. They raised their guns and shot him," said Susan.

The assailants crouched over John's lifeless body, removed his ring and his watch, and went through his pockets. Suddenly they remembered Susan and started toward her.

"Pan? Oro?" — "Bread? Gold?" asked a soldier. She looked at him closely and realized he was none other than the man who had been in her store the previous day to buy the *pantalones*. The Mexicans grabbed her by either arm and gestured at her rings — a plain gold wedding band, a diamond solitaire engagement ring, and a monogram ring set with diamonds.

As she struggled to remove the jewelry, her thoughts were racing. She was certain that she would be killed just like her husband. "Then the thought came to me that I might surprise or outwit them. The next thought that came to me was to scream. I screamed twice, at the same time I looked towards Mr. Moore and the front of the house, to attract their attention away from me, and to give the impression that someone had come." Her captors loosened their grip as they turned to see what she was looking at. Susan jerked free, picked up her skirts, and fled out the back door. Several soldiers were in the garage trying to start the Ford.

"Mira, mira, señora!"

They fired at her. She felt a stinging sensation in her right leg and knew that she had been shot, but kept running. A second bullet slammed into her right hip. She fell, but got up and continued. Running and falling, she eventually reached the barbed-wire fence that enclosed their immediate property. Somehow she managed to heave herself over the fence and she crawled toward a clump of mesquite.

As the gunfire grew intermittent and then stopped altogether, the sweet sound of morning rushed in. Susan Moore lost consciousness. When she awoke, she realized that she was bleeding profusely and tore a ruffle from her petticoat to bind her wounds. Then she passed out again. When she came to, she heard the sound of horsemen and realized it was the American soldiers. She hung her handkerchief on a bush and called out weakly to them.

Captain Smyser and two privates found her. "Why, it is a woman. My God, it is Mrs. Moore!" he shouted. "Are you hurt?"

In a calm voice, she responded, "Yes, Captain, I am shot, but I can wait, if you will go to the house and take Mr. Moore in. They have killed him and you will find him on the front step."

Soon other soldiers arrived. They pulled off their coats and made a bed for her. Someone gave her brandy. Another brought her water in a milk pan. A third shielded her face from the sun. As they were tending her, she noticed a dirty young American woman standing nearby. It was Maud Wright.

"She was dressed in a coarse linen dress with a little Dutch bonnet and was very, very dirty. However, I was glad to see a woman, especially an American, and she came up to me and said she had been a prisoner of Villa for nine days. I looked at her, she looked like she was hungry to me, I asked her if she had had any breakfast, she said no, I told her when we got to town to go to any of these restaurants and get whatever she wanted and have it charged to me, and I asked her to stay with me, and go to town with me in the ambulance, which she did."

Together, Susan Moore and Maud Wright rode into Columbus. By then it was about ten o'clock in the morning. The sky was hard as enamel and the morning sun felt like shards of glass in their eyes. Susan lifted herself up and saw the smoldering remains of the hotel, the half-burned automobile that belonged to Charles DeWitt Miller, the bodies of horses and soldiers. She lay back down and closed her eyes.

There were other survivors. Milton James's stepsister, Myrtle Wright Lassiter, lay unconscious near the Hoover Hotel with a head injury and bullet wounds in her thigh and right hip. She was picked up later that morning and taken back to Milton's house, where she would eventually regain consciousness. Milton himself had managed to crawl to the east side of the hotel, where a man named Gardner picked him up and carried him down to the railroad tracks. Gently he laid Milton down on the embankment and then continued on his way. Later that morning, the train conductor, John Lundy, spotted Milton as the train began inching its way into Columbus. He was delirious and begging for water. Lundy lifted Milton onto the train and transported him to the army hospital. One of the bullets had passed through his penis and scrotum and into his right leg. A second bullet had slammed into his left leg, carrying with it bits of his clothing that were driven deep into the wound. But he would live.

As the sounds of the battle receded, the people of Columbus crept from their hiding places. The children ran ahead, excitedly fingering bullet holes in the thick adobe walls and grabbing up swords and guns. The Hoover Hotel served as a temporary hospital, the bank as a temporary morgue. In all, eighteen U.S. civilians and soldiers had been killed and ten others wounded.

FROM THE KNOLL south of the railroad tracks, Colonel Slocum and the other officers of the Thirteenth Cavalry had watched the dissolving shapes of the horsemen. Behind them Columbus still burned. Major Frank Tompkins had asked for permission to chase the attackers. Slocum had nodded, and in a few minutes thirty-two men were mounted and moving.

As Tompkins and his men galloped south, they could see the fleeing Villistas off to their right. They tried to catch up to them but their progress was greatly hampered by barbed-wire fences. As the Villistas retreated through a twenty-foot gap in the boundary fence, Lieutenant Clarence Benson and his men, who had been sent out the night before to patrol the border, killed eighteen fleeing Mexicans. Also killed at this point was Harry Wiswell, a thirty-eight-year-old corporal from Long Island, who just two weeks earlier had remarked upon the hostile attitudes of the Mexicans in a letter to his mother.

Upon crossing the international line, Tompkins spotted a low hill that was occupied by a rear guard of Villistas who had been left behind to cover the retreating troops. He ordered his soldiers to draw their pistols. "Charge!" he bellowed. The horses galloped up the hill. The Mexicans fired on them but their bullets went high and the Villistas broke and retreated just as the cavalrymen reached the lower slopes. When the troopers gained the top of the hill, they dismounted and trained their Springfields on the Mexicans. Their aim was far more accurate and dozens of Villistas and horses fell to the ground.

Realizing that they were now in Mexico and had violated standing orders from the War Department, Tompkins dashed out a note to Colonel Slocum asking for permission to continue the chase. In forty-five minutes, a messenger galloped back with an ambiguous answer: Use your own judgment.

Deployed at wide intervals, moving at a fast trot, the Americans charged the Villistas three more times. Each time, the rear guard of Villistas returned the fire and then continued their southerly flight. Eventually the U.S. soldiers found themselves on an open plain that was devoid of cover. The main body of Mexicans saw now that they outnumbered the cavalrymen by ten to one and prepared to counterattack. Tompkins and his men fell back about four hundred yards and waited, but Villa's men, it seemed, were too exhausted to launch another offensive. Tompkins debated whether to continue the pursuit, but his troopers were almost out of ammunition and the horses were badly in need of water so he decided to return to Columbus.

They arrived back in town about one o'clock in the afternoon. In all, they had traveled between five and fifteen miles into Mexico and had made four stands. The chase had been deeply satisfying; Tompkins's official report would claim seventy-five to one hundred Villistas had been killed during the pursuit. The number is probably exaggerated but points to a vexing aspect of the raid: the reported number of dead Villistas varied wildly. In Slocum's official report, he stated that a total of sixty-seven Villistas were killed in the town, the military camp, or in the desert leading to the international line, and later upped the figure to seventy-eight. Whatever the number, there was no dispute that those charged with protecting Columbus had failed.

*　　*　　*

IN THE RUNNING gun battle back to Mexico, the Villistas dropped their loot, littering the desert with jars of chewing gum and cigars; spurs and bridles and saddles; wedding rings and gem-studded brooches; shoes and socks and underwear; tablecloths, sheets, and pillowcases, which caught on the sharp thorns of mesquite bushes and billowed gently in the dawn air. The Mexicans toppled from their horses into the brush. Most of them died, not as Villa would have hoped — as gladiators with their faces to the sun — but face-down in the sand, their mouths filled with vomit and soft pitiful moans that rose into the air and were carried off with the heat of the new day. Among the dead were two boys, both no older than fourteen. One was holding several pounds of candy, the other a pair of girls' black patent-leather slippers.

At Arroyo del Gato, roughly sixteen or seventeen miles south of Columbus, the Villistas stopped and unsaddled their horses for a two-hour rest. Pablo López was suffering greatly from his wounds and so was a colonel named Cruz Chávez, who had been shot in the abdomen. The two officers were placed on stretchers and *cargadores* assigned to carry them. Nicolás Fernández gave Villa the sad news: sixty men were missing and unaccounted for, eleven of whom were his beloved Dorados. In addition, twenty-six were wounded, including López and Chávez.

Villa regarded Chávez mournfully. Then he turned to Candelario Cervantes and said, "It has come to this, Cervantes. I gave way to please all of you." Cervantes, in turn, lashed out at Nicolás Fernández, saying it was Fernández who kept reassuring everybody that the attack would be successful. Martín López shook his head in disgust, adding that it had been a "futile effort for a few dollars."

✦10✦

VERY UNNATURAL DEATHS

LAURA RITCHIE SLEEPWALKED over the charred rubble, her three daughters trailing behind, their white faces fixed in the anxious new expressions that they would carry into old age. The raiders had withdrawn and now her husband lay dead in the street, his legs almost burned off in the fire. Broken dishes, quilts, and a squarish hump of something that might have been the piano or organ were visible in the ruins. Puzzled and confused, she hailed Roy Stivison, the school principal, and the Reverend C. H. Boddington as they made their way through town. In a low voice filled with disbelief, she told them that her husband had given the raiders all the money he had in his pockets — and they had killed him anyway.

Rachel Walker, too, returned to identify her husband. Only nineteen years old, she had no way to negotiate around the image of her husband lying in the street, an octopus-shaped puddle of black, sticky blood spreading out beneath him. His corpse was wrapped in a quilt and taken to John Peak, an undertaker who had come from El Paso. After returning home to bury his "few pitiful remains," Rachel suffered a complete nervous breakdown. She remained in bed for weeks, bruised and sore, tortured by insomnia, her face swelling and breaking out in mysterious eruptions. Her nervous system was so "badly perverted" that her physician, E. C. De Moss, predicted she would never recover. She was "in a highly excited nervous condition, almost insane, very ill, suffering from shock of the gravest nature," he wrote, adding, "she was the most unnerved person that he [De Moss] has ever seen, during the period of thirty-two years that he has devoted to the practice of medicine."

Edwin Dean found his father's body in the street among the dead Mexicans and had the task of returning home and telling his mother what had happened. There was no easy way for Edwin to break the dreadful news and when Eleanor opened the door, he blurted out, "Mama they got Papa, he's killed." In a sorrowful letter to her other sons, Eleanor wrote, "We got the auto out & went to him. He lay in the street in front of Walkers store with Mexicans dead all around him but all I saw was Jimmie dead, dead shot like a dog. They tried to keep me from him but I went to him just the same, oh so white and covered with blood & all shot to pieces but his face not hurt only on one side." She and Edwin loaded the body into their automobile and returned home. Still stiff with unprocessed grief, they had to return to work almost immediately because their grocery store was one of the few places in town where people could buy food. "People were crying bread, bread, bread," remembered Ozella Stanfield, who worked in the store and would eventually marry Edwin.

Members of the Elks Lodge came over from Douglas, Arizona, to help identify the remains of Dr. Harry Hart. Beneath one body, a friend found a small piece of patterned cloth. "Now I know that this is Hart's body," he exclaimed, "for he and I ordered suits from this same cloth. It was the last of the bolt and we said at the time, 'No one else can have suits like ours!' " Another friend remembered his ring and they continued digging until they found it. The gold had been darkened by the flames but the rubies and diamonds still gleamed brightly in the sun.

Charles DeWitt Miller's brother and several companions drove down from Las Cruces. Miller's body had been pulled from the wreckage of his car and moved to the bank building. His body, too, had been burned but was still recognizable. Confirmation also came in the form of a Scottish rite ring with his name engraved on the inside.

Bodies were strewn everywhere, particularly on Broadway, where the fighting had been heaviest. Some Mexican raiders were still alive and twitching or moaning weakly and a few had taken out their crucifixes and placed them upon their breasts. The soldiers' wives regarded them with a cold indifference. "I passed any number of dead Mexicans, they were lying all through town, and I could look at their shattered bodies with only an unwomanly joy," Alice Tompkins wrote in a letter to her parents. Mary Slocum, the colonel's genteel and refined wife, experienced similar emotions. "When we came out of the house, the dead and wounded were everywhere. I did not know I could have such hate in my heart. I saw Mexicans horribly wounded and suffering terribly and did not care how much they suffered."

George Carothers and E. B. Stone, a Federal Bureau of Investigation agent, hurried to Columbus to make separate investigations of the attack. They were particularly eager to question Maud Wright and Bunk Spencer in order to confirm that Villa was indeed the mastermind behind the assault and to evaluate the military strength of his forces. Maud was taken to Colonel Slocum's house, where a number of women and children had sought refuge, including Laura Ritchie and her daughters. Mary Slocum helped Maud bathe and gave her lotion to rub on her sore, swollen feet. After Maud had bathed and put on fresh clothes, Bunk Spencer was asked to pick her out from a group of women standing in a lineup. He identified her correctly, confirming both his story and Maud's.

The townspeople and the soldiers walked through the town, looking over the destruction and stopping occasionally to examine the bodies of the dead Mexicans. They kept the rifles, pistols, swords, and bandoliers of the slain raiders as souvenirs. One of the townspeople, Leo Lemmon, stooped down to examine the body of a man who was lying in the ditch that ran parallel to the Deming–Palomas road. He was obviously an officer of some sort and was wearing a khaki uniform, leggings, and a band around his hat. A commission tucked into one of his pockets identified him as Captain Francisco Prado. Lemmon also found a small leather diary on his body, which consisted of a series of short entries, beginning on January 1, 1916, and ending on March 7. Since Lemmon could not read Spanish, he turned the diary over to a companion, Roy Johnson, who read and translated it. The entry for January 10 leaped out at him: "Today about eleven o'clock we assaulted two trains at Santa Isabel, killing 17 Gringos; leaving afterwards, sleeping at Lago." The words were the first hard evidence that Villa had been behind the train massacre. On the body of another dead raider, the soldiers found a leather wallet with the name T. M. Evans stitched on the inside. The wallet belonged to Tom Evans, the young man who had tucked his gold watch into his underwear before getting off the train. It was the second piece of evidence definitely linking Villa to the massacre.

A bulky portmanteau, which had apparently been dropped by Villa's orderly, was also found in the street. It contained recent commissions bestowed on various officers and numerous receipts for expenditures made by the División del Norte. The cash disbursements showed that Villa, although dubbed a bandit, had been spending every penny he had on his army. In the months leading up to the raid, for example, he had purchased large quantities of flour, corn, sugar, salt, chickpeas, and sardines; requisitioned 150 pack mules; shod 300 horses; disbursed funds to doctors who had taken care of the wounded; purchased lamps, tents, quilts, and clothing; distributed fourteen thousand dollars to his troops and doled out countless smaller amounts as bonuses, commissions, and rewards.

But the most significant document found in the portmanteau was the letter written from Villa to Emiliano Zapata in which he suggested they join forces to fight the gringos. In a letter to Secretary of State Robert Lansing, George Carothers wrote, "I attach importance to this letter, as it clearly proves that Villa has had the intention of declaring war against us for several months, and has sent emissaries all over the country to incite the people." Carothers also warned the secretary of state that the United States would have to capture Villa quickly or run the risk of having to pacify the entire country. "A very large percentage of the Carranza troops fought under Villa at different times, and deep in their hearts admire him. Furthermore, they are all the same breed, and deeply resent any invasion of their soil by a foreigner."

Carothers made the same points in a subsequent letter to General Hugh Scott at the War Department and threw in a few salient observations about Villa: "He is crazy, from what I could find out among the prisoners, goes about with his mouth open, and looks dazed. His obsession is to kill Americans, and he has undoubtedly what the Mexicans call 'Delirio de Grandesa' or Delirium of Greatness. He inspired his whole column with the conviction that they could conquer the United States, and that they would be in Washington in six months. This is a different man than we knew. All the brutality of his nature has come to the front, and he should be killed like a dog."

Seven Villistas who had been wounded were taken to the military stockade, including a twelve-year-old boy named Jesús Paez, who had been shot in the leg. Jesús was a handsome youth, with shining black eyes and a scholarly gravity, and seemed eager to cooperate with authorities. E. B. Stone, the Bureau of Investigation agent, was so impressed with him that he planned to charge the captured Villistas with murder, using the boy as a witness. Unfortunately, only two of the seven wounded raiders would survive: Jesús and a sixteen-year-old youth named Juan Sánchez, so small and slender that he seemed hardly more than a boy himself.

On the southwestern edge of town, the soldiers and cowboys gathered up the partially burned wood from the Commercial Hotel and whatever other combustible material they could find and laid it out in a grid. Then they dragged the dead Mexican raiders onto the woodpiles. Kerosene was poured over the bodies and they were set on fire. An oily smoke rose into the air and a terrible smell spread through the town. When the fires went out, several soldiers and their girlfriends, who wore immaculate white dresses, squatted at the edge of one of the funeral pyres, where some of the human shapes were still discernible. One of the soldiers lifted a blackened corpse into a sitting position and held a revolver to its head while another snapped a picture.

*   *   *

MANY TOWNSPEOPLE and military officials, including Herbert Slocum, were convinced the Villistas had been aided by Mexicans living in Columbus. The raiders knew where all the officers lived, where the horses were stabled, where the bank, hotel, and stores were located. Even more curious, none of the homes or businesses belonging to Mexican-Americans had been damaged in the raid. Wrote the *Columbus Courier,* "Only one Mexican store had the plate-glass broken in, and there is strong suspicion that it was broken in by the owners of the store. They have left town under orders. In the Sanford building near the depot there is a restaurant and jewelry shop in the west part, pool hall in the center, and a store on the east that has always been occupied by Mexicans. Only the west part of the building, occupied by Americans, was touched."

Although the people of Columbus had lived through the same droughts and sandstorms and crop failures as their Mexican neighbors, the closeness had not bred affection or trust and the thin veneer of civility that characterized relations between them evaporated after the raid. "Local old-timers speak in hushed voices, warning that they are not to be quoted, saying that many of the wounded Villistas were murdered after the fighting. Some were said to be relieved of their suffering by having their heads slammed against wagon wheels. Other disabled were piled amidst the lifeless bodies," wrote William Cobb in a paper for the Columbus Historical Society. No written evidence has surfaced confirming these allegations, but two letters and a story published in the local newspaper in the days following the raid suggest strongly that some Mexicans who were rounded up by the military and ordered to leave town were killed as they fled toward the border.

Following the raid, Slocum declared the town under martial law and ordered the soldiers from the Thirteenth Cavalry to search every Mexican household. Weapons were seized and Mexicans who looked "suspicious" were arrested. Alfredo Aregon, who worked as a waiter in the Columbus Hotel, was hauled in for questioning because he was absent from his job for several hours prior to the attack. Authorities claimed afterward they had found some of the loot taken from the stores and a U.S. military uniform in his possession. A young man named Pablo Sánchez was charged with espionage and thrown into the guardhouse after he was discovered to be in possession of field glasses. Others were arrested for even flimsier reasons. Slocum gave the detainees until sundown to get five miles beyond the city limits and most "have not been heard from since," wrote agent Stone. An elderly man named Hidado Vavel did not heed the warning. "About 9:30 p.m. this night he was seen in the brush about ½ mile from the camp here by the sentries who ordered him to halt; instead of halting, the old man kept running; the sentries shot him down and killed him," Stone reported.

The tension was still palpable when Marcus Marshall, the son of the wealthy investor who owned the Palomas Land and Cattle Company, stepped down from the eastbound Golden State Limited two days later. He had come from Los Angeles to assess the property damages from the raid. Marcus immediately rounded up all the ranch employees and any other witnesses he could find and questioned them closely. Foreman James Fonville told him how he had seen Villa's men on Tuesday evening. Bunk Spencer described the hangings of Arthur McKinney and William Corbett, noting how they had laughed and joked with the Mexican troops. And Antonio Múñez recounted his spying mission for Colonel Slocum, emphasizing that he had told the colonel that Villa was "headed this way."

Marcus then proceeded to do an inventory of property losses. The ranch's commissary and one of its houses, which were located in Columbus, had not been touched, but Villa's troops had made off with saddles and harnesses and sixty-two horses. Marshall and several ranch employees rode out into the desert, looking for the animals. "We counted eleven dead horses, three being ours. We also counted six dead Mexicans lying in the brush but we laid no claim to any of them. As I rode out yesterday on the Mexican side I counted nine dead Mexicans who had not yet been picked up and in a pile burning were the bodies of 69 Mexicans. My horse came near throwing me as we came suddenly upon the body of a dead Mexican lying behind a sage bush."

Then, in the same matter-of-fact tone, he informed his father that twelve Mexicans had been killed on the three consecutive nights following the raid. "The past two nights have just about cleaned this town out of Mexicans; Thursday night five were shot; Friday, four, and last night, three." The younger Marshall was so concerned about the safety of the ranch's Mexican employees that he told his father that he was keeping them on the ranch property and planned to send them out of town as soon as "passes" could be secured. "Cashier Forzan left Columbus with his wife on Friday, thinking it best for him not to remain while feeling was running intensely against Mexicans."

Perrow Mosely, the founder of the *Columbus Courier,* who would die soon after the raid, intimated in a letter to his sister that the army was complicit in the vigilantism: "Most of our Mexicans have been made to leave, and many of them have died very unnatural deaths since the battle. Our people are very bitter and the soldiers are letting them (our people) do pretty much as they please — all the Mexican Prisoners were taken out of camp and turned loose — our citizens were informed of what was to be done and shot them as they were turned loose."

The *Courier* also alluded to the killings in its news columns. "All Mexicans," the newspaper reported, "who were not personally known by American citizens were ordered to leave town, and every suspicious character was forced to leave, with instructions that they would be executed if they came back here. Those who returned are now numbered with the dead."

Marcus's letter was reprinted verbatim in the *New York Times.* But none of the regional or national correspondents apparently thought the deaths newsworthy enough to merit a follow-up story. Similarly, official army records mention nothing about these killings. In fact, Colonel Slocum actually went out of his way to assure his superiors that everything was under control. "All peaceful as summer morning at this writing," he reported in one of his first telegrams to the War Department.

From the beginning, Slocum sought to portray the attack in the best light, noting how quickly the cavalrymen organized to fight off the invaders and the large number of Villistas killed. Although both statements were true, the attack nevertheless must have been humiliating to him, as well as to the other higher-ranking officers of the Thirteenth Cavalry and the army as a whole. Not only had a small force of foreign-born raiders stolen into town under cover of darkness, setting fire to the buildings and killing civilians and soldiers, but most of the senior officers of the Thirteenth were huddled behind mattresses, doors, or bushes, and had missed the opportunity to display the gallantry and bravery that the old cavalry was known for.

Slocum no doubt realized that there would be criticism; Juan Favela said later that Slocum sent for him a few hours after the raid and gave him a pass to go anywhere in the United States. " 'Just get out,' " Favela quoted the colonel as saying. " 'I don't want you talking to the newspapermen who will be pouring into town.' " Favela went north to Deming for a few days, before returning home to his wife.

Members of Colonel Slocum's family immediately recognized the potential damage to his career and reputation. His wife, Mary, in what appears to be an official interview on March 14, said, "Down here *everyone* understands conditions, but I was afraid in the North they would think it queer that the 13th was *surprised*." And his son, Ted, dashed off a quick letter to General Scott on the day after the attack, imploring him to protect his father's name "in whatever way you can."

One of the most public critiques came from Marcus Marshall. "The blame for the Columbus affair should rest on the U.S. Army. They had been forewarned not only by foremen Fonville and Antonio, our men, as to Villa's whereabouts and the directions being followed by Villa on his march, but had information from other sources. . . . The U.S. Army was extremely lucky in having so few soldiers killed — I believe seven in number, and luck is all that it can be called. . . . Over-confidence and the thought that Villa would not dare attack a detachment of U.S. troops no doubt lulled our soldiers into a feeling of security."

General Funston, ignoring his own culpability, was trying to sort out in his mind whether Slocum had taken adequate precautions to protect the town and camp. "On the face, it looks to me like a bad piece of business, especially if it is true, as stated in the *New York Times* clipping, that he had been warned by civilians," he confided in a letter to General Scott. "I know that if I had been in command there and had heard that Villa was anywhere near the border, I would have had the town and camp protected by heavy guards and have had out strong patrols from the town in addition to those along the border from the border gate."

In addition to Funston's remarks, Scott had in his files excerpts from a letter written by a Columbus resident: "You have seen from the papers, I guess, all that has happened and the papers are lauding Colonel H. J. Slocum, but he did not get out until the battle was over and the Mexicans were retreating. He should, in my opinion, be tried for murder, for he had notice that night, before twelve o'clock, that they were coming and took no precautions to protect the town, nor the boys of his own regiment. I don't care what the papers say to the contrary, he deserves no credit for what was done, nor what has been done since, for Major Tompkins was in command of all the actual work. It will never be safe here as long as they leave Colonel H. J. Slocum in command."

The colonel's reputation grew more tarnished when reporters in Washington began asking about a fifty-thousand-dollar reward that Slocum was said to have offered personally for the head of Villa. The War Department claimed it had no knowledge of any such reward nor had the government authorized one. "It was learned, however," wrote one reporter, "that the Secretary of War had directed the Chief of Staff to send a message to General Funston asking him to make inquiries and to report the facts as to the reputed offering of a reward. Army officers generally expressed strong doubt that Colonel Slocum had offered any such reward. He is an officer of long experience and high reputation and knows very well that such an act would not be regarded with favor or likely to be condoned by the Secretary of War."

The rumor played into a sense that Slocum had blundered and was now rather desperately trying to make up for it. Slocum did have responsibility for what happened in Columbus but to focus on him alone was to ignore the fact that virtually everyone in the military chain of command had been informed of Villa's approach to the border. Still, Scott had no choice but to order an investigation. "Hints of carelessness and even cowardice on the part of some officers have been made and the inquiry may develop an army scandal that will amaze the country," promised the *Rocky Mountain News,* providing no explanation of the titillating pronouncement.

BESSIE JAMES AND JAMES DEAN were buried in the little cemetery northwest of town. Both mourners and preachers carried guns. The caskets of the slain cavalrymen and civilians who would be buried elsewhere were loaded aboard a train. The cavalry post had only enough flags to drape three of the caskets and one of them still bore bullet holes from the raid. Behind the caskets stood several horses, their saddles draped in black and stirrups reversed. As the train pulled out of the station, the trumpeters played taps.

Laura Ritchie accompanied her husband's body to El Paso, where he was buried. She kept seeing his hands, trembling like pink rabbits at the ends of his arms, as he marched down the stairs. Her youngest daughter, Blanche, was so traumatized by the raid that she had to consult a "nerve specialist" in Philadelphia. William Ritchie had earned about three hundred dollars a month, a good wage for the times, but now Laura and her three children were destitute, escaping the hotel with only the clothing on their backs. To make matters worse, Mayor William Hoover, who was also the local agent for the Connecticut Fire Insurance Company, informed her that the company would not pay anything on the small policy she had taken out covering the hotel furnishings. The insurance company had taken the position that it was not liable for losses incurred as the result of an "invasion, insurrection, or civil war." Still grieving, she was forced to sit down and write them a letter: "I cannot believe that Mr. Hoover is correct in saying you would decline my claim, which is so small considering my loss, but which seems a large amount to me at present."

Susan Moore accompanied her husband's body to his hometown of Bucyrus, Ohio. When the train stopped in Chicago, news-paper reporters crowded around her and she covered her face with a handkerchief. Susan kept seeing the gloating cruelty on the faces of her husband's attackers as they stabbed him, then shot him at such a close range he sounded like a pillow being fluffed. With one bullet still lodged in her body, she dragged herself back to Colum-bus, determined to pay off the bills that she and her husband had incurred. "I was badly crippled but managed to hobble around by holding on to the tables and chairs. I could not live in the home, on account of the tragedy, and it was not safe." She rented out her Ford runabout and Mooreview and lived in the back of the store. She kept a gun under her pillow and another under the counter. "I just lived in fear all the time, I was afraid of a nervous breakdown," she would later tell a congressional committee.

Milton James spent two weeks in Sisters Hospital in El Paso. He lay flat on his back, unable to turn over, listening to the funereal whispers outside the door. When did they tell him Bessie was gone? Or did he already know it the moment she flung away his hand as they ran toward the hotel? Milton also returned to Columbus car-rying a bullet in his body. He had always been thin, but now he was cadaverous, and so weak that it would be months before he could do any physical labor. "Since his injuries, he has been extremely nervous, has been weak physically, and is unable to enjoy sound sleep; his nervous system was severely shocked by seeing his wife shot down, and as a result of the wounds received by him," his attorney would later write.

Archibald Frost spent six days at a hospital in Deming. Both sides of his body had swelled badly from the bullet wounds and it was days before he could get around without help. He carried his left arm in a sling and could barely move his right arm because of the shoulder wound. One of the bullets had penetrated almost to his spine and doctors were afraid to remove it, making him the third survivor carrying a bullet from the raid. He, too, suffered from "nervous prostration," and in the years to come would expe-rience debilitating bouts of inflammatory rheumatism.

Maud left Columbus and went to El Paso to stay with friends while she awaited the arrival of her little boy. Venustiano Carranza had instructed his representatives to make sure that Johnnie was put on a train and brought safely out of Mexico. When the child reached Juárez, the Carrancista soldiers made Maud sign numerous papers and snapped a photograph of the boy to prove he had been returned unharmed to the mother. Maud swept the child up in her arms and for the first time since the ordeal had begun, she cried. "Oh, my baby, my baby," she murmured, oblivious to the armed soldiers, as well as the reporters who had dogged her every step. Wrote one, "She gathered her baby, smudgy gingham dress and all, to her breast, and turned and left the cuartel."

The raiders who had fallen into the brush would remain where they lay for weeks. H. N. Gray, the man who worked for the Mexican consul's secret service bureau, drove out into the desert with a wagon, determined to find his young friend, José Pereyra, who had tried to protect the women at the Commercial Hotel. Vultures rose up lazily into the sky as he passed by and then sank back down to their feeding. Pereyra's body was unrecognizable but Gray was able to identify him by his new gray suit and his Stetson, which was lying nearby. He had been shot in the back and the bullet had pierced his heart.

VILLA AND HIS TROOPS, meanwhile, continued their flight south. Everyone was exhausted, even Villa, whose heavy body pitched forward in the saddle, his mind swept clean, the rage momentarily gone. He wanted a warm bed, a woman, food, maybe red enchiladas stuffed with sausage or a roasted sweet potato, its skin blackened by fire, and a glass of milk. The Villistas reached Ascención, a small town roughly sixty to seventy miles south of Columbus, on the afternoon of March 10. The troops were billeted in the houses and all available forage rounded up.

Cruz Chávez died on the afternoon of their arrival. Pablo López's wounds had grown "alarmingly dangerous," but he was still hanging on. The other Villista generals — Nicolás Fernández, Candelario Cervantes, Francisco Beltrán, and Juan Pedrosa — had escaped without injury and scoured the countryside for fresh horses and farm wagons for the wounded. Working swiftly, the soldiers transferred the injured men into the wagons and resumed their march. Villa's Dorados served as guards for the wagons and they moved slowly in order to lessen the suffering of the wounded.

On the evening of March 12, the Villistas stopped at the Corralitos hacienda, passing beneath the ancient cottonwood trees that arched over the driveway. The ranch, located a hundred miles south of Columbus, encompassed more than a million acres and was owned by Commodore E. D. Morgan and several other New York investors. Villa billeted his troops in the ranch house, a sprawling edifice that included a ballroom and more than three hundred rooms. They slaughtered cattle in the outlying fields and commandeered a small buggy for Pablo López.

While he was at the hacienda, Villa contacted the Carrancista official in Casas Grandes and told him that he would be passing by during the night. He reassured the official that "the Carrancistas need not consider him an enemy; that he was true to his previous utterances of no desire left on his part to fight Mexicans; that the only ambition he had left was to kill Americans." Then he had the members of the Polanco family, who managed the ranch, brought before him and demanded to know where the fresh horses were kept. When he was informed that there weren't any horses left, he ordered the men stripped and beaten with wet ropes. Then he ordered his soldiers to hang them, saying, "they were too damned American to live."

In a small chapel courtyard, the ropes were draped over a beam that held several beautiful bronze church bells. The men were repeatedly hauled up into the air. Just as they were about to lose consciousness, they were lowered and interrogated. One of the men, Mucio Polanco, managed to break free and leaped on Villa and began to strangle him but was pulled off and beaten. Enraged, Villa ordered five of the six men lined up against an adobe wall and executed. Afterward, he told the frightened bystanders, "You may bury them or not, as you please." He took the sixth member of the family, Gregorio Jr., twenty-one, back to the mother and said, "I am going to leave you this one son to support you. You ought to thank me for leaving him." It was a gesture typical of Villa — a small, courtly courtesy after an unthinkable act of violence.

Continuing south, Villa and his men spent the night in the prosperous hamlet of Galeana, 140 miles from the border. In the morning, from the open window facing the plaza, he harangued the crowd: "Brethren, I have called you together to inform you that in an endeavor to enter the United States I was stopped by the gringos on the line and was compelled to fight large numbers of them. I repeat to you, I shall not waste one more cartridge on our Mexican brothers but will save all my ammunition for the 'guerros': prepare yourselves for the fight that is to come. I want to ask you to assist me in caring for the wounded I have with me suffering for the good of our beloved country."

The people of Galeana responded generously to Villa's call, giving him food and clothing and even money. But they were unwilling to join his ranks and five residents were forcibly pressed into service. Villa knew he and his band would be vulnerable to capture unless they found fresh horses, so once again he dispatched Nicolás Fernández and a small detachment to scour the countryside.

At the town of El Valle, 170 miles south of Columbus, Villa left most of the wounded in an adobe schoolhouse. They had suffered severely and the only treatment they had received was from General Francisco Beltrán, who apparently had some medical training. It had also become obvious that Pablo López could no longer keep up. Villa ordered ten men to escort López to Las Animas, a village located some forty-five miles southeast of El Valle. Three days later, with a detachment of Carrancistas closing in on him, López was forced to mount a horse and flee to a cave ten to twenty miles farther south.

While at El Valle, Villa made another incendiary speech and demanded that the townspeople join him: "War is being declared and from this moment I want to see how many will join me, how many will incorporate themselves with me. I have people with me from all the towns excepting El Valle from where I haven't a single one and it is necessary that this town will give me no opportunity for complaint. Do not fear, I promise you that I will not fire again, not even a single shot, against the Mexicans, and if some day I do it, you may say that I am a malefactor."

Forty additional men were pressed into service. "His custom," the *New York Times* drily noted, "has been for either himself or one of his lieutenants to line up most of the male population for inspection. The best physical specimens have been pulled out of line and told roughly that they were honored above the others because they had become 'Villa's men.'"

At Namiquipa, 240 miles south of Columbus, the Villistas got into a pitched battle with Carranza's troops. Despite their exhaustion, Villa's men succeeded in routing the Carrancistas in less than two hours and captured a hundred rifles, two machine guns, a hundred horses, and about sixty prisoners. The victory went a long way toward restoring Villa's confidence. Feeling charitable, he let most of the prisoners go, but kept the rifles and machine guns. Villa knew he would need the weapons to fight the gringos who would soon be coming after him.

PART II

THE HUNT

→→11←←

To the End of
the Furrow

NEWTON DIEHL BAKER, a diminutive man dressed in black derby and imbued with the same flat, slightly elongated features as President Wilson, was just leaving the White House on the morning of March 9 when a throng of reporters surrounded him and began peppering him with questions.

"Are you the new Secretary of War?" one asked.

Newton Diehl Baker nodded.

"All hell's broken loose in Mexico!" they shouted.

And so, Newton Baker, who had never played with toy soldiers and had hesitantly accepted Wilson's offer to be secretary of war only moments earlier, was plunged into his first military crisis. "My coming was taken advantage of by Villa," he wrote ruefully to a friend, "and I have a deep grudge against him for the days of anxiety and discomfort already given me. Perhaps a man who has accumulated so many grudges, however, is indifferent to adding one from me."

Wilson had approached Baker about serving as secretary of the interior in his first cabinet but Baker had made it clear that he

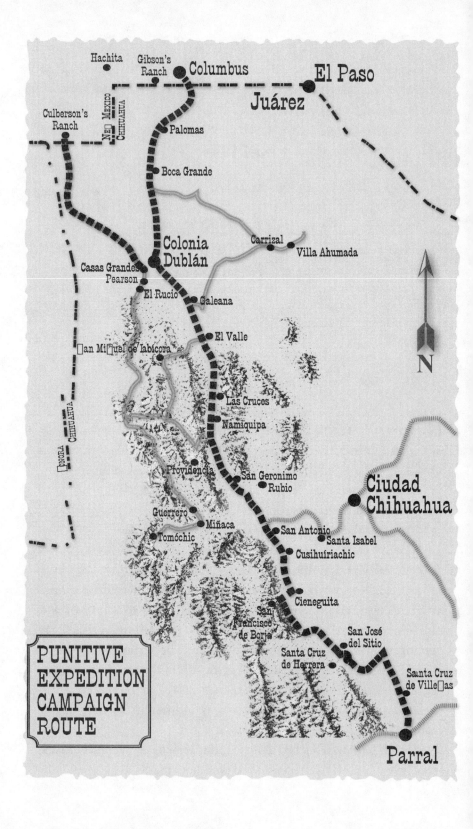

wanted to finish out his term as mayor of Cleveland. When Wilson approached him again, this time inquiring if he would be interested in becoming his secretary of war, Baker had patiently explained to him all the reasons that he wasn't qualified for the post. He pointed out that he was a member of three pacifist organizations and had absolutely no knowledge of the army or how it was organized. Furthermore, Baker confessed, he had been rejected by the army because of his poor eyesight when he tried to enlist in the Spanish-American War.

But Wilson was undeterred and Baker finally agreed to accept the job. "His friends insisted that, whereas Theodore Roosevelt had been born with a chip on his shoulder and a pirate sword in his formidable teeth, Newton Baker had arrived in the world with a book under his arm," writes historian Bruce Johnson.

The brief happiness that President Wilson felt upon getting Newton Baker to join his cabinet evaporated as news of the Columbus raid reached him. Once again, events would compel him to act in a way that went against everything he believed in. A progressive thinker, professor at Princeton and later its president, Wilson was brimming with ideas about domestic reform when he was sworn into office. On the eve of his inaugural, he remarked, "It would be the irony of fate if my administration had to deal chiefly with foreign affairs." But that is precisely what happened.

Certainly, the administration's plan to checkmate the Germans by recognizing Carranza had backfired terribly; Villa's rage was just what the Germans had been angling for and they responded gleefully to the news. With the United States being drawn ever closer to the European conflict, the last thing that Wilson wanted was a war with Mexico. But citizens who lived far from the border were calling for revenge and Wilson knew he would have to do something. National honor required it. Besides, it was an election year. Following the Santa Isabel train massacre, the president had managed to hold back the clamorous sea of interventionists, adventurers, and Manifest Destiny agitators who wanted to extend the United States' border down to the Panama Canal by reassuring the American people that Mexico's de facto government would bring the perpetrators to justice. But Pancho Villa had demonstrated just how empty those promises were. "It was the feeling in the Cabinet circle that unless the government met the situation by vigorous action," wrote the *New York Times,* "Congress would be likely to take matters in hand and adopt a resolution calling for armed intervention. This was exactly what the Administration desired to avoid."

The most powerful voice of the interventionists belonged to Albert Bacon Fall, the Republican senator from New Mexico, who, one day after the Columbus raid, vowed to introduce a measure in Congress calling for recruitment of five hundred thousand volunteers to invade Mexico. Often clad in a string tie, wide-brimmed cowboy hat, and long, dark duster, Fall seemed to personify the Old West. "He has no bonhomie and his face is marked by lines of harshness; his speeches are tart and rasping and his demeanor is sour," a contemporary observed. Fall had first gone into Mexico on horseback in 1883 and over the next twenty years acquired financial stakes in mining, lumber companies, and railroads. In 1906, he claimed to have divested himself of his Mexican interests, with the exception of a power of attorney he held for an unidentified partner "who had a great many million dollars invested there." Such a fuzzy arrangement was not surprising from a man who, in a few short years, would be indicted in the Teapot Dome scandal.

President Wilson had a number of choices in responding to the raid, ranging from doing nothing to mounting a full-scale invasion. He opted for something in between: a narrowly defined mission — a punitive expedition — whose purpose would be to seek out and destroy Villa and his band. Following a cabinet meeting on March 10, the White House issued a carefully worded press release designed to satisfy its domestic audience and reassure the Mexican government that the United States was not invading its country. "An adequate force will be sent at once in pursuit of Villa with the object of capturing him and putting a stop to his forays. This can and will be done in entirely friendly aid of the constituted authorities in Mexico and with scrupulous respect for the sovereignty of that Republic." Using a metaphor that spoke to a nation of small farmers, President Wilson told reporters, "We have put our hands to the plow and must go to the end of the furrow."

PANCHO VILLA had done a good job of boxing in his rival. If Carranza refused to let the U.S. Army into Mexico, he would be popular at home but risked starting a war that he could not win and one that would undoubtedly topple him from power. If he simply acted as a doormat, however, he might wind up losing the presidency anyway. Agents from the U.S. State Department delivered a tersely worded message to the First Chief at his headquarters in Irapuato at four o'clock in the afternoon on the day of the raid. "You may say to him," instructed Secretary of State Robert Lansing, "that this appears to be the most serious situation which has confronted this government during the entire period of Mexican unrest and that it is expected that he will do everything in his power to pursue, capture, and exterminate this lawless element which is now proceeding westward from Columbus."

Instead of offering condolences, Jesús Acuña, Carranza's secretary of foreign affairs, told State Department representative John Belt that the attack proved how strong the First Chief's forces had become — the inference being that the Carrancista troops were pursuing Villa so vigorously that he had crossed the border to escape capture. Taken aback, Belt then presented Acuña with a list of questions drawn up by the State Department, which, among other things, inquired into the de facto government's knowledge of Villa's whereabouts prior to the raid and what specifically had been done to capture him.

In his second communication with the State Department, Acuña was more sympathetic, saying that Carranza was "pained to hear of the lamentable occurrence at Columbus, New Mexico." But he did not back down from his initial remarks and pointed out that twenty-five hundred soldiers under the command of General Luis Gutiérrez had been pursuing Villa when he crossed over into Columbus. In an almost rambling aside, Acuña went on to say that the raid was similar to the Indian attacks of the 1880s when Indians from reservations in the United States crossed the border into Mexico and attacked settlers in Chihuahua and Sonora:

> In both these cases an agreement between the governments of the United States and Mexico provided that armed forces of either country might freely cross into the territory of the other to pursue and chastise those bandits. Bearing in mind these precedents and the happy results to both countries yielded by the agreement above referred to, the government over which the citizen First Chief presides, desiring to exterminate as soon as possible the horde led by Francisco Villa, who was recently outlawed, and to capture Villa and to adequately punish him, applies through you, Mr. Confidential Agent, to the government of the United States and asks that the Mexican forces be permitted to cross into American territory in pursuit of the aforesaid bandits led by Villa, upon the understanding that, reciprocally, the forces of the United States may cross into Mexican territory, if the raid effected at Columbus should unfortunately be repeated at any other point on the border.

The reciprocity agreement clearly referred to some event in the future, but the Wilson administration chose to view it as being applicable to the current situation. On the thirteenth of March, U.S. officials sent Carranza a memo acceding to the arrangement and stating that they considered the agreement to be in effect immediately. The War Department promptly moved ahead with preparations for the Punitive Expedition.

Newton Baker relied heavily on two imposing and white-haired generals to guide him: Major General Hugh L. Scott, chief of staff, and Major General Tasker Bliss, his assistant chief of staff. Both were born in 1853 and had attended West Point, Bliss graduating in 1875 and Scott the following year. As the years leached the color from their hair and the whiskers grew up around their faces, the West Pointers had come to resemble two huge and gentle brothers. Although the Wilson administration had vowed to catch Villa "dead or alive," General Scott urged Baker to rethink that goal. After all, there was nothing stopping Villa from boarding a ship and sailing to South America. Then what would the U.S. military do? Follow him? Baker saw the logic of Scott's argument and modified the expedition's mission, saying its purpose was to pursue and disperse the bands that attacked Columbus. Few, however, would remember that distinction when it came time to evaluate the expedition's success.

Frederick Funston, who commanded the army's Southern Department, which had jurisdiction over a wide swath of border territory, including Columbus, wanted desperately to head the expedition himself. At first glance, he seemed a perfect fit for the job. He was fluent in Spanish and had gained a familiarity with Mexico while presiding over the military occupation of Veracruz. Though he stood only five feet four inches tall and weighed little more than a hundred pounds, Funston was a towering figure in the War Department and one of the army's most colorful generals. Born in Ohio in 1865, Funston grew up in the small town of Iola in southeastern Kansas. His mother, Ann, was a great-grandniece of Daniel Boone and his father, Edward Hogue Funston, six feet two and weighing more than two hundred pounds, was a Civil War veteran and Kansas congressman known as "Foghorn" Funston. The young Funston had helped write his father's speeches, but politics held no interest for him. It was adventure he craved, and while still in high school he applied to West Point. Unfortunately, he flunked the entrance exam and failed to meet the minimum height requirement. Disappointed, he taught for a while at a little schoolhouse called Stony Lonesome but soon grew bored with the job and returned to high school himself. Upon graduation, he enrolled in the University of Kansas and became fast friends with an aspiring journalist named William Allen White. While still in college, the two worked together briefly on a Kansas City newspaper. ("We roamed the city like sheep-killing dogs," White would later say.) Funston was a competent student but too impatient to finish his degree and he launched out into the world again, working as a surveyor, ticket collector, and itinerant reporter, traveling as far north as the Arctic Ocean and as far south as Mexico.

In the early summer of 1896, at Madison Square Garden in New York City, he heard a rousing speech about the Cuban revolt against Spain and decided to join the rebel cause. In his Cuban uniform, which consisted of a starred sash and soft battered hat, Funston resembled a petite Shakespearean actor or a prince from some Lilliputian kingdom. He had porcelain cheeks, bowed red lips, and a regal hauteur to his uplifted chin that would have been comical but for the deadly seriousness that blazed from his eyes. Funston spent nearly two years in Cuba and fought in twenty-two battles. He was shot twice, almost died from malaria, "and finally, in a cavalry charge, had large shards of wood thrust into his hips from the roots of an upturned tree when his horse rolled over," writes fellow Kansan Dave Young.

When he returned to the States, in 1898, he weighed eighty pounds. Upon his recovery, the governor of Kansas appointed him colonel of the Twentieth Kansas Regiment and he shipped out to the Philippines. There, the members of his regiment participated in nineteen battles and won three Medals of Honor. During a second tour, Funston came up with a daring plan to capture the insurgent Filipino leader, Emilio Aguinaldo, in which he and several of his comrades would penetrate Aguinaldo's lair disguised as POWs. General Arthur MacArthur, Douglas MacArthur's father, reluctantly approved the plan, saying, "Funston, this is a desperate undertaking. I fear that I shall never see you again."

But Funston's plan succeeded brilliantly. Although he was greatly debilitated by the effort, he returned to the United States a hero and was awarded a general's star in the regular army. Almost immediately, he was enveloped in a swirling controversy when soldiers testifying on Capitol Hill accused him of atrocities and the execution of prisoners in the Philippines. Newspaper editors called for his court-martial and Funston fought back, suggesting that the editors be hung from lampposts. President Theodore Roosevelt, whose jingoistic philosophy mirrored Funston's, ordered him to be quiet and a letter of censure was placed in his military file.

As he aged, Funston lost his haughty demeanor. His cheeks softened into jowls and his lithe little body grew barrel shaped. Some of his wild edges had been smoothed out, but his memos still gave off sparks of anger and impatience that the more political generals, steeped in history and cognizant of their place in it, were savvy enough to edit out. When it came to stamina, brains, and reckless courage, Frederick Funston was certainly a match for Francisco Villa.

But this expedition was going to be extremely delicate; one misstep could result in an all-out war. President Wilson was already trying hard to reassure the highly nationalistic Carranza that the United States was not launching an invasion or an intervention, but simply sending a few thousand men into Mexico's heartland to disperse some bandits. Little Freddy Funston could disrupt the delicate, diplomatic minuet. In addition to his being too hotheaded and blunt spoken, Scott and Bliss thought it was best that Funston remain at Fort Sam Houston in San Antonio to keep tabs on the entire border. The field assignment, they declared, should go to one of his subordinate officers. Perhaps Brigadier General John Pershing?

Newton Baker knew nothing about Pershing but if the old generals thought Pershing was the best man for the job, then Pershing it was. On March 10, he sent General Funston the official orders:

> You will promptly organize an adequate military force of troops under the command of Brigadier General Pershing and will direct him to proceed promptly across the border in pursuit of the Mexican band which attacked the town of Columbus. . . . These troops will be withdrawn to American territory as soon as the de facto government of Mexico is able to relieve them of this work. In any event the work of these troops will be regarded as finished as soon as Villa band or bands are known to be broken up. . . .

With his lean body, erect posture, riding boots and crop, Pershing seemed the very image of what a soldier should be. He was dry-looking physically and dry in some deeper way, too, as if a small banked fire within him had burned off all his emotions. His hair was sandy colored, his skin the color of sand, and deep drought lines ran from the corners of his eyes and down his cheeks. He had a thin, down-turned mouth that in another man might be interpreted as disappointment but in Pershing signaled only determination.

Scott and Bliss were confident that Pershing, a disciplinarian and a highly competent general, would be able to maintain firm control over his men and hold his temper in the tricky business ahead. But there was another reason why the two kindly old generals wanted him to lead the expedition: the assignment might ease his crushing grief.

The eldest of nine children, Pershing was born in 1860 in Laclede, Missouri, a town of six hundred residents. He was a descendant of Frederick Pfoerschin, an indentured servant who emigrated to the United States from Europe in 1749 and changed his name to Pershin, then added a *g* to give it a ring. When John was just twelve, his father lost everything in the 1873 depression and he pitched in to keep the family afloat, working as a farmhand and schoolteacher. When he saw a notice of a competitive examination for West Point, he decided to take it, even though a military career did not really appeal to him. "No, I wouldn't stay in the Army," he told a friend. "There won't be a gun fired in the world in a hundred years. I'll study law, I guess. But I want an education and now I see how I can get it."

He took the exam, beating out the nearest contender by scoring one point extra in the grammar section of the test. Pershing was already twenty-two — the cutoff age for cadets entering West Point. To get around that obstacle, he lied about his age, pushing his birth date back by nine months. Once admitted, he proved to be a competent student, graduating thirtieth in a class of seventy-seven. Upon receiving his diploma in 1886 from General William Tecumseh Sherman, he left for the western frontier where the U.S. cavalry was in the process of subduing the last of the Indian tribes. He was assigned to the Sixth Cavalry in New Mexico and participated in General Nelson Miles's campaign to round up Geronimo. Later the regiment was sent to South Dakota to help suppress the last great uprising of the Sioux, which culminated with the massacre at Wounded Knee. Though Pershing's regiment did not participate in the massacre, it was part of the cordon that subsequently kept the Indians from escaping the reservation.

In 1891, he exchanged his saddle for a slot at the University of Nebraska, where he taught military science and tactics and earned a law degree. Upon promotion to first lieutenant, in 1895, he went west again and this time joined the Tenth Cavalry, one of the six all-black regiments authorized by Congress following the Civil War. Commanded by white officers, the black troops consisted of two cavalry and four infantry regiments. The Indians called them Buffalo Soldiers because they wore jackets made from buffalo hide and had hair that was similar to the animals' curly coats.

Pershing returned to West Point in 1897 for a teaching stint. A hardened soldier by now who had weathered Montana blizzards and New Mexico droughts, he seemed a cheerless martinet to the ebullient young cadets and they dubbed him "Nigger Jack," because of his assignment with the Tenth. Later the name was modified to "Black Jack" and remained with him for the rest of his life. When the Spanish-American War broke out, in 1898, he was sent to Cuba and earned the admiration of his commander, who stated, "Pershing is the coolest man under fire I ever saw." From there, he was dispatched to the Philippines to help pacify the Moros, Muslim tribesmen who had been fighting the Spaniards for three hundred years. To prepare for his assignment, Pershing learned several native dialects and actually took the time to study the Koran.

He returned from overseas with a greatly enhanced military reputation and was assigned to the army's general staff. At a social function, Theodore Roosevelt introduced him to the powerful Wyoming senator Francis E. Warren, chairman of the Military Affairs Committee, but it was the senator's daughter, Helen Frances, just twenty-five and young enough to be his own child, who attracted him. The following evening they went dancing and a year later they were married in a huge wedding that included Roosevelt among the guests.

Roosevelt promoted him in 1906 to brigadier general, bypassing 862 more senior officers. The promotion was met with howls of indignation and charges that his family connections — not his ability — were responsible for the huge career leap. To the critics, Roosevelt tartly responded: "To promote him because he married a senator's daughter would be an infamy; to refuse him promotion for the same reason would be an equal infamy."

In 1913, he returned from another tour in the Philippines and was stationed at the Presidio in San Francisco. By that time he had four children: Helen, eight; Anne, seven; Mary Margaret, six; and a five-year-old son named Warren. With the occupation in Veracruz, conditions along the Mexican border were growing increasingly unstable and he was soon ordered to Fort Bliss in El Paso. When Pershing realized that the posting would be for an indefinite period, he made plans to have his family join him. On August 27, 1915, a week before they were to depart, he got a telephone call at head-quarters:

"Telegram for you, sir," said the orderly.

"Yes?" responded the general.

"Shall I? Shall I read it to you, sir?" the orderly stammered.

"Yes," responded Pershing.

The young man halted again.

"Go ahead," Pershing muttered impatiently.

The stammering, frightened voice began speaking of a fire that had broken out in the Pershings' flimsy wooden home back in San Francisco. A relative who was staying with the family was awak-ened by heat and rushed to her door to alert Mrs. Pershing but was driven back into her room by the inferno. She and her maid and two children jumped to safety, but Helen and her three daughters suffocated to death from the smoke. Five-year-old Warren was found unconscious on the floor of his bedroom by Pershing's aged African-American servant, identified in newspaper accounts only as "Johnson," who led a rescue party into the burning house. The boy was the only member of the family to survive.

"Is that all? Is that everything?" Pershing asked when the orderly was finished.

"Yes sir."

Then the waters of grief and sorrow closed over him. Pershing buried his wife and three daughters in the plots belonging to the Warren family in Cheyenne, Wyoming. As the funeral procession passed, citizens bowed their heads and businesses throughout the state closed. "From that time on his countenance took on a certain grimness, and more than ever his attitude bespoke a 'no nonsense' philosophy," writes historian Bruce Johnson. "A lean, tanned, hard man, Pershing was not close to his troops; he was no father figure to them. But they respected his fairness, his ability, his total lack of hypocrisy."

Pershing returned to Fort Bliss, accompanied by his sister, May, who volunteered to help take care of his son. For weeks, he wandered through the rooms and porches of the rambling house, wondering how he would go on living. Time, he told a friend, had not dimmed the pain at all.

In the spring of 1916, when his grief had abated somewhat, he began dating Anne "Nita" Patton, twenty-nine, the sister of George Patton, then a brash, young lieutenant with the Eighth Cavalry, which was also stationed at Fort Bliss. Nita was tall and blond like her brother, but with a matronly padding to her hips and a lovely, expressive mouth. Though Pershing was fifteen years older, Nita nevertheless found him exceedingly attractive, drawn in part by the tragic air that now surrounded him.

George Patton, thirty, had mixed feelings about the relationship; already a superb horseman and expert marksman, Patton was determined to advance through the army on his own merits. At the moment, however, his advancement seemed stymied by the fact that his regiment had not been called up for the expedition. Knowing how much Pershing valued physical fitness, Patton blamed it on his colonel, who was overweight. ("There should be a law killing fat colonels on sight," Patton fumed in a letter to his father. "It is hell to be so near a fine fight and not get in it.") Determined to go anyway, Patton contacted Pershing's adjutant general, Major John Hines, and his aide, Martin C. Shallenberger, and finally the "Old Man" himself.

"Everyone wants to go; why should I favor you?" Pershing asked.

"Because I want to go more than anyone else."

"That will do," said Pershing, dismissing him.

Patton lobbied Pershing again that evening, pointing out that he was "good with correspondents." Although the general remained noncommittal, Patton returned to his quarters and packed his bedroll and saddle. At five o'clock on the morning of March 13, Pershing called.

"Lieutenant Patton, how long will it take you to get ready?"

Patton replied that he was already packed.

"I'll be goddamned. You are appointed aide."

Pershing cautioned that the assignment was only temporary; once James Collins, his regular aide and longtime confidant, returned from leave, Patton would have to go back to his own regiment. But Patton was determined to make the assignment permanent, and in the months to come would look after countless details associated with the expedition and become one of the general's regular hunting partners and riding companions in Mexico.

Patton's assignment began that very day. In his shiny new "machine," he picked up the general and his entourage and ferried them to the train station. Patton said good-bye to his wife, Beatrice, a beautiful and wealthy New Englander, and Pershing spent a few minutes alone with Nita. Then they boarded a train for Columbus, arriving at ten thirty on the evening of March 13. Patton unloaded Pershing's luggage and waited at the station until five o'clock the following morning for their horses.

Although only five days had elapsed since the raid, the little town had already undergone a stunning transformation. The depot was crowded with milling troops and the high, anxious cries of mules and horses being unloaded from boxcars. A pall of dust hung over the village as gray army wagons rattled over the dirt streets. The town fathers began to complain of the "Speed Maniacs" who careened through Columbus's dirt streets. "One sometimes feels he carries his life in his hands on the simple journey to get the mail," complained G. E. Parks, the newspaper editor, whose wife, Susie, had so bravely tried to get word to the outside world during the raid.

Brown pup tents were staked out on the parade grounds, where the daytime temperatures could exceed 112 degrees. The soldiers stuffed their bed sacks with straw, used the sun-heated water in their canteens for shaving, and showered whenever thunderstorms raked the desert. North of the railroad tracks, civilians also pitched tents, which were surprisingly commodious and often furnished with Mexican rugs, Coleman lanterns, and chintz-covered crates.

Moving-picture men and reporters hungry for scoops stalked through the town and camp. Their news-gathering efforts would be greatly hampered by the military in the first days and weeks of the expedition. One of Funston's first orders to Pershing was to seize the telegraph office in Columbus, guard the telephone wires leading out of town, and closely watch all automobiles headed for telegraph stations in other communities. "The man who gets a scoop is an arch criminal," Major W. R. Sample warned. With a virtual blackout on news, reporters had little to do but exchange rumors and monitor the frantic activity.

GENERAL FUNSTON had been disappointed to learn that he would not lead the hunt for Villa, but always the good soldier, he had plunged into the massive preparations for the Punitive Expedition. The area of Chihuahua in which they would be hunting Villa was approximately one hundred miles wide and five hundred miles long. It was bordered on the west by the Sierra Madre and on the east by the National Railroad of Mexico. The terrain was extremely rugged, devoid of roads, and consisted mostly of alkali deserts and soaring mountains. Since much of the area was unmapped, the expedition's military leaders would have to rely on an assortment of native scouts, cowboys, adventurers, and revolutionaries to guide them. Water would be difficult to find and food for animals and men would prove almost nonexistent. "The desert is support for some wild ducks and geese but mainly for lizards, horned toads, tarantulas, scorpions and rattlesnakes — the repulsive outcasts of the animal world," wrote Colonel H. A. Toulmin in a 1935 military account of the expedition. In order to avoid antagonizing the Mexican people, the soldiers would not be allowed to occupy any villages and towns and the Carranza government would soon make it clear that it had no intention of allowing the United States to use Mexican railroads to transport supplies to the troops, a move that would greatly complicate military planning.

The initial cavalry regiments tapped for service included the men of George Custer's fabled Seventh, the Buffalo Soldiers of the Tenth, the horse soldiers of the Eleventh, and the troopers of the Thirteenth. Accompanying these mounted regiments would be the Sixth and Sixteenth infantries and two batteries of the Sixth Field Artillery.

The heavy artillery hardly seemed worth the trouble: "To transport one gun required ten animals, which needed shoeing and forage, plus a dozen men to look after the mules as well as assemble and fire the gun," points out military historian Herbert Molloy Mason. Supporting the combat troops would be a signal corps to establish communication, an ambulance company and field hospital for the wounded, engineers to build roads and bridges, and two wagon companies to haul supplies. (A wagon company consisted of 36 men, 27 wagons, 112 mules, and 6 horses.)

Army quartermasters from around the country worked frantically to locate supplies and ship them to Columbus. A boxcar of Missouri mules was requisitioned from Saint Louis. Twenty-seven new trucks were purchased from the White Motor Company in Cleveland and the T. B. Jeffreys Company of Kenosha, Wisconsin. Newly broken horses were entrained at Fort Bliss. Strange-looking vehicles that were actually the military's first tanks were loaded onto railroad cars. Wagon parts, ordnance, radio sets, medical supplies, rations, and forage were also hunted down and shipped to Columbus.

Troops were sent from Fort Riley, Kansas; Fort Huachuca, Arizona; and Fort Oglethorpe, Georgia. At the request of President Wilson, Congress passed emergency legislation to increase the strength of the regular army from 100,000 to 120,000 men. Nearly all the additional men would be assigned to guard duty on the border or the expedition itself. Also dispatched to the border were Captain Benjamin Foulois and the country's entire air force, which consisted of the First Aero Squadron and its eight Curtiss JN-3s, or Jennies. Flimsy as negligees and notoriously unreliable, the planes were dismantled and shipped by train. Captain Foulois posted ten riflemen at the front of the train and scattered more soldiers armed with rifles and pistols throughout the sleeping cars and the rest of the compartments.

Foulois was another of the larger-than-life officers who seemed to fill the ranks of the Punitive Expedition. He had shown no particular promise or aptitude for anything beyond a curious interest in birds, and eventually joined his father's plumbing business. Fixing toilets might have become his life's work except for an inner restlessness that led him to enlist in the army. Like Funston and Pershing, he wound up in the Philippines and took part in numerous battles. Upon returning to the States, he gravitated to aviation and learned how to fly dirigibles. In an academic paper, he made a number of far-fetched statements about the future of the new flying machines, including the prediction that the airplane would someday replace the horse in reconnaissance missions and that it would be possible to transmit words and pictures between people on the ground and men in the air. The ideas seemed wildly improbable, but they nevertheless attracted the attention of the army's chief signal officer, who instructed Foulois to conduct airship and aircraft trials. In 1909, he test-flew a plane with Orville Wright. Foulois wanted to believe that he had been selected because of his intellectual abilities but realized it was more likely his slender, five-foot-six-inch frame that had garnered him the coveted seat.

Wright and Foulois managed to stay aloft for about forty minutes. That was good enough for the army and Foulois was ordered to take the plane to San Antonio and learn to fly it. Whenever he had a problem, he would dash off a letter to Orville Wright, asking him for advice. Later, he joked that he was the only pilot in history who learned to fly by taking a "correspondence course."

Maintaining communication and supply lines that would eventually reach nearly five hundred miles into Mexico's interior would present Funston and Pershing with formidable obstacles. But the biggest hurdle would be the hostility of the Mexican people. Wilson and his cabinet members were under the illusion that they would be welcomed into the country, but the reality proved to be exactly the opposite. The Columbus raid actually led to an upsurge in Villa's popularity and the Mexican people were not about to help the invaders capture or kill a native son.

George Carothers had warned of the hostility in his letter to Secretary of State Lansing immediately following the raid: "They all believe we are cowards, and have a lurking desire to try a tilt with us. My fear is that no matter how hard we try to keep out of it, once our soldiers commence an invasion in pursuit of Villa, we will be drawn into the greater task of pacifying the whole country."

On March 15 — only six days after the Columbus raid — a

great, confused body of men and horses and mules floundered to its feet and started down the flat, sloping plain into Mexico. Major Frank Tompkins and his little horse Kingfisher had the honorary position of advance guard and were followed by Colonel Slocum and the troopers of the Thirteenth Cavalry. A train blew its horn, a military band played, and the townspeople and the soldiers' wives gathered along the dirt road to cheer the troops. But it was unseasonably warm, nearly eighty degrees, and there was something grim and dispiriting about the whole affair. The pessimism only deepened when the news rippled through the crowd that a young private named Dean Black had been accidentally shot in the stomach when he failed to give the proper countersign to a border guard. He was rushed aboard a train headed for El Paso but died on the way.

The sweating backs of the army mules "shone in the sun like anthracite," wrote Frank Elser, a *New York Times* correspondent. "One by one they passed through the gate, and once through it they were in Mexico. The land dips away from the boundary line to the south and the transports in their neutral colors soon faded away." No one really believed that General Pershing would ever capture Pancho Villa. He was a ghost, a phantom, returned to the brown hills of Mexico.

⊹⊱12⊰⊹

SUNBURN, FROSTBITE, AND BLISTERS

THE COLOR GUARD of the Thirteenth Cavalry crossed the border at 12:13 on the afternoon of March 15. Although the Carrancista officer in Palomas had threatened to block the entry of the U.S. soldiers, General Pershing, anxious to avoid any last-minute glitches, had apparently "bought off" the commandant by hiring him as a guide. The village consisted of a scattering of adobe huts and was brown and lifeless except for a thatch of brilliant green grass that grew up around a spring. A few chickens pecked in the dirt and an old couple with leathery, impassive faces told the troopers that all the inhabitants had fled. One correspondent commented on the malodorous air and likened it to the stench of "stockyards, abattoirs and tannery combined."

The column made camp a mile south of the little settlement. The wagons were arranged so they formed a hollow square, machine guns were stationed at the perimeter, and the animals picketed in the center. The soldiers fried bacon and potatoes in their mess kits and boiled coffee in their tin cups. Night fell quickly, dropping like a black cloth over the red-tinged sky. The troops shivered in their thin, army-issued blankets and on the picket line the horses swayed, filling the darkness with their rippling sighs. When the white rays of the sun appeared, reveille was sounded and the soldiers rose and broke the ice from their water pails, stirred the fires to life, cooked their breakfasts, and continued on their way.

E. A. Van Camp, the telegraph operator and partner of George Seese, tagged along with the soldiers as far as Palomas. He dallied the next morning when the troops broke camp, thinking he would have no trouble catching up to them. As he trotted out of town with his two packhorses, he picked up the wrong trail and found himself in the small settlement of Lake Guzmán, where Carrancista soldiers shouted and cursed him. Once they realized he was a journalist, they calmed down and permitted him to file a story at the telegraph office. When Van Camp caught up with the American expeditionary forces, he was placed under arrest for having sent out an uncensored news story and escorted back across the border with instructions not to return. His sojourn in Mexico had been brief but he had discovered something that would soon become apparent to the rest of the country: Carranza's troops were as hostile to the Americans as the Villistas were. General Pershing just might wind up fighting both.

The U.S. soldiers were following roughly the same trail that Villa and his men had taken north. At one of his abandoned camps, they found a pile of cartridges and a small expense booklet belonging to Charles Rea Watson, the third piece of evidence linking Villa to the train massacre. Near the Boca Grande River, the soldiers came across the body of one of the cowboys slain by the Villistas, which may have been the camp cook, James O'Neal, who had been trampled to death. "It looked like an old suit of underclothing stretched on boards, a scarecrow perhaps. But when alongside you could see that it was a man, stiff and stark, face jammed down hard in the dirt," remembered C. Tucker Beckett, an army photographer. Later they came across the body of Arthur McKinney, lying below a tree limb with a severe rope burn. His hanging, it seems, was not the lighthearted affair that Bunk Spencer had described. He had been shot and stabbed multiple times and had been hanged with such force that his head had been completely severed from its torso. McKinney's remains were returned to Columbus in a light spring wagon and buried in the little cemetery alongside the fresh graves of Bessie James and James Dean.

Both the cavalrymen and the infantrymen wore wool shirts, wool sweaters, pegged breeches, peaked brown hats, leggings, and leather-soled shoes. The wool was hot and itchy and soon grew soaked with sweat; the leggings, which fitted over the top of the shoe, often caused severe damage to the Achilles tendon, and the shoes themselves, with their smooth leather soles, did little to protect the feet from rocks and produced such enormous blisters among the infantrymen that many were forced to fall out and wait for the ambulances.

Each soldier was issued a Springfield rifle with ninety rounds of ammunition, an automatic pistol, which was carried on a web belt, a first-aid pouch, canteen, cup, fork, knife, and spoon. In their backpacks or saddles, the troops carried shaving equipment, tooth powder and toothbrush, undershirts and underwear, two pairs of socks (which could be used to carry coffee or sugar), a towel, cake of soap, handkerchief, tobacco and rolling papers, matches, toilet paper, writing paper, envelopes, fountain pen, pocketknife, shoelaces, buttons, shelter tent, and blanket. The horsemen also carried a saber, lariat, grain bag for their animals, and two extra horseshoes, tacked beneath the stirrups.

By day two of the expedition, the novelty had rubbed off and the soldiers began to think longingly of the comforts of even poor, ransacked Columbus. The sun melted the bacon in the knapsacks and the grease poured down the soldiers' backs. The infantrymen who followed the horse soldiers were nearly blinded by the billowing clouds of dust. The troops doused their bandannas with water and draped them over their hats or around their faces. Some even tried to shield the delicate nostrils of the animals with wet cloths. A few of the lucky soldiers had brought along "sand goggles" and those who hadn't wrote to family members immediately, begging them to send the eyewear. William P. Harrison, a trooper with the Thirteenth, remembered: "Most of the fellows rode along with their eyes shut to keep out the dust and glare. Many of the men were half-blind by noon. My eyes began to itch soon around the edges; then they felt as big as camp kettles, and everything got dark. You could feel the blood beating back of your eyeballs. Then the headache would begin." On one of the laps, Colonel Slocum briefly took charge of the advance guard and they raced ahead to the Casas Grandes River.

Shortly after midnight, twelve hours after the first, or eastern, column departed Columbus, a western column, consisting of mostly the Seventh and Tenth cavalry regiments and Battery B of the Sixth Field Artillery, marched into Mexico from Culberson's ranch, which was about forty-five miles southwest of Columbus. This column was led by Pershing himself and had originally planned to depart at 9:30 p.m. on March 15 but was delayed when Pershing was involved in an automobile accident on his way to the ranch. He was not injured, and when he arrived he gave the order to saddle up. The soldiers were instructed not to smoke or talk "so that caused us to leave the good old U.S.A. very quiet," recalled trooper Henry Huthmacher.

There was no moon and the soldiers dozed in their saddles, reins loose in their hands, lulled by the clink of bridles, the squeak of wheels, the muted squeals of a close-packed herd moving together. Temperatures plummeted and the wool shirts and sweaters that the troopers wore now seemed far too flimsy. Some of the soldiers pulled out their blankets and draped them Indian-style around their shoulders. As daylight broke, a captain in the Tenth Cavalry looked back at his African-American troopers and saw that dust had covered them so thoroughly that the only color left was in their eyelids, which "stood out like flies in a pan of milk."

The column rode for twenty-five miles, going into camp at 6:00 a.m. at a place called Geronimo Rock. At noon, they saddled up and rode for another fifty miles, finally resting for the night at the ranch where Bunk Spencer had been taken hostage. The soldiers erected their dog tents next to the irrigation ditches and purchased hot food from women who worked on the ranch. It was the first time many of them had ever seen tortillas, and the young Henry Huthmacher struggled to describe them in a letter to his sister: They were "kind of a corn cake that looks something like flap jacks and they tasted like good old pound cake." While they were eating, someone stole Patton's saddle blanket. Pershing lent Patton one of his blankets. And later, Patton wrote in his diary, "I stole another one for him."

The next morning, the troopers struggled to their feet. As the hours passed, the fatigued packers soon began discarding hardtack and whole cases of army bacon — the weight was too much and abandoning the supplies seemed momentarily sensible. The soldiers jettisoned their oil slickers and blankets, the picket ropes and steel pickets that they used to stake out their horses, and their long, straight French sabers. A few of the old-timers had enough sense to grab up the discarded blankets and it was they who would sleep most soundly in the months ahead.

At about eight o'clock on the evening of March 17, the western column made camp near the Mormon settlement of Colonia Dublán. Located about a hundred miles south of Columbus, Dublán was one of nine large colonies that had been established in Mexico by the Mormons at the turn of the century after they ran into conflict with U.S. authorities over polygamy laws. Their wide streets, two-story brick houses, fruit trees, and green lawns made them seem like prosperous midwestern communities that had been disassembled and reassembled in Mexico.

With no wagon trains or infantry to slow him down, Pershing's column had actually beaten the eastern column to the agreed-upon rendezvous point. The march had been relatively uneventful; two mules and eight horses had died and George Patton's mount had fallen on top of him, breaking his flashlight, but leaving him with only a few bruises. Three days later, the eastern contingent arrived in Dublán. When all the stragglers were finally assembled, the expedition's combined strength was 192 officers, 4,800 men, and 4,175 animals.

Upon arrival in Colonia Dublán, Pershing handed his fine bay horse to his orderly. From that point on, he would travel by more modern means: a low-slung Dodge touring car with an American flag on one bumper and his brigadier general's guidon flying from the other. Riding in the car with him were his orderly and his personal cook, who was confronted nightly with the task of creating an appetizing meal from hardtack and grease and whatever else he could scrounge from the countryside. Tagging along with Pershing and his headquarters staff were the national correspondents and their "gasoline steeds." They were a good-humored bunch, well bred and well educated, and thrilled to be covering a story that promised some blood and a lot of color. They included Frank Elser of the *New York Times,* whose copy had a distinctly poetic touch; Floyd Gibbons of the *Chicago Tribune,* who had good sources on both sides of the border; and Robert Dunn of the *New York Herald Tribune,* who had spent the previous year covering the war in Europe. George Seese, the Associated Press reporter who had scooped his peers on the Columbus raid, also accompanied the troops into Mexico, but by the end of March he had either been fired or resigned and a correspondent named H. W. Blakeslee had been sent as his replacement.

GATHERING UP A BASKET of food, Bishop A. B. Call and several Mormon elders called on Pershing. The general was still sleeping in his tent, but rose immediately and went out to greet them. Together they visited a Carrancista commander in nearby Casas Grandes before returning to the bishop's house for dinner. Pershing asked for several Mormon scouts to guide the expedition. The church elders were hesitant because they felt cooperation might jeopardize their relationship with the Mexicans, who, after all, would continue to be their neighbors long after the American troops had departed. Reluctantly, they agreed to provide Pershing with the men he needed. One of them was a rakish daredevil named Lem Spilsbury, who not only spoke Spanish but knew Villa well and had even been an overnight guest in his house. Other scouts, lured by the promise of a regular paycheck, needed no arm-twisting. They included a Chickasaw Indian named Bill Bell, a trapper, guide, miner, hunter, and, most recently, deputy sheriff in Columbus; Henry Vaughn, a young Texan who boasted of being a vaunted Dorado and claimed to have executed nine prisoners at Villa's request; and Dr. A. E. Gates, who had practiced medicine in Mexico and had once been a member of Madero's dynamite squad.

By lantern light, Pershing pored over a crude map of Mexico and plotted his campaign. He had received information that Villa and his men were on a fertile plateau some sixty miles to the south-west, reportedly replenishing their food stocks and replacing their worn-out ponies at Luis Terrazas's fabulous spread, San Miguel de Babícora, or farther south, at one of the three lovely ranches belonging to the Hearst family. By now, the few working ranches in Mexico that had not been destroyed or seized had come to resemble military forts and the heavily armed vaqueros spent as much time fighting off revolutionaries as they did rounding up cattle.

The main house on one of the Hearst ranches, for example, consisted of a central building of stone and adobe that opened onto a patio. The walls and doors of the house, as well as the corrals, which could easily accommodate hundreds of animals, were equipped with portals for rifles. Had Villa actually been heading for one of these ranches, he would have been in for a nasty fight. But Pershing had no way of evaluating the information and ordered three columns to move out immediately. On the evening of March 17, after resting for just a few hours at Dublán, 675 soldiers of the Seventh Regiment struggled to their feet and departed. The following day, two smaller squadrons composed of troopers from the Tenth Cavalry left. The plan was for the three columns to surround Villa on the plateau, blocking his escape to the south and cutting off his routes to the east or west.

Pershing sent a telegram to Columbus on March 19, instructing Captain Benjamin Foulois and his airplane squadron to join them at Dublán. The enthusiastic Foulois took the instructions literally and at five o'clock, just as the sun was setting, the eight Jennies roared off on their great adventure. The pilots had no lights, no navigation equipment, and no maps to guide them, and only one man had any experience flying at night. In place of a stick, the pilots used a wheel that was set on a movable bar in front of their bodies. Turning the wheel changed the direction of the plane and pushing or pulling on it made the plane climb or dive. A foot pedal, much like the accelerator found in an automobile, controlled the speed.

One plane had barely gotten off the ground when its engine malfunctioned and the pilot was forced to return to Columbus. The other seven JN-3s flew on in loose formation, guided by the planes in front of them. They could see the bluish shapes of the mountains, the North Star, the moon. As darkness blanketed the earth, Foulois realized that he had made a tactical error by leaving so late and decided to land at Ascención, one of Villa's first stops upon fleeing Columbus and some sixty to seventy miles south of the international line. Three other planes followed him down. The four Jennies landed without damage — a "remarkable" event, Foulois would later write in his war diary, given the fact that a cavalry regiment had just rolled over the ground and produced a cloud of dust ten feet high.

The other three planes, which were flying perhaps one to two thousand feet above the pack, flew on. Lieutenant Joseph Carberry finally landed his plane on the road leading to the small hamlet of Janos, forty miles beyond Ascención. Lieutenant Robert Willis, a flying enthusiast who had left the Sixth Infantry for the aviation corps, crash-landed farther south and walked for thirty miles until he caught up with a detachment of U.S. troops. The third pilot, Lieutenant Edgar S. Gorrell, kept going, lured by an orangey smudge on the horizon. Gorrell thought the glow was from fires that the pilots were told would be lit to guide them to their makeshift landing strip. Instead, he found himself flying over a raging forest fire. He reversed course, heading north again. Near the town of Ojo Caliente — "hot eye" — some thirty miles northeast of Ascención, he ran out of gas and brought the plane down in a pasture filled with horses and cattle. Grabbing his revolver, canteen, and compass, he cautiously crept away from the herd, filled his canteen at a nearby stream, and set off on a brisk march, hoping to cross the trail of the southerly moving troops. He walked for about six hours, then lay down and slept. At dawn, he resumed his march but soon grew so thirsty that he decided to return to the plane. Once there, he filled his canteen and choked down some dry rations. Refreshed, he noticed for the first time several adobe houses nearby. Eventually he persuaded one of the residents to lend him a horse and take him to Ascención. There, he found a group of American soldiers and spent the night with them. The following morning, he borrowed some gasoline, hitched a ride back to the plane, filled his tanks, and resumed his flight. The plane had gone only about thirty miles when Gorrell spotted a convoy of trucks and decided to land and beg for more gas. The truckers were more than happy to oblige and Gorrell refueled quickly and taxied down a dirt road. As his plane was climbing into the air, one of the wings struck a gasoline drum and tacks began to fly off the cloth covering. Finally beaten, Gorrell set the plane down and hitched a ride to Dublán with the truckers. The ordeal had taken four days. By then, the horse soldiers of Seventh and Tenth regiments had already moved on.

THE TROOPERS OF THE SEVENTH had not yet recovered from their arduous march into Mexico, and whenever halts were ordered, the men tumbled from their saddles and fell asleep. "Until daylight," remembered young Henry Huthmacher, "I tried to get some sleep but awoke time and again by someone growling at his horse telling him to get off his arm or out of his belly."

The two smaller detachments of the Tenth Cavalry had been on the move since the day after the raid and their horses were already feeling the strain on their legs. To give them a rest, Pershing decided to send them part of the way by train and asked the manager of the El Paso Southwestern Railroad to send some rolling stock to Dublán. The train arrived in terrible condition, filthy and unventilated, with large gaping holes in the floors where campfires had been built. The soldiers tore down nearby stock pens and used the wood to repair the flooring. Working rapidly, they loaded the horses and the train began inching south. Scores of soldiers rode "Mexican style" on the tops of the cars, bales of hay stacked along the edges to keep them from falling off.

The train crew was not imbued with the same urgency as the soldiers and stopped frequently for water or fuel. When the train reached the town of El Rucio, twenty-eight miles south of Dublán, a disgusted Colonel William Brown off-loaded his squadron of 272 men and took off across country. Major Ellwood Evans, meanwhile, continued south with his 212-member squadron, only to meet with tragedy when two cars loaded with horses and men overturned on a switchback. Troopers and their mounts were flung down a steep embankment. Several horses had to be destroyed and eleven men were injured, including a saddler, who later died of his injuries. Evans left the injured men behind with a medical corpsman after receiving assurances that a train would be sent the following day to convey them back to Dublán, and struck out on horseback with the rest of his detachment.

A few days later, Pershing hurled four more columns south. Their mission was to back up the troops in the field, occupy territory already searched and vacated by the cavalrymen, and guard the mountain passes. Pack mules laden with food and grain were sent after them, though trucks eventually became the most efficient way of supplying the columns. "The pursuit of Villa was a triple chase," recalled Sergeant John Converse, an observer who accompanied the Thirteenth. "Villa fled south, the cavalry after him and the motor trucks after the cavalry."

The trucks traveled in long convoys, moving at about fourteen miles per hour. "Their tops are always visible above the gray and green chaparral, their bulk is impressive, and their speed, combined with the rifles of the guards who ride on top of the loads, make them seem some dangerous engines of offense," noted one correspondent. With no signs to mark the routes, the truck drivers used mesquite branches, laid diagonally across the ground, to indicate a turn or a dangerous pothole. Somehow they managed to find goggles and even respirators to protect themselves from the dust. At night, over their campfires, they sang Broadway songs and sipped "cowboy coffee," a bitter, dark brew made by boiling water and coffee together and then allowing the grounds to settle to the bottom.

The columns carried enough food to last two or three days — hardtack, bacon, a little coffee, and perhaps a potato or two. When the rations were gone, they tried to buy whatever they could find, with the officers often paying for the provisions with their own money. Using mortars and pestles purchased from the locals, the cooks ground up corn, mixed it with water, and fried it into cakes. Sometimes the cornmeal was mixed with the broth from beef bones, which were transported from camp to camp and boiled over all-night fires. The few stores that existed had been thoroughly looted but occasionally residents would come to the camp to sell eggs, tortillas, tamales, or sweets. Soon the Americans' diet came to resemble that of the Villistas they were chasing: beans, corn, and half-cooked beef — "the last run down and killed in the hot sun of the afternoon and eaten the next day, tough, stringy and indigestible," remembered Major William Eastman.

Eastman was a young doctor assigned to the Seventh Cavalry who also served as the regiment's dentist and veterinarian. He had only scant supplies to treat his patients: tincture of iodine, phenol, bismuth, soda bicarbonate, magnesium sulfate, licorice tablets, and Vaseline. Fortunately, the water was pure and clean and despite an occasional attack of dysentery from the beef, the soldiers' health remained good. Dental cavities turned out to be the biggest problem and Eastman plugged them with cotton soaked in phenol or tincture of iodine.

When breeches wore out, the soldiers patched them with cloth from their saddle blankets or tents. New shoe soles were fashioned from stirrup covers, hats were constructed from the lining of saddlebags. Once the writing paper was gone, the soldiers used the cardboard from the hardtack cartons. The temperature changes were extreme, plunging as much as ninety degrees during the night, and sleep was often elusive. To keep warm, the men dug trenches and built fires within them. When the ground was thoroughly warmed, they raked away the coals, spread a tarp, and lay down fully clothed, piling blankets and saddles on top of themselves. They also slept in pairs, one blanket underneath, a second on top, and a fire at their feet. Sometimes tents were used as windbreaks and strung up between two trees. A log was placed parallel to the tent, a fire built next to the log, and bedding placed as close to the flames as possible. At many campsites the native grass was almost four feet high, and fires broke out frequently. "In spite of precautions we seemed to be continually setting fire to the country wherever we went. The grass was dry as punk and if it got a good start with the wind blowing, it was almost impossible to put out," remembered Sergeant Converse.

The horses suffered the most. They were not the tough little ponies that the Villistas rode, but large-boned thoroughbreds or crosses between several breeds. They were big and powerful, but fragile, too. Nearly all of them were classified as "bays," a stingy army description that failed to capture the many hues of a brown horse. In actuality, they were the color of ginger, cinnamon, and cloves; rich, warm chocolate, coffee, and the watery tannic of tea. Only their eyes were the same, huge dark pools revealing an animal capable of great fear and great courage.

Horses have a grazing animal's nature; they are self-reliant and content enough to live alone, in the middle of a great plain, with only the wind and crows for company, but happier still with another horse that they can stand parallel to in the buggy months of summer, noses and rumps reversed, the tail of one swatting the flies from the face of the other. They are creatures of habit and thrive on the monotonous turning of day into night, looking forward to a pat of hay for breakfast, a pat of hay for lunch, a pat of hay for dinner, and grass in between. They become cantankerous when their feeding time is altered, startle at loud noises and sudden movement, and are made uneasy by changes in their environment. Yet these were precisely the travails that they would have to endure on the expedition.

Soldiers are expected to stand and fight, but everything in a horse tells it to flee when confronted with danger. Horses are gentle and unaggressive by nature, but their dispositions can turn rebellious in the hands of the wrong rider. Their mouths open willingly for the bit, which sits at the corners of their lips. If this most intimate of spaces is violated, if the reins are jerked or pulled repeatedly, horses can become tough mouthed and nonresponsive, or even worse, clamp the bit between their teeth and run away with their passenger. Their flesh is extremely sensitive — who has not seen a horse shudder under a fly's weight? — yet ignorant riders think it necessary to pummel them with whips and spurs until the animal retreats into some reptilian corner of its brain and refuses to move at all.

A horse's back — the beautiful curve that begins at the top of the head, slopes down across a smooth plain, and gently rises into the tail — must be carefully tended. Horses that experience pain and discomfort while being saddled learn to jig and prance and fill their bellies with air so that the girth strap needs to be repeatedly tightened. The long, twisting rivers of muscle covering the leg bones are susceptible to strains and microscopic tears, and an injury in one leg often means the other three have to compensate, with one injury frequently leading to a second. Even more impractical are a horse's ankles, dainty as a ballerina's and prone to wind puffs — swollen tissue that subsides only with rest and liniment.

The hooves, which are hard as stone, seem to be perfectly adapted to withstand the enormous impact of walking and trotting and cantering. At their center, though, is a wedge-shaped "frog" prone to drying and bruising. The wrong kind of food can flood the thick horny material with heat and cause permanent damage. Regular trimming and properly fitted shoes are essential. Unfortunately, the animals ridden into Mexico received neither, and their hooves grew long and added to their fatigue and the strain on their legs. The cavalrymen were considerate of their horses and tried to lessen their suffering. They brushed them twice a day and turned them loose to graze whenever possible. (The young Patton was adamant about the need for grazing and wrote scorching memos whenever he saw horses standing on the picket line.) But even the most tender, loving care could not make up for the lack of rolled oats and green alfalfa. The horses chewed up leather bridles, saddlebags, halters, and ropes. The soldiers purchased native corn, but before the grain could be fed to the horses, it had to be dumped onto blankets and the many small pebbles found in the mixture laboriously picked out. Starved though they were, many horses simply stopped eating if their teeth struck a rock. As the flesh melted from their bones, extra blankets were needed under the McClellan saddles to protect their backs. "Great care was taken of the horses' backs," remembered Sergeant Converse. "Blankets were folded carefully, saddles packed so the weights were distributed evenly and the men not allowed to lounge in the saddle."

Many of the horses taken into Mexico were debilitated from the trauma of being boxed up and transported in railroad cars and they suffered from shipping fever and lice. During the campaign, they developed constipation, diarrhea, and life-threatening colic. Some fell to their deaths when they lost their footing on the mountain trails, or were dragged off a cliff by the wagon they were pulling. Many more were killed in the running gunfights, for they were always the largest targets on the battlefield. The majority, though, died of exhaustion and hunger. Quickly, like the little Villista ponies, they gave up their lives. A few were let go on the trail, to fend for themselves, but most were put out of their misery by a merciful bullet to the head. The soldiers grieved their deaths. Poor beasts, they muttered as they passed the huge, ungainly forms, bloated and barrel shaped, a blasphemy of the graceful creatures that they had been in life. With each one lost, Pershing's challenge became greater. And the fighting had not yet begun.

ON MARCH 21, Colonel George Dodd, a cigar-chomping West Pointer and classmate of Colonel Slocum, took charge of the Seventh Regiment south of Galeana, one of the string of towns that Villa had passed through on his flight south. Dodd was sixty-three years old and yearned for one more good fight before he reached the army's mandatory retirement age of sixty-four. He had been twice cited for gallant conduct under enemy fire and was a veteran of San Juan Hill and the Philippines, where he had participated in twelve pitched battles. He was an experienced soldier, physically fit with a craggy handsomeness, and every bit as driven as Pershing himself.

Dodd's orders were to move directly south and then veer west toward San Miguel de Babícora and connect with the other columns. On March 23, he passed the town of El Valle, a picturesque community of adobe homes and flower gardens. Colonel Jorge Salas, a Carrancista commander, rode out and demanded to know by whose authority the U.S. troops were in Mexico. Dodd showed him a proclamation from General Obregón himself, which stated in part that the Mexican government had "entered into an agreement with the government of the United States, so that their respective troops may cross the International boundary in pursuit of bandits who are committing depredations along the frontier."

Seemingly satisfied, Salas confided that Villa was reportedly holed up in Namiquipa, the little town that was home to Candelario Cervantes and many of the raiders who had attacked Columbus. Buoyed by the news, Dodd raced on. As the column neared Cruces, an ardent Villista community fifteen miles north of Namiquipa, he struck off the dirt road and followed an arroyo to avoid detection.

Dodd planned to surround Namiquipa the following morning, March 24, and take Villa by surprise. While bivouacked, he learned that Villa had already fled. "I was in doubt, which of the many divergent rumors to follow, at this juncture, and will admit being perplexed," he later wrote. Dodd decided to stick to Pershing's plan and proceeded to march west across the mountains toward the Hearst properties. A late winter storm suddenly swept down from the Sierra Madre, bringing sleet, high winds, and bone-chilling cold. Sand mixed with snow and ice was driven into the tender, sunburned faces of the horse soldiers. "It cuts like a knife, filling the eyes and hair and mouth, filtering through the clothing and into boots and shoes," wrote correspondent Frank Elser. "Even the horses are suffering. They have turned their backs to the wind, and with heads down, like cattle drifting before a blizzard, they stand dejected at the picket lines."

The Seventh Cavalry soldiered on, following a steep rocky trail up and over the Continental Divide. The elevation was between ten and eleven thousand feet and icicles grew from the mouths of both soldiers and horses. Despite the intense cold, the troopers could not help noticing their beautiful surroundings.

The hills and valleys were filled with virgin forests teeming with deer, bear, wolves, and wild turkeys. It was as if they were looking back in time at an untouched piece of the American West. Upon reaching one of the Hearst estates, Dodd learned Villa had not been seen anywhere near the place for months. Wearily, the Seventh went into camp and continued on the following day. "It was bitter cold in the morning when the march began," the regiment's narrative reads, "some cases of frost-bitten fingers being reported. The regiment walked several miles to keep warm. Later in the day and afternoon coming down into the valley east of the mountains the weather was very hot."

The Seventh crisscrossed mountains, canyons, and wind-scoured plains, hoping to pick up Villa's trail. Messengers from other columns periodically caught up with them, sharing their latest information regarding Villa's whereabouts. Dodd also sent his Spanish-speaking guides into the towns to query the residents and the Carrancista commanders about Villa's location. The reports were maddeningly vague and often unreliable. Dodd finally stopped listening to the reports and went by instinct, confident they were still on the right trail when they passed fresh graves, the worn-out carcasses of dead ponies, or cattle from which a few cuts of meat had been taken, the rest left for the coyotes.

WHILE DODD'S TROOPERS floundered through the mountains, wearing out their mounts and expending valuable energy, Villa's men were recuperating in the small town of Rubio, almost three hundred miles south of Columbus. "The abundant supplies found here cheered us considerably," recalled one raider. Villa knew from his spies that the gringos were already on his trail, but what he didn't know was how fast they were moving and how close they actually were to catching him.

Since the skirmish with Carranza's troops at Namiquipa on March 19, his band had continued south, but they were traveling east of the region that the Americans were searching. On the evening of March 24, Villa and his men changed direction, swinging to the southwest toward the town of Guerrero, a Carrancista stronghold in a fertile valley located in the Sierra Madre.

At 3:00 a.m. on March 27, Villa gathered his troops together to inform them of his daring plan: they were to attack Guerrero and the neighboring settlements of San Ysidro and Miñaca simultaneously. His loyal officers nodded and the main body separated and rode through the darkness. At Miñaca, Francisco Beltrán and Martín López caught 80 sleeping Carrancistas, who surrendered without firing a shot. But Nicolás Fernández's detachment encountered 250 Carrancista soldiers under the command of General José Cavazos at the pueblo of San Ysidro. Surprised and badly outnumbered, they fell back toward Guerrero, where Candelario Cervantes and Pancho Villa and their troops were engaged in a furious firefight. At about six o'clock in the morning, on a sweeping mesa, Villa jumped out of an arroyo, and ran on foot toward the opposing line. As he did so, one of the conscripts taken in El Valle raised his rifle and shot him from behind. "It was our intention to kill him and go over to the Carrancistas," recalled Modesto Nevárez. "But just at the time when he was shot, the Carrancistas gave way and ran, leaving us with no possible way to escape, so we again assumed the pretense of loyalty and declared that if he had been shot by any of us it was purely accidental."

Villa had been shot with an old-fashioned Remington rifle, which uses a very large lead bullet. His right leg had been in a forward position as he ran, and the bullet entered from behind, opposite the knee joint, and ricocheted down, coming out through the shinbone directly in front and about four inches below the knee. The bullet had made a big hole where it went in and a much larger hole where it exited. "The shin bone was badly shattered and I afterward saw them pick out small pieces of bone from the hole in the front," Modesto recalled.

Villa instructed his officers to tell the rank and file that he had been thrown from his horse. Then several of his most trusted Dorados hurried to the home of a doctor, where they were given cotton bandages and a coarse-grained drug, which was dark blue in color and turned red when dropped into water. Villa's pant leg was cut back nearly to the hip, the wound was washed, and the leg bound with splints and bandages.

Villa spent the night on the outskirts of Guerrero in the home of a trusted sympathizer. Although he believed that Dodd's men were in El Valle, some 150 to 200 miles to the north, he was still anxious to get away. The following evening, March 28, Villa slipped out of town with a small group of trusted soldiers. Since he could no longer mount a horse, he rode in a carriage with fifty of his Dorados riding in a tight cluster around him. Three other wagons carrying wounded officers, including Juan Pedrosa, who had been shot in the foot, rattled along behind him. Nicolás Fernández and his detachment rode alongside the wagons, watching for potential ambushes. Occasionally, members of the advance guard would stop to remove large stones from the road so Villa's ride would be less jarring.

On the same day that Villa's entourage left Guerrero, Dodd's men captured a native who said that Villa had been badly wounded in a battle there. Dodd considered the information reliable and decided to head for the town at once. Lieutenant Herbert A. Dargue, flying one of the still-operational Jennies, arrived in camp with a message from Pershing. The general advised Dodd that he was sending fresh troopers to pick up the chase and instructed him to turn over his pack animals and recuperate for a few days. But Dodd wrote back that he would break off the chase after Guerrero. Before taking off with the message, Lieutenant Dargue passed out candy and tobacco and gave his shoes to one of the soldiers.

Dodd decided to make a forced night march of thirty-six miles through the mountains in order to attack the town at dawn. It was a daring and almost reckless thing to do, given the condition of the soldiers and horses. By then, the regiment had been on the march for fourteen straight days, covering nearly four hundred miles and subsisting on corn, beans, fresh beef, and whatever else they could find. Their guide hadn't been to Guerrero in years and no reliable native guides could be enticed to join the column. Despite the single-digit temperatures and their inadequate knowledge of the terrain, Dodd nevertheless set off on the march shortly before midnight. The column was forced to make frequent stops in order to figure out which way to go. During the halts, the troopers sank to the ground, reins in hand, and slept. "Words cannot describe the tedious effort demanded of the tired trooper when he is forced to dismount and lead his weary horse over a difficult trail on a dark night, making effort to keep in touch with the horse in front, for to lose contact in the dark means going astray, causing long delays in reassembling the column," Major Tompkins later wrote.

He must carry his rifle in one hand and lead the horse with the other. Many times the horses are so played out that they hang back and make the troopers pull them along. The soldier is animated by the prospect of meeting the enemy but the poor horse has nothing to stimulate him to abnormal effort except the instinct of service which is born in him. It is too dark to see the trail, so horses and men go stumbling along, drunk with sleep and fatigue, with the horse sometimes on top of the man. No wonder it is a common saying "he swears like a trooper." The trooper learns to swear when leading his mount in a long column, on a night march, over a rough trail.

At dawn on the morning of March 29, Dodd and his men finally spied the rosy domes of Guerrero's two whitewashed churches. The Americans, as it turned out, had taken an unnecessarily long route to Guerrero and had emerged from the trail south of the little settlement. On their right was a grassy plain with the faint outlines of fence posts, indicating barbed wire. To their left was a cliff that dropped down one hundred to two hundred feet to a river. The town itself was strung out on both sides of the river about half a mile north of where the troopers were standing. The bluff that led down to the river was cut by deep arroyos. More bluffs rose to the west of the town and blended into the mountains. These, too, were cut by deep arroyos. Dodd realized immediately that the terrain would make a surprise attack difficult, if not impossible. Everywhere, it seemed, were obstacles.

In Guerrero, several residents spotted the "strange mounted force approaching" and rushed to the cuartel to warn the remaining Villistas. Although Villa had instructed his troops to leave for the state of Durango immediately, Candelario Cervantes and Martín López and a combined force of two hundred men had dallied. Cervantes ordered his men to retreat, designating a town in the mountains to the west where they would rendezvous. López slipped out of Guerrero and galloped to San Ysidro to warn Francisco Beltrán and his 120 soldiers. Beltrán's detachment quickly saddled up and headed south.

Dodd ordered his squadrons to circle the town, with instructions to cut off all escape routes. As his troopers were working their way down the bluff, they saw a large body of soldiers moving out of town at a leisurely pace and carrying the Mexican flag. The U.S. soldiers suspected that they were Villa's men masquerading as members of the Carrancista army but didn't dare fire upon them until they were absolutely sure. When the American troops drew closer, however, the Mexicans broke and ran, confirming they were indeed Villistas.

Dodd ordered the men to attack. He no doubt envisioned a glorious pistol charge, but the horses were incapable of moving faster than a "slow walk." Two collapsed beneath their riders as they were being urged forward. The troopers dismounted and inflicted what damage they could from a distance, using their Springfield rifles and machine guns. By the time the engagement was over, Dodd estimated that thirty of the enemy had been killed and an even larger number wounded. By contrast, only five cavalrymen had sustained injuries and they were so superficial that the men were soon returned to action. The Seventh also captured forty-four rifles, two machine guns, and thirteen horses. Two of the horses were confirmed as having been stolen in the Columbus raid and were in such terrible shape that they had to be shot. The Americans also captured twenty-three mules, including one that the troopers jokingly referred to as "Villa's drug store." The animal was carrying quinine capsules, antiseptics, bandages, and coffee — which both sides considered almost as important as medicine in conducting a military campaign.

When the U.S. troops entered Guerrero, they discovered that it had been completely sacked by the Villistas. "Such a mess I had never seen," recalled William Eastman, the physician assigned to the Seventh. "Men lying around wrapped in dirty serapes, ragged women squatting over fires cooking 'Jerky' or making tortillas. Sorebacked ponies, dogs and pigs with their refuse, scraps and bones and drying hides." He treated a Carranza officer who was ill from a "debauch," as well as soldiers suffering from ulcers, infected wounds, or fevers, and one man who had come down with bronchitis, "which he said he had contracted about a week ago from having taken a bath." In a courtyard behind one of the more successful stores, they found the body of a Frenchman. The shop-keeper had displayed an ear purportedly belonging to a Villista in his store window, offering five hundred pesos for its mate. Unfortunately, the man had neglected to remove the display when Villa's men arrived and they hanged him from a tree.

Although the Guerrero fight had been a small one, it made big headlines back home. President Wilson nominated Dodd for promotion to brigadier general and the nomination was quickly approved by the Senate. Dodd's victory was bittersweet. After the skirmish he had learned that Villa had, in fact, been in Guerrero but had left only hours earlier. If Dodd had had more reliable guides on that cold march, he might well have caught *el jaguar* himself.

THE CARRIAGE CARRYING VILLA clattered south. In agony, Villa guzzled gin in large quantities to dull his pain. He wept and cursed, slipping in and out of consciousness. At one point, he asked to be shot. At another, he ordered that the driver of the wagon be shot. Remembered Modesto, "I noticed that after that he entirely lost his courage and at times seemed to be unconscious; he would cry like a child when the wagon jolted and cursed me every time I hit a rock."

Villa's party was now moving to the southeast, following a route that would take them to Parral, a town of twenty thousand inhabitants located approximately 150 miles southeast of Guerrero and the southernmost town of any size in the state of Chihuahua. The residents of Parral had been among the first to answer Francisco Madero's call. During the long-running revolution, the town had been bombarded and plundered by various factions and the residents subjected to threats and torture and terror. Through it all, they had maintained their revolutionary fervor. Villa had lived in Parral for many years and considered it his hometown. He knew he would survive if he could get to Parral, which was five hundred miles south of Columbus, but getting there was the challenge.

Like the American troops, the Villistas were also caught in the freezing sleet and snow that had swept down out of the mountains. The trails were treacherous and men and animals staggered from exhaustion and hunger. The Mexicans were wet and cold but could not build fires because the countryside was crawling with Carrancista troops. One of the most aggressive detachments was led by José Cavazos, who had repelled Fernández's men at San Ysidro. Cavazos hated the Villistas; they had killed 250 of his men following a battle in February and he wanted revenge. Once again, the Villistas were forced to restrict their movements to darkness.

On March 29, they paused at a small ranch house on the outskirts of the mountainous town of Cusihuíriachic, the destination point for the ill-fated mining party and 350 miles from Columbus. In the grayish light of dawn, they shook the stiffness from their limbs only to feel their muscles tightening again at the sounds coming from Villa's carriage. Villa's leg had swelled grotesquely and had begun to turn black for about twelve inches above and below the bullet wound. Villa refused to go into the villages where medical care and a warm bed might be found, camping instead in the shadowy bottoms of arroyos or in mesquite thickets. "They traveled almost day and night," Modesto remembered. "When they wanted to stop, General Villa would not stand for it. He was the worse scared man I ever saw." To compound their gloom, one of the wounded officers was found dead in his carriage. A second officer was so close to death that they were forced to leave him behind. Once past Cusi, their progress slowed considerably and they covered only a few more miles before going into camp. On March 30, they killed four cattle and spent almost all day resting. The Mexicans had not eaten or slept since leaving Guerrero and six men deserted at this point.

The following day, the entourage stopped and a litter was made for Villa from tree limbs and rope. A litter was also prepared for General Pedrosa, though his was not so elaborate or sturdily built as Villa's. Sixteen men, all staff officers or personal friends, were detailed to carry Villa. His brother-in-law rode next to him, leading his horse, a beautiful blue roan pinto. "He is a very strong, well-built man and he lifted Villa around in his arms like a child," remembered Modesto.

Their progress was unbearably slow. Even under the best conditions, the two litters, each carried by four men, could not travel more than two miles an hour. The *cargadores* tried to be gentle, but a certain amount of jostling was inevitable. "When I last saw him," continued Modesto, "his big fat robust face was very thin and frail. His staff officers hunted everything dainty for him that they could find for him to eat. He ate very little, and seemed to grow weaker day by day."

On April 1, the Villistas approached the Hacienda Cieneguita, twenty miles south of Cusi. It was still snowing and the road was very slippery. Two miles before they got to the ranch, the driver of Villa's carriage lost control of the horses and the vehicle flipped over and was smashed so badly that it was left behind. Villa was in such great pain that he failed to notice his close brush with death. Instead, he put two poison tablets in a gin bottle and swigged down the mixture. His staffers waited for him to die, but noticed later that he had not given the pills time to dissolve.

At the ranch house, the Villistas were cheered by the food they found — corn, sugar, rice, cheese, and coffee. On April 2, still moving in a southeasterly direction, the group passed the settlement of San Francisco de Borja. They continued on for another ten miles, bivouacking in an arroyo on the outskirts of the tiny village of Santa Ana. It was here, according to a detailed map prepared by the Punitive Expedition's intelligence section, that the Villistas decided to split up.

Juan Pedrosa wrapped his wounded foot in a blanket, remounted his horse, and headed south. Nicolás Fernández and his men proceeded separately in the same direction. Villa and a small escort, meanwhile, were taken in extreme secrecy to a place called Ojitos, five miles to the southeast. To get there, Villa had to mount a horse and travel over extremely rugged terrain. His purpose, wrote the expedition's intelligence officers,

> was concealment for a period long enough to enable him to recover from his wound. He could not have accomplished this if he remained in contact with his forces, deserters were frequent enough even when in command, now that he was wounded they would occur with much greater frequency. His location, if surrounded by his troops, would undoubtedly have

been known sooner or later. His decision, it appears, was to lose temporary contact with everyone, except the close relatives with him and to remain at a place known only to them.

Villa remained in Ojitos for only four days — not nearly long enough for his leg to heal, but ample time for General Pershing to reorganize and send more troops against him.

->13-<-

PERSHING'S INDIGESTION

GENERAL PERSHING WAS CONFIDENT the reports that Villa had been shot were accurate and was determined to keep up the pressure. His columns galloped on, fluid fingers moving parallel to each other, detouring frequently to search villages and ranches, hoping to catch the wily guerrilla leader before he disappeared forever. They passed looted haciendas, where the corpses of vaquero *soldados* filled the arroyos, and the few chickens and hogs that had not been butchered roamed the fields. The Americans searched house after house, proceeding ever more cautiously after having been directed to several homes that allegedly harbored Villistas only to find men suffering from smallpox.

Like Colonel Dodd and the men of the Seventh, the other columns also made arduous night marches, appearing in the dawn light on the outskirts of sleeping villages only to find their quarry had vanished or, even more frustrating, that they had deliberately been given false information. The commanders of the provisional columns were skilled counterinsurgency fighters and their bleary eyes wandered restlessly over the brush and rock looking for the telltale scuff and half-moons of horseshoes. But the Villistas had

To Santa Cruz de Villegas

Line of retreat

Hill

Maj. Frank Tompkins
and rear guard

Hill

PARRAL
SKIRMISH
April 12, 1916

N

Parral

Mexican troops

many advantages; this was their country, their people. They had been toughened by six years of privation and war and could go two to three days without food or water. The Mexicans doubled back on their tracks, made fake trails, planted rumors and false stories with the villagers. And the weather, particularly in the mountains, was still frigid.

Pershing and his small entourage followed the columns in their heavy automobiles. From Dublán, they motored south to El Valle, 170 miles south of Columbus; then to Namiquipa, 240 miles; on to San Geronimo, 265 miles; and then Bachíniva, 285 miles below the border. Pershing was "on the prowl" constantly, writes historian Clarence Clendenen. "Little mention is made in any official record of this habit, but letters and diaries of veterans of the expedition frequently speak of his sudden appearances, usually after dark, observing closely, questioning closely, and occasionally giving terse orders. People who 'were on their toes' and performing their duties to the best of their abilities had nothing to fear, but his tongue was a sharp goad to all others."

Pershing traveled like a gypsy, washing up in a collapsible canvas bucket, using overturned cans for camp chairs, a box for a desk, and the headlight of the touring car for a lamp. He was lashed by the same cold winds, slept on the same hard ground, and ate without complaint his nightly repast of "slum" — a stew made from beef jerky, potatoes, and carrots.

With each passing day, George Patton's admiration for Pershing grew. He was especially impressed by Pershing's efforts to maintain a fastidious appearance. "No frost or snow prevented his daily shave so that by personal example he prevented the morale destroying growth of facial herbiage which hard campaigns so frequently produce."

Pershing also found much to admire in the young lieutenant. Patton was enthusiastic and tackled his assignments without complaint. Knowing how much his young aide craved action, Pershing sent him on frequent missions to deliver messages to the columns in the field. Patton used the excursions to do a little military sleuthing of his own. While delivering dispatches of Dodd's fight to other military commanders in Namiquipa, for example, he made a detour to a hacienda, where he found all the occupants drunk. He took into custody a man who was wearing shoes identical to those issued to the American soldiers. "On the way to town he told me he lived in Namiquipa and that his children had small pox. They did, so I let him go."

To aid them in their hunt, Pershing sent for Apache scouts from the White Mountain Reservation in Arizona, who were known for their uncanny tracking abilities. "On a rock ledge that seems to show nothing they will find some little stone lying in a position they know is unnatural. That is enough to establish the new direction of the trail. They seemed to know unfalteringly which way a man will logically turn under certain conditions," one supervisor said. The scouts had skin the color of "well-used saddles" and waist-length hair and went by the names of Chicken, Ska-lah-hah, Nonotolth, Loco Jim and Chow-big, Skitty Joe Pitt and B-25. Comfortable as they were outdoors, they also enjoyed their creature comforts and demanded moisturizer for their lips, sand goggles for their eyes, pistols, web belts, regulation uniforms, and watches, which they referred to as "time on wrist."

One of Pershing's biggest challenges was coordinating and directing the chase over hundreds of rugged, poorly mapped miles. Telegraph wires were frequently cut by Villa's allies; telephones were scarce, and field radios had a range of about twenty-five miles. He often found himself unable to communicate with General Funston in San Antonio, or the jittery folks back at the War Department. More often than not, that suited him just fine but he needed to communicate with the soldiers in the field. Most messages between the columns and field headquarters were delivered by human messengers traveling alone and unprotected on horseback, or by the pilots of First Aero Squadron. But the Jennies were so poorly designed and ill suited for the mission that four weeks into the campaign, almost the entire fleet had been destroyed or permanently grounded. With their small, ninety-horsepower engines, the planes were unable to attain the altitude necessary to fly over the Sierra Madre. They were frequently sucked up into whirlwinds and dashed toward the trees in precarious downdrafts. The dry climate wreaked havoc on the wooden propellers, and the water in the radiators often became so hot that the motors would splutter and stop in midair. "All officer pilots on duty with Squadron during its active service in Mexico were constantly exposed to personal risk and physical suffering," Benjamin Foulois would later write. He continued:

> Due to the inadequate weight-carrying capacity of the airplanes, it was impossible to carry even sufficient food, water or clothing on many of the reconnaissance flights. During their flights the pilots were frequently caught in snow, rain, and hail storms which because of their inadequate clothing, invariably caused considerable suffering. In several instances, the pilots were compelled to make forced landings in desert and hostile country, 50 to 70 miles from the nearest troops. In every case, the airplanes were abandoned or destroyed and the pilots, after experiencing all possible suffering due to the lack of food and water, would finally work their way on foot, through alkali deserts and mountains, to friendly troops, usually arriving thoroughly exhausted as a result of these hardships.

The maiden voyage into Mexico was just the beginning of the squadron's harrowing experiences. The very next day, March 20, Lieutenant Thomas Bowen was turning to make a landing when his machine was caught in a whirlwind, stalled, and went into a partial nosedive. Bowen managed to escape with a broken nose and numerous bruises, but the airplane was completely destroyed.

In early April, two airplanes flew from San Geronimo to Chihuahua City to deliver dispatches to Marion Letcher, the American consul. In one airplane was Lieutenant Herbert Dargue with Captain Foulois as observer. The second airplane was flown by Lieutenant Joseph Carberry with Captain Townsend Dodd as observer. By prearrangement, Dargue and Foulois, who were carrying the original dispatches, were to land on the south side of the city. Carberry and Dodd, who were carrying duplicate copies, were to land on the north side.

The two planes reached their prearranged locations without any trouble. Foulois got out to take the dispatches into town and instructed Dargue to fly to the north side of the city and join the other plane. "As I left the ground," Dargue later told a correspondent for the *Washington Post*, "I saw a squad of Carrancista soldiers drop to their knees and fire at my plane." Upon hearing the gunshots, Foulois raced back, began screaming at the soldiers to stop, and was promptly arrested. As he was marched to jail, followed by a surly mob, he saw a U.S. citizen and urged him to contact the American consul and tell him what had happened.

Dargue managed to fly to the north side of the city, where he met Carberry and his plane. (His partner, Captain Dodd, had already left to deliver his duplicates.) The two airplanes soon attracted another mob. "There was quite a crowd of natives and Carrancista soldiers standing around, and it was easy to see that they weren't any too friendly. Carberry and I had both seen a larger field near an American factory (about six miles from the city), and we decided to fly over there, where we would have protection," Dargue continued.

While the two pilots discussed their plans, the crowd drew closer. "The natives were crowding around the planes, cutting off pieces of fabric for souvenirs, burning holes in the plane with cigarettes, and tampering with the rigging. We inspected Carberry's plane and found that they had taken the pins for the elevator and rudder, so we fixed them up with nails," Dargue remembered.

Carberry cranked up his engine. With the mob shouting, he taxied down the field and rose into the air. Dargue took off next, the crowd pelting him with stones. He had only flown a short way when the top section of the fuselage blew off, requiring a forced landing. When he got out, he saw people jumping up and down on the aircraft part and chased them off.

At that moment, a photographer appeared to take a picture of the aviator and his plane. Playing for time, Dargue would move just as the photographer was about to snap the shutter, blurring the image. The photographer would then have to repose him and return to his camera. "For more than 30 minutes, he kept the photographer on the verge of hysterics and the crowd interested by moving just as the shutter was about to be snapped. He posed and reposed, and the crowd forgot its ire," the *Post* reported. Finally a group of more sympathetic Carrancista soldiers arrived and dispersed the crowd. The airplanes were repaired and a few days later they returned to Pershing's advance base.

Dargue soon found himself in trouble again. While reconnoitering roads near Chihuahua City with Robert Willis, he recalled, "We passed over a precipice and hit the most terrific air bump I have ever met. It was so severe that it bent the crankshaft and put the motor out of commission. I saw a little sandbed below and headed for it. There wasn't enough room for a landing and I knew a crash was coming, but I had enough control to turn on a wing and light in a clump of trees which broke our fall."

The two men were both knocked unconscious. Willis was the first to awaken. His feet were caught between the engine bed and gasoline tank and he had a deep gash in his head. "I thought he [Dargue] had probably thought me dead or gone off for help. After a time I heard him groan."

After they had bandaged each other, they burned the plane and began walking in the direction of the nearest U.S. Army camp, which was sixty-five miles away. They tried to maintain a schedule of walking for an hour and then resting for ten minutes but soon grew delirious from thirst and hunger. "There was a little town ahead of us called Bustillos," remembered Dargue, "and we were both watching it when we fell asleep. We slept for exactly an hour and then occurred the most peculiar experience I have ever had. We both awoke suddenly, both sitting upright and both staring toward Bustillos. There we saw four American Army automobiles, moving in our direction, as if they were searching for us. I knew both of us saw them, for we sat there for some time and discussed them, wondering how they had happened to become anxious about us when there was no check on our movements and no way of knowing where we were. Then, while we watched them, the cars slowly disappeared and the town was as empty as ever." It was the first of many hallucinations they would suffer before finally reaching safety.

*   *   *

To General Pershing, the hostility that Foulois and his pilots encountered was just one more piece of evidence that proved the Carrancistas had no intention of helping him capture Villa. In fact, it seemed that troops of the de facto government were doing everything to obstruct his efforts. Similarly, the inhabitants in the villages and towns were also turning against the U.S. soldiers. As one captain put it, "The sentiment of the people in this section is growing stronger and more bitter against Americans on account of the presence of U.S. troops in Mexico."

Occasionally, though, friendly residents visited his camp, mostly to sell food or gawk at the large horses and equipment. One evening, when spring had returned to the land, a wagon materialized in the blue dusk and began slowly rolling toward him. It was filled with musicians — a violinist, guitar player, cornetist, and bass viol player — dressed in rough cotton garb of peons. They were on their way home from a birthday party and wondered if the soldiers would like to hear some music. The men nodded enthusiastically and the visitors arranged themselves in a semicircle and began to play.

The musicians played Spanish love songs, full of yearning and pathos, and quick-tempoed tunes of *bailes*. This was the music that Pancho Villa had often danced to; even as his troops were laying siege to one city or another he would slip away to a dance, lumber around the floor in his great heavy field boots, and return at dawn to direct the military campaign. Glancing slyly at their hosts, the musicians ended their performance with "La Cucaracha," the many-stanzaed song that celebrated Villa's military victories and romantic exploits:

La cucaracha, la cucaracha	*The cockroach, the cockroach*
Ya no puede caminar	*Can no longer walk*
Porque no tiene,	*Because it doesn't have,*
Porque le falta	*Because it needs*
Marijuana que fumar	*Marijuana to smoke*
Ya murió la cucaracha	*The cockroach has already died*
Ya la llevan a enterrar	*They are taking it to be buried*

Entre cuatro zopilotes	*Between four buzzards*
Y un ratón de sacristán	*And a sacristy mouse,*
Con las barbas de Carranza	*With Carranza's beard*
Voy a hacer una toquilla	*I'm going to make a scarf*
Pa' ponérsela al sombrero	*And put it on the sombrero*
De su padre Pancho Villa	*Of your father Pancho Villa.*
Una panadero fue a misa	*A baker went to Mass*
No encontrando que rezar.	*Not resting there to pray*
La pidio a la Virgen pura,	*But to ask the pure Virgin*
Marijuana pa' fumar.	*For marijuana to smoke.*
Una cosa me da risa	*One thing makes me laugh*
Pancho Villa sin camisa	*Pancho Villa without a shirt.*
Ya se van los carrancistas	*The Carrancistas have already gone*
Porque vienen los villistas	*Because the Villistas are coming*
Para sarapes, Saltillo;	*For serapes, Saltillo*
Chihuahua para soldados	*Chihuahua for soldiers*
Para mujeres, Jalisco;	*For women, Jalisco*
Para amar, toditos lados.	*For love, all the little ways.*

A hat was passed and the soldiers filled it with silver. Someone begged the musicians to play one last song: *"La Paloma," por favor.* Shrugging their shoulders, they began. The melody was beautiful and filled with longing that matched the fading light and the mood of the homesick soldiers. Suddenly one of Pershing's aides held up his hand. Confused and alarmed, the musicians stopped and the journalists looked uncomfortably at one another. The song, it seemed, had been a favorite of the general's late wife. Everyone looked toward Pershing, who had moved farther away to study the mountains. For a moment, the peaks glowed with a red transparent light and the flat, pale rocks on the hillsides resembled fish scales. Then the color vanished and the mountains resumed their immutable shapes. Pershing returned to the campfire and asked the musicians to keep playing. So they finished the song, passed the hat once more, climbed back into the creaking wagon, and disappeared into the night.

* * *

DYSPEPTIC AND DISTRACTED, always distant from his men, Pershing was not a man who inspired affection. But respect he had plenty of, for he shared equally in the hardships, and although he was meticulous and reserved in his personal habits, he understood the needs of his soldiers and let them have their dice and poker games and even went so far as to establish a "sanitary village" — a sanctioned whorehouse — at the expedition's field headquarters, which was guarded by the military police, and where both customers and local prostitutes were regularly inspected for venereal disease.

Such entertainment was not for him. Pershing kept his focus on one thing: the hunt for Pancho Villa. Suspecting that Villa might be heading toward Parral or the Durango state line, Pershing again sought to entrap him. Leaving Colonel Dodd and the horse soldiers of the Seventh to scour the mountainous country southwest of Guerrero, he sent three more columns south. The three roving squadrons formed a trident pointing toward Parral: Colonel William Brown and a squadron of Buffalo Soldiers from the Tenth would search the roads to the east; Major Frank Tompkins, who had chased the Villistas from Columbus, would drive down the middle; and Major Robert Howze, Eleventh Cavalry, would hunt the rugged trails to the west.

Within a day or two, Frank Tompkins and his provisional squadron of one hundred men had left the others behind. Tompkins was a distinguished-looking soldier, with thick hair going gray at the temples and an arrogant thrust to his chest. The son and grandson of West Point graduates, he had eschewed his own slot at the academy in order to enter the army early and speed up his advancement. He was a brave and energetic officer, but extremely contemptuous of all things Mexican. Now this pugnacious and opinionated man was the spearhead of the new advance.

Exultant at his new freedom, Tompkins ordered the horses into a trot, a gait that, paradoxically, was less tiring than a walk and allowed them to make about seven miles per hour. The rider at the front of the column used hand signals to indicate the pace: the right hand, raised briskly several times, was the signal to trot and the same hand held horizontally above the head meant slow down. The soldiers rode two abreast whenever the trail allowed and the horses eyed each other with a competitive playfulness. The countryside streaked by in muted tones of grays and greens. The horses that had managed to survive the first few weeks in Mexico had grown leaner and stronger and were now capable of marching for thirty to thirty-five miles a day on half rations. The nights were warmer, too, and both man and beast slept better and awoke less fatigued. Only the pack mules, which stood perhaps fourteen hands high and weighed eight hundred pounds, continued to lag behind. Their pace was somewhat understandable; they were often loaded down with machine guns and supplies that were equal to half their weight, and no amount of cajoling could make them go faster.

Tompkins breezed by the villages that Villa's escort had skirted just a few days earlier — Cusihuíriachic, Cieneguita, and San Francisco de Borja — impoverished communities consisting of flat-roofed adobe homes and inhabited by burros, old men, women, children, and dogs, all hollowed out by hunger and revolution. Near San Borja, a group of Mexican soldiers rode out to meet Tompkins, bringing a note from their commander, José Cavazos, the Carrancista officer who had been aggressively searching for Villa. In polite language, Cavazos asked Tompkins to halt until he had talked with his superior. "I would esteem it very much if you would suspend your advance until you receive the order to which I refer."

Tompkins rejected the request and rode on to the outskirts of San Borja, where he instructed one of his lieutenants, James Ord, who spoke Spanish fluently, to proceed into town and ask Cavazos to come out for a conference. While he was waiting, he ordered some of his men to dismount and take control of a nearby hill so that they would have the military advantage in the event Cavazos and his men "should think of indulging in any little act of treachery."

After a while, the general and his entourage trotted out to meet him, the bright colors of the Mexican flag waving in the breeze. In comparison to the villagers, the Mexican troops were well armed and smartly clad, wearing khaki-colored uniforms, leggings or chaps, and gray felt sombreros with smallish peaks and tasseled horsehair bands. They carried six-shooters on their hips and thirty-thirty carbines in their saddle boots. Slung around the pommels were more belts of ammunition. Long, cruel-looking spurs hung from their boot heels and heavy, curved bits weighed down the mouths of the ponies — pintos, roans, sorrels, and bays.

Cavazos said he could not allow the U.S. troops to go through town. Besides, he said, Villa was dead, buried at Santa Ana, and his troops were just leaving to search for the body. (Cavazos was lying; by then he knew Villa was hiding at Ojitos and was on his way to search the area, but he wasn't about to share his information with the gringos.) Tompkins reluctantly agreed to halt his journey south. As a show of friendship, Cavazos pulled out a quart of brandy, took a long drink, and handed it to Tompkins. "I took a good long pull and handed it to Ord who got his share and handed it to another of my officers who all helped to lower the line. When the bottle got back to Cavazos he took one look at it, made some exclamation in Spanish, which sounded like strong language, and threw the bottle in the bush."

Tompkins and his men swung east toward the town of Santa Rosalía and then resumed their southward march toward Parral. They stopped at clear streams to water their horses and let their animals graze whenever possible on the tender new grass. At each place he camped, Tompkins would summon the leader — or "head man," as he preferred to call him — from the nearest village and inform him that if the Americans were fired upon, Tompkins would promptly burn down his house. "These head men did not like this arrangement and put up the plea that they could not possibly know in advance of any such hostile intent toward my camp. I would only reply: 'Then you are out of luck,' and terminate the conference. I used this method when camping near any settlement and never had my camp disturbed. Other commands were not so fortunate."

The cavalrymen had been given the usual rations of hardtack and bacon, a few potatoes, as well as some flour and salt, which they mixed with water and fried in grease to make "cowboy bread." To supplement the fare, Tompkins ordered the local officials to bring them food. Although he always paid for the meals with Mexican silver, his arrogance and threats did not endear him to the inhabitants. One village official, who had been ordered to deliver a cauldron of hot beans to the camp, protested that the villagers had no beans and no pot to cook them in. "I told him we would have nice hot beans for breakfast or his house would burn. The beans came on time and were paid for in Mexican silver. There were enough for breakfast and luncheon, too."

WHILE FRANK TOMPKINS and his troopers were eating their beans, Major Robert Howze and his squadron had succeeded in picking up Pancho Villa's trail. Howze, a Texan, was in some ways the opposite of Major Tompkins. Unfailingly polite, he preferred to win allies through friendship and used intimidation only as a last resort. Like most of the other officers on the expedition, he was also a West Point graduate and greatly respected by his men. Accompanying him was a Mormon scout named Dave Brown, who spoke Spanish fluently, was also courteous in his dealings with the local inhabitants, and was almost as skilled as the Apaches when it came to tracking humans.

In San Borja, Howze and Brown conferred with the *jefe político*. Although the man was unwilling to share any information, Brown managed to get his wife to talk. Despite her husband's hostile glares, she told the Americans that Villa's troops had split up and Villa himself was going south. Howze's troopers trotted out of town and soon found bloodstained bandages, cotton, and the remains of a campfire. The following day, they came across two more abandoned campsites and judged that they were moving four times as fast as Villa's entourage.

As it turned out, Villa had been forced to leave his lair in Ojitos on April 6 after a sympathizer had rushed to warn him that General Cavazos was on his way. Still in great pain, he mounted his beautiful pinto and started south. On April 7, he stopped in the tiny settlement of Aguaje, ten miles directly south of Ojitos.

The following day, Howze arrived in a village that was just five miles to the northwest of Aguaje. Howze bivouacked in a deep canyon, and at daybreak, after being forced to shoot five horses, resumed his march. The American troopers passed within a mile of the village where Villa was staying and were now on a collision course with the rebel leader's southerly moving escort. Then, the Americans came to a fork in the road. The left fork was covered with hoofprints, suggesting that a large contingent of mounted soldiers had taken it and were going east toward the village of San José del Sitio, which was nine miles away. A smaller group of shod horses had taken the right fork. Major Howze was inclined to take the left fork, in part because he was in desperate need of food and forage. But Dave Brown, the scout, suspected that the Villistas had deliberately driven a large herd of riderless horses up the left fork to throw the Americans off the trail and recommended that they take the right fork instead. After a long, agonizing discussion, the troopers decided to take the left fork. This enabled Villa, who undoubtedly knew exactly where the Americans were, to hurry down to Santa Cruz de Herrera, where he had been told that he would be safe while his leg healed.

The trip to San José del Sitio turned out to be fruitless for Howze and his men. The residents refused to sell the gringo soldiers food or forage. Desperate, Howze ordered the Mormon scout to round up and butcher some cattle anyway. As they were preparing to eat them, "a slender, mean-looking fellow" came into camp and demanded payment. They would later find out that the scowling visitor was a Villista, who undoubtedly had used the rustled cows as an excuse to scope out the troop strength and equipment of the gringos.

On the morning of April 10, Howze's squadron left San José del Sitio. Knowing they were surrounded by spies, they marched east out of town and then reversed direction and cut back toward their old trail. Eventually they arrived on the ledge of a mountain. Spread out in the valley below them was the settlement of La Joya. Through their binoculars, the U.S. soldiers watched as several mounted men galloped into the town plaza, dismounted, and went inside the church. Soon they reemerged and began moving slowly away. A man mounted on a sorrel horse and wearing a large sombrero rode in the middle of the horsemen and appeared to be receiving a lot of attention. On the outskirts of the village, the

Mexicans split up, with most of them, including the important-looking man, going south. A few headed in the other direction toward a canyon. Was this man Villa? Or a decoy? By the time Howze's squadron had worked its way down the cliff, all the villagers had fled except for a Tarahumara Indian, dressed in white muslin, who had been circulating among the horsemen at the church. He was immediately taken into custody and questioned intently, but responded with a "perpetual smile."

Howze dispatched soldiers to search the canyon. A young lieutenant took his rifle and hid in some bushes. When two mounted Mexicans appeared, he stepped out and demanded that they halt. Instead, they wheeled their horses and began galloping away. The lieutenant fired, dropping both men. One was wounded, the other killed. The villagers later identified the dead man as Captain Manuel Silvas, an officer who had participated in the Columbus attack. Back in La Joya, Howze's troopers searched the homes and found several articles of clothing taken during the Columbus raid. As usual, the problem was trying to distinguish friend from foe; a Villista without a gun became just another Mexican. Howze's men nevertheless tried to elicit what information they could before leaving town to follow the trail of the Mexicans who had gone south.

As they were meandering across a relatively flat piece of land, the troopers were caught in a vicious ambush. Two lieutenants galloped up the ridge where the enemy fire was coming from and eventually succeeded in dislodging the snipers. This time, the Villistas' aim was more accurate: several troopers were wounded and a young private from Tennessee killed by a bullet through the head. His body was wrapped in a blanket and buried. The troopers, who had brought no shovels with them, used mess kits, forks, sticks, and even their bare hands to dig the grave. By the time they had finished, it was nearly ten o'clock at night and the squadron decided to rest for a couple of hours.

The ambush had obviously been staged by Villistas to slow down Major Howze's progress. As the Americans bandaged the wounded and buried the dead, Villa reached Santa Cruz de Herrera and went to the home of Dolores Rodríguez, the father of a Villista general killed by the Carrancistas several months earlier.

Sometime after midnight, the cavalry troops arose and saddled their horses and marched sixteen miles south to Santa Cruz. They reached the village at 3:00 a.m. on April 11 — only hours after Villa's arrival. As the Americans approached the settlement, they were fired upon and returned the fire, killing two men. At daylight, they searched the houses and then rode a few miles out of town and camped. The command, "being more or less exhausted," remained there for the rest of the day.

Afterward, one of Howze's aides, Lieutenant Summer Williams, went into town to buy food and saw a group of Yaqui Indians, unarmed but wearing face paint, exiting from a ranch house a mile away. Knowing that some Yaquis had allied themselves with Villa, he became suspicious and returned to camp and urged Howze to attack the ranch house at once. "No one of us could get him to listen to the possibility of Villa and a small band being in hiding in this house. He prohibited any of us from going to this ranch house, and the following morning we marched south," the frustrated lieutenant would later write. "I fully believe that this is where Major Howze and his column lost Villa and also lost our great opportunity."

It's not clear why Major Howze, who had been so dogged in his pursuit, stopped short of searching the house. But one thing was certain: both the men and the horses were on the edge of starvation. "Our animals were low in flesh, lame and foot sore; our men were nearly barefooted; the country was nearly devoid of food, and wherever we turned, we found less horse feed," he would later write. Howze decided to head to Parral, fifty miles to the southeast. Though it was a two-and-a-half-day march away, he hoped to find there the supplies he so desperately needed.

BY APRIL 11, General Pershing and twenty members of the headquarters staff were camped in a cornfield on the outskirts of Satevó — four hundred miles south of Columbus, eighty-three miles north of Parral, and midway between his roving columns. The entourage, which consisted of four automobiles and three trucks, made a defensive square in the cornfield. Pershing ordered shallow

Maud Wright was taken hostage on the evening of March 1, 1916, at her ranch in northern Chihuahua and forced to ride with the Villista troops to Columbus, New Mexico. After the raid she went to Juárez, where she was reunited with her son, Johnnie. This photo was taken by the Carrancista government to prove the child had been returned safely to Maud. *(Courtesy of Johnnie Wright)*

Nicolás Fernández, seated on Villa's right, was the officer who took Maud Wright hostage. He was one of Villa's closest confidants and was present when Villa was given amnesty in 1920 by the Mexican government. *(Courtesy of Gloria Roach)*

Villa loved sweets and often stopped at the Elite Confectionary in El Paso for a bowl of ice cream with his friends. *(El Paso Public Library)*

(From left to right) Alvaro Obregón, Pancho Villa, and General John Pershing meet for a friendly visit in El Paso in 1914. Standing behind Pershing is the young George Patton. *(El Paso Public Library)*

Pancho Villa and the War Department's chief of staff, Hugh Lenox Scott (mustached and wearing glasses), met often to settle border issues. The man in the cape next to Villa is Rodolfo Fierro, who was dubbed "the Butcher" after he personally killed several hundred prisoners. *(El Paso Public Library)*

Some of Mexico's wealthiest citizens were forced to flee their homes during the revolution. Many moved to El Paso, where they contributed greatly to the economy and established schools, churches, and social clubs. *(El Paso Public Library)*

Prisoners seized by the various revolutionary factions were often taken out into the brush and summarily shot. *(El Paso Public Library)*

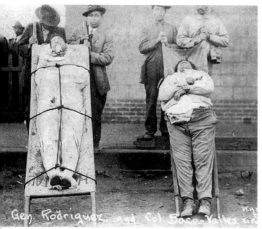

Venustiano Carranza, the de facto leader of Mexico, frequently ordered the bodies of Pancho Villa's officers to be put on public display in order to discourage towns-people from joining Villa's army. *(Courtesy of Robert Bouilly)*

A copy of the Mexican passport issued to Charles Rea Watson, who led the party of miners massacred by Pablo López's troops on January 10, 1916, in a remote area west of Chihuahua City. *(National Archives)*

Arthur McKinney, range foreman on the sprawling Palomas Land and Cattle Company, inadvertently stumbled into the Villistas a few days before the Columbus raid. McKinney and two other cowboys were killed as the Mexicans moved toward the border. *(Courtesy of Richard Dean)*

Juan Favela, a cowboy-rancher, repeatedly warned U.S. military authorities that Villa was headed toward Columbus, but his warnings were not heeded. *(Courtesy of Richard Dean)*

Colonel Herbert J. Slocum, a West Point graduate, was in charge of the Thirteenth Cavalry based at Columbus. His reputation was greatly damaged by Pancho Villa's surprise raid on the military camp and town. *(Courtesy of Lynn Rivard)*

Lieutenant John Lucas was awakened by the sound of Villa's soldiers moving past his window. He managed to get out of his house, rouse his troops, and set up machine guns at strategic points in the camp and along the railroad tracks. *(Pancho Villa State Park)*

Lieutenant James Castleman led a contingent of soldiers into Columbus during the predawn raid. After making sure his wife was safe, Castleman and his troopers set up a defensive line near the Hoover Hotel and fought valiantly. Although the people of Columbus viewed him as their savior, Castleman probably violated military procedures by not first helping to secure the camp. *(Courtesy of Richard Dean)*

James Dean, a grocer, was killed during the raid. *(Courtesy of Richard Dean)*

Archibald Frost was shot twice on the morning of the raid as he tried to get his wife, Mary Alice, and infant son to safety. Frost, who survived his wounds, operated a store that sold furniture, hardware, and munitions. *(Courtesy of Richard Dean)*

An aerial view of Columbus after the raid. The burned areas represent the locations of the Commercial Hotel, a grocery store, and several smaller buildings, which caught fire during the attack. *(New Mexico State Records Center and Archives)*

William Ritchie and his wife, Laura, operated the Commercial Hotel, where five men, including Ritchie, were executed. *(Pancho Villa State Park)*

Soldiers from the Thirteenth Cavalry gathered up dozens of dead raiders and burned them on the outskirts of town. *(New Mexico State Records Center and Archives)*

U.S. soldiers and their girlfriends used the charred bodies of Villistas as macabre props in photographs taken after the raid. *(Columbus Historical Society Museum)*

The sleepy village of Columbus turned into a boomtown following the attack. The railroad depot, which looks much the same today, was one of the busiest places in town as troops, horses, foodstuffs, trucks, and even aircraft parts were offloaded for the Punitive Expedition. *(National Archives)*

General Pershing sent small, fast-moving columns into the uncharted deserts and mountains of Chihuahua in an effort to surround Villa before he escaped. The cavalrymen moved so quickly that it was often weeks before supplies reached them. *(Gallery of the Open Frontier)*

General Pershing shared in the hardships endured by his troops, sleeping on the frozen ground, using the fender of his touring car as a desk, and eating whatever his cook could scrounge together. *(National Archives)*

The Punitive Expedition employed trucks to transport supplies after the Mexican government made it clear that it would not allow the U.S. Army to use its railways. It was the first time that trucks were used in a major military campaign, and the lumbering vehicles aroused the curiosity of villagers and soldiers alike. *(National Archives)*

Apache scouts were used to hunt down the Villa bands. They were extraordinary trackers but demanded such civilized amenities as sand goggles, wristwatches, and emollients for their lips. *(National Archives)*

A Mexican farmer helps a U.S. officer across a stream. *(Gallery of the Open Frontier)*

Mexicans flocked to the army camps to sell the soldiers foodstuffs and other items. *(Deming Luna Mimbres Museum)*

A barbershop, Troop C, Eleventh Cavalry, Dublán, Mexico. *(National Archives)*

Colonel Herbert Slocum, shown holding a cigar, lost thirty pounds during the Punitive Expedition and eventually left Mexico for health reasons. *(Courtesy of Eileen Slocum)*

U.S. soldiers assigned to border duty adopted cats and dogs and often kept them in their tents. Note the sand goggles perched on the hat of the young man on the right. *(Columbus Historical Society Museum)*

Workmen put the finishing touches on the gallows from which six Villistas were hung in Deming, New Mexico, in June 1916. *(Deming Headlight)*

Jesús Paez, age twelve, was shot during the raid and later was forced to undergo an amputation. He claimed his father was a member of Villa's vaunted Dorados, but his story was full of contradictions, and many years later one of the raiders said Paez was actually a resident of Columbus who had been accidentally shot by the U.S. troops. *(Deming Luna Mimbres Museum)*

José Rodriguez was one of the seven Villistas convicted of murder in the Columbus raid but escaped the hangman's noose when the governor commuted his death sentence. *(New Mexico State Records Center and Archives)*

Juan Muñoz, one of the nearly two dozen Villistas captured in Mexico by General Pershing's troops, had attended college and was the son of one of the leading citizens of Namiquipa. Documents show that he later served as an informant for the U.S. Army. *(New Mexico State Records Center and Archives)*

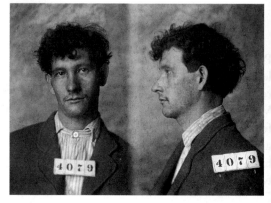

Sergeant Benjamin McGhee was fatally wounded during the Parral fight when a bullet entered his mouth and lodged in his throat. Shown here are members of the Hospital Corps carrying him toward a waiting ambulance. *(Gallery of the Open Frontier)*

A truck filled with high-spirited U.S. soldiers near the town of Namiquipa, Mexico. *(Gallery of the Open Frontier)*

Pablo López, shot through both legs during the Columbus raid, returned to Mexico with the fleeing Villistas, but eventually he was forced to hide in a cave. Exhausted and malnourished, he finally gave himself up to the Carrancistas and was executed by a firing squad in Chihuahua City. *(Courtesy of Robert Bouilly)*

Candelario Cervantes, seated in the front row and holding a sword, was one of Villa's most loyal officers and got many of the men from his hometown of Namiquipa to reenlist by threatening to kill their families. To his right is José Bencomo, who was killed along with Cervantes by U.S. troops in May 1916. *(Columbus Historical Society Museum)*

Lem Spilsbury, a Mormon guide, was captured along with numerous U.S. soldiers following the disastrous battle at Carrizal. Spilsbury believed the U.S. Army was deliberately trying to provoke a war with the de facto Mexican government. *(El Paso Public Library)*

Mormon children living near Colonia Dublán, the expedition's main headquarters, visit the U.S. Army camp. Many Mormons emigrated to Mexico after polygamy was banned in the United States. *(Gallery of the Open Frontier)*

trenches dug and inspected the small group, including the correspondents, to make sure their rifles and sidearms were in working order. The *Times* correspondent, Frank Elser, had lost his rifle.

"Soldiers don't lose their rifles," Pershing growled.

"No, sir, they don't, soldiers," responded Elser.

Pershing slept outside the square, on a dinky cot by himself. In the distance, he could see the flickering lights of the Carrancistas' campfires. "The big moon, rising higher, touched everything with a luminous and breathtaking beauty. Sentries paced the hills. The coyotes yipped, a thousand of them," wrote Elser.

Pershing could sense his troops were close to *el jaguar* now and wanted to be in on the kill. Driving toward Parral were Howze's troopers, the swashbuckling Frank Tompkins, and Colonel William Brown, another magnificent officer in his sixties. A fourth detachment led by Lieutenant Colonel Henry Allen had been ordered to cut the weak men and animals from their squadron and concentrate on finding Pablo López.

On the way to Parral, Major Tompkins and his troopers had encountered an amiable Carrancista captain named Antonio Mesa who had offered to telephone ahead to arrange for a campsite and forage for the tired troopers. Given Parral's history, it seemed highly unlikely that its inhabitants would look kindly upon the foreigners, but Captain Mesa assured Tompkins that they would be treated well. Urging their tired horses forward, the officers thought longingly of the amenities awaiting them. "We pictured the hot baths we should have, the long cool drinks, and the good food," remembered Tompkins.

Sometime around noon on April 12, Tompkins reached the outskirts of the town. No representatives of the Carrancista government were on hand to meet him so the major left the main body of his troops outside the town and proceeded with a small group to the guardhouse, where he asked to be taken to the headquarters of the *jefe de armas*. When he arrived, he was introduced to General Ismael Lozano, who invited him upstairs for a private conference. Also present at the gathering was José de la Luz Herrera, Parral's civilian mayor. The room had French windows overlooking the street and Tompkins could see his squadron down below, looking impressive and alert. The Mexican officials were agitated and alarmed by Tompkins's presence. ("Their entrance into the city was so sudden and unexpected that it was regarded as an act of hostility," Mayor Herrera would later explain.)

General Lozano asked Tompkins why he had come. Tompkins responded that he had been invited into the city by Captain Mesa, who was supposed to have sent a message in advance notifying the town officials of their arrival. Lozano said he had received no such message and emphasized that Tompkins and his men would have to leave immediately. Tompkins replied that they would go, but not until they had received the food and forage they had been promised.

Lozano called a man to his office to arrange for the supplies. As they were finishing their business, Tompkins heard a ruckus and looked out to see a mule hitched to a heavy cart bolting down the street, which he interpreted as an effort to cause confusion among the soldiers. "A big Yank grabbed the mule by the bit and stopped that little act," remembered Tompkins. "This incident was so indicative of treachery that I slipped my holster in front in anticipation of immediate need."

By the time Tompkins and Lozano had reached the street, a huge mob led by a beautiful young woman named Elisa Griensen had gathered. *"Viva Villa! Viva México!"* they shouted. As the troops started out of town, other women leaned out of their second-floor windows and dumped their slop jars and spittoons onto the soldiers. Tompkins was infuriated and dropped behind to keep an eye on the crowd. One compactly built man, with a neat Vandyke beard and mounted on a very fine Mexican pony, seemed to be exhorting the mob to violence. *"Todos! Ahora! Viva México!"* he shouted. Tompkins thought the man looked German and made up his mind to shoot this "bird" first if violence did erupt. Then Tompkins did something that seemed totally out of character: wheeling his horse around, he shouted, *"Viva Villa!"* If his aim was to confuse, he momentarily succeeded. The mob stopped and laughed. Then it surged forward.

Lozano was at the head of the U.S. troops, leading the soldiers in a northeasterly direction out of Parral. They were moving toward the railroad tracks and a depression between two smallish hills when gunfire erupted at the rear of the cavalry column. Tompkins realized his troops were being fired upon by someone in the crowd and raced ahead to notify General Lozano. *"Los hijos de la chingada!"* cursed the general, retracing his steps. Lozano slashed at the mob with his saber and another Carrancista officer fired into the crowd, shooting four or five people. The Parral residents instantly turned their wrath on the Mexican soldiers, yelling obscenities and throwing fruit and stones at them.

The ever-suspicious Tompkins thought Lozano had been deliberately leading them into a trap and ordered two groups of troopers to take the two hills. Then he deployed his rear guard under First Lieutenant Clarence Lininger along a railroad embankment. While the troops were moving to their new positions, a group of Carrancista soldiers had gathered on a third hill some six hundred yards to the south. Lozano begged Tompkins to retreat at once. But Tompkins would not be budged: After we get our food and forage, he responded. The Mexican troops on the hill advanced toward them. Tompkins stood and waved his arms and screamed at them to go back. When they refused, he ordered a captain and three armed men to drive them back and to fire upon the Mexican soldiers when they had them within range.

Tompkins decided his first target would be a soldier waving a Mexican flag. He turned and borrowed the rifle of Sergeant Jay Richley, who was lying behind him, his forehead peeping above the railroad embankment. When the flag suddenly disappeared from sight, Tompkins turned to hand the rifle back to Richley, but the young man was dead — a bullet had struck him in the eye and passed out the back of his head.

Now the fight began in earnest, and Tompkins, who had been secretly yearning to do something more than threaten to burn a poor man's house down, was ready. With Mexicans converging on his flank, he realized their position was extremely vulnerable and ordered his men to withdraw across country toward the dirt road leading north to the small village of Santa Cruz de Villegas (not to be confused with Santa Cruz de Herrera, where Villa was holed up). As the main body retreated, Tompkins flung a line of troopers across the road to fend off the Carrancistas, who continued to follow them for the next sixteen miles. The U.S. forces were outnumbered by three to one and forced to fight a rearguard action the entire way.

Before they had reached the dirt road, Private Hobart Ledford, a tenderhearted man who had befriended a little white dog on the way to Parral, was shot through the lung and toppled from his horse. The detachment's medical officer, First Lieutenant Claude Cummings, leaped off his mount and dressed Ledford's wound while bullets sputtered into the ground. Cummings managed to get Ledford back onto a horse and then he turned to minister to Corporal Benjamin McGhee, who been shot in the mouth and was bleeding profusely.

Meanwhile, Lieutenant Lininger and his eight men continued to hold the Mexican troops at bay while the main body retreated. The Mexicans returned the fire, but their aim was so inaccurate that Tompkins's men were able to withdraw in an orderly fashion, marching two abreast down the road.

Enraged by the deaths of their fellow soldiers, the Carrancistas continued to dog the U.S. forces, traveling parallel to the road that the Americans were on. The land was flat and rolling, the fields separated by stone walls four feet high and four to six feet thick. At each wall, the Mexicans had to dismount, remove the stones, get back on their horses, and gallop to the next barrier.

Tompkins's aide, Lieutenant Ord, noticed that Hobart Ledford, the lung-shot private, had fallen off his horse again. He raced back and pushed Ledford onto the mount. Slowly they returned to their lines, with Ord holding Ledford on one side while a second soldier propped him up on the other. Major Tompkins followed the threesome, urging Ledford's horse forward with his whip. "Ledford begged us to go on and leave him. His agony was great," remembered Tompkins. "I gave him a pull from my canteen, told him the ranch was just ahead, to hold on for five minutes more and we would have him where the doctor could make him comfortable."

Moments later, another bullet slammed into Ledford, entering through his back and coming out near his belly. He tumbled from the horse dead. The three soldiers hurried to catch up with their disappearing column, leaving the young man's body where it had fallen.

Convinced that the Carrancistas would make one last charge, Tompkins deployed his men across the road. "In a minute or two they came," he wrote, "without formation, hellbent-for-election, firing in the air, yelling like fiends out of hell and making a most beautiful target." The U.S. soldiers went into action and Mexican soldiers and their mounts rolled in the dust, screaming in agony; only a few Carrancistas managed to check their horses and turn away at the last minute.

Upon reaching the village, Tompkins ordered his best marksmen onto the roofs and sent other soldiers to try to make contact with the American columns that were marching behind them. The Carrancistas gave no indication that they were about to give up the fight and Tompkins suddenly had images of the Alamo in his head. But when one of the army's best rifle shots picked off a Carrancista sitting on his horse eight hundred yards away, the Mexicans stopped their advance.

Soon a messenger carrying a white flag and a note from General Lozano rode into Tompkins's camp. "I supplicate you to leave immediately and not bring on hostilities of any kind," the Mexican general wrote. "If on the contrary, I shall be obliged to charge the greatest part of my forces." Tompkins dashed off a response in which he laid the blame for the altercation on the Mexicans:

> I have just received your letter and regret very much that you were unable to control your soldiers. We came to Mexico as friends and not as enemies. After you had left us, I awaited in good order for the grain and fodder contracted for. When your soldiers, without provocation, fired upon mine, killing one and wounding two, as from this moment it became a question of self-defense, I also opened fire to permit my main body to retire, it still being my intention to avoid a general fight. It was

your soldiers who followed me five leagues firing at every opportunity. I did not answer their fire until those who fired came
dangerously near.

He added that he was willing to continue his journey north, provided that he would not be molested. Two hours later, the besieged
troops heard a trumpeter from Colonel Brown's Tenth Cavalry
bugling Attention followed by Officer's Call. The trumpeter for the
Thirteenth answered, his wavering notes going out across the dark-
ening plain. Once the U.S. soldiers realized the fight was over, they
grew exhilarated, but many were saddened, too, by the deaths of
Hobart Ledford and Jay Richley and the suffering of Benjamin
McGhee, who would soon die from his wounds. (In addition to
these three fatalities, a fourth soldier would eventually be listed as
missing in action.) The skirmish also took its toll on the horses,
with five killed and sixteen wounded.

Two days later, Major Howze and his exhausted troopers of the
Eleventh Cavalry reached the Tompkins camp. In all, his squadron
had marched 691 miles since leaving Columbus. One man had
been killed and four wounded, and thirty-six horses and five mules
were dead.

A few days later, Parral's mayor, José de la Luz Herrera, rode
out to the cavalry camp to apologize for the incident. Herrera
wanted Villa captured or killed as much as the Americans; his two
sons, Maclovio and Luis, had fought under Villa, but had switched
sides when Villa broke with Carranza. The elder Herrera had publicly declared Villa a bandit and knew that his life was in danger as
long as the rebel leader lived. Nevertheless, Herrera still believed
that Tompkins provoked the fight by going into town unan-
nounced. The mayor also pointed out that it was the citizens of
Parral — not the Carrancista troops — who were the aggressors.
Here again, he was telling the truth, although it was doubtful that
cavalry officers believed him. After the U.S. troops had withdrawn,
some thirty Parral residents who were purportedly sympathetic to
the Villistas were arrested and two would eventually be executed.

Troopers from the Tenth and Thirteenth regiments retrieved the
body of Hobart Ledford. His corpse had been stripped of shoes,

pants, shirt, and valuables, but the little white dog was still at his side. The animal had been without food and water for nearly twenty-four hours. Touched by its loyalty, the soldiers adopted the dog as the official mascot of the Thirteenth Cavalry's Troop M.

Ledford's body was wrapped in a blanket and buried in the local cemetery, along with a sealed bottle that contained his name and military record. Lieutenant Lininger composed his eulogy and recited the Twenty-third Psalm. Three volleys and taps followed. The next day, Jay Richley's body, enclosed in a casket, was brought by hearse from the town of Parral and was also interred in the cemetery. Over the next ten months, the army's Burial Corps would make repeated trips into Mexico to recover the bodies of some thirty-one soldiers or civilians who had died on the expedition. But for some reason, six bodies were left behind. One of them was Private Ledford.

The news of the Parral fight reached Washington first. On April 13, with Pershing still ignorant of what had happened, Secretary of State Lansing received two notes, one from Carranza's secretary of foreign relations and another from Don Venustiano himself, protesting the incident and blaming it on Tompkins's "imprudence."

Pershing finally learned of the situation on April 14 when Benjamin Foulois, who had gone to Chihuahua City with dispatches, hurried back to give him the news. "Uh," he grunted, rubbing his chin in characteristic fashion. But he was furious and told the correspondents that they could write whatever they wanted. "Nothing should be kept from the public. You can go the limit," he declared. Pershing dispatched two members of his headquarters staff to investigate the incident, instructed all cavalry columns in the field to make haste toward Parral, and ordered the Sixth and Sixteenth infantries and the Fourth Field Artillery to start south from the base camp at Colonia Dublán. Tompkins rejoiced to see the reinforcements. "We now felt as though our force was strong enough to conquer Mexico, and we were hoping the order to 'go' would soon come," he wrote.

But Pershing realized that he could not keep the soldiers there for long. With the Carranza government still adamantly opposed to allowing the Punitive Expedition to use its railroads, it would soon become nearly impossible to feed the men and animals converging on Santa Cruz de Villegas, which was 484 miles from Columbus. The combined cavalry units consisted of 34 officers, 606 enlisted men, 702 horses, and 149 mules. The animals alone required six tons of hay and nine thousand pounds of grain daily to say nothing of the two thousand pounds of food required by the humans.

Pershing decided he had no choice but to order the troops to move north, at least temporarily. "On Saturday, April 16, 1916, we piled in the cars and headed toward our own border. We drove all day and all night. Pershing sat grim and silent, his big frame taking the jounces of the rocky trails. He was suffering from indigestion," Frank Elser wrote.

The hunt for Pancho Villa had come to a standstill. "Whether the halt is to be permanent or not depends upon circumstances beyond the control of General Pershing," wrote Elser. "But from a military standpoint he has for the time being come to the end of his lane."

EVEN BEFORE the Parral incident, President Wilson's cabinet had been debating the question of how long Pershing should remain in Mexico. Secretary of State Lansing and Secretary of War Baker thought the troops should be withdrawn before a full-scale war between the two countries erupted, with Baker voicing the opinion that it was "foolish to chase a single bandit all over Mexico." General Scott was also in favor of withdrawing the troops, pointing out that Pershing's orders had been merely to disperse and punish the marauders and that the objective had been accomplished in a "very brilliant way." But Wilson's attorney general, Thomas Gregory, and Franklin Lane, secretary of the interior, thought Pershing should remain where he was until Villa was captured or until Carranza could prove to them that he could control the raids across the border.

Wilson himself was conflicted about what to do. Although he found the First Chief infuriating, he had no desire to see him fail and knew the presence of the U.S. troops in Mexico was destabilizing his presidency. But the border was still lawless and Pancho Villa was still at large. Wilson worried that a premature withdrawal might make the United States appear weak, not only to its southern neighbors but also to Germany. In addition, he was reluctant to give interventionist opponents such as Senator A. B. Fall ammunition in an election year. After Parral, however, Wilson knew there was no way that the troops could be withdrawn. National honor was at stake. The Punitive Expedition, he decided, would have to remain in Mexico for a while longer.

The president's decision was fraught with risks. Military troops on both sides were edgy and one wrong move could ignite a war. And the American officers in the field were beginning to think that a larger war might not be a bad thing. While Pershing jounced north in his touring car, munching on crackers to stanch his indigestion, he was silently formulating a plan to pacify the state of Chihuahua and then the whole country. Once he was settled in his new camp, he sent a telegram to General Funston laying out a litany of complaints against the Carrancista government. "My opinion is general attitude Carranza government has been one of obstruction. This also universal opinion army officers this expedition. Carranza forces falsely report attacks against Villa's forces and death of Villa leaders. Activity Carranza forces in territory through which we have operated probably intentionally obstructive. Marked example obstruction refusal allow our use of railroads. Captious criticisms by local officials against troops passing through towns prompted by obstructive spirit."

The columns, he continued, were often delayed when hot pursuit was important and he noted that the Guerrero fight would have been a success but for the "treachery" of the Mexican guide. The natives, he wrote, had also obstructed their efforts to catch Villa at every opportunity, circulating false rumors and even going so far as to help him escape. "Inconceivable that notorious character like Villa could remain in country with people ignorant his general direction and approximate location. Since Guerrero fight it is practically impossible obtain guides even from one town to another except by coercion."

Pershing also reported that the animosity toward the U.S. troops was growing. "At first people exhibited only passive disapproval American entry into country. Lately sentiment has changed to hostile opposition." The de facto government was in a complete shambles and unable to control the local warlords, he added. "In fact anarchy reigns supreme in all sections through which we have operated." He concluded the telegram with the following suggestion:

> In order to prosecute our mission with any promise success it is therefore absolutely necessary for us to assume complete possession for time being of country through which we must operate and establish government therein. For this purpose it is imperative that we assume control of railroads as means of supplying forces required. Therefore recommend immediate capture by this command of city and state of Chihuahua also the seizure of all railroads therein, as preliminary to further necessary military operations.

Following up on his idea, Pershing two days later sent a second telegram to Funston outlining how U.S. troops could take control of the entire country. Soldiers from Fort Bliss could seize Juárez, he suggested, and working in tandem with his own men, they could drive the Mexicans south. Once Chihuahua City was taken, he recommended taking Torreón in order to secure Monterrey and other points to the east. "The tremendous advantage we now have in penetration into Mexico for 500 miles parallel to the main line of railway south should not be lost. With this advantage a swift stroke now would paralyze Mexican opposition throughout northern tier of states and make complete occupation of entire Republic comparatively easy problem."

To Funston, Pershing's suggestion wasn't particularly radical. On April 10, two days before the Parral attack, he had telegraphed the War Department, asking to lead a new expedition into Mexico starting from Marfa, Texas. His request was curtly denied by the War Department, which noted that a second incursion into Mexican territory would engender certain "political difficulties." The cooler heads within the War Department also quashed Pershing's plan. General Tasker Bliss later attributed the ideas to the army's sense of frustration and its desire to capture *something, someplace anything!"*

Parral was the farthest south that U.S. troops penetrated into Mexico and the clash there marked the end of the first phase of the Punitive Expedition. Occurring only a month after the troops had crossed the border, the skirmish also marked a turning point in the military logistics. Pershing dissolved the columns and ordered the men to reassemble under their original regiments. Then he divided the occupied territory into five districts, with each regimental commander charged with policing a district and destroying any scattered remnants of Villa's army. He issued the following instructions to his officers:

> It is also desirable to maintain the most cordial relations, and cooperate as far as feasible, with the forces of the de facto government. Experience has taught, however, that our troops are always more or less in danger of being attacked, not only by hostile followers of Villa, but even by others who profess friendship, and precaution must be taken accordingly. In case of unprovoked attack, the officer in command will, without hesitation, take the most vigorous measures at his disposal, to administer severe punishment to the offenders, bearing in mind that any other course is likely to be construed as a confession of weakness.

With the American troops out of the way, Villa could now concentrate on getting well. Some historians maintain that Villa mounted a burro and proceeded to a cave known as Cueva de Cozcomate. But intelligence officers for the Punitive Expedition believed that Villa remained at the Rodríguez ranch until the first of June. Whether he was actually in the house where the Yaqui Indians were seen leaving is unknown, but he did tell a Japanese businessman, who worked as a "confidential agent" for the army, that he had watched in alarm as U.S. troopers searched the houses. "It was the closest call to capture I have ever had in my life; I was actually in very great danger."

As for his generals, Nicolás Fernández and Francisco Beltrán continued south to the state of Durango. Pablo López remained hidden in a cave while his brother, Martín, drifted toward their hometown of San Andrés. Candelario Cervantes and his men loitered in the hills west of Guerrero, watching the American troops with field glasses. And Juan Pedrosa received some medical treatment from a French doctor and went into seclusion at a home that was just a few miles north of General Pershing's advance base at Satevó.

➤➤14◄◄

No One to Seek For

FOLLOWING THE PARRAL FIGHT, Hugh Scott and Frederick Funston were dispatched to El Paso to meet with Álvaro Obregón. Officials in Washington hoped the three generals could speak frankly to one another and halt the slide toward all-out war. After some hesitation, Carranza had reluctantly agreed to let his talented military chieftain attend, even though he was growing suspicious that he and Obregón were after the same prize: the presidency of Mexico.

The residents of Juárez and El Paso, who had lived for six years with revolution and counterrevolution and the almost daily rumors that they were about to be bombarded into rubble, greeted the news with a mixture of anticipation and irritation. Following the Columbus raid, El Paso had resembled an armed military camp. Soldiers from Fort Bliss had patrolled the downtown streets, sheriff's deputies had tramped the muddy banks of the Rio Grande, extra men had been hired by the police department, and more than a hundred Villa sympathizers and ex-officials had been rounded up in nightly dragnets. The suspects had been placed in the city jail and bonds were set so high that their captivity had been assured for an indefinite period of time. In a moment of candor, the police chief had acknowledged that the measures being implemented were not always legal. "We are not always proceeding according to law. If we did, we would not accomplish anything. We are out to keep peace along the border and prevent Villa's sympathizers from aiding him in evading our soldier boys. Dealing with bandits you have to take extraordinary measures."

The mayor of El Paso had also taken steps to limit free speech, prohibiting public discussion of the Columbus raid or the expedition. "We all want to demonstrate patriotism and love of country, but futile conversations about this war benefit nobody," he said. The police had cracked down on the small Spanish-language newspapers publishing in El Paso. Fernando Gamiochipi, the editor of *El Paso del Norte,* had been jailed on suspicion of inciting a riot and all copies of his newspaper were confiscated. Several other Spanish-language newspapers operated by Mexican expatriates were also suppressed "as a precaution against possible disorder resulting from inflammatory utterances." The typesetting equipment was returned a few days later but the chief of detectives had warned that police officials would continue to censor the news.

Ironically, El Paso owed much of its prosperity to the Mexican refugees who had fled across the border during the revolution. Restaurants opened and became wildly successful, clothing stores did a brisk business, bank deposits increased dramatically, and barbershops were filled with military generals waiting for shaves and haircuts. In the southern part of town, known as Little Chihuahua or Chihuahuaita, the boardinghouses and hotels were filled with spies, smugglers, arms dealers, soldiers of fortune, reporters, revolutionists and counterrevolutionists who called themselves Maderistas, Huertistas, Villistas, or Carrancistas, or *científicos* of the old Díaz regime. "Young revolutions have started from it; shattered revolutions have ebbed back into it; plots and counterplots have been darkly hatched within the corridors of its hotels," James Hopper wrote.

Luis Terrazas, the fabulously wealthy Chihuahua landowner, arrived in the city with twenty wagons filled with goods and an extended family that included forty-eight women and children, and rented an entire floor of the luxurious Paso del Norte Hotel. Upon his arrival, intelligence agents from nearby Fort Bliss proceeded to bug the rooms. The agents grew numb with boredom as they listened to the chatter about women's hats and gowns and were no doubt relieved when the clan rented a commodious house overlooking the city that happened to belong to New Mexico senator Albert Fall. Grand as it was, the house in no way could accommodate the extended family and their servants, which numbered some 150 people, and nearby houses were leased or purchased for the overflow. "After breakfasting," writes author Victor Macias-González, "don Luis held court, receiving family members, friends and acquaintances in seigneurial style in the mansion's salon. Seated at a large and comfortable chair that must have appeared to visitors to be a throne, he welcomed those who sought his advice and money. He reached into a large pouch on a table at his side to disburse small cash gifts of 25 and 50-cent American coins."

WHEN ÁLVARO OBREGÓN'S entourage pulled into the Juárez train station, residents tramped down to look at his locomotive and then returned home, singularly unimpressed. Unlike Villa's old train, Obregón's was nondescript and consisted of a mix of boxcars, flatcars, coal cars, private cars, and passenger coaches. One coach, dubbed the "Celaya," was the same car from which Obregón had directed the decisive battles against Villa and the car to which he was brought after his arm had been torn away by a Villista shell. A second railroad car, from which a long banner hung, was called the "Siquisiva," named after the Hacienda Siquisiva, General Obregón's birthplace. A third carried the heavy, cream-colored automobile that Obregón would use for trips across the river to meet with Hugh Scott and Frederick Funston.

A military band formed up on a platform to welcome Obregón's party, which included several new brides. "The drummer was all set, the bass fiddler ready to saw away on the strings, and the clarinets and cornets, and slide trombones were all tuned for the 'triumphal march' which the band was to play," a journalist reported. "Just as the diminutive director in beard and glasses, looking like an understudy of John Philip Sousa, was about to rap with his baton for attention, a green baize curtain of a car window was brushed aside and a command was given in sharp staccato sounds." The general, it seemed, was having his siesta and the band was encouraged to serenade someone else down the line.

Several hours later, Obregón, now known throughout Mexico as *el manco de Celaya* — the one-armed man of Celaya — appeared on the platform, freshly shaved, wearing a dark gray uniform buttoned up to his chin and a gold fountain pen in his pocket. Surrounded by his aides and his personal bodyguard, who wore red bands on their sombreros and trim gray uniforms made in New Jersey, he strolled over to the customhouse and waited for General Scott and General Funston, who were to pay him a courtesy visit.

As the two cars bearing the U.S. generals rolled over the international bridge and toward the customhouse, Mexican troops stood at attention and trumpets and drums were played. The visit was strictly social in nature and one of the first things that Funston did was express condolences to Obregón for the loss of his right arm. Obregón smiled graciously, looking every part the war hero, and said that at least he hadn't lost the rest of his body.

The following morning, the Mexican general returned the courtesy call at Scott's private railroad car in El Paso. Accompanying him were General Plutarco Elías Calles, the governor-general of Sonora, who had defeated Villa at Agua Prieta; General Gabriel Gavira, who commanded the Juárez garrison and had warned Pershing of Villa's approach to the border; and Consul Andrés García, the amiable civilian, who acted as interpreter and master of ceremonies.

Now it was the U.S. troops who were lined up smartly along both sides of the street. Obregón was saluted with a volley of nineteen guns and several bands played "The Imperial Potentate" march. As soon as the automobiles crossed the international line, the bands switched to the popular march "Under the Double Eagle."

Obregón stepped from his automobile and began walking toward the railroad car where General Scott awaited him. He swung up onto the platform using his good arm. He extended his left hand sideways from his body and General Scott clasped it with his right hand, which itself had been crippled from an old bullet wound.

Scott and Funston had been given detailed instructions from the War Department on how to handle the negotiations. They were to open the discussion by emphasizing that the expedition's presence in Mexico was for the sole purpose of "removing a menace to the common security and the friendly relations" of both countries. Then the two generals were to suggest to Obregón that their armies work cooperatively to capture Villa, with the Carrancistas driving Villa's band north into the arms of the U.S. troops. "The government of the United States has no pride involved in who makes the capture, and its only interest is that it should be done expeditiously so that American troops can be withdrawn and the peace of the borders assured."

The War Department emphasized that under no circumstances were Scott and Funston to address the question of the withdrawal of U.S. troops. If Obregón broached the issue, they were merely to say that any withdrawal of troops was a diplomatic matter. The two generals were also to make clear to Obregón that "so long as the possibility of further depredations by Villa exists the withdrawal of American troops would increase the danger and in any event be very difficult."

At the insistence of the Mexican government, the first official negotiating session was held at five o'clock on April 29 in the green room of the Juárez customhouse. The two U.S. generals took a seat below a painting of Benito Juárez, Mexico's liberator. Outside, a throng of reporters gathered, trying to discern through the windows what was being said. One of the windows had a "very clean cut" bullet hole. Several bands played and the crowd listened appreciatively. "The music was psychological," a reporter wrote. "It was sweet and sensuous and disconcerting to ill feelings and hostilities. The spell of Mexico settled down upon the group. Who could quarrel with 'Samson and Delilah' ringing in their ears and the melodic folk songs of the Mexican people?"

But a quarrel did occur, almost immediately, when Scott and

Funston brought up the problem of supplying their troops and pressed Obregón for use of the railways. Obregón, working from an entirely different script, politely turned aside the request and demanded the immediate withdrawal of the U.S. troops. He maintained that Villa was dead, or had been rendered innocuous, and his troops also killed or scattered. "There is no one to seek for now," he said, adding that the presence of U.S. soldiers was only making his job more difficult. As the meeting wore on, the reporters peering through the windows noticed Funston gesticulating in an excited manner. With a deadlock imminent, the Americans ended the conference. The meeting had lasted two hours.

Afterward, Obregón talked with journalists, tapping his foot impatiently during the question-and-answer session and dodging questions about the purpose of the conference. When asked if his troops could capture Villa, he responded, "It is not a question of troops. Now it is only a question of a hunt, not a campaign. There is no need for a great column of troops to catch a single man."

The negotiations might have ended there, but a mutual friend arranged a second meeting between General Obregón and General Scott at the Paso del Norte Hotel. (Funston was not present, Scott later wrote, because "he allowed his real sentiments to be expressed so brusquely that he lost his influences in those conferences, and he thought it best for him not to attend anymore.")

The Paso del Norte Hotel was the city's pride and joy. Fake marble, which could be manufactured in any color of the rainbow, had just come into use and the hotel's builders had taken full advantage of the technological breakthrough. The dome in the lobby was "turquoise blue," the pillars were "rice-field green," the walls "ox-blood red" and the "yellow found in underdone boiled eggs," and the whole mess trimmed in "delicate French mochas and 'Ladies Home Journal' frosting," wrote James Hopper of Collier's.

In order to evade reporters, Scott strolled uptown, occasionally stopping to purchase small items. When he was certain he was no longer being followed, he hailed a laundry wagon and asked to be dropped off at the service entrance of the hotel, where he took the elevator up to the eighth floor. Somehow, though, he wound up in the wrong corridor. "A Hearst correspondent, coming out of his room unaware of my presence, spied me and called out, 'I got you!'" In just a few minutes, twenty-seven reporters were standing outside the room where he was to meet Obregón. Scott ducked inside and slammed the door. Wrote the *El Paso Herald,* "The closing of that door at the 'mystery room' started the longest diplomatic session and the longest drawn out siege of newspaper men since Francisco Madero received the peace envoys from Mexico City in the little 'casa blanca' across the river from the smelter."

Scott was determined to get Obregón to sign an agreement that would allow Pershing to stay in Mexico "without his being assaulted by the Mexicans" for as long as President Wilson wanted. The two generals talked nonstop, pausing only long enough to devour sandwiches at 2:00 p.m. and steaks and salads at dinner. Hotel employees carried up pitchers of ice water and pots of strong coffee. In the hallway, the reporters waited, pitching pennies and shooting craps with the house detective. When one of the generals would go to the door to clear his head or receive telegrams, the reporters would leap up from their gambling games and ask for news. Downstairs, a bellboy walked through the fake-marble lobby carrying a silver tray in his hand and shouting at the top of his lungs, "Francisco Villa! Francisco Villa! Call for Mr. Villa." After he had paged the grill, the smoking room, and the dining room, someone told him to go up to room 828 and ask for General Obregón, who might be able to shed some light on the whereabouts of the rebel leader.

Behind the closed doors, documents were drawn up in English and Spanish, argued over, changed, and rewritten. At 12:30 a.m., after twelve solid hours of "mental struggle," the two generals arrived at an agreement. Only one page and eight paragraphs long, the document acknowledged that Villa and his band had been destroyed or dispersed. That said, the de facto government promised to aggressively patrol the border, and in exchange, the U.S. agreed to pull back its troops "commencing the withdrawal immediately." Although the Mexicans still refused to allow U.S. troops to use their railways, Obregón nevertheless promised Scott that his Mexican troops would not "molest" the U.S. soldiers while they remained in Mexico. "So, instead of ending up with a clash," Scott wrote in a letter to a friend, "we are on better terms now that we have been since the Columbus raid."

Scott told Newton Baker that the conference was "not equaled by any similar struggle with the wildest and most exasperated Indian heretofore encountered." In a letter to a colleague, he added, "I could not afford to let him get away from me without signing my papers because he would fall into the hands of a very hostile Mexican sentiment and I would lose everything I had gained. I do not know how I held him, for if he had said he was tired and wanted to go home and go to bed I could not have held him, but somehow or other I managed to keep him and he finally signed the papers."

The two men opened the door and walked down to their parked cars on San Antonio Street. The moving-picture operators lit their torches, illuminating the street in a ghostly splendor. "General Obregón," wrote one reporter, "sat in his big automobile like a fighter under fire. The brilliant light gave his olive skin a ghastly look and brought out his finely chiseled profile." Obregón allowed the movie men to take their pictures, then he gave a sharp order to his driver, slouched behind the wheel in a cape coat, and the car leaped forward into the darkness.

Scott, red eyed and drained, returned to his railroad car, where a stack of messages from the War Department awaited him. He sank into his chair and began to read. "I had not known how intense my concentration had been until it was over and I began to relax, to find that every muscle was taut, my fingers clenched and my teeth likewise. Both hands and jaws ached with the intensity of the effort."

But Scott's effort turned out to be futile. The United States approved the agreement on May 4, 1916, but the de facto Mexican government did not. Carranza continued to insist that the U.S. troops withdraw immediately or face the military consequences. A memo, which had been intercepted by U.S. officials, suggested that he meant it: "Dispose your troops that they shall be in a position to cut off American expeditionary forces now in Chihuahua. The action must be sudden and will take place after the Scott-Obregón conference. It will make no difference what else may be decided upon in conference unless there is absolute withdrawal of American troops the above plans will be carried out. The Sonora troops will be assisted by troops in Chihuahua."

Funston, in a defensive mode now, ordered Pershing to withdraw north to Colonia Dublán. Pershing balked, saying he would no longer be able to supply the troops hunting Pancho Villa and that such a withdrawal would result in a "serious loss of American prestige."

Two days later, on May 5, a group of Mexican raiders crossed the border and attacked two tiny settlements in the Big Bend area of Texas. Three troopers and a seven-year-old boy were killed at Glenn Spring and six hostages were taken at Boquillas. A smaller version of the Punitive Expedition was hastily organized and spent two weeks in Mexico hunting the marauders. Convinced now that Carranza was dealing with them in bad faith, President Wilson called up the National Guard troops in Texas, Arizona, and New Mexico and ordered them to the border. In response to the events, Funston dictated a forceful memo to Pershing:

> War with de facto government almost inevitable. You are liable to be attacked at any time by large force reaching Chihuahua by train from central Mexico as well as by Sonora troops. Your line is too long and troops scattered too much. For a time we cannot support you. Fall back along your line of communications with view to general concentration of entire force at Colonia Dublán. Such action imperative. No question of prestige can be entertained as military considerations must govern. If attacked do not allow any preliminary success to induce you to advance too far as danger meeting overwhelming force and having your line of communications cut is too great. Acknowledge and report daily.

On May 19, Funston telegrammed him again, warning of the anti-American sentiment and the heavy movement of troops north "for ostensible purpose of suppressing bandits but movements suspiciously large for needs." He continued, "If any part of your forces is attacked by an organized body of de facto government troops you will attempt to destroy all of their forces within reach taking care not to become too deeply involved or exposing your line of communications. . . . In case of such attack on you rush information to me without waiting to give details as it is essential that we learn of it before Mexicans."

Carranza's generals were daily becoming more bellicose. General Luis Herrera in Parral stated publicly that he would begin attacking Americans still in the country on June 1. And General José Cavazos, who had shared his whiskey with Major Tompkins, had verbally abused the expedition's civilian scouts and ordered his men to fire on any American soldiers they saw. Funston urged Pershing to avoid anything that would bring the two sides into conflict. "You are instructed to act conservatively."

Seething, Pershing nevertheless obeyed orders. Penned up in northern Chihuahua, he suffered alongside his troops through the sandstorms, the growing heat, the flies, the boredom. "We have been very idle," George Patton confided in a sad letter to his father. "It is most tiresome sitting out on a bluff over a river in the sun and dust. We can't go to town because they shoot at us now and then and the gen. does not want to start something unless he can finish it."

PART III
REVENGE AND REVIVAL

⤛15⤜

Gasoline Baths and
Confessions

MORNING SUNLIGHT POURED THROUGH the window of the hospital ward, falling on the chamber pots and sour sheets and faces of the sleepers. Slowly the patients awakened from their drugged dreams. Jesús Paez, his black hair still smelling faintly of kerosene and his skin raw from disinfectants, heard the birds outside the window, and for a moment his heart soared with a twelve-year-old's exuberance. Then the terrible knowledge that nagged at him even in his deepest sleep rushed in: his left leg had been amputated, foot, ankle, calf, knee, and most of his thigh lopped off by a surgeon's saw while he lay etherized on the operating table.

For nearly a week after the Columbus raid, Jesús had languished in the hospital tent with the other wounded Villistas. Two men taken on the battlefield had already died of their wounds. On the fifteenth and sixteenth of March, Jesús and four others were transported to the jail in the basement of the Deming courthouse. Jesús's femur had been fractured by the impact of the bullet and his wound had become badly infected. He was taken to Ladies Hospital, where the leg was amputated. For days, before and after the operation, he had lingered in a feverish state of near death, but he was young and strong and the danger eventually passed. When word of his miraculous recovery got out, newspaper correspondents came to interview him. He propped himself up in bed and his obsidian eyes filled with tears as he talked about his father, Emilio. During the raid, Jesús said, he had remained with the rear guard, holding his father's horse. When his father did not return with the others, Jesús had gone to look for him. A bullet struck him in the left thigh, shattering the bone, and he fell to the ground in excruciating pain. *"Yo soy un buen muchacho"* — "I am a good boy," he screamed as a cavalryman approached him.

The correspondents soon dubbed Jesús the *"buen muchacho"* and the "baby bandit" and the people of Deming brought him crayons and notepads and coins, which went into a small piggy bank next to his bed. But Jesús, it seemed, was not the docile creature that the newspapers made him out to be. When his guests departed, he hounded Mrs. Emma Duff, the hospital matron. Wrote a Deming resident:

> The Mexican boy who belongs to the bandits and who was taken prisoner and brought here to the hospital severely wounded, is proving a terror for poor Mrs. Duff to manage. The foolish people here insisted upon making a young hero of him and rushed to see him in perfect squads, carrying all sorts of delicacies to him and other gifts. He is only 12 years old, or so they say, but is a hardened young tough and has become dreadfully spoiled. He has been treated with the care and kindness of a valuable young prince and he has not the gratitude of a buzzard. Mrs. Duff says he would shoot her in the back if he only had the chance. In addition, a Mexican priest, who made his appearance here only after the raid, visits him seven or eight times a day and the boy has become more and more unmanageable under this man's ministrations, who talks to him in Spanish. Mrs. Duff is convinced he is no priest but a spy, and thinks the authorities ought to take some steps about it, but it seems no one feels authorized to do anything. The boy calls constantly for cigarettes and a stiff drink of whiskey and Mrs. D. at any hour in the night must get up and answer his

bell, give him the cigarette and then stay until he finishes it lest he burn something with it. If she refuses him, he raises a yell that lifts the roof and alarms every patient in the hospital. His leg had to be amputated at the hip and I suppose that and his apparent youth make people pity him. Poor Mrs. D. is almost crazy with the trouble of him.

Jesús's story was filled with inconsistencies. In one interview, he said his father had been forced to join the column. In another, he boasted that his father was a Dorado and paymaster in Villa's army. Yet Villa would hardly have made a forced conscript a member of his Dorados much less entrusted him with money for his troops. Years later, one of the Villistas who participated in the attack said Jesús was not a member of their band at all but lived on the east side of Columbus with other poor Mexican families and was accidentally shot by the Americans as he fled from his house. *"De una de esas casas salió corriendo y gritando que no tiraran, un paisano y, luego, un chamaco lo siguió."* — "From one of these houses, a peasant and later, a kid, came running and screaming not to shoot."

Civil authorities in Deming had been eager to try someone for the atrocities committed in Columbus, but by March 23, three more raiders had died, leaving only Jesús and Juan Sánchez, sixteen, still alive. Since they were mere boys, it would be difficult to hold them solely responsible for the brutal murders. Still, the desire for vengeance was strong and someone should have to pay. But who?

The answer came on April 11, when a second group of wounded Villistas was brought up from El Valle to Columbus. No formal extradition process was followed, nor was the de facto government consulted before the men were removed from Mexico. An army document simply states that six men were being transferred on orders of the chief of staff of the Punitive Expedition. All of them had been left behind as Villa retreated south and were suffering from badly infected gunshot wounds. The most severely injured were José Rangel, who had bullet wounds in both legs and couldn't walk, and Francisco Álvarez, whose handsome features had been ruined by a bullet that had penetrated his cheek and mouth. They were dressed in filthy rags and a medical officer with the expedition had difficulty getting them to take the gasoline baths that were supposed to rid them of vermin. "The Mexicans knew enough of gasoline to fear it, and after the Columbus raid some bodies of Mexicans were burned in the vicinity. They wailed and begged and dragged back from the gasoline, in scarcely intelligible Spanish, imploring the army men not to burn them alive," a correspondent wrote.

Upon arriving in Columbus, the six men were taken to a hospital tent where an army nurse named Lurid Fillmore watched over them. While they lay on their army cots, a parade of citizens and law-enforcement officials trooped in to question them. The prisoners answered the questions freely without having the benefit of an attorney or anyone else to represent them. A few days later, those same officials were called as witnesses before a Luna County grand jury. The men related what they had learned from the prisoners in the hospital tent and the information was sufficient for the grand jury to hand up a raft of criminal indictments. All six Mexicans were indicted on two counts of first-degree murder each in the deaths of James Dean, John Moore, Charles DeWitt Miller, and Corporal Paul Simon, the soldier who played clarinet in the band.

In a separate group of indictments, Juan Sánchez, Jesús Paez, and Pablo Sánchez, the man who was arrested on suspicion of being a spy, were charged with the same murders. Although the evidence was flimsy, Pablo Sánchez was also charged with being an accessory before the fact in the murder of Charles DeWitt Miller. Finally, the grand jury indicted Pancho Villa himself for the murders of James Dean, John Moore, and Charles DeWitt Miller. (He was not indicted for the murder of the soldier, possibly in an effort to avoid military complications.)

As soon as the indictments were handed up, arrest warrants were issued and the six wounded prisoners were taken into custody by the sheriff of Luna County and transported to jail. The trial was set to start four days later, on April 19, before Judge Edward Medler, a no-nonsense judge from Lincoln County who had been reassigned to the district court in Luna County that spring by the state supreme court.

The day before the trial, Medler got a call in his hotel room from the Luna County district attorney advising him that E. B. Stone of the Bureau of Investigation wanted to confer with him about the case. Stone was the federal agent who interviewed many of the prisoners and the two hostages, Maud Wright and Edwin Spencer, immediately after the raid. Medler seemed irritated by the request and two years later, in a letter to Senator Fall, he noted with some satisfaction that Stone was serving time in Leavenworth for soliciting a bribe from Leona Grace, a "boss madam" in El Paso. At the time, however, Stone was still a reputable agent and Medler agreed to hear what he had to say at eight o'clock that evening in the courtroom.

At the appointed time, Stone made his appearance and said he had a statement to make from the United States attorney general, Thomas Gregory. Stone produced three telegrams: one from Gregory, a second from General Funston, and a third from Newton Baker. "The substance of the telegrams," recalled Medler, "was that these various departments protested against the trial of the Villa raiders, or the Columbus raiders, as we called them, on the ground that it would involve the United States in international complications with Mexico."

Medler viewed Stone's remarks as a reflection on his court and responded testily that the Mexican prisoners had been indicted by a properly impaneled grand jury and were in the legal custody of the sheriff of Luna County. He also explained that the county was not in a position to cope with a postponement because a previous grand jury had found that the Luna County jail "was unsanitary and not a proper place to confine prisoners." Furthermore, he added, "I saw no reason why the court could not proceed to try this case on the following morning; that General Pershing was in Mexico with his expedition trying to arrest Francisco Villa, a co-defendant named in this indictment; and that if the trial of these raiders would involve the United States in international complications, to my mind it would seem that the United States was already involved. In other words, I practically told him there would be no 'watchful waiting' around my court."

When Medler had finished, agent Stone asked the judge if he would be willing to talk with Summers Burkhart, the U.S. attorney in Albuquerque. The judge agreed and they reached him by telephone. "I had known Mr. Burkhart for quite a number of years and easily recognized his voice. Mr. Burkhart, when he found I was on the telephone, advised me he had received instructions from the Attorney General to go to Deming and protest against the trial of these Villistas."

"Upon what grounds?" barked Medler.

"Upon the ground that you will not give them a fair trial."

Medler considered the remark to be in contempt of court and informed Burkhart he had until ten o'clock the following morning to repeat his statement in open court. "He [Burkhart] then apologized, stating he did not intend to make any reflections upon the court, but stated that the public feeling was such that he did not feel the defendants would get a fair trial. I assured him that as far as I had anything to do with it as judge of the court that they would have a fair trial."

The following morning, April 19, the six Villistas filed into a courtroom on the second floor of the Luna County courthouse. The room was large and spacious, with an embossed-tin ceiling and tall arching windows. The judge sat behind a wooden bench, which still had the old territorial seal of New Mexico carved upon it. To the left of him were the jury box and witness stand, made from the same wood. The Villistas were clad in jeans and blue shirts that were buttoned up to their necks. Their heads had been shaved, making them appear very young. The county physician reported to Medler that the six men could handle the rigors of a trial, but in fact, only two of the raiders could stand when the indictments were read aloud.

E. B. Stone took a seat in the audience, which was crowded with female spectators. J. S. Vaught, the assistant district attorney for Luna County, was the lead prosecutor. Buel Wood, an attorney from Carrizozo, New Mexico, represented the Villistas. He would have had a hard time mounting a vigorous defense; he had been appointed to the case only the day before the trial began.

Twelve potential jurors, all men with Anglo-sounding names, filed into the jury box. Prosecutor Vaught asked them a brief series of questions about their ages and occupations, where they lived, how much they knew about the case, and their feelings toward the death penalty. One was excused when he said he would not sentence anyone to death.

Defense attorney Wood asked the group collectively to withdraw from the case if they had any prejudices. "Now, if any of you gentlemen bear any malice against the Mexican race or if any of you gentlemen suffered in a property sense or had any of your relatives or close friends hurt, wounded, or killed at Columbus during the raid, or if you know of any other fact connected with the raid on Columbus that would naturally create in your mind an impression . . . I will ask you gentlemen as a matter of your own personal conscience that you will voluntarily withdraw from the jury box when your name is called as juror." None of the men volunteered.

Eventually twelve jurors were seated. The panel reflected small-town America at the beginning of the twentieth century and included a cigar dealer, a stock handler, seven farmers, a livery-stable operator, a machinist, and a man who operated an "automobile livery" business.

J. S. Vaught delivered his opening statement, which lasted perhaps thirty seconds. The state, he told the jurors, decided to try all six defendants for the murder of Charles De Witt Miller. Each indictment contained two counts: the first charged that one or all of the defendants had actually fired the weapon that killed Mr. Miller, and the second alleged only that the defendants had "aided and abetted" in the killing. Conviction on either count carried the death penalty and it was clear from his statement that he intended to prove only the second count.

"Call your first witness," snapped Medler.

The prosecution then proceeded to put on the witness stand the same law-enforcement officials and civilians who had tramped into the hospital tent and questioned the wounded Villistas. Only one of those witnesses — Constable T. A. Hulsey — said he actually saw Charles DeWitt Miller being murdered, but admitted that he had witnessed the killing from the ignominious vantage point of a tree hole in his backyard. The other prosecution witnesses did not see any of the actual killings, nor were they able to positively identify the defendants as being among the raiders. Curiously, none of the actual eyewitnesses to the raid — including Maud Wright, Bunk Spencer, Arthur Ravel, Rachel Walker, Laura Ritchie, or Laura's three daughters — testified.

When it was Buel Wood's turn to put on his defense, he didn't call any of these eyewitnesses either. Instead, he put on only the defendants themselves, a strategy that turned out to be a colossal error. The first was José Rodríguez, a Carrancista soldier from the state of Nuevo León who had been taken prisoner by Villa in mid-February following a fight at one of the lovely haciendas in the Hearst empire. Rodríguez was only twenty, but seemed prematurely aged, lacking in all frivolity.

"Now, what did you do the morning of the ninth?" asked Wood.

"I didn't do anything. They left me where the horses was, and when they started to run I started to run ahead of them. When we was on our retreat, that is when they wounded me."

Prosecutor Vaught cross-examined Rodríguez closely, hoping that he would reveal himself to be a more willing and knowledgeable participant in the raid, but Rodríguez stuck to his story. He testified that he had no idea that the troops were attacking Columbus until he heard the shooting and saw the fires.

But you knew, Vaught persisted, that Villa did nothing else "except fight, didn't you?"

"I just knew that he fought against Mexico; I didn't know that he was fighting the Americans."

The second defendant, Eusevio Rentería, twenty-four, had thick, taciturn features and a scowling, embittered profile. Rentería talked of his long military career, beginning with his forced service under Porfirio Díaz, his imprisonment by the Yaqui Indians, and his capture by the Villistas at the Cabrado mining camp. Villa "was very cruel to us," he said. "If we would not obey what he ordered us to do, he would have killed us."

"And that is why, is it not, that you boys and the rest of Villa's command was kept in ignorance of the true movements and the real design that Villa and his officers had in mind?" asked defense attorney Wood.

"We were always ignorant as to what he intended to do. We just marched along when he told us to."

José Rangel, twenty-three, suffering from gunshot wounds in both legs, was moved to the front of the courtroom on his cot so that jurors could hear his testimony. Rangel testified that Villa and his men captured him as he was coming out of a store in Chihuahua City about two and a half months prior to the raid. He was given a Mauser and some cartridges and served as an orderly. He insisted that he did not come into town during the attack.

The fourth defendant, Juan Castillo, twenty-six, was another Carrancista soldier who had been captured by Villa. "When they ordered us to do anything we would have to do it; if we would not, they would beat us up," he testified.

Judge Medler then interrupted Wood's questioning to ask Castillo if he was paid anything.

Nada, Castillo responded.

Taurino García, a twenty-one-year-old bricklayer with big, round eyes and a wispy, tentative mustache, told jurors that he was kidnapped by Villa's men on a dusty road in Chihuahua. "He stood me up there in a ring. He formed a ring of some men and had a fellow beat me up," he testified. Five days before the raid, he continued, Villa gave him a gun and fifteen cartridges. He said he knew it would probably be used in a battle but he could not resist taking it. García was wounded as he advanced into Columbus. He lay on the ground until one of his fellow soldiers picked him up and carried him to the rear.

After García's testimony, the judge halted the trial and the manacled prisoners were taken downstairs to the filthy jail where three of their countrymen had died just a few weeks earlier. The next morning they were returned to the courtroom. Francisco Álvarez, twenty-two, took a seat on the witness stand. His face was still swollen and wrapped in bandages. Álvarez denied being in Columbus during the raid and denied knowing Villa. Apparently frustrated with his answers, defense attorney Wood turned to the prosecutor and said, "Take him."

During the cross-examination, Álvarez grew more voluble and reversed several of his earlier statements. He admitted that he was, in fact, in Columbus and that he was given a gun and ammunition and had gone with the main troops into town.

The state called only one rebuttal witness — Jesús Paez, who resembled a Charles Dickens character as he hobbled to the front of the courtroom on his crutches. Jesús's testimony was brief, possibly an indication that Vaught already knew the boy's story was problematic. Nevertheless, hoping to inflame the all-male jury, the prosecutor prodded Jesús into saying that Villa had promised each of the raiders an "American wife" when the attack was over.

Afterward, both sides rested and the judge and lawyers retired to prepare their instructions to the jury. Although Buel Wood maintained that the defendants were simply soldiers following orders, Medler went out of his way to demolish this defense in the instructions to the jury. Jurors were told that threats of duress and imprisonment or even "an assault to the peril of life" did not constitute "legal excuse or justification" for murder. No state of war existed at the time between Mexico and the United States, he added, "and unless a state of war did exist, there was no justification in law for a military expedition."

The jury retired to deliberate at 11:29 a.m. Thirty minutes later, the panel filed back into the courtroom. The foreman handed a piece of paper to the judge. Medler read it and then turned to the defendants: the jury, he intoned, finds you guilty of murder in the first degree.

AT 2:00 P.M. on the same day, Juan Sánchez, the sixteen-year-old boy who was picked up on the battlefield, went on trial. (The charges against Jesús Paez appear to have been dismissed in exchange for his testimony, and the trial of Pablo Sánchez, the alleged spy who was named in the same indictment, was postponed "on account of lack of sufficient evidence.") Although no transcript of the second trial has been found, newspaper reporters observed that Sánchez's trial proceeded even more quickly than the first: "The state developed such a weight of evidence in the trial ending in the conviction of the first raiders placed on trial that it did not place all of its witnesses on the stand." After just two hours of testimony, a jury retired to deliberate his fate. Thirty minutes later, they returned, grim faced. Juan Sánchez was also found guilty of murder in the first degree.

ON MONDAY, APRIL 24, the seven Villistas returned to the courtroom for sentencing. Before passing sentence, Judge Medler noted that the convicted prisoners had been provided with competent counsel and a fair trial. But just how competent the defense was and how fair those trials had actually been is a matter of debate. Defense attorney Buel Wood would later tell reporters that the admissions the defendants made on the witness stand "supported the verdict" and Judge Medler himself later called their testimony "practically a confession." Another tactical error made by Wood was trying all six defendants at once, which even reporters at the time described as highly unusual.

Nevertheless, a trial had been held and a verdict delivered. Medler gaveled the courtroom into silence. The defendants, Medler instructed, were remanded to the custody of the Luna County sheriff until May 19, 1916. On that day, in an enclosure to be erected by the sheriff, "you Eusevio Rentería, Taurino García, José Rodríguez, Francisco Álvarez, José Rangel and Juan Castillo be then and there by the said sheriff of the said county of Luna, hanged by the neck until you are dead, and may God have mercy on your soul." Juan Sánchez, looking almost as small and wan as Jesús Paez, was also sentenced to be hanged.

With the judge's pronouncement of the death sentence, a sigh of relief went up from the spectators and they hurried out into the wide breezy hallway. Wrote one reporter, "The attention of many was arrested however, by the quivering form of José Rangel who could no longer stand the ordeal. He buried his face in the varied hue quilt that covered his rickety cot and wept hot salty tears. As the folding doors bounded open and the sheriff's assistants hurried past bearing the crippled foreigner, many paused and turned away when they beheld him concealing his tear-stained face in his handkerchief."

Instead of returning the condemned men to the local jail, Judge Medler ordered the sheriff to take them to the penitentiary in Santa Fe for safekeeping. He also ordered Luna County officials to clean up the jail at once: "The present state of affairs, which has been characterized by your grand jury as a disgrace to the county must be remedied," he told the Luna County commissioners.

The seven prisoners were taken to the penitentiary by a train provided by the Santa Fe Railroad. The railroad car was old and rickety and prisoners and their guards had to ride for miles in darkness. "It is true that a faint and evil smelling light was obtained at each end of the car after about six attempts had been made to ignite the lamps, but in the middle of the car, where the prisoners were herded, it was black as the inside of a cow," the *Deming Headlight* reported.

->>16<<-

JERKED TO JESUS

WITH THE EXECUTION DATE fast approaching, a Santa Fe lawyer named Edward C. Wade Jr. took it upon himself to send a telegram to President Wilson, entreating him to contact the governor of New Mexico and ask for a reprieve for the condemned men so that a thorough investigation of the Villista cases could be made by federal authorities: "They are ignorant, illiterate and like children mentally; one is seriously wounded. They were, I am informed, taken prisoners in Mexico by Pershing's expedition and were brought out of Mexico without extradition proceedings and turned over to the state authorities for punishment. They contend they are military prisoners, entitled to the protection of the United States. They have no friends, are in a strange country and have no financial means to assert their innocence in higher court or to urge their contention that they are prisoners of war and should be so treated."

Judge Medler was incensed by Wade's appeal and so were the local newspapers. "The people of New Mexico and the entire Southwest owe no debt of gratitude to E. C. Wade, Jr. for interesting himself, without compensation, on behalf of the seven Mexicans convicted at Deming and sentenced to be hanged in just fifteen days," fumed the *Deming Graphic* in an angry editorial. Calling the seven prisoners "murderous scoundrels," "Mexican curs," and "yellow devils," the editorial writer reminded readers of John Moore, shot to death at his home; his wife, Susan, gunned down in "sportive fashion"; and William Ritchie, the genial host of the Commercial Hotel, bleeding to death on the front steps of the hotel.

The White House felt differently, however, and Joseph Tumulty, President Wilson's close adviser, sent a telegram to New Mexico governor William McDonald asking for additional information on the seven condemned men. McDonald replied that he would investigate the cases and get back to him. Keeping his word, the governor then made a special trip to the penitentiary to interview the prisoners, accompanied by a stenographer and the secretary of state, Antonio Lucero, who also acted as interpreter. In their discussions with the governor, all the condemned men now claimed that they were Carrancista soldiers who had been captured by Villa and were given the choice of joining him or facing the firing squad. They pointed out that during the raid they were left holding the horses because Villa was suspicious of their loyalty and was unwilling to take them into town. But McDonald was not convinced. The horse holders, he theorized, were actually of great strategic importance because the horses "represented their only means of getting away after the massacre."

Following up on his inquiry, President Wilson then sent McDonald a letter and formally asked him to postpone the executions:

> Would it not seem, in view of the existing conditions, that the executions of these men be deferred pending the active field operations for the capture of the principal offender, Villa, whose case should be disposed of along similar lines? In view, too, of the highly excitable conditions on the border and among the Mexican people, may not grossly misrepresented and exaggerated accounts of the execution be circulated and lead to acts of so-called reprisal being committed upon American citizens resident in Mexico? I respectfully request that you

consider the propriety of reprieving these men for a reasonable period in order that their present execution may not complicate the existing conditions in the manner stated above.

McDonald replied that the president's suggestion was "in accord" with how he planned to handle the cases, adding that he was awaiting a copy of the trial transcript. "I scarcely think that their execution would result in any serious reprisal on the part of the Mexicans, though of course no one can tell just what might happen," he wrote. "You will readily understand that there is considerable feeling in New Mexico, and I believe these cases should be handled carefully in order to prevent, so far as possible, any objectionable developments here as well as in Mexico."

The following day, May 13, the governor granted a twenty-one-day reprieve to the condemned men, pushing back the execution date to June 9.

WHILE THESE HIGH-LEVEL DISCUSSIONS were going on, a remarkable undercover operation was unfolding at the state penitentiary. At about midnight on the evening of May 11, Ben Williams, owner of a detective agency in El Paso, appeared at the gates of the New Mexico penitentiary with a handcuffed prisoner. The captive gave his name as Antonio Vásquez and was turned over to the captain of the guard. Once in custody, the man was ordered to take a shower, then given a prison uniform ("with a number on the back") and locked into a cell with Juan Sánchez, the sixteen-year-old. The next morning, when the alarm bell rang, the two woke up and began to talk. When Sánchez asked Antonio what he was in for, the older man said he was a Villa spy. In truth, Antonio was a gumshoe named Samuel Geck, who worked for the El Paso agency. The firm had numerous clients with business investments in Mexico and Geck's assignment was to make friends with the Villistas in order to find out more about the Santa Isabel train massacre and "the plans of their leaders for possible other depredations on American properties in Mexico."

Suspecting nothing, Juan Sánchez talked freely about his life with the Villistas. He said he was an orphan, born on a hacienda in San Luis Potosí, a state in south-central Mexico, and had voluntarily enlisted in Villa's army. He had accompanied Villa to Agua Prieta and remained with him through the disastrous Sonoran campaign. He positively linked Villa to the train massacre, saying that Villa had learned from one of his spies that a number of Americans were on their way by train to Cusihuíriachic to reopen a mine and that no Carrancista soldiers were guarding them. Villa had then sent several officers and fifty men to attack the train, "with instructions to kill all the Americans that he found on the train." The boy ticked off names of other participants in the train massacre, but the detective later wrote that he couldn't remember them all because "I had no way of making notes."

Sánchez told him that he did not fire any shots while in Columbus and didn't want to go there, but was forced to go by Pancho Villa. During the retreat, he couldn't find his way back to the horses and was picked up by the cavalry soldiers about daylight.

Having gotten what information he could from the teenager, the detective sent word to the prison superintendent that he wished to see his attorney, a signal that meant he was ready to be moved someplace else. At 11:00 p.m. he was transported to the hospital room where the other six wounded Villistas were sleeping. In the morning, they awoke and breakfasted together. Afterward the detective tried to get the prisoners to talk. José Rangel was the first man he spoke to and the story he told differed significantly from his courtroom testimony. Rangel had testified that he had been pressed into Villa's army, but now said that he had joined Villa voluntarily and had accompanied him to Agua Prieta. Some parts of his story, however, remained unchanged. He insisted that he had had no idea that Villa was going to attack the United States. "If he had, he would have deserted Villa, but was afraid that he would be caught and killed," the operative wrote, adding, "Rangel claims to be innocent, but that if the authorities thought he was guilty of the crime that he was ready to die. Rangel seems to be a leader among the six men, and is not disposed to talk very much. He spoke about the gringos being cowards."

Eusevio Rentería stuck to the basic outline of his story. So did José Rodríguez, Juan Castillo, and Taurino García. "Rodríguez admitted he was in the raid at Columbus, but would not talk about the fight, except that he was wounded in the running fight with the American soldiers. Juan Castillo only said that if he had to die that he was ready, and would not talk about Villa or any of the fights. Taurino García did not talk much, claimed he had been with Pancho Villa four or five months, and had been forced to join the Villa army."

Despite his mouth injury, Francisco Álvarez was the most voluble. He said he joined the federal army at age fifteen, but soon deserted with his colonel's horse and saddle after being ordered to salute a superior. Four years later, he got into a fight with his cousin over a woman, shot him, and was sent to prison. Upon release, he joined Villa's troops and participated in several battles. Álvarez boasted that he was close to Villa during the Columbus raid. "He and Villa and about eighty men were about the last ones to leave Columbus," Geck quoted him as saying.

Sensing he was not going to get more information, Geck stated that he wanted to see his attorney. Back in the receiving room, he exchanged his prison garb for his street clothes. Then, he and his boss, Ben Williams, exited the penitentiary.

BUEL WOOD had been paid $250 by the court for representing the seven Villistas at trial and had not filed an appeal. But now he had a new paying client: the de facto Mexican government and the Mexican ambassador, who had retained him to investigate the cases and make a special plea for the governor to grant executive clemency. His initial public comments, however, suggested that he was more concerned with currying favor from Judge Medler than keeping his clients from the gallows. "I am fully and firmly convinced that no man or set of men in the history of the American justice ever received a more impartial and fair trial. . . . The record of their cases as tried and made, contains no error sufficient to obtain a new trial, and if that record would be and could be reviewed by a higher tribunal, the only comment of the record made would be a dismissal of the appeal with thanks to the trial court for his fair and impartial administration of justice. . . ."

While Buel Wood was making his obsequious remarks, Samuel Geck was busily typing up his report. When it was finished, his boss sent a courtesy copy to J. S. Vaught. The prosecutor was excited by its contents and asked for permission to share it with the governor: "The report you sent me is very interesting and throws considerable light on the question of their guilt and also as to whether or not they should be punished in the manner in which they have been ordered punished. Of course I am interested in seeing that the sentence of the Court be carried out, and want to do everything in my power to have it done."

It is likely that McDonald did see the report; by June 3, he seemed to have made his mind up about the prisoners' guilt and sent another telegram to President Wilson, advising him that his investigation had showed that the seven men had indeed received fair trials. Wilson thanked the governor for consulting with him, but made one last effort to influence him, enclosing a letter written by Newton Baker to Joseph Tumulty. In the letter, Baker expressed strong reservations about the pending executions on both moral and legal grounds:

> I still have a feeling that Villa is the responsible criminal and these men were his ignorant dupes, and that therefore the extreme penalty is too severe. . . . In view of the fact that Villa has not yet been apprehended, and in view of the additional fact that these men were captured on Mexican soil, brought to the United States without the consent of the Mexican Government or of the men themselves, and therefore without a resort to the ordinary processes of extradition, which would be the usual way for the United States to secure custody of Mexican citizens who had offended her laws, it would seem to me better if Governor McDonald would simply commute their sentences to life imprisonment, so that if in the round-up the Republic of Mexico undertakes to object to our abducting her citizens without going through the formalities of extradition as provided by treaty between that Republic and ours, she will at

least not be able to say that we carried off her citizens and executed them.

As a postscript, he added, "It may well be that my feeling on this subject is in part affected by my complete aversion to capital punishment, but I do not think it is."

The letters and telegrams show clearly that Wilson and his cabinet members had grave concerns about the cases. Yet they did nothing to assert federal jurisdiction when the prisoners were still in the custody of the U.S. Army, and a few months later, when another twenty-one Villistas were taken out of Mexico in the same informal way, Wilson once again would allow them to be tried by local authorities.

As carpenters in Deming were hammering together the scaffold from which the prisoners would be hanged, Governor McDonald on June 7 issued a second twenty-one-day reprieve. But this time it was for only five of the condemned Villistas. Juan Sánchez, who had confessed during his trial to being in the vicinity of the Commercial Hotel when Charles DeWitt Miller was killed, and Francisco Álvarez, who had boasted of fighting at Villa's side in Columbus, would go to the gallows as scheduled. Leading the charge to hang them was their former defense attorney, Buel Wood: "We are convinced of the guilt of the two who are to hang tomorrow and believe they should pay the penalty," he declared.

A LARGE CROWD had gathered at the Deming train station to see the prisoners arriving from Santa Fe, but the sheriff put one over on them by stopping the train a mile or so out of town and conveying Sánchez and Álvarez to jail by automobile. Rumor had it that Villa had vowed not to let the men hang and the residents of Deming were taking no chances. Well-armed citizens of the Deming Vigilantes Committee, which was organized by local merchants in the aftermath of the raid, patrolled the surrounding streets, and members of New Mexico's National Guard stood sentry at the entrance to the jail, their guns loaded and bayonets mounted.

In the West, hangings always stirred the poetic imaginations of reporters and they often recorded in great detail the last hours of a man's life — what he ate for breakfast, what he wore, and his final words. When invited to speak, some prisoners spewed out curses while others launched into monologues that sometimes lasted for an hour or more. A priest or minister and the sheriff usually accompanied them to the gallows. More often than not, the prisoners found themselves drawing closer to the sheriff in their final moments, for it was he who oversaw the mechanics of the hanging and whom they depended upon to ferry them as painlessly as possible into the next world.

Hanging a man seemed like a simple procedure but in reality it took a great deal of skill to make sure the death would be quick and painless. The rope had to be stretched beforehand, the noose coiled properly and positioned in the correct spot in the hollow of the neck. The force of the fall, which depended in part on the length of the rope and the weight of the condemned man, had a lot to do with whether the neck would break cleanly. Many prisoners wound up strangling to death, and there were recorded cases of hanged men suddenly awakening after they had already been cut down and laid in their coffins.

The headline writers struggled to find new ways to describe the moment the trapdoor opened: the condemned men were "launched," "ushered," "dropped," or "swung" into eternity. One "stepped" confidently into the void, a second was "jerked on the New York plan," and a third fell through the trapdoor, "kicking himself to death in the light air."

At four thirty on the morning of June 9, the Reverend Joseph Carnet and the Reverend Alfonso Romero went to the jail to pray with the condemned men. Francisco Álvarez smoked cigarettes and made jokes but Juan Sánchez was more serious and spent his last hours in "semi-silent prayer." At around six o'clock the witnesses began arriving. Two physicians took up their positions beneath the gallows with stethoscopes around their necks. The law required that twenty people witness the hangings, but Sheriff Simpson had sent out invitations to more than fifty, including Milton James, Lieutenant Castleman, and G. E. Parks. Laura Ritchie had been invited to cut the rope, but when the time came, she found that she just couldn't bring herself to do it.

In Mexico, the way a man comports himself at the moment of death has such immense importance that an expression has evolved for it: *hombrearse con la muerte* — to face death like a man or, more figuratively, to push death around. Francisco Álvarez was determined to die with the courage and dignity so admired by his countrymen and he maintained his composure to the end, asking for one last cigarette as he was led up the steps of the scaffold. Captain A. W. Brock read the death sentence in Spanish and then asked Álvarez if he would like to make a final statement. "*Yo no quiero*" — "I don't want to," he responded. He cocked his head obligingly as a black cap was drawn down over his face and the noose tightened. At that moment, his body began to shake and he involuntarily backed away. Gently he was guided back under the rope. At 6:36 a.m. the trap was sprung. Twelve minutes later, he was pronounced dead.

Now it was Juan Sánchez's turn. He limped slightly and his small size coupled with his infirmity made several witnesses look away. At 7:13 a.m. the trapdoor was sprung, and Juan's body plunged down through the opening. He weighed no more than a hundred pounds and the clean snap that the hangman had hoped for did not materialize. "He just gurgled so they cut him down. He was revived and they called the captain immediately," remembered a young guardsman named George Washington Hudiburgh Jr., who witnessed the spectacle:

Soon the district attorney and the judge were summoned and an argument ensued whether to hang the poor fellow again or let him go. The short of it was that they wired the governor and he said to read him the death warrant. It said, "hung until dead." So they took the little Mexican back up the gallows and dropped him again but his neck still wouldn't snap. Now the hangman was mad and without the usual ceremony he pulled the Mexican up by the rope through the trap and upturned him, and drove him with great force head first down through the trap. A loud snap told the story and that did the trick. He was dead.

The witnesses left quickly, some talking loudly and brashly, others subdued and thoughtful. The bodies were cut down, wrapped in quilts, and taken to the cemetery, where they were buried in unmarked paupers' graves. Governor McDonald issued no more reprieves for the Villistas and three weeks later, on June 30, four more prisoners were transported back to Deming under heavy guard. They ate a hearty dinner and slept well but refused breakfast. They went to the gallows in pairs, with Eusevio Rentería and Taurino García going first. When the sheriff asked Eusevio if he had any last words, he merely shrugged and said he had nothing to say. But Taurino was very frightened. His eyes were huge, his lips dry and cracked. He swept his tongue over the interior of his mouth and what came out were words of forgiveness.

"I hope you people will pardon me like I pardon all of you."

Eusevio tried to cheer him up. "Don't be afraid to die," he said. "We all have to die sometime, just as well die now."

As the brilliant light of morning filled up the sky, the trapdoors opened and the two prisoners plunged through. They lost consciousness immediately but their hearts continued to beat for another twenty minutes. The doctors, positioned beneath them, periodically put their stethoscopes up to the hanged men's hearts to see if they had stopped. When their bodies were finally cut down, their necks were ringed with rope burns, their mouths and eyes wide open.

Juan Castillo and José Rangel ascended the scaffold next. When asked if they had any last words, Rangel remained mute. Juan Castillo said, "I know I am going to die. I am going to die in justice. I pardon all of you." Black masks were drawn down over their faces. A moment later, the trapdoor opened. Their necks broke with audible cracks and their deaths were almost instantaneous.

José Rodríguez was the only condemned Villista who escaped the hangman's noose. Convinced that he hadn't fired a shot in Columbus, McDonald commuted his sentence to life and he was put to work at the prison brickmaking plant. "Rodríguez," wrote the *Santa Fe New Mexican* on June 30, 1916, "now appears to be in good health and gives promise of becoming a good worker around the brick kiln. "

José Rangel's will was made public ten days after the hanging. He wrote that he had neither friends nor family to console him in his sorrow and expressed his love for Mexico. He admitted that he had, in fact, participated in the raid but was only following the orders of his commander, Pancho Villa. Like the other raiders, he was buried in an unmarked pauper's grave.

⇥17⇤

A Ripe Pear

WHILE THE SEVEN VILLISTAS were going through the criminal-justice system, General Pershing and his troops captured another three dozen or so men suspected of having participated in the Columbus raid and incarcerated them in crude, barbed-wire stockades on Mexican soil. Some of the enclosures resembled open-air pens and offered scant protection from the blistering sun and the thunderstorms that periodically swept over the desert. Wearing cheap straw hats and loose cotton clothing, the prisoners watched the comings and goings of the cavalry soldiers. Pershing issued orders stating that only authorized personnel would be allowed to have contact with the prisoners and also made it clear that they were not to be put to work cleaning up the camps or doing other odd jobs. Still, the incarceration proved unbearable for some of the captives. A man named Adolfo Manquero bolted from the stockade in mid-April and was shot and killed by a sentry. A few days later, his nephew, Jesús Camadurar, "a tubercular," died after stabbing himself in the chest with a knife.

When the prisoners were interrogated by the expedition's intelligence officers, nearly all of them admitted to having participated in the raid. Like their ill-fated companions, the majority claimed that they had been forced to join the column after Villa's men had threatened to kill them or their families. Using the intelligence gained from the prisoners, General Pershing refined his hunt for Pancho Villa and his top officers, sending out night patrols to conduct surprise searches of homes and ranches.

On a routine excursion to purchase corn, Lieutenant Patton decided to make a surprise visit to a ranch where Julio Cárdenas, the head of Villa's vaunted Dorados, was said to be living. Cárdenas had remained at Villa's side until the guerrilla leader went into hiding. Then he had joined Nicolás Fernández's detachment. Fernández had been excessively secretive about their destination and Cárdenas had grown impatient with him. "This is as far as I shall accompany you," he said one morning as they were breaking camp, departing for home with his men.

Now, watching three vehicles filled with gringo soldiers approaching, Julio Cárdenas may have wished he had remained with Fernández. The automobiles rumbled to a halt and the Americans leaped out. Patton was one of the first to reach the main gate. Three armed Villistas burst from the entrance on horseback and Patton yelled at them to halt. Instead, the Mexicans reversed direction, only to find themselves facing another contingent of soldiers. They veered back toward Patton, firing their weapons. He returned the fire, hitting both a rider and his horse.

As Patton was reloading, another Mexican exited the yard on horseback. Remembering an old cowboy's adage to always aim at the horse of an escaping enemy, Patton shot the animal, waited for the rider to disentangle himself, then killed him, too. When the skirmish was over, three Villistas, including Cárdenas, lay dead. The bodies were strapped onto the hoods of the cars like deer and taken back to camp.

Pershing was delighted and dubbed Patton the "Bandit" and let him keep Cárdenas's silver-embossed saddle and saber. "The Gen. has been very complimentary telling some officers that I did more in half a day than the 13th Cav. did in a week," Patton said in a letter to his wife. He continued, "You are probably wondering if my conscience hurts me for killing a man. It does not. I feel about it just as I did when I got my swordfish, surprised at my luck."

Another coveted prize was Candelario Cervantes, considered almost as important as Villa by the headquarters staff, who continued to receive tantalizing reports of his whereabouts. Around April 20, Colonel Dodd learned that Cervantes and about 150 men were headed for Tomóchic, a remote village that was surrounded by mountains rising to more than ten thousand feet. The village was home to mostly Tarahumara Indians, who lived in terrible poverty and suffered from typhus and smallpox. Dodd plunged into the mountains, following trails that were so narrow and steep that his soldiers had to dismount and each hang onto the tail of the horse in front of him. Although it was nearly Easter, the air at that elevation was still unbearably cold. The troopers grew numb from the knees down and developed excruciating headaches, nausea, and bleeding from the nose. Dr. Eastman, who accompanied the marchers, wrote of the startling beauty of the land and the intense suffering of the men:

> Traveled three days through a wonderful, mountainous country, in fact this was the Continental Divide, very picturesque, heavily wooded with pines, many of them magnificent great trees. Saw wild turkeys, the tracks of bear and deer and heard the lobo wolf howl at night. Camped late in the afternoon of the third day within a few miles of our destination and waited for the moon to rise. Started on again at eleven and had three hours of the most heartbreaking marching I had ever experienced, walking and leading and no halts, stumbling along through deep cañons where the old moon failed to penetrate, up over steep rocks and along narrow ledges where we would look down into utter blackness and a misstep meant destruction. The elevation here was between eight and nine thousand feet and we had no time to filter and warm and moisten the air through our noses, but took it in great gulps through wide open mouths.

On the afternoon of April 22, the Seventh Cavalry exited the mountains and sent scouts into the small village. Cervantes had apparently received advance warning of Dodd's approach from local residents and had slipped away, leaving a rear guard in the hills to slow down the Americans. While Dodd's troopers were finalizing their plans under the cover of trees, one of the men accidentally discharged his weapon, alerting the Villistas to their position and leaving Dodd no choice but to attack. The packmaster rang his bell to call the troop train together and the U.S. cavalry charged. One platoon was sent to the left, the other to the right, sealing off the town. The Villistas fired upon the U.S. troops from the roofs of houses and from the hills. Two troopers were killed, three others badly wounded.

After dispersing the enemy, the soldiers spent the rest of the day taking care of the wounded and searching the houses. They found U.S. military uniforms that had been taken during the Columbus raid and took two men into custody. Official reports state both captives were killed that night while trying to escape. But Henry Huthmacher suggested in a letter to his sister that the troopers of the Seventh had adopted the Mexican practice of *ley fuga,* that is, killing their prisoners and then proclaiming they had been shot while trying to escape. "One case was pulled off good by telling the Mex. to pull out, that they were through with him. He walked not over a dozen feet before he was hit 12 times starting at the top of his head and ending by shooting off his heel. Another case, we turned one loose and he hadn't gone 200 yds. from camp when he built a fire and started signaling. The man that watched him, shot only once and came back to camp."

The Seventh Cavalry hit the trail the following morning. "The dead were carried on pack mules and the wounded compelled to ride horseback and suffered severely in spite of all we could do," wrote Dr. Eastman. "All wounded parts were immobilized as securely as possible, we moved slowly and rested frequently."

As they rode along, they found traces of blood from the wounded Villistas who had preceded them and freshly dug graves. Dodd put the enemy's losses at twenty-five, then upped it to thirty-one. He was later told that the Tarahumara Indians gathered up eleven wounded Villistas, poured pitch over them, and burned them alive.

Although Candelario Cervantes had escaped from the fight unscathed, the encounter had badly demoralized his men and one of his colonels soon departed, taking with him about ninety followers. That left Cervantes with about fifty men, whom he split into three commands. His band moved from camp to camp, occasionally spending the night in a house with a trusted sympathizer. Eventually he gravitated back to Namiquipa, but the little town was one of the most dangerous places for him to be; Pershing had established one of his advance bases on the outskirts of the town and five detachments of horse soldiers were sent out regularly to hunt for him.

From his various hideouts in the hills, Cervantes watched in disgust as peasants drove their oxcarts to the Americans' camp, carrying *huevos* and *pan dulce* to the troops. They traded the foodstuffs for baling wire, which was used to make wheels, and for empty kerosene cans, which became cooking braziers and water receptacles. Cervantes viewed the peasants as traitors but they could hardly be blamed; Namiquipa had suffered greatly during the revolution and many of the residents were on the verge of starvation.

Cervantes tried to rouse the residents to fight the Americans and even appealed to the Carrancistas to join him. "We hope that if you do not unite with us like the great family, since by force we can succeed, at least you will leave us free to fight the miserable North American invaders; the only cause of our disagreement and national disgrace." Instead of joining the rebels, many of the *namiquipenses* formed a civil guard, called the *defensa social,* to protect themselves against the depredations of bandits.

Although almost all of Cervantes's troops had deserted him or been captured, he remained defiant. On the morning of May 25, dressed in a black plush jacket with white piping and a fancy Mexican sombrero turned up at the brim, he spotted a small group of American soldiers scattered through a canyon, mapping the terrain and hunting for wild pigs. He decided to ambush the soldiers and capture the mules. With eight or nine other companions, he swept down through the canyon, firing his weapon. The Americans returned the gunfire, but not before one of them had been killed. The shooting soon brought other cavalry troopers to their assistance. By that time, the Mexicans were withdrawing, leaving their companions where they had fallen. A young intelligence officer searched the pockets of two dead rebels and removed several papers from the body of the well-dressed Mexican. As he headed back down the canyon with two fellow soldiers, he skimmed the documents and stopped in midstride when he realized that the dead man was Candelario Cervantes. The other was Cervantes's close friend, José Bencomo. "We must have those bodies for identification," he said, instructing one of his companions to go back and get them.

Filled with apprehension and scanning the cliffs, the American hurried back up the canyon. When he got to the site of the ambush, the two Mexicans and their horses were still lying on the ground. He dragged one body alongside the other and hastily tied the legs together with a buckskin thong. Next, he took a braided lariat from one of the Mexican saddles, wrapped it around the joined legs of the Mexicans, and tied it to his own saddle. Then he proceeded to drag the bodies back down the canyon. By the time he caught up with the rest of the troops, the faces of the two Mexicans were so battered that they were unrecognizable. The U.S. soldiers buried the bodies and sent a note to Pershing's headquarters informing him of the incident.

The following morning, several staffers from headquarters returned to the burial site and exhumed the bodies. They had been informed by a prisoner that Cervantes had a bullet wound below the left shoulder and another on the right leg above the knee. Sure enough, one of the corpses had two old bullet wounds exactly where the prisoner had said they would be. "The death of the notorious and dangerous leader, Candelario Cervantes," Pershing exulted, "ranks in importance next to the death of Villa himself."

The bodies were eventually returned to their families. To their sorrow, the local priest would not allow the funerals to be conducted in church and only "meager" ceremonies were held. The corpses were dressed in cheap clothing and placed in pine coffins built by local carpenters and stained black by a local painter who did not have enough pigment to give both boxes a full coat. Then the coffins were loaded onto two-wheel carts and hauled by burros to a weed-choked *campo santo*. Twelve mourners, wearing black shawls and threadbare clothing, struggled along behind the carts, the only dark spots on that jewel-bright May morning.

A few days later, members of the Mexican civil-defense group led Pershing's cavalry to a weapons cache, where Villa had hidden four hundred rifles and eleven machine guns. The cavalrymen were jubilant over the discovery, but it would have dreadful ramifications for the people of Namiquipa.

Pershing would receive more good news a few days later from Chihuahua City, when the Carrancistas sent him a telegram stating that Pablo López, the architect of the Santa Isabel train massacre, had been executed.

PERSHING AND HIS HEADQUARTERS staff knew from their informants and prisoner interrogations that Pablo López had been wounded and was exceedingly vulnerable to capture. Lieutenant Colonel Henry Allen, with a provisional squadron of eighty-four men from the Eleventh Regiment, had come across his tracks on April 9. Allen suspected the tracks belonged to López because the Mexican was supposed to be riding a cavalry horse that was missing its right front shoe. The U.S. troopers searched the hacienda where López's parents worked and then picked up his trail again on a faint path leading to some caves. Allen had been on the verge of searching the caves when he learned of Frank Tompkins's skirmish with the Carrancistas. Fearing for the safety of the major and his men, Allen had reversed course and raced to Parral to back him up.

López had indeed been living in a cave, though it's not clear whether it was one of the locations that Colonel Allen was about to search. When López's supplies ran out, old friends in the hills brought him what food they could spare. In late April, feverish and malnourished, he could stand the isolation no longer and gave himself up to Carrancista troops. He was taken to the penitentiary in Chihuahua City and informed that he would be executed as soon as he could walk to the firing squad. While he was waiting, an

Associated Press reporter went to his jail cell to interview him. López was dozing on a cot, clad only in an undershirt, cotton trousers, and black socks. His left leg was wrapped in bandages. "Well, señor, what do you wish? Have you also come to gloat over the poor captive for whose blood your soldiers are so eagerly thirsting? A number of other curious gringos came to see me recently, but I refused either to see them or talk to them."

When the reporter mentioned that he was of Irish descent, López consented to an interview. "Ah," he said. "You are not then a gringo. Well that makes a little difference; you have revolutions in your own land, is it not so? Yes, my friends keep me posted on outside news. If it were not for them I would starve."

The reporter offered López a cigarette and he took it, remarking how expensive tobacco had become in Mexico. Then he settled back and began to talk. His voice was low, his words deliberate, his sentences forming like drops of water in the pooled darkness. He seemed like an intellectual, not the unlettered peon that he professed to be, and in no way did he resemble the frightened, craven bandit he had been portrayed as in some newspaper accounts. Mesmerized, the reporter would later write that it was as if Villa himself were speaking.

López inhaled the smoke deep into his lungs and blew it out. He had been extremely handsome once but malnutrition and suffering and war had aged him. He was a scarecrow, arms and legs emaciated, his hair like thatch, his skin soft as a curing tobacco leaf thanks to so many long, sunless days. He said he entered life as a poor, ignorant peon. "My only education was gained in leading the oxen and following the plow. However when the good Francisco Madero rose in arms against our despotic masters, I gladly answered his call." Villa, he said, "was the object of worship of all who were ground under the heel of the oppressor. When the call came I was one of the first to join him and I have been his faithful follower and adoring slave ever since."

"Don Pancho," López continued, was convinced the United States was too cowardly to try to win Mexico by arms and believed that it intended to "keep pitting one faction against another until we were all killed off, when our exhausted country would fall like a ripe pear — *como una pera madura* — into their eager hands." Villa, he added, was convinced that Carranza had sold out to the Americans and wanted to trigger an intervention before the "Americans were ready" and while "we still had time to become a united nation."

López said he was forced to surrender because he was literally starving to death. "Would I have surrendered to the gringos? No, señor, many times no. I have been often in tight places when wounded, but have never thought of surrendering. If the gringos had found me I would have fought to the last and kept one cartridge for myself."

When asked about the train massacre, Lopéz sighed. "Things might not have gone as they did if it had not been that there were other jefes there among whom there was a spirit of deviltry. Perhaps we would have been content with only the Americans' clothes and money. But, señor, they started to run, and then our soldiers began to shoot. *El olor de la polvora nos enciende la sangre* — The smell of powder makes our blood hotter. The excitement grew and — ah, well señor, it was all over before I realized. Yes, I was sorry when I had time to cool down and reflect."

Speaking in the same candid tone, he also admitted that the Columbus raid had netted them little. "Were we disappointed over the Columbus raid? Well, all we got there were some horses, many bullets and a lot of hell." But none of that mattered now, he said, shrugging his shoulders. "I am bound for Santa Rosa [Chihuahua's execution place] when I am able to walk there. I would much prefer to die for my country in battle, but if it is decided to kill me, I will die as Pancho Villa would wish me to — with my head erect and my eyes unbandaged — and history will not be able to record that Pablo López flinched on the brink of eternity."

On June 5, when the clock in the cuartel struck eleven, López was marched from his prison cell to the place of execution. He smoked a cigar with his guards and then walked up to the blood-stained, pitted wall. A friend supported his right side and he used a homemade crutch on his left. López was carefully dressed, wearing a brilliant white shirt that would help his executioners find their target and dark, pin-striped pants that would hide the unmanly stains that would come afterward. He removed his plain straw sombrero, threw away the crutch, and smiled until all his white teeth showed. His unbandaged eyes looked at the firing squad. *En el pecho, hermanos, en el pecho* — In the breast, brothers, in the breast.

The commander barked an order and the soldiers lifted their rifles to their shoulders and fired. Five points of red appeared on his white shirt and López toppled over dead. The firing squad had done its job well and there was no sign of the writhing that sometimes followed the executions. But the commander walked over to the upturned face anyway, pulled out his pistol, and gave the dead man the *tira de gracia* — the coup de grâce — the same mercy shot that López had once ordered at Santa Isabel for the naked, squirming miners.

→18←

A TERRIBLE BLUNDER

PERSHING'S ELATION over the deaths of the high-ranking Villistas was short-lived as the tension between the Carrancistas and the expeditionary forces continued to grow. Large numbers of Mexican troops were massing to the east and west of Pershing's line and Venustiano Carranza continued to press for the immediate withdrawal of the U.S. troops. On June 16, General Jacinto Treviño, commander of the Carrancista forces at Chihuahua City, sent Pershing the following telegram: "I have orders from my government to prevent, by the use of arms, new invasions of my country by American troops and also to prevent the American forces that are now in this state from moving to the south, east, or west of places they now occupy. I communicate this to you for your knowledge for the reason that your forces will be attacked by the Mexican forces if these indications are not heeded." In order to make sure that Pershing understood the gravity of the situation, three Carranza officers then visited his camp and went over their orders by lantern light. The threat was like waving a red flag in front of Pershing. He bade the Mexican officers a curt good night and fired

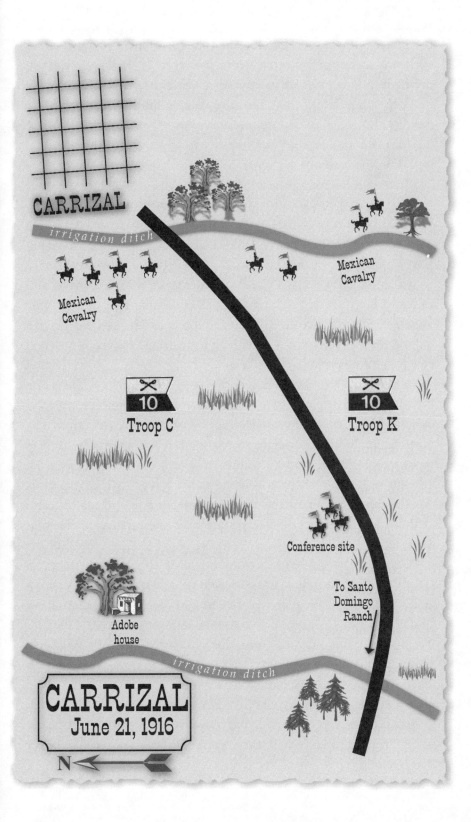

CARRIZAL

irrigation ditch

Mexican Cavalry

Mexican Cavalry

Troop C
10

Troop K
10

Conference site

Adobe house

To Santo Domingo Ranch

irrigation ditch

CARRIZAL
June 21, 1916

N

off a terse telegram to Treviño. The U.S. government had placed no such restrictions on his movements, he wrote. "I shall therefore use my own judgment as to when and in what direction I shall move my forces in pursuit of bandits or in seeking information regarding bandits. If, under these circumstances, the Mexican forces attack any of my columns, the responsibility for the consequences will lie with the Mexican government."

Two days later, on June 18, President Wilson called up the militia from forty-four additional states. Secretary of the Navy Josephus Daniels ordered sixteen warships to both coasts of Mexico as a "precautionary" measure. And Secretary of State Robert Lansing put the finishing touches on a scalding, six-thousand-word message in which he flatly refused Carranza's demands for withdrawal and rebuked him for his insulting and bellicose language. U.S. citizens began fleeing Mexico and General Obregón sent out a message, calling upon all Mexicans to enlist in the armed forces in order to repel the "foreign invaders."

In a highly provocative move, General Pershing on this same day decided to dispatch two cavalry patrols to reconnoiter the land around Villa Ahumada, eighty miles east of his base camp. His spies had told him that eight to ten thousand Carrancista soldiers were massing there and he wanted to check out the rumors, even though he knew such patrols could ignite a war. "Cavalry patrols for the safety of our forces must be sent out day and nightly, and if there is a fight it will likely start over these patrols," he told reporters.

Captain Charles Boyd, a white officer in the African-American Tenth Cavalry Regiment, was selected to lead one patrol. Pershing had known Boyd for many years and considered him a competent and industrious officer. Boyd seemed almost a carbon copy of Frank Tompkins, proud, ambitious, and spoiling for a fight. He was a graduate of West Point, but noticeably fat now, with a mouth filled with gold crowns and a long, aquiline nose that cleaved down through two slackening cheeks. No written copy of Pershing's instructions has been found, but Boyd was jubilant when he returned from a meeting with the general. He waved a piece of paper in front of his fellow troopers and said teasingly, "I've got peace or war" right here.

For reasons that are not clear, Pershing ordered Troop K, also from the Tenth Cavalry, which was stationed at Ojo Federico, about two days' march from headquarters, on the same mission. A slender and cautious-looking officer named Captain Lewis Morey, also a West Point graduate, led this contingent. The two troops started east from their separate locations, moving across the arid and sparsely inhabited scrubland.

Boyd's second in command was Lieutenant Henry Adair, aristocratic, confident, nearly bald except for a few strands of dull red hair hanging from the back of his head. Also accompanying him was Mormon scout Lem Spilsbury, who still bore a childhood scar on his cheek from where he had been gored by a bull. His mother had stitched up the wound, dousing it first in turpentine and then sewing it with stiff thread, but the hole never closed completely and became a great source of amusement to Lem, who often forced water through the opening to entertain his friends and family.

As they jogged along, Boyd confided to Spilsbury that U.S. troops were poised to counterattack if Pershing was molested. "If the Mexican troops fire on us without provocation," he said, "just as soon as that word gets back to the line, General Pershing will attack on the south all along the line and General Funston will immediately attack along the border." In fact, the War Department had drawn up much more detailed plans than that. In the event of outright war, the United States planned to immediately occupy the international bridges and the Mexican border towns, seize Mexico's railroads, and dispatch another ten thousand troops to Pershing's camp. Then, three columns of soldiers composed of regular troops and militia would be assembled in El Paso, Brownsville, and Nogales. The El Paso column, working in tandem with Pershing's beefed-up troops, would push south, driving the Carrancistas south of Chihuahua City; the Brownsville column, together with five thousand soldiers who would come ashore at Tampico, would force the Mexican troops from the states of Coahuila, Nuevo León, and Tamaulipas; and the Nogales column would sweep the Carrancistas from the state of Sonora.

Spilsbury had lived in Mexico all his life and didn't like what Boyd was hinting at. In a statement to army investigators, he would later say, "I only accepted work for General Pershing to help catch Villa if possible and as soon as I saw that the Americans were likely to force war with Mexico I tried repeatedly to get away but General Pershing would not let go and I was afraid to try and escape and return home to my people's ranch near Casas Grandes for fear they might punish me."

Morey's detachment was moving through country that was much drier than that being traversed by Boyd's troopers. Although the horses and men were in much better shape than they had been at the beginning of the campaign, they nevertheless experienced a few moments of anxiety at the end of the second day's march when they came upon a river that was supposed to have water but was completely dry. Fortunately, they found a fresh spring about a mile and a half upstream. Worried that even worse conditions awaited them, Morey sent a wagon and some extra horses and men back to camp so he would have fewer mouths to feed and lightened his load by caching some of his hard bread, bacon, and grain on the prairie, intending to pick it up on the return trip.

Morey's troopers reached the Santo Domingo ranch about five o'clock on the afternoon of June 20, where they found Captain Boyd and his men already relaxing in the shade. The two captains compared their orders and discovered they were virtually identical. Morey was baffled and couldn't understand from a "tactical point of view" why they had both been sent on the same mission. Boyd responded, "Well, I think I do understand it and know why it is." He did not elaborate. Since Morey was the junior officer, he agreed to place himself under Boyd's command. The combined forces now amounted to three officers and about eighty men.

The foreman of the ranch, an American named W. P. McCabe, told them that roughly two hundred Carrancista soldiers were garrisoned in the little town of Carrizal, which was located seven or eight miles to the east of the ranch. He said another 250 to 300

Mexican soldiers were at Villa Ahumada, a few miles to the northeast of Carrizal. The figures were much lower than what Pershing had been told. At that point, the general would later write, his officers could have returned to their base camps with their reconnaissance missions accomplished. But Boyd announced that he had orders to go through Carrizal to reach Ahumada and that was what he was going to do. "We'll go through the town, and if they fire on our rear guard, we'll go back through the town and clean them up," he said.

Morey warned Boyd that the Mexicans would likely fire on them "from the tops of the houses, from windows, and from behind doors, the houses lining both sides of the streets."

But Boyd shook his head. "It is not likely that they will want to bring on war between the United States and Mexico."

McCabe then jumped into the debate, pointing out that the narrow lanes and bulletproof adobe houses posed a "nasty trap." He urged Boyd to go to the east of the town where there were few buildings and the ground was open. He also pointed out that two other roads would take them to Ahumada and one of them was actually shorter than the road through Carrizal.

But Boyd could not be dissuaded. Both he and his lieutenant were convinced that the Mexicans were cowards and wouldn't fight. "That's been the main trouble with our work south," Adair observed; "we didn't send troops around to head them off and the Mexicans always ran and could get away."

Lem Spilsbury cautioned that Carrizal posed an entirely different situation. "The Villistas were on the run, while these men if they are under orders, they will have to fight, and it was my opinion they were under such orders."

With no consensus having been reached, the meeting broke up and the officers went about their chores. At supper, the debate resumed. "Morey," said Boyd, "what I want is to go through that town, and we are not going to have a repetition of the Parral incident."

"Well, that's good dope," Morey responded, explaining later that he simply meant the instructions were clear. Morey took fifty-five dollars from his saddlebags and gave it to Mr. McCabe for safe-keeping, saying that he didn't want it to fall into the hands of the Mexicans. He sensed the other officers thought the gesture was unnecessary but no one said anything to him and the atmosphere remained cordial.

The officers and civilians then got into a discussion about whether Boyd should request permission to march through Carrizal. Nearly everyone present at the meeting felt it was the proper thing to do. So Boyd wrote out two identical notes in English, one to the *jefe político* of Carrizal and another to the *jefe político* in Villa Ahumada asking for permission to go through their towns: "I am passing through your town engaging upon a peaceful mission. The usual authority is requested. Please inform chief military official of my movements. C. T. Boyd, Captain, 10th Cavalry."

Captain Morey, who had attended the same tactics class as Captain Boyd at West Point, said jokingly, "You are violating one of the first principles of tactics by planning these messages so far ahead."

"Well, we may be making history tonight," replied Boyd. "I want these notes properly written and do not wish to be bothered with them in the field."

At about four o'clock the following morning, the troops saddled up and rode east toward Carrizal. Halfway there, Boyd stopped and ordered the troopers to load their pistols and check their rifles. He repeated his determination to go through town and warned the men that if they were fired upon they should kill whoever did it and then continue through the village at a leisurely pace. Once they reached the other side, they would turn back and attack.

About 8:30 a.m. they stopped at an irrigation ditch on the outskirts of Carrizal to water their horses. Directly to the east of them was an open field, then another irrigation ditch that ran in a north-south direction and some cottonwood trees. On a slight hill beyond the trees they could see the flat-roofed adobe houses of Carrizal and the little Catholic church.

Captain Boyd sent one of their Mexican interpreters into town with his note asking for permission to go through. Before the messenger returned, Lieutenant Colonel Genovevo Rivas Guillén and about eight Mexican soldiers rode out to meet them.

"Adónde va?" asked Rivas.

With Spilsbury acting as interpreter, Boyd rattled off two lies: he said that they were looking for a deserter and were also searching the area for bandits. Rivas, who somehow intuited that Boyd was lying, regarded him skeptically. The deserter, he responded sarcastically, was probably in El Paso and if there were any bandits in Carrizal, they were looking at them. Abruptly, he added, "I have orders to stop your advance until further conference."

While they were talking, the messenger returned with a note from General Félix Gómez inviting the U.S. soldiers into town for a conference. "Please come over to this [town] with the force which you have in order that we may have a conference." Boyd considered the invitation a trap and told Rivas that he would like to speak to the general right away. A Mexican soldier was promptly dispatched to retrieve him.

Boyd then instructed the troopers to move east across the open field until they were perhaps six hundred yards from the trees. While the men were moving into their new positions, General Gómez rode out onto the field. He asked Boyd the same questions that Rivas had posed and was given the same evasive answers. Then he abruptly changed his tone. "I have orders from General Treviño to stop any American forces going east, west or south," he said, adding that Boyd was no doubt aware of the ultimatum. Boyd acknowledged that he was, but insisted that he had orders to go through town.

Gómez repeated his own orders and said that if the Americans advanced, he would have no choice but to fire on them. Then, in one last effort to avoid a fight, he suggested that Boyd wait while he conferred with Treviño himself to see if an exception could be made.

Instead of taking up the offer, Boyd rejected it, thinking that Gómez was simply stalling until reinforcements arrived. "Tell the son of a bitch that we're going through," he ordered Spilsbury.

Gómez glared at him. He understood those English words. *"Bueno,"* he responded. "You may go through, but you'll have to walk over our dead bodies before you do!" Then he turned and rode back to his command.

Boyd also returned to his troops. "It looks very promising," he said, apparently pleased that a confrontation was imminent. "The general says that we can go north or west but not east. We are going east."

Adair and the other members of Troop C were spread out on the left side of the dirt lane leading to the little village. Two hundred yards away, on the right side of the lane, were Morey and Troop K.

While the conferences were being held, the cavalrymen noticed that dozens of Mexican soldiers, both mounted and unmounted, were taking up positions behind the ditches and cottonwood trees. Several Mexican women, also carrying rifles, had appeared beside them. Two machine guns were brought forward and aimed at the cavalrymen and snipers appeared on top of the houses in the little town. Protected by the trees and the ditch and situated on rising ground, the Mexicans had an enormous tactical advantage. Some of the Mexican horsemen had also begun to edge around Boyd's left flank and other soldiers on foot had begun to move around Morey's right flank.

The U.S. troops advanced on horseback another three hundred yards. Boyd cautioned the men not to fire the first shot or he would spend the next fifty years trying to explain it. Then he yelled, "Prepare to fight on foot!"

The troopers dismounted and the horses were led to the rear. The Americans moved up another hundred yards. Suddenly the Mexican machine guns roared to life. Boyd's line wavered, as if all his soldiers had been hit at once. As it turned out, the volley was high and the horses and mules caught most of the bullets.

"Commence firing!" Boyd shouted.

Boyd had rushed forward perhaps fifteen feet when he was shot in the hand. "I've been wounded, you've got them on the go, so go to 'em boys!" he yelled.

He waved his hat and hollered at Adair and Morey to join him, seemingly determined to draw as much fire onto himself as he could. A second bullet struck him in the shoulder, opening a hole that was big enough for Lem Spilsbury to see the white bone. Boyd took no notice of the wounds and dashed in front of his own line of fire and then back to the rear, where he swung his hat in the direction of Morey's troopers. "Come on K troop!" he screamed.

Then he turned back to his own troops and hollered, "Come on boys! Let's get a drink out of the irrigation ditch!" The words were hardly out of his mouth when a third bullet plowed through his eye, killing him instantly.

Generalized panic and fighting broke out everywhere. Many of the horses stampeded about the field, their entrails falling from gaping stomach wounds. Dust and smoke obscured everything. Boyd's troopers were cut to pieces. Four men were killed and four others injured in the first moments of battle.

Adair and three soldiers managed to scramble across the irrigation ditch and make their way into the trees, where they engaged in close fighting with the Mexican troops. Adair was shot in the left side but didn't seem to notice. When they ran out of ammunition, he calmly handed his pistol to a comrade and returned to the line to retrieve ammunition belts from the wounded.

As he was crossing back over the drainage ditch, a second bullet slammed into his chest. "Oh, I'm hit!" he screamed. He fell backward and was caught by two privates. "I held his head up out of the water until he died," remembered Private Melvin C. Covington.

On the other side of the dirt lane, Morey and the soldiers of Troop K were faring no better. They had managed to advance perhaps fifteen or twenty feet before taking cover in a shallow roadbed. Caught in a deadly cross fire, fired upon from the front, both flanks, and possibly from behind, they flopped on their stomachs, aiming their Springfields toward the trees. One platoon concentrated upon the Mexicans in front and to the left of them and a second focused on the Mexican soldiers who were moving on their right flank. Bullets whizzed through the air, taking a terrible toll. In the first minutes of the fight, three of Morey's troopers were killed and seven wounded.

Morey looked for Boyd's troops but it seemed as if they had all moved into the trees or were lying flat on the ground. He could see Boyd's horse and his trumpeter's horse galloping wildly around the field. Morey returned his attention to his own line and spotted the

Carrancistas coming at them from the left. "Corporal Houston, look out for your left flank!" Morey screamed.

Corporal Houston had his sights on a Mexican officer who was walking back and forth between the trees, peering at the battlefield through his field glasses. The corporal thought the man was General Gómez and he squeezed the trigger carefully and saw the officer topple over.

Suddenly Morey yelled again. "Sergeant Page! Good god man! There they are, right up on you! Rapid fire!" The Mexicans were fifty yards away, threatening them from the right.

Page screamed back, "Captain, we can't stay here!"

Morey commanded him to hold steady and keep firing. Another ten or fifteen minutes passed and Page yelled again that they were in danger of being massacred. At that moment a bullet slammed into Morey's shoulder, knocking him backward. When he got up, dazed and bleeding profusely, he realized they were indeed about to be overrun and ordered a retreat. The withdrawal was orderly at first and then the U.S. soldiers broke and ran, followed by about fifty Mexican troops.

"Scatter out men! Don't bunch up! You make too good a target!" a sergeant yelled. The soldiers moved to the northwest, crossing the line followed by Boyd's retreating men. Morey asked a soldier where Boyd was and was told he had been killed. Nobody seemed to know what had happened to Adair. Morey fainted once and was helped back up on his feet. He slipped into the irrigation ditch where they had watered their horses earlier that morning, thrashed his way out, and stumbled to an adobe house where several injured soldiers and other troopers had gathered. A trumpeter sounded To Horse, To Recall, and Assemble but all the cavalry calls were ignored.

"You boys make your getaway, if you can, because I am done for," Morey gasped.

The Mexican cavalry, meanwhile, had swung around behind the soldiers. The panic-stricken men who had been holding the extra horses kicked their mounts into a gallop, flying through a narrow gate and over a hill. Some didn't stop until they reached the

Santo Domingo ranch. Rather than pressing their advantage, the Mexican troops stopped to loot the fallen bodies, including Captain Boyd's.

Morey stumbled off the field with several men — one of whom was badly wounded in the knee — eventually stopping at a limekiln. Morey sank down against the cool stone and dashed off a telegram to his superior officer. He related the events leading up to the battle and closed by saying, "I am hiding in a hole two thousand yards from field and have one other wounded man and three men with me." After he had finished his message, he turned to his companions and said, "You men may do as you please."

Several soldiers chose to remain with him. At dusk, the small band started out for the ranch, walking for perhaps a minute or two, then lying down and sleeping. Morey finally became too exhausted to go on and forcibly ordered the others to leave, handing them his map, field glasses, and compass. After they were gone, he lay down and slept for two hours. When he awoke, he felt suddenly refreshed. By alternating his marching with short, intense periods of sleep, he was able to make it back to the Santo Domingo ranch at around 4:00 a.m. He sprawled facedown in a mud hole and drank sparingly, then stumbled toward an adobe building where, as if by miracle, he found beefsteak, coffee in a pot, and corn bread.

The ranch had been the scene of intense activity earlier but was now completely deserted. McCabe would later tell army investigators he had watched in disgust as groups of badly frightened men straggled back from Carrizal that day. "I told them they were doing a mighty poor thing to run off and leave their comrades, and tried to get them to stop and remain there. They replied that there were more of their men coming towards the ranch, and that they were going for re-enforcements."

Throughout the day, more exhausted and scared troopers had stumbled up to the ranch. They fed and watered their horses and were given something to eat. About 4:00 p.m., a rumor had circulated that fifteen hundred Mexican soldiers were headed for the ranch and the U.S. soldiers panicked. McCabe had begged them to stay, but they left en masse, leaving him alone with two Chinese workers and three Mexican laborers. Fearful of an attack themselves, McCabe and the ranch hands had gone out in the bushes and hidden.

Back on the battlefield, the Mexicans had swept down on the remaining Americans. "Who are you and why are you fighting us?" one Carrancista soldier had asked an African-American trooper named Willie Harris. Lem Spilsbury, seeing himself surrounded, had thrown up his arms and surrendered. Throughout the day, the Carrancistas continued to round up fleeing soldiers until they had captured twenty-four troopers. The men were stripped of their shoes, hats, clothing, money, and jewelry. Then they were taken to a little cuartel and locked up in a dark room. "While we were in this house," remembered Spilsbury, "we heard a number of shots, one or two at a time, and the Mexican guard asked me if I knew what they were. I said, 'No.' Then he said that they were killing the wounded."

The prisoners were marched to Villa Ahumada, where a train was waiting to take them to the penitentiary in Chihuahua City. The Mexican passengers swarmed around the Americans, threatening to kill them. "The Mexicans got so close in around us — there were only sixteen men guarding us — that we could hardly move. This man stepped out among the crowd and addressed them as 'patriots and brothers' and said that we had killed their general and were enemies but that we were prisoners of war and should be respected as such. He was a civilian and his speech quieted the crowd considerably," Spilsbury recalled.

When the prisoners reached Chihuahua City, another crowd was waiting for them and pelted them with stones. They directed their fury mostly at Lem Spilsbury — the "Mexican Tejano" — the only white face among the black prisoners. "They wanted to hang me and burn me at the stake and threatened to rope me and drag me. But they did not do anything to us but throw stones at us."

At the penitentiary, Spilsbury scrubbed out his cell and settled down to wait. The Mexican guards treated them decently, feeding them beans and rice and bread. Each day the British consul and an

Associated Press reporter paid them a visit to see how they were doing and to make sure they were not being mistreated.

Once again, news of the battle reached Funston and officials in Washington before Pershing could piece together what had happened. In an angry telegram, Funston asked Pershing:

> Why in the name of God do I hear nothing from you the whole country has known for ten hours through Mexican sources that a considerable force from your command was apparently defeated yesterday with heavy loss at Carrizal. Under existing orders to you why were they there so far from your line being at such distance that I assume that now nearly twenty-four hours after affair news has not reached you who was responsible for what on its face seems to have been a terrible blunder.

President Wilson learned of the Carrizal fight from newsmen hawking "extras" on the street. In all, twelve Americans were killed or missing in action, another twelve were wounded, and twenty-four were captured. Although the Mexicans refused to reveal their casualties, they were estimated to be even higher, with anywhere from forty-two to fifty-two killed and thirty-nine wounded.

It seemed to Wilson that the dreaded break with Mexico had finally come. Through diplomatic channels, he demanded an immediate release of the prisoners and prepared a message to Congress asking for authority to use whatever military force was needed to secure the frontier, including, if necessary, the occupation of all the Mexican states along the U.S. border until a responsible government could be constituted. If Mexico had possessed a legitimate government, he wrote, he would have asked Congress for a formal declaration of war. "But we are not dealing with such a government. There has been no such government in Mexico since February, 1913. At no time since the tragic assassination of President Madero have we had any certain evidence that those who were assuming to exercise authority in that distracted country represented anybody but themselves."

The bellicose Carranza was pragmatic enough to see his own

potential demise in the rapidly escalating situation and he soon ordered the prisoners released. Several days later, his representatives suggested that formal negotiations be held to reconcile the differences between the two countries. The United States quickly agreed. By then, the details of the Carrizal incident had become better known and Wilson and his aides realized that the incident had largely been instigated by Boyd. Three representatives from Mexico and three representatives from the United States were named to the negotiating panel, which was scheduled to begin meeting in the fall in New London, Connecticut. With that, the air began to clear. In an eloquent speech, given on July 1 at the Press Club in New York, the president said: "Do you think the glory of America would be enhanced by a war of conquest in Mexico? Do you think that any act of violence by a powerful nation like this against a weak and distracted neighbor would reflect distinction upon the annals of the United States?" He added, "I have constantly to remind myself that I am not the servant of those who wish to enhance the value of their Mexican investments, that I am the servant of the rank and file of the people of the United States."

The U.S. prisoners were taken to Juárez and released on the international bridge. A throng of reporters were on hand to observe them. Some of the captives were barefoot, others were wearing riding jodhpurs cut off at the knees. Lem Spilsbury presented one of the most eccentric figures of all, wearing soiled white duck trousers, a yachting cap, and a serape over his shoulder. The soldiers were taken to a fumigation shack where their clothes were burned and they were scrubbed down with kerosene and vinegar. Then they were allowed to take soap-and-water showers and don fresh clothing. As they departed for Fort Bliss, the African-American residents of El Paso handed the troopers delicate bouquets of sweet peas. The soldiers held them in their fists and grinned widely as the photographers snapped away.

The Carrancistas had dumped the bodies of the twelve troopers listed as killed or missing in action, including Boyd and Adair, into a hole and buried them, but U.S. authorities demanded that the bodies be exhumed and returned to the United States. The weather was sweltering and by the time the corpses reached the border, they were so badly decomposed that health authorities in El Paso refused to open the caskets and fingerprint them so that proper identification could be made. The surviving members of the two troops were eventually able to identify all but one body. The remains of Boyd, Adair, and a private named DeWitt Rucker were returned to their families and the other soldiers were buried with full honors in Arlington National Cemetery. The bodies of four troopers from the Tenth Cavalry were never recovered.

Morey left Mexico by automobile. In Columbus he boarded the eastbound Golden State Limited and went to Fort Bliss for a brief reunion with his old command. The men were delighted to see him and crowded around, smiling and slapping him on the back. He left after only a few moments, telling reporters that he was still in a weakened condition from his wound. But in truth, he was probably discouraged and frightened. An internal investigation of the Carrizal incident had begun and Morey could already feel the great weight of the army's disapproval settling upon him. Eventually sworn statements would be taken from nearly every participant in the fight, including Lem Spilsbury and W. P. McCabe. Army investigators concluded that Boyd was largely responsible for the debacle but nevertheless praised him and Adair for their bravery. As for Morey, they wrote, "he did not stand forth as a leader."

The investigators sidestepped General Pershing's role in the whole affair and left many questions unanswered. For example, why did Pershing order two detachments on an identical mission a hundred miles away after General Treviño had issued his ultimatum? Why was Captain Boyd, well known for his aggressive soldiering, chosen for the mission? Why were Boyd's orders oral and Morey's written? And finally, why were they not told of each other's assignments?

Only Lem Spilsbury, a civilian, had the temerity to suggest that the U.S. military was deliberately trying to provoke a war with Mexico. As for General Pershing, he professed himself to be heartsick when he learned of the disastrous battle and Boyd's role in it. "No one could have been more surprised or chagrined than I was to learn that he had become so seriously involved." He also insisted that he had urged Boyd to use caution. "I told him, among other things, that the Mexican situation was very tense, and that a clash with Mexican troops would probably bring on war and for this reason was to be avoided."

In fact, Pershing's orders had produced a debacle that would result in the end of his mission. And somewhere, hidden from friends and enemies, his leg wound slowly mending, Pancho Villa was plotting his comeback.

19

Whore Dust and a Rabid Dog

THE CARRIZAL INCIDENT was the last fight of the Punitive Expedition. Forbidden by his superiors to even send out patrols, Pershing had nothing left to do but await orders to withdraw, which did not come for another seven months. In some ways, the dormant period proved more challenging for him than the active hunt for Pancho Villa. His task now became trying to keep an army of ten thousand men occupied and out of trouble. The troops were divided into two camps, with roughly six thousand men at Colonia Dublán and another four thousand troops stationed sixty-five miles to the south near the town of El Valle.

The Dublán camp, enclosed by a fence and patrolled by sentries, soon came to resemble a small thriving town. A river ran along its western edge and to the east were irrigated fields and a few of the brick houses belonging to the Mormons. Dozens of Chinese entrepreneurs descended upon the camp, opening up laundries and concession stands, which sold hot doughnuts and the sugary treats that the soldiers had craved during the long, cold marches. The cooks often took their shotguns and hunted for wild turkey and quail and ducks and rabbits to supplement the officers' messes. In the neighboring pastures, the horses fattened and grew serene. The troops built sturdy shelters from adobe bricks and stretched their canvas tents over the walls for roofs. They stuffed grass beneath their bedrolls and made "ice boxes" by draping wet gunny-sacks over crates. Long truck trains rumbled in and out of the camp from the dirt road leading north to Columbus, bringing letters, food supplies, and packages from home that included navel oranges, English walnuts, writing tablets, candles, and Ivory soap.

An arena for boxing and wrestling was built and a field laid out for baseball and football games. In the evenings, there were min-strel shows and one-act plays and long hours of letter writing. Per-shing turned a blind eye to the craps and high-stakes card games, but drew the line at allowing intoxicating liquors into the camp. As a consequence, cantinas sprang up outside the fence and a lively bootlegging business developed. One of the largest cantinas and dance halls was run by Greeks from Juárez. The "sanitary village" south of the camp continued to do a land-office business. The com-pound was roughly an acre in size and consisted of a restaurant and about forty one-room cabins where prostitutes worked and slept. Pershing approved a similar restricted district for the troops in El Valle. In a letter to General Scott, he said he saw no other way to resolve the "woman question" and pointed out that the arrange-ment had actually lowered the rate of venereal disease. Some of the medical officers, though, found the arrangement appalling. "As some of the men remarked, 'Whenever the wind blows we get cov-ered with whore dust,' and while that is putting it rather vulgarly, yet it was the way we felt about it," William Eastman concluded.

With the growing heat and large concentrations of men and ani-mals, the risk of disease and illness grew. Meat was dipped in boil-ing water and hung in drying huts swabbed down with kerosene. Latrines were fired daily, manure swept up and deposited far from the camp, and the men encouraged to rinse their eating utensils in boiling water. The sanitary inspectors were particularly worried about typhus, which was endemic throughout Mexico. The illness was transmitted by lice and the troops were instructed to air their tents three hours a day, change their bedding, shave their beards, cut their hair, put on clean underwear, and bathe "all over at least twice a week."

Pershing despised idleness and drilled the troops relentlessly in the use of overhead machine-gun fire and mounted pistol charges. The young Patton abhorred idleness even more. "We are rapidly going crazy from lack of occupation and there is no help in sight," he groused in a letter to his father on July 12, 1916. Patton blamed their predicament on the U.S. president and his vacillating policies. "I should like to go to hell so that I might be able to shovel a few extra coals on that unspeakable ass Wilson."

On August 31, Pershing decided it was time for a vacation for himself and his restless young aide. Together with members of the headquarters staff and several newspaper reporters, they drove from Dublán to Columbus over a deeply rutted road. There, they met Beatrice and Nita Patton and spent the rest of the week as tourists. There was much to see; the raid had put Columbus on the map in a way the civic boosters could never have dreamed of. "We are well advertised now," sighed the *Columbus Courier.*

"Eat houses," drink stands, shooting galleries, tonsorial parlors, cigar stands, Turkish baths, ice cream parlors, poolrooms, laundries, and new grocery stores had been established. The Hoover Hotel was booked to capacity, with two guests to each room and overflow consigned to the lobby. Miller's drugstore had reopened under new owners who were skilled at compounding the latest medicine; Sam Ravel had begun planning a new hotel that would feature "steam heat baths." And the lot next to the Commercial Hotel, where two donkeys nosed through tin cans, was being offered for a shocking one thousand dollars.

"There are dozens or more eat houses that feed hundreds and hundreds of people every day," the newspaper reported. Many of the eat houses were forced to open in large canvas tents. For fifty cents, a customer could buy a T-bone steak, sirloin steak, or hamburger steak, and twenty-five cents bought an omelet or a piece of apple pie. The food was often covered with a fine layer of sand, the dirt floors covered with rain puddles, and the tables obscured by roiling steak smoke, but business was so good that customers frequently were turned away.

Alfred Everett Wilson, a teenager who dreamed of becoming a writer but was already suffering from the tuberculosis that would claim his life in a few years, went to work in his father's eating tent and recorded in his diary the windstorms that thinned the soldiers into shadows; the fist-sized tarantulas; the adventurous truckers, who outfitted both themselves and their dogs with sand goggles; and the violent fights among the kitchen help, particularly a dishwasher named Mac, a former juggler who suffered from pleurisy, biliousness, neuralgia, catarrh, asthma, bronchitis, and drunkenness.

For entertainment, there was a movie house with a rouged blonde at the ticket counter and moving pictures powered by a sputtering gasoline engine; five marching bands in the army camp; and private drinking clubs that featured such names as the Benevolent Order of the Bees, the Loyal Order of Moose, and the Fraternal Order of Grizzly Bears. Into the wee hours of the night, the patrons could dance the Bool Weevil Wiggle, the Texas Tommy Tango, the Bunny Hug, the Buzzard Flap, or the Pappy Huddle.

Pershing and Patton had only a week's leave, not nearly enough time to savor all the amenities, and before they knew it they were jouncing back to Dublán. Pershing could not stop talking about Nita. "He's all the time talking about Miss Anne. Nita may rank us yet," Patton told his wife.

The budding romance energized Pershing but did not distract him from his duties, and he continued to monitor closely political and social conditions in Mexico. A lawless anarchy existed in northern Chihuahua. The Carrancista troops preyed on the local people, extorting money and robbing them in broad daylight. "No discipline among either officers or men," an informant told Pershing. "The latter are un-uniformed, dirty, and ragged, with but scant clothes of any kind. They are paid in Carrancista money, which merchants do not want at any price, but under coercion exchange at 100 for 1, or practically as so many pieces of blank paper. Among these so-called soldiers are boys from apparently 12 years of age to old men — a deaf mute, a hunchback, and a one-legged boy."

More disquieting was the knowledge that *el jaguar* — Pancho Villa — was on the prowl again.

Although the expedition's mission, as amended by General Scott, was simply to disperse Villa and his band, Pershing and the members of his intelligence staff nonetheless concocted a secret plot to assassinate the guerrilla chief. The plan called for Japanese agents posing as peddlers to infiltrate Villa's hideout and poison him. (Villa loathed the Chinese but the Japanese government had made repeated overtures to him and he had many friends among the Japanese expatriates living in Mexico.) E. B. Stone, the controversial federal agent, had first come up with the idea of using Japanese agents to kill or capture Pancho Villa. The expedition's intelligence division, which included an officer who spoke Japanese fluently, had hit upon a similar idea.

ACCORDING TO THE U.S. ARMY's intelligence reports, Villa had remained in the house on the outskirts of Santa Cruz de Herrera until the first of June. Though his leg was not yet healed, he then marched south into the state of Durango and established a new headquarters at the Hacienda de Torreón de Cañas. Green fertile fields, cottonwood trees, and flowers of all kinds surrounded the farmhouse. By inquiring of peasants along the route, two Japanese agents named Tsutomo Dyo and A. Sato tracked Villa to the hacienda. Dyo and Sato had run a mining operation in Chihuahua that had been looted by the Villistas, and from that unlikely beginning a friendship developed between Villa and the two Japanese men.

The agents were escorted into the farmhouse, where they found Villa sitting in an armchair. Dyo was greatly startled by Villa's physical appearance. In his diary, he wrote, "His long untrimmed jet black beard first attracted my attention and beside him were two crutches; he wore only one shoe, the right, the swollen left foot was covered with light woolen sock." When Villa asked Dyo why he was so far from his ranch, Dyo replied that he had run into Villa's wife, Luz, in El Paso and she had asked him if he could take some bandages to her husband. He had readily agreed, telling Villa,

"It occurred to me that our former good relations and friendship counted for something so I consented."

Villa seemed to pay little attention to what Dyo was saying. Abruptly he changed the subject and asked if the two agents were hungry. When they nodded, Villa said that he had already given orders for his troops to move out but would have his cook prepare them a meal. His isolation and long period of recuperation had left him immensely curious about the outside world and he peppered his visitors with questions. "During the meal, Villa grew inquisitive as to the relations between the United States and Mexico and propounded numerous questions concerning the location of their forces. I gave him what information I knew on the subject. I was especially astonished when he asked me point blank: 'What does the world think about me; what is the consensus of opinion as to whether I am dead or alive?' I replied that the consensus of opinion was that he was dead but that a large number did not believe it."

When they were finished, Villa rose from the table and announced in a loud voice that he was leaving to attack Parral. Before departing, however, he said he wanted his leg dressed with the bandages that his wife had sent him. Dyo volunteered, adding that he had once taken a first-aid course:

This was my first opportunity to examine in detail the wound of which we had heard so many varied tales. I removed the soiled calico bandage from the left [actually the right] leg below the knee, which was separated from the flesh by two wild leaves, the name of which I am not familiar; as the leaves were removed considerable pus matter oozed out from the open sore. I observed that the bullet had entered from the rear, penetrating the leg bone midway between the knee and heel and had come out in the corresponding part of the leg in front. The bullet hole in the rear is closed and to all appearance healed. The hole in front is also closed but the pus hole is just above it and as I touched this part I could feel the fragments of broken leg bone. The leg is considerably swollen from the knee to the toes so Villa is unable to wear a shoe. For very short distances about the house he moves with the aid of crutches. The wound pains him considerable when he rides a horse, and does so only when necessary. In order to cover any considerable distance, he rides in a buggy.

While Dyo was wrapping the leg, Villa told him that he had been struck by a stray bullet fired by the Carrancistas — a statement that suggests that he still had no idea that one of his own conscripts had fired on him. In a musing voice, Villa continued, "No one will ever know how much I have suffered with this. You know I am a total abstainer but I have fallen three times in my life; once when my mother died, the second time when my father passed away, and the third time when wounded at Guerrero. No amount of stimulant seemed to remove my pain."

It was dusk when Dyo finished his ministrations. The troops were already saddled and marching toward Parral and Villa invited Dyo to accompany him in his buggy. Fifty Dorados rode three hundred yards ahead of the carriage. Francisco Beltrán and Nicolás Fernández, who had done more than anyone else to keep the movement together while Villa was recuperating, were in charge of the main body of troops. The soldiers moved in a northwesterly direction toward Parral, but as soon as enough distance had been put between them and the hacienda, Villa suddenly switched directions and struck east across the open country. Dyo realized that his loudly announced plan to attack Parral had been a ruse to throw off any spies who might be listening. Villa's real goal, as it turned out, was to attack Jiménez, located about fifty to sixty miles east of Parral, and seize the huge cache of ammunition stored there. "He took occasion to explain to me that what he sought was ammunition and popularity and that he needed the former to ensure that latter," Dyo wrote.

The soldiers marched over mesquite-covered hills that were devoid of even the faintest of trails. When the terrain became too rugged, Villa got out of the buggy and walked or rode his horse. After traveling about eight miles, he ordered a halt in an arroyo and instructed the men not to smoke or build fires. That evening,

he asked Dyo to change his bandages again. Watching the procedure, Villa said, "I see no marked change for the better with the
application of the bandages sent me by my wife." Dyo replied that
he should have an operation to remove the bone fragments in his
leg. Villa shook his head. "I have never had any use for doctors.
I would rather wait that nature do her duty. I believe that the leaves
that grow in the mountains are much more effective than your
doctors."

The following day, Villa was in an expansive and talkative
mood and shared with Dyo some of his military philosophy. The
knowledge of terrain was the single most important factor in winning military battles, he said. "For that reason," wrote Dyo, "he
selected as advance guard commander the leader acquainted with
the ground on the line of march. When the time for attack arrived,
he allowed this leader to have a prominent part in the disposition
of forces and when he thought it advisable, he did not hesitate to
place him in absolute command under his supervision."

Villa and his army, which had now grown to about twelve hundred men, made several stops on the way to Jiménez. At a hacienda
owned by Luis Terrazas, Villa drove off the overseers and distributed the furnishings and land to the peons. Then he continued
marching until he reached the small village of Río Florida. There,
he ordered the mayor to assemble the townspeople and gave a
short speech in which he once again alleged that Carranza had sold
out the Mexican people to the United States. "I am here to urge
you all to join me in overthrowing this usurper of Mexican right
and liberty; we shall then be free to challenge the United States of
North America and demonstrate to them that the Mexican people
will not allow themselves to be bought and sold in bondage." The
speech lasted perhaps ten minutes and Villa repeated himself several times. Yet, the speech was sufficiently inspiring for nearly a
hundred men to join him voluntarily.

Villa had hoped to take Jiménez by surprise but that hope was
dashed when a group of Carrancista soldiers quartered at a nearby
hacienda discovered his presence. Villa decided to attack the troops
at once, and easily defeated them. The *tira de gracia* was applied

liberally to the officers. Villa decided to release about 180 of the rank and file but not until they had been "branded." Wrote Dyo: "General Balderio [probably Baudelio Uribe] who is known as the 'inventor' of the Villa forces, suggested the singular punishment for the prisoners of branding them by cutting pieces of flesh from one or both ears so that if caught a second time in the service of the Carranza government their identification would be easy. Balderio produced shears, knives and scythes from the farm houses, which he handed to volunteer privates to carry the idea into effect. About fifty or sixty of the Carranza prisoners were abused and punished in this manner." Villa ordered the property, which belonged to U.S. businessmen, burned but rescinded the order when General Beltrán suggested that doing so would harm the tenant farmers.

Villa then sent some of his troops on to Jiménez, which they captured on July 4 without firing a shot. The following day, Villa entered the town himself, still riding in the carriage. He ordered all the stores looted and the proceeds distributed among the poor families and his troops. An official of the British vice consulate later prepared a report on the incident from the statements of eyewitnesses. "They proceeded then to commit every manner of atrocity upon persons and property there. They killed civilians and soldiers wantonly and capriciously, ransacking every house and store, stripped clothes from passersby in the street, and even proceeded, in a number of notorious cases to the barbarous practice of clipping off men's ears." The Villistas, he wrote, were covered in vermin, dressed in rags, and half starved. One of their main objectives was to find a doctor. "The man looked sickly, and likely to die, but still preserved much of his extraordinary old-time energy," the British official said of Villa. "When he dismounted from his coach he was compelled to use crutches, his right leg being so swathed in wrappings as to indicate inflammation, and it was said, blood poisoning had set in."

Villa went to the local telegraph station, where he dispatched a number of messages designed to confuse the Carrancistas. Then he returned to the plaza and delivered a fierce harangue, claiming again that Carranza had sold Mexico to the gringos. Wrote the

British official, "He made the usual promises to the mob for relief from the hunger and suffering that they have endured, with wealth for them all, and was cheered to the echo."

Villa remained in Jiménez for two days, then faded back into the countryside. The Japanese agents, meanwhile, proceeded to put their poisoning plan into action. Dyo had been given three tubes containing twenty poison tablets each. The tablets had no taste or smell and took effect in three days. Dyo had tested the poison on a dog, giving the animal two tablets with "apparent good result." He planned to administer thirteen pills — nearly seven times as much — to Villa.

At some point, Dyo apparently succeeded in mixing the pills into a cup of coffee and gave it to Villa to drink. But Villa, who for years had worried about being poisoned, poured half the coffee into the cup of one of his aides and waited until the man drank before he sipped from his own cup. Without waiting around to see what happened, the agents slipped away from Villa's camp and returned to expedition headquarters. Whatever ill effects the drink had on Villa is unknown, but the concoction certainly didn't kill him.

With Pershing's troops penned up at Dublán, Villa's fortunes began to rebound and in mid-September he dashed a note off to the Carrancista commander, General Jacinto Treviño, in Chihuahua City promising that he would be in town on the sixteenth of September, Mexico's Independence Day, to shake hands. He added that "he might be hungry and would like to have something to eat."

Villa kept his word, once again displaying the insolence and audacity that had brought him so much fame. In early September, he disguised himself and slipped into the city to check out the location and strength of the Carrancista forces. At two thirty on the morning of September 16, Villa's troops stormed the city. He freed two hundred prisoners at the penitentiary, who promptly joined him, took over several federal buildings, and continued on to the governor's palace, where he appeared on the balcony and made a speech to the wildly cheering crowds. "I will give you liberty for I am your brother!" he shouted. Treviño gathered up his escort and started toward the palace but his men deserted him and joined the Villistas instead. Never intending to hold the city, Villa retired leisurely with sixteen carloads of booty and numerous captured artillery pieces, which were guarded by other Carrancista soldiers who had switched sides.

Throughout his military career, Friedrich Katz writes, Villa had the uncanny ability to snatch victory from the jaws of defeat and defeat from the jaws of victory, and his resurgence in the fall of 1916 and early spring of 1917 followed that pattern. He rebuilt the División del Norte until he once again had a full-fledged army consisting of five to six thousand soldiers. He stopped the looting and began to reassert the old discipline that he was once known for. "Subordinate failure to carry out instructions no matter how trivial was punishable by death," U.S. Army intelligence officials later wrote.

Two weeks after his dramatic appearance in Chihuahua City, he delivered a much more serious manifesto to the Mexican people in which he cited the recent heroic efforts of the people of Belgium to defend their country from the German invaders and called upon the Mexicans to do the same in repelling the "Barbarians of the North." He continued, "Victory will crown our efforts, do not forget it, because just causes always triumph, but, if destiny proves adverse to our cause, we will fall with our faces to heaven as the gladiators fell. . . ."

Pershing continued to urge his superiors to let him resume his hunt for Pancho Villa. When the requests were denied, he seems to have resigned himself to the fact that no more serious efforts would be made to apprehend Villa. In a letter to General Scott, he said Villa was holding his own simply because there was no energy being put into his capture. "You are familiar with Villa's terrorizing methods of enforcing service," he wrote drily. "He kills if men refuse to follow, and threatens to burn their families at the stake if they desert."

And that was not the most heinous of Villa's crimes. In the town of Camargo, he shot a woman point-blank when she flew into a rage upon learning that her husband had been killed by his troops. At the urging of his supporters, he then ordered the execution of ninety additional Carrancista women.

Villa briefly occupied the city of Torreón in mid-December and confiscated numerous goods, including thirty boxcars of soap, cottonseed meal, and cottonseed cake from the soap factory of Patrick O'Hea, the British vice-consul. In a highly emotional and graphic report describing Villa's activities, O'Hea wrote, "His career is that of a dog in rabies, a mad mullah, a Malay run amok."

❯❯20❮❮

AN OLD COLONEL

THE FIRST WEEKS IN MEXICO had been hard on Herbert Slocum. Unlike General Pershing, he had grown soft in middle age; he smoked cigars, he was overweight, and he was sixty-one years old. In the evenings, he retired early and slept so deeply that sometimes he didn't even remember when his adjutant shook him awake to ask him a question. With the limited rations and rigorous exercise, Slocum shed thirty pounds and felt better physically than he had in years. Psychologically, though, he was still under great stress. The investigation into the Columbus affair was dragging on. To compound his misery, Pershing had developed an extreme antipathy toward him and had instructed his chief of staff, Colonel DeRosey C. Cabell, to monitor Slocum's activities. As a consequence, Cabell was busily writing him up for various infractions of army regulations, such as leaving his camp filthy; removing horses from the picket line that belonged to other troops; losing a military codebook; failing to establish adequate outposts; and not following orders.

Slocum wrote long letters to old West Point chums Hugh Scott and Ernest Garlington, inspector general of the army, asking for their help in finding him a new position. While waiting, he carried on as best he could. One of his closest allies was Captain James Ryan, the Thirteenth Cavalry's intelligence officer. Ryan, who wore a toupee, had also felt the sting of Pershing's malice while on a reconnaissance mission in Mexico. One hot afternoon, Pershing ordered his staff, including the bewigged Ryan, to undress and accompany him on a cool swim. Ryan objected but was overruled and soon the entire headquarters staff was innocently splashing water on him while he gingerly made his way into the river "trying to balance his wig," remembered Pershing's former aide James Collins.

Ryan was also close to Hugh Scott and often wrote letters to him, hinting broadly that he should do something to get Slocum out of Mexico. "Slocum is in better health because we have a good camp and he keeps in the shade during the heat of the day. He cannot stand any more hard campaigning down here in the sun and I have urged him to pull out as soon as he can, without being criticized."

Slocum was eventually cleared of the infractions written up by Cabell, but he still had to cope with the much more serious allegations revolving around the Columbus raid. Unlike in the Carrizal incident, when more than seventy sworn affidavits were taken from soldiers on the battlefield, the army conducted a very limited investigation of the attack. No effort was made to explain how Villa and five hundred men slipped past the roving patrols, none of the cavalry officers living in town were questioned about their activities or whereabouts during the actual attack, and none of the civilian eyewitnesses who had warned of Villa's approach were questioned. Instead, the inspector general's investigation focused only on the precautions that the colonel took to protect the town and camp and Slocum himself appeared to be the only witness questioned. He vigorously defended his actions, describing the mounted and dismounted guards scattered about the camp and the troops that he had dispatched to the border:

> To have had scattered out of immediate concentration in case
> of need, any greater portion of my small command, would have
> been, under the circumstances, most unwise, and was so con-

sidered by me. The facts developed by the Mexican attack in the extreme darkness of March 9, 1916, has [*sic*] not changed this view in any way. The small town of Columbus has no lights, no electricity, and but little kerosene being used. On a dark night, such as the hour selected for this attack, a sentinel or member of a patrol could not see twenty feet in front of him. It was an easy matter for lightly shod Mexicans to sneak into the stable sheds in this darkness and cut the horses loose, as there were no lights around the stables. A requisition for oil and street lamps for this purpose having been previously disapproved.

Colonel Slocum also pointed out that there were no restrictions on the "floating Mexican population" in Columbus. A sketch of the camp was found on one of the dead Mexican soldiers, he added, indicating that many hostile Mexicans in Columbus joined in on the fight. "It was an easy matter," he continued, "for an enemy to concentrate immediately south of the border line without being disturbed, and attack the camp and Columbus, when notified by spies there of the most favorable opportunity." Only the machine guns were kept under lock and key, he said, adding that the men had access to their rifles and ammunition. He went on:

> I consider that every possible precaution was taken to protect American interests both civil and military by my command at Columbus, and the readiness and quickness with which the troops turned out, and met the attack, drove the Mexicans out of town and camp, with a loss known to me to be 78 killed, number of wounded unknown, except the ten or twelve wounded that were found in Camp, that the town of Columbus nor the Palomas Cattle Co has no just cause for feeling they were not amply protected by the troops. Further: had it not been for the braveness and thoroughness of the troops which met the attack, Columbus today would be off the map.

Slocum hung tough with the investigators, but by early July he was ready to quit and said as much in a letter to General Scott.

"Mrs. Sage in ill health, and my father feeble, and must go on and size up situation, possibly my retirement may be found necessary — of course, I will not leave here while there is any chance of a scrap, but the Mexicans do not want it and if we only play fair there won't be any with the Punitive Expedition." In a postscript, he added, "If you have any duty in U.S. [illegible] for an old colonel, ring me up!"

Three weeks later, he received a telegram from General Scott saying that he was reassigning him to Brownsville. "God be praised!" Slocum exploded in a July 25 letter. "I am so overjoyed! This service was truly getting on my nerves and I was about all in — Didn't want to quit under circumstances and now I can continue in harness for a while longer and finally retire from the firing line."

More good news followed a few days later when Slocum received a packet from Washington containing the inspector general's findings in the Columbus investigation. "You have been hammered from various directions a good deal by the press about Columbus, and we have not been able to take your part heretofore, but now the papers have come in and we have gotten the whole matter cleared up, about ten days ago," Scott wrote on July 29. "I have the permission of the Secretary of War to put it out in the public press, which I hope will have the effect of remedying any damage which may have been done by different people who rushed into the newspaper without cause."

The final report made no mention of any negative findings, and all the generals — including Pershing and Funston — stood solidly behind Slocum. "Colonel Slocum seems to have made every endeavor to obtain accurate information of the whereabouts and intentions of Villa," General Pershing said. "Although a brigand, Villa was not presumably an enemy of the United States nor were Mexico and the United States at war. Although Villa's approach to the border excited the curiosity of our officers along the border, it is not believed that many thought that Villa would have the audacity to attack a regimental garrison of American troops."

For his part, Funston retracted his earlier remarks about Slocum not having posted adequate guards. "The matter had not seemed clear to me before reading Colonel Slocum's statement, but it is now my opinion that there was not sufficient grounds for alarm to have made incumbent on him to increase materially the guards at the camp and town."

Inspector General Garlington added that Slocum had followed correct military procedures. "The fact that he was barred from sending patrols across the boundary line into Mexico deprived him of the only sure means of discovering the presence of bandits or others with hostile purpose in time to adequately protect his territory from sudden incursions by them." And General Scott summed it up: "I recommend that Colonel Slocum be advised that no stigma rests upon his conduct of command at Columbus, N.M., at the time of Villa's attack, and that he and his command are highly commended for their prompt and valorous action in the repulse of Villa's force and pursuit of the same."

ALTHOUGH PERSHING publicly supported Slocum, privately he was still fuming. He wrote two highly negative critiques of the colonel, one of which he sent to Funston and the second to Tasker Bliss, Scott's aide in the War Department. "He is old for his years, and thinks too much of his comfort," he told Bliss. But Pershing's harsh opinion was not shared by everyone. Colonel Dodd, the crusty officer who had led the Seventh Cavalry deep into Mexico and almost captured Villa, considered Slocum's regiment to be the best in Mexico. And Slocum's loyal friend, Captain Ryan, in an August 1, 1916, letter to Scott, continued to praise him. "He is too good a man and one of such fine character, high sense of duty and greatness of heart that he should not be risked in these out of the way parts on expeditions of this kind. I miss him very much but for his sake I am glad he is safely out of Mexico." As far as the U.S. government was concerned, Herbert Slocum had done just fine.

A REBORN TOWN

BACK IN COLUMBUS, a white sun hovered in the sky. Thunder-heads boiled up over Tres Hermanas in the late afternoon and then drifted away. It was what local residents referred to as the monsoon season, but the rain seemed to fall everywhere but Columbus. The faithful were convinced that the town had fallen out of favor with the Almighty and the settlement did seem a less innocent place: the music of cabarets tumbled from the doorways and newly deputized watchmen swaggered through the streets, wearing roweled spurs and guns. The watchmen were a brutal lot, recruited by an even more brutal sheriff who enjoyed chaining his prisoners to trees. The watchmen had recently pistol-whipped an army major, con-tributing to the growing animosity between the soldiers and the locals. In addition to the increasing number of burglaries, assaults, thefts, and embezzlements, organized criminal enterprises such as bootlegging, gambling, drug smuggling, and gun running were also flourishing. As always, there was prostitution.

In the tumbled-down shacks and cribs of Columbus's red-light district, flies swarmed over the open latrines and whores lay in sticky embrace with their customers. Lieutenant Colonel Charles Farnsworth, the commander of the military base in Columbus, concluded, like Pershing, that it was more efficient to regulate prostitution than to try to stamp it out altogether and two red-light districts — one for whites and one for African-Americans — were established. By late summer, fifty prostitutes were working in Columbus. Their teeth were crowned with gold, their arms and legs decorated with blue, fuzzy tattoos, their hair scorched by harsh dyes. They suffered from tuberculosis and tonsillitis, infections and venereal disease. Thomas Dabney, the town's physician and also the newly elected mayor, examined the girls himself and collected $2.50 for each examination. But the women soon began complaining to military authorities that Dr. Dabney was actually contributing to the spread of venereal disease because he used only Vaseline or alcohol to clean off his instruments as he went from woman to woman. Eventually a military doctor took over the exams and the disease rate declined.

Alcohol was another huge problem. Two years earlier, the village board of trustees had passed an ordinance limiting the sale of liquor to "near beer," which contained 2 percent alcohol. But a loophole still allowed private clubs to sell alcohol, which was one reason they grew so quickly. Military authorities, working with Mayor Dabney, succeeded in getting voters to pass an ordinance prohibiting the sale of liquor in the private clubs, as well. Several months later, the sale of near beer was also banned. The grips of passengers debarking from the train were searched, automobile trunks were inspected, freight offices were watched. One day in September, thirty-three joints were raided. "We haven't been able to put liquor out of Columbus, but we've made whiskey cost $2.00 a pint in a back alley and it's a certainty soldiers on $15.00 a month can't afford to drink long at that figure," asserted one officer.

Drug use among soldiers was also growing. Truckers smuggled cocaine and morphine across the line in the vehicles returning from Mexico. "The business of selling drugs has been so little molested by the proper authorities that men have been seen 'decking' (putting into small-size packages) cocaine and morphine, in public saloons in the presence of customers at the bar," the commander of the military police advised his superiors in Washington.

Gun smuggling was another lucrative business. Military intelligence officers in Columbus soon grew suspicious of Sam Ravel, the general-store owner whom the Villistas had hoped to find in the Commercial Hotel. In July, Ravel was arrested by civil authorities after crossing the border with six men, all of whom were alleged to be "notorious saloon keepers." The automobile they were riding in contained, among other things, ninety-six pints of whiskey, a keg of wine, a Colt revolver, a Mauser and two rifles, a hundred rounds of Mauser ammunition, forty-five rounds of thirty-thirty ammunition, and thirty-five rounds of pistol ammunition. Ravel insisted he was innocent and vowed to go to Washington to get his passes back.

The violence against Mexicans continued through the summer. A laborer working on the Deming road was shot through both legs. Three Mexicans employed by one of the infantry regiments were pistol-whipped. And on July 23, the bodies of two Mexicans were found two miles west of town. They had been killed on the railroad tracks and dragged into the bushes. Next to them were two Mexican hats with a bullet hole through each crown. An inquest panel composed of six local citizens fatuously concluded that "two unknown Mexicans" had come to their death by "unknown causes."

PERSHING APPLIED FOR PROMOTION to major general in late September. Newton Baker recommended the promotion to President Wilson, who approved it on September 25. George Patton couldn't have been happier, and at a lemonade reception in Mexico he toasted the new two-star general enthusiastically. A week later, Patton was working in his tent when his kerosene lamp exploded, burning his face and ears. "My face looks like an old after-birth of a Mexican cow on which had been smeared several very much decomposed eggs," he advised his wife in one of his typically colorful missives. Though the burns were healing quickly, Patton nevertheless went on sick leave to California, where his father, a

Democrat, was campaigning for the U.S. Senate. The elder Patton lost the race, but George believed his father's campaign had helped President Wilson carry the state of California. When his father was offered no consolation prize, such as a cabinet post, he grew even more embittered toward Wilson. Pershing urged Patton to be cautious in his public statements. "You must remember that when we enter the army we do so with the full knowledge that our first duty is toward our government, entirely regardless of own views," he wrote in an October 16, 1916, letter.

Patton returned to Mexico in mid-November. He was cold, miserable, and bored. In a letter to his wife, he confided that he was actually considering getting out of the army. "If I was sure that I would never be above the average army officer I would, for I don't like the dirt and all except as a means to fame. If I knew that I would never be famous I would settle down and raise horses and have a great time. It is a great gamble to spoil your and my own happiness for the hope of greatness. I wish I was less ambitious, then too some times I think that I am not ambitious at all only a dreamer."

Pershing, the hard-eyed realist, was busy shaping his image for posterity. Even before the expeditionary troops pulled out of Mexico, he had begun framing a response to the critics who would claim the expedition had been a wild-goose chase and a failure. In truth, the expedition had actually fulfilled its amended mission by killing or dispersing nearly all of Villa's band, but many would remember only the administration's flamboyant promise to capture Villa "dead or alive," and conclude that the whole affair had been a waste of taxpayers' money. In a well-crafted letter to General Scott, which Pershing undoubtedly knew would be made public someday, he put the blame squarely on the Carrancista government. "Going back to the early days of the campaign," he wrote, "you will recall that the Parral incident halted the expedition and under our instructions it was necessary to wait on diplomatic action between the two governments. I want to invite your attention to the fact that at that time we had four cavalry columns converging toward Parral, which, as you know, is near the Durango line. These columns were all south of Villa and if we could have continued the pursuit, there is little doubt but that Villa would have been captured."

But perhaps one of Pershing's most remarkable efforts to manipulate the historical record was his "major damage control operation" to cover up the assassination plot to poison Villa. Charles Harris and Louis Sadler, the two New Mexico historians who discovered the plot, maintain that public knowledge of the assassination attempt would most certainly have jeopardized Pershing's military career and possibly President Wilson's reelection campaign. The two historians found evidence that documents had been removed from the expedition's intelligence files at the National Archives as late as 1926:

> The identity of the person who weeded the files is not known. However, a memorandum in the Punitive Expedition records dated November 19, 1926, states that General Pershing, who had retired as Army Chief of Staff two years earlier, had possession of two operational folders, and that the files of the Punitive Expedition Intelligence section were checked out to Colonel Aristides Moreno, a senior Intelligence officer who had served under Pershing in Europe during World War I. Whether or not General Pershing or Colonel Moreno removed certain telegrams and intelligence reports from the Punitive Expedition files is unclear. What is clear is that a number of telegrams and several reports of the Japanese agents are missing.

By the time 1917 rolled around, the expedition forces were making preparations to return home. At Dublán, the adobe huts were broken up, the refuse collected and burned, the camp raked clean so that the prairie looked the way it did when they had first come upon it. When the cavalry regiments and the infantry started north, they were accompanied by five hundred Chinese refugees and fifteen hundred Mexicans, who carried their worldly possessions in wagons and pony carts and on the backs of worn-out burros. On February 5, the troops crossed back into the United States. Covered with dust, footsore, deeply weathered, they passed beneath the reviewing stand where Pershing had gone ahead to receive them. His stiff, erect body was enclosed in a heavy coat and he stood before them and saluted crisply, still unbowed and unbeaten.

That evening he had dinner with the Farnsworths, who were living in a converted store that still bore the bullet holes of Pancho Villa's raid. A new Edison telephone sat on a table in the living room and two outlets had been drilled in the ceiling for electricity, which now came on for a few hours each day. Pershing rose early the next morning and boarded a train for Fort Bliss. As he sat on a dusky pink cushion, doing paperwork, the morning sun illuminated the tar-paper shacks and tents receding behind him. The little town glinted for a moment and then faded into the mica wash of the desert. After ten months and three weeks in Mexico, General Pershing had completed his duty.

TWO WEEKS LATER, General Funston was dining with friends at the elegant St. Anthony Hotel in San Antonio. The brief Texas winter was giving way to a hot, yellow spring and Funston was enjoying himself, the crushing worry over Pershing and his troops finally lifted. The hotel orchestra was playing the familiar notes of the "Blue Danube" waltz and Funston listened appreciatively. "You know," he said, turning to a friend, "there is no music as sweet as the old tunes." Then his breath caught in his throat and he collapsed onto the floor and died. He was fifty-one years old.

Pershing was ordered to Fort Sam Houston in San Antonio to take over the army's Southern Department. There, he would encounter some of the remarkable men who had not gone into Mexico but would play important roles in the years to come, including Captain Douglas MacArthur and a young lieutenant by the name of Dwight Eisenhower. And fate was not yet finished with General Pershing. On April 6, 1917, the United States declared war on Germany, and one month later Pershing was named head of the American Expeditionary Forces in Europe.

After Pershing's troops had exited Mexico, Villa returned to Namiquipa to punish the townspeople who had revealed the location of his weapons cache and cooperated with the gringos. The men fled to the hills, so Villa simply had all the women rounded up and then allowed his troops to rape them. Nicolás Fernández was revolted by the barbaric act, and took several women under his protection, threatening to kill any man who came near them. It was yet one more atrocity committed by Villa, and he no longer had to worry about an American reprisal.

→→22←←

VICTIMS OR BANDITS?

WHILE THE SOLDIERS CELEBRATED their homecoming in Columbus's dance halls, twenty-one Villistas squatted on their haunches in the military stockade south of the railroad tracks, wondering what would become of them. These were the men who had been captured in Mexico by Pershing's expedition and were sent back to Columbus prior to its withdrawal. The youngest was seventeen, the oldest forty-eight. Unlike the sad young conscripts who had gone to their deaths six months earlier, most of these men were veterans of Mexico's long-running revolution. Nineteen had served in the División del Norte for anywhere from six months to two years or more. And two-thirds, or fourteen prisoners, were from the revolutionary town of Namiquipa or nearby villages and had been under the command of Candelario Cervantes.

Although the U.S. Army was eager to close the books on the Columbus raid, civilian authorities were not yet finished. On February 6, 1917, a federal agent arrived in Columbus and interrogated the captives. The agent seemed most interested in finding out where, exactly, Pancho Villa was stationed during the raid. But if he had hoped to come away with a definite answer, he was sorely disappointed. Villa seemed to be everywhere and nowhere all at once. Some prisoners said they saw him with the advance guard, others reported him in the rear with the horse holders, and a few said they never saw him at all.

Once again, the Villistas were turned over to local authorities in Luna County for punishment. Nineteen were indicted for the murders of John Moore, James Dean, Charles DeWitt Miller, and Paul Simon. Afterward, probably due to the horrendous conditions in the Deming jail, they were transferred to a jail in Silver City, where they languished for eight months. On August 27, 1917, seventeen of the prisoners appeared before District Judge Raymond Ryan and pleaded guilty to second-degree murder in a plea bargain arranged by J. S. Vaught, the same prosecutor who tried the first group of prisoners. No defense attorney was on hand to represent them. In exchange, they escaped the hangman's noose and were sentenced to from seventy to eighty years in the state penitentiary. As for the other prisoners, their fates are unclear. One of those men, Guadalupe Chávez, decided at the last minute to rescind his guilty plea. Later, in a letter to the governor, J. S. Vaught expressed great frustration with the defendant, saying that he had not been able to set the case for trial because "most of the witnesses in this case are somewhere in France with the American Army."

Following the sentencing hearing, the seventeen men were transported to the penitentiary in Santa Fe, where they joined José Rodríguez, whose death sentence had been commuted by Governor McDonald. Sentiment was still against the Villistas and the *Santa Fe New Mexican* railed against the "worthless pelados" who now had to be fed and housed at the taxpayers' expense. "It seems to us that hereafter bandits from another country invading the United States and slaughtering its citizens ought to be dealt with by the military forces of the United States."

On November 22, 1920, in one of his last acts as a lame-duck governor, New Mexico's Octaviano Larrazolo granted a "full, complete and unconditional pardon" to José Rodríguez and the fifteen remaining inmates who were sentenced to life. (Prison records state a sixteenth, Silvino Vargas, had been pardoned earlier and a seventeenth, Enrique Adame, had escaped.) In a lengthy executive order, Larrazolo laid out his reasons for the pardons, focusing on the question of whether the attack on Columbus was the work of bandits or an act of war by an organized army. This was the same issue that Buel Wood, the hapless defense attorney, had tried to emphasize in the first trial and the issue that Judge Medler denigrated in his instructions to the jury.

Governor Larrazolo believed strongly that the prisoners were not free agents but common soldiers in the ranks of the army commanded by Pancho Villa. Whether the convicts were voluntary recruits or conscripts didn't make any difference, he said, because the bottom line was that they had to obey orders or face death:

> . . . there must be malice, that is, ill will, meaning a willful deliberate and perverse intention and desire to do wrong. Can we say that such motives were in the hearts of these men who did not know where they were going, what they were going to do, or why; but who, on the other hand, were simply carrying out the instructions, orders and commands of their superiors, when they well knew that a failure to comply therewith and disobedience to such orders might mean their death? It is perfectly plain to me that under the circumstances, these men were not guilty of murder.

To buttress his argument, the governor then referred to a similar incident in Texas in which Carrancista soldiers crossed the border and fought with U.S. troops. A number of men were killed and six of the Mexican soldiers were charged with murder and sentenced to death. But the state appeals court reversed the decision, arguing that the defendants were clearly soldiers following orders and that the state courts didn't have jurisdiction to try the cases. Larrazolo said it was also clear to him that the Villistas had no understanding of the difference "between murder in the first degree or any other degree." Once the pleas were entered, he pointed out, Judge Ryan had no choice but to pass sentence. Had the cases gone to trial, he added, Ryan would have directed them to be acquitted because he "told me personally that in his opinion these men should be pardoned."

The prisoners were scheduled to be released on Thanksgiving Day, but an attorney for the American Legion secured a temporary injunction from a Santa Fe district judge, arguing that the pardons were illegal because they had not been sanctioned by the Board of Penitentiary Commissioners. The injunction was soon made permanent and the question was referred to the state supreme court.

Intent upon keeping the Villistas in prison, representatives of various civil organizations approached officials in Luna County and asked them if they would be willing to reindict the prisoners on additional murder charges growing out of the raid. The county wasn't eager to expend twenty-five thousand dollars for another trial but eventually bowed to public pressure and ordered the sheriff to go to Santa Fe and rearrest the men. Now a second legal issue had been raised: could the county reindict the convicts on new murder charges stemming from the same incident for which they had already been convicted? This question, too, was referred to the state supreme court.

On December 28, the state high court issued a ruling that satisfied no one: the governor did indeed have the authority to pardon the prisoners without the consent of anyone, the justices wrote, and Luna County officials also had the authority to rearrest the prisoners on additional charges.

The stage was now set for one more trial. Dressed in clean clothes and wearing leg irons and handcuffs, the sixteen Villistas were returned to the Deming jail by train on February 11, 1921. Two months later the trial opened. Five years had passed since the Columbus raid and this time the state planned to put on a much more comprehensive case. The new prosecutor was a young man named Forest Fielder, who was aided by his father, J. H. Fielder, one of the state's most experienced trial lawyers. The court-appointed defense attorney was R. F. Hamilton, Deming's mayor. Presiding over the trial was Judge Raymond Ryan, who had taken the guilty pleas in August of 1917.

No transcript has survived of the trial but several newspaper reporters were in the courtroom and wrote about it. The El Paso Herald reported that picking a jury had proved difficult because almost every potential juror questioned had formed an opinion about the case. Eventually a panel was seated that included three farmers, a plasterer, a painter, a carpenter, a jeweler, a garage owner, a hotel owner, a railroad worker, and a laborer. The father of one of the jurors, George Maisel, had served on the jury that had convicted the first group of raiders. And as a sign of the changing times, Frank Torres, a man of "Spanish-American" blood, had also been selected.

María Rodríguez, whose husband and brother were sitting among the double row of defendants in the front of the courtroom, had come from Mexico to watch the trial. She wore a long black coat, blue dress, black silk mantilla, and soft, leather shoes with French heels. "Mother of God," she exclaimed through an interpreter. "How I wish there had never been a Villa and a revolution! We were so happy in the old days, though we were quite poor and greatly oppressed."

"Spectators in the court room commented on the improved appearance of the prisoners and the contrast they present to their former appearance in court here," wrote the *Albuquerque Morning Journal*. The newspaper also reported that the defendants had pleaded guilty to second-degree murder on the advice of a Silver City deputy sheriff, who assured them that they would be sentenced to only three or four years.

The most dramatic witness for the prosecution was Laura Ritchie, who described how the invaders battered down the hotel door and dragged her husband from her, shot him on the sidewalk, and left him to die. Also taking the stand were Major N. W. Campanole, who interrogated the prisoners in Mexico, and Colonel E. C. Abbott, who had commanded the New Mexico infantry of the National Guard. Their testimony was designed to rebut the notion that the defendants were ignorant conscripts who didn't know they were in the United States. Campanole pointed out that a train had passed through town fifteen to thirty minutes before the raid and would have alerted the men they were on U.S. soil. Colonel Abbott also testified that at least one Villista — Juan Muñoz — had told him that he knew he was in the United States. Nevertheless, Campanole may have inadvertently buttressed the defense's case when he confirmed that defendants had been forcibly conscripted. "I did not see the recruiting order, but according to information I received, it called on all former followers of Villa to again take up arms under penalty of death."

The testimony continued for two days. When it was concluded, the attorneys gave their closing arguments and then retired to the judge's chambers to draw up instructions to the jury. The panel initially had four verdicts to choose from: first-degree murder, second-degree murder, manslaughter, or acquittal. Taking a gamble, the defense asked that the second-degree murder and manslaughter verdicts be stricken from the instructions. Ryan agreed and the jury retired to deliberate. Their choices were stark: a guilty verdict would result in the death of the defendants and a not-guilty verdict would give them their freedom. The jury was out for only thirty-five minutes — about the same length of time that jurors in the earlier trial had spent in deliberations. When they filed back into the jury box, Judge Ryan asked the foreman, Hugh Ramsay, if they had reached a verdict.

We have, Your Honor.

The verdict was passed to the clerk, who read it in English and then passed it to the interpreter, who translated it into Spanish:

Inocente.

Stunned, the defendants at first showed no change in their facial expression. "Like men drawing back from the brink of the grave they neither spoke nor smiled, but as one man they rose in their places while one of their number, Mariano Jiménez, thanked the jury," the *Deming Graphic* wrote.

As spectators rushed up to shake hands with them, the men became visibly affected. David Rodríguez broke down in tears. Francisco Solís thanked them again. "Señores, we are most grateful. On behalf of my comrades, I wish to express our gratitude. You have been most gracious to us and we were constantly sustained during this trial by our faith in your justice and your desire to be fair to us poor men. We will be most happy to again return to our families and enjoy freedom in our country. We assure you we were innocent."

The following day, the prisoners were delivered to Mexican authorities on the international bridge leading to Juárez. Writing of the trial several days later, the *Deming Graphic,* which had thundered and railed against the prisoners, mused that the verdict was evidence once again that Americans didn't like to take life, even in a legal setting. "Perhaps this inability of Americans to nurse hate through the years is a weakness, yet it has proved to be the salvation of the nation."

✦23✦

DEATH COMES FOR

THE HORSEMEN

WHEN GENERAL PERSHING returned from World War I, Congress passed a special law re-creating the rank of general of the armies of the United States and bestowed it upon him, along with a sixth star. Only one other man in U.S. history had ever held that title: George Washington. There was talk of a bright political future, but Pershing curtly put the speculation to rest, stating emphatically that he had no interest. He became chief of staff of the army in 1921 and retired three years later when he turned sixty-four. He lived quietly and without fanfare for the next two and a half decades, surviving long enough to see the world convulsed in a second global war and the dropping of two atomic bombs on Japan. Though he had a closet filled with medals and ribbons, he often wore only one in public: the Victory medal awarded to every man who served in any capacity in the armed forces. He died in 1948 at Walter Reed Hospital after a long illness. He was just two months shy of his eighty-eighth birthday.

Many of the men who served under Pershing went on to great distinction in World War I and World War II. The most famous was his gawky aide, George Patton, who had occasionally shared a blanket with him during the Mexican campaign. Patton was assigned to the U.S. Tank Corps during World War I and was wounded by machine-gun fire while trying to get assistance for tanks mired in the mud. But his greatest military victories would come in World War II when he led troops in successful campaigns in North Africa, Italy, and Europe.

Major Frank Tompkins was given command of an infantry division and sailed for Europe on July 8, 1918. Six months later, he was gassed and received severe burns. He retired in 1920 with the rank of colonel. Herbert Slocum nominated him for a Medal of Honor, but he received instead a Distinguished Service Cross for his pursuit of the Mexican troops and a presidential citation. He taught at Norwich University in Northfield, Vermont, the nation's first private military college, and went on to serve two years in the Vermont legislature.

The people of Columbus considered Lieutenant Castleman their true savior, but his career was probably hurt by the fact that he had taken his troopers into town to check on his wife instead of first helping to secure the army camp, violating one of the basic rules of military engagement. Once he and his soldiers were positioned at the intersection near the Hoover Hotel, however, they fought bravely, running dangerously low on ammunition as they drove the invaders west into the machine-gun fire of Lieutenant Lucas. Castleman, who also received a Distinguished Service Cross for his part in the Columbus raid, was promoted to captain in July of 1916 and a year later transferred to the Fourteenth Cavalry. During World War I, he went to France, where he served as assistant to the quartermaster general and roamed all over Europe, looking for food and supplies for the American Expeditionary Forces. He remained in the army until 1932, retiring after thirty years of service.

Lieutenant Lucas received no medals for his role in the Columbus affair but would become a highly decorated and much-loved officer in the years to come. During World War I, he was detailed to the Signal Corps and received a severe head wound that would result in headaches for the rest of his life. He remained in the army when armistice was declared and eventually achieved the rank of major general. During World War II, he commanded the American and British forces in the Anzio landing but was relieved of duties for making insufficient progress. ("They will end up by putting me ashore with inadequate forces and get me in a serious jam," he wrote in his diary. "Then, who will take the blame?") He received two Distinguished Service Medals, a Purple Heart, a Silver Star, and numerous other honors during his long military career.

Although Herbert Slocum had been officially exonerated of any blame in the Columbus raid, he was not promoted in the great expansion of the army leading up to World War I nor did he go overseas. The War Department apparently had no quarrel with him and his name topped the list of colonels selected by the board of general officers who were entitled to promotion to brigadier general, but someone crossed his name off the list. In a letter to one of his sons, Slocum spoke of being passed over with a studied nonchalance and also alluded to the reasons for it: "I am not worrying at all about promotion, knowing as I do that my name headed the list of Colonels selected by the board of General officers as those entitled to promotion and my name was 'blue penciled' by those in authority on account of circumstances over which I had no control and I was made a victim of such circumstances, together with politics, which is a part of our great Government. The wound is still there, of course and always will be there, but I do not intend to embitter my remaining days and I shall finish my remaining service until next April and give my country my best efforts as I have always tried to do."

In April of 1918, while Slocum was stationed at Brownsville, a young army officer named J. J. Dickinson passed through on an inspection. Afterward he went to dinner with the colonel and Mrs. Slocum and several other officers and their wives. Out of a "sense of delicacy," Dickinson carefully avoided all mention of the Columbus raid. To his surprise, Slocum himself brought it up when they were having their after-dinner coffee. Dickinson listened carefully and wrote a lengthy story based upon the conversation that was published a year later in the *Mississippi Valley Magazine*.

According to Slocum's version, George Seese, the intrepid Associated Press reporter, had made arrangements for Villa to give himself up to his old "amigo" — Slocum — who, however, knew nothing of the plan. "But when Villa's men learned of the plan, they threatened to mutiny and Villa convinced them the report was a lie and vowed to proceed with the attack that night." One of the primary targets of the raid was Slocum's wife, Mary: "The only object of Villa's raid was to seize Mrs. Slocum, after Villa personally had murdered Col. Slocum, carry her off to a virtually inaccessible fastness in the Sierra Madre and hold her for a huge ransom. Villa knew that Col. Slocum was one of the principal heirs of the great fortune of Russell Sage, of whose widow, only recently dead, Col. Slocum was a nephew and a designated heir and trustee of the immense Sage estate, one of the world's biggest fortunes." The Slocums learned of the plot from Maud Wright, who had been taken to their house after the raid. "It was from her that the Slocums obtained the first faint hints of the amazing plot. She understood Spanish, and heard the whole tragic plan discussed in the Villa camp — both the original plan that meant safety for Villa, and the changed plan upon which the murderous chieftain made the raid."

Dickinson went on to say that Slocum had obtained affidavits from George Seese, which were then forwarded to the State Department, the Department of Justice, and the War Department. But those affidavits have never been found, nor have any other documents supporting Colonel Slocum's version of events. What's more, Maud Wright, in her statements to George Carothers and E. B. Stone, made no mention of such a plot.

Still, Slocum's story, particularly the part about Villa's plan to hold his wife for ransom, seemed somewhat plausible. Villa had often held prominent citizens and foreigners for large ransom payments, which he used to help finance his army. Mary Slocum also talked of the noise that the bullets made as they struck the walls of their house on the morning of the raid and clothing shredded by bullets — evidence that Villa's men had been there.

Slocum retired on April 25, 1919, and moved back to Washington, D.C., where he lived another nine years. When he died, on March 29, 1928, he left an estate valued at roughly three to four million dollars, which was divided principally among his wife and two sons and a few close friends. He was buried at Arlington National Cemetery with full honors. One of the pallbearers was his old friend Hugh Scott.

THE LEADERS of the Mexican Revolution all died violent deaths. Venustiano Carranza assumed the presidency in mid-March of 1917 and returned to Mexico City. Emiliano Zapata, who had carried on his fight for agrarian reform in nearby Morelos, had continued to taunt Carranza, writing insulting letters to him that were published in the daily newspapers. In an intricate plot, Carranza succeeded in having Zapata and his bodyguards assassinated on April 10, 1919.

The relationship between Carranza and Álvaro Obregón grew strained as the presidential elections of 1920 drew near. Obregón, who had done more than anyone else to ensure Carranza's triumph, expected Carranza to step aside so that he could become president. But Carranza was reluctant to give up power, especially to a military man like Obregón. The Mexican Constitution banned the reelection of the president so Don Venustiano, unable to run again, did the next best thing and threw his support to Ignacio Bonillas, a minor politician whom he thought he could control. In response, Obregón's home state of Sonora declared that Carranza was no longer Mexico's legitimate president and named Adolfo de la Huerta, the Sonoran governor, as the interim leader. Other leaders throughout Mexico joined the revolt.

Carranza, realizing his time had come, decided to leave Mexico City. But first he systematically looted the government treasury, exhibiting the "quiet, tireless sleepless greed" that Edith O'Shaughnessy had once spoken of. (During his tenure, theft was so common that a new verb, *carrancear*, was coined.) Onto a long train, he loaded millions of dollars in gold and silver, priceless antiques, presses and ink used to print paper money, and even disassembled airplanes. As the train chugged toward Veracruz, it was attacked by insurgents and smashed by a locomotive loaded with dynamite. High in the mountains, the presidential entourage was finally halted at a point where the tracks had been torn up. Carranza proceeded on horseback, carrying what he could on pack mules and leaving millions in gold and silver behind. In the remote village of Tlaxcalantongo, he took refuge in an earthen hut. He ate with his usual deliberateness and then retired for the evening. At four o'clock on the morning of May 21, 1920, he awoke to the sound of gunfire and the cries *"Viva Obregón!"* and *"Muera a Carranza!"* He screamed at his guards to save themselves as multiple bullets slammed into his chest, killing him. He was sixty years old.

The Mexican legislature appointed Adolfo de la Huerta to serve as interim president until the elections could be held. An urbane and friendly man, de la Huerta wanted to heal the wounds of the revolution and granted amnesty to numerous revolutionaries. To Spanish author Vicente Blasco Ibáñez, de la Huerta seemed like "a virgin lost in a crowd of rabid and shrewd old hags who think they can become young again by rubbing against her."

With his bitter enemy dead, Pancho Villa was eager to reach some sort of peaceful resolution with the Mexican government. His army had once again dwindled to a few hundred guerrilla fighters and he was living the hunted-animal life he so despised. He had managed to retain his puckish sense of humor, though, and had named one of his favorite mules President Wilson. But the days of Wilson were drawing to a close; a presidential election was pending and Villa was worried that a new effort to catch him might be launched. Adolfo de la Huerta, who had no entanglements with Villa, was in favor of granting him amnesty and managed to persuade Obregón and other generals that it would be best for their war-torn country if he could be enticed to lay down his arms.

The actual process of reaching a peace accord was a treacherous dance. Villa had been almost captured twice while making friendly overtures and knew that to get what he wanted he would have to negotiate from a position of strength rather than one of weakness. In a desperate and audacious gamble, Villa embarked on a forced march to Sabinas, Coahuila, a town located roughly 120 miles west of Laredo, Texas. To get there, he traveled for three days through a fierce desert in the middle of July. Water holes and springs were dried up and both men and horses died from thirst. The troops reached Sabinas at about four o'clock on the morning of July 26. As dawn broke over the pretty little town, it seemed as if they had entered the promised land. Coahuila had not suffered the depredations of Chihuahua and was enjoying a mild prosperity. Crops were ripening in the fields and horses moved across the green pastures.

Villa immediately sent for the president of the Sabinas brewery and ordered him to shut down the plant. Next, he summoned the owners of the bars and cantinas and ordered them to close, warning that any merchant caught selling or giving liquor to any of his men would be shot. Then, his auditors were dispatched to inspect the books of all the grocery and clothing stores in town and report back with the names and locations of the most profitable enterprises. From the most affluent stores, he "requisitioned" twenty thousand dollars' worth of shoes, hats, breeches, underwear, socks, shirts, food, forage, horseshoes, nails, leather, pack mules, and horses for his troops.

While his men were being fitted out, he went to the telegraph station and contacted President de la Huerta in Mexico City and said he was ready to discuss amnesty terms. He asked de la Huerta to send General Eugenio Martínez, a former officer whom he knew and trusted, to the bargaining table. De la Huerta, who harbored his own political ambitions, immediately agreed. While waiting, Villa put his troops into position so they could guard the town and fend off any attackers. Martínez was to leave his troops three miles outside of town and come into Sabinas with a hundred men. Villa's bodyguard would consist of roughly an equal number.

Flanked by five generals, including Nicolás Fernández, Villa opened the conference on July 28 by emphasizing that he did not want the meeting to be considered a "surrender but a peace conference" between himself and the new government. He cursed the leaders of the Mexican government, calling them "grafters and traitors." Stating once again that he had killed his own people long enough, he took out a folder and gave it to General Martínez. The folder contained the number of men he had killed with his own hands or during battle; Villa estimated that he was responsible for the deaths of forty-three thousand men. "He stated that he had been a bad man for years, and that this government was the first that had tried in any way to do the right thing." Villa said he was willing to make peace with the government but if they were unwilling to accept his olive branch, he was prepared to make "more trouble." Wrote Gus Jones, a congressional investigator:

> He further stated that the time had come when Mexico needed men, imbued with the spirit of patriotism, and not selfish interests, and that if they all got together, they would again build their country up and place it where it should be. He further stated that one of his main reasons for making peace was because the days of Mr. President Wilson in Washington were short and that soon the Republican party would be in power and that they would immediately take as a pretext for intervention, Villa and his past deeds, and this he wished to avoid, stating that if the United States wished intervention, they would have to drum up other causes.

By that evening, the two men had reached an accord: in exchange for laying down his arms, Villa would receive the hacienda El Canutillo. Villa knew Canutillo well; it was in the state of Durango, only fifty miles from his beloved Parral, and encompassed fertile grasslands and thousands of acres of rich, irrigated farmland. For a short period during the revolution, one of his chieftains, Tomás Urbina, had occupied it. Under the terms of the agreement, Villa also would be allowed to keep a bodyguard of fifty men, whose salaries would be paid by the Mexican government. The rest of his army would receive six months' to a year's worth of wages, as well as adjoining hacienda land, or have the option of joining the federal army at their current rank.

It was a sweet deal and Villa knew that he was not likely to get anything better. Both sides approved the arrangement, which provoked "heated resentment" from Obregón and grudging admiration from U.S. officials. "It would appear from this that Francisco Villa has again outgeneraled his opponents," a U.S. Army intelligence report stated. And William Blocker, the U.S. consul, said much the same thing in a memo to the State Department: "The organization of this ignorant man is wonderful, and I cannot conceive how he has so easily made infants out of the Mexican commanders."

Although many on both sides of the border doubted that Villa would refrain from politics, he kept his word and lived quietly at Canutillo. His own bedroom was simply furnished, with the exception of a tray of unopened perfume bottles, an odd touch for a man who had once professed such disdain for *perfumados* — sweet-smelling men. He built a school, imported modern machinery, and planted vast crops of wheat and corn and beans. He ran the hacienda much as he did his army, with regular inspections and bugles sounding at dawn and dusk. At one point, Villa actually asked the government to reimburse him two hundred thousand pesos for the damages suffered by his hacienda during the revolution. "The peculiarity of the situation is that the ranches were practically worthless and that the destruction was caused by Villa's own followers," wrote U.S. Army intelligence officials, who continued to closely monitor his activities and remained suspicious of everything he did.

Villa had many enemies and plots were constantly being hatched to kill him. Yet the would-be assassins could not penetrate the veritable fortress that he had erected. "It is said that no one can approach Villa's ranch without advance permission or knowledge as all the approaches to the place are continually guarded by a system of guards and outposts," the U.S. Army wrote. Nevertheless, as the months went by, Villa's animal cunning and vigilance lessened. He grew stout in middle age and spent more time with the children who had been born of his many "wives." On the morning of July 20, 1923, almost exactly three years to the day since he had laid down his arms, Villa was returning to Canutillo from Parral. Villa himself was driving his low-slung Dodge touring car and his driver was standing on the running board. The passengers included his secretary and four bodyguards. As the vehicle slowed for a narrow turn, a pedestrian raised his fist and shouted, "*Viva Villa!*" The old war cry was the signal for assassins hidden in a house across the road, who raised their rifles and fired. Nine bullets struck Villa, killing him almost instantly. Everyone else in the automobile was also killed, except for one man, who was badly wounded but managed to escape back to Canutillo. Two and a half years later, someone opened Villa's grave and cut off his head. Neither the perpetrator nor the head was ever found.

As Mexico emerged from the wreckage of the ten years of civil war, it seemed that Álvaro Obregón would be the only high-ranking revolutionary leader to escape the violent death that all his compatriots had suffered. Obregón served as president from 1920 to 1924 and then stepped aside for fellow Sonoran Plutarco Elías Calles, who had delivered the crushing defeat to Villa at Agua Prieta. As Calles's term drew to a close, Obregón's supporters in the Mexican legislature wrote an exception into the no-reelection clause of the Constitution so that Obregón could run for president for a second time. On July 17, 1928, two weeks after he was elected, he was celebrating his victory at a fashionable resort twelve miles south of Mexico City. Bow tied, mustached, and florid faced, he had come to resemble the prosperous chickpea farmer that he had been when the revolution began; only the pinned and empty right sleeve was a reminder of what Villa's troops had taken from him. After a speech, a young artist stood by humbly, hat in hand, waiting to show him his sketches. The artist was actually a Catholic fanatic and member of the Cristero Rebellion, a violent revolt that had erupted in the mid to late twenties after the Mexican government had attempted to forcibly curb the influence of the Catholic Church by closing seminaries and churches, expelling hundreds of foreign-born priests and nuns, and depriving clergy of their civil liberties. When Obregón turned toward the artist, the man pulled a gun from the hat and shot him five times.

SEVERAL YEARS AFTER the raid, Nicolás Fernández's wife and three children changed their last name and moved to El Paso. Fernández loved them dearly but would go no farther north than Ciudad Juárez because he was fearful of being arrested. He slipped across the border to El Paso only once, in 1926, when his wife was dying. Eventually he resumed his military career and became a general in the regular army. He was active in politics, the confidant of Mexico's presidents, and was addressed respectfully as *"mi general"* everywhere he went. "He was a very Victorian, very stoic man," said his grandson, Rudy Herrera, who lives in Washington State.

When Fernández retired from military life, he turned his attention to farming. He grew cotton and raised breeding bulls and horses for the army. He continued to carry a pistol and was chauffeured from place to place in a Dodge station wagon. He never learned to drive, for cars held no interest for him; horses remained his passion. Though he must have suffered physical damage from his years of fighting on horseback, his posture remained ramrod straight, his face wintry and austere, and he continued to shun both alcohol and tobacco. Like Villa, he was concerned for the welfare of the soldiers who had been under his command and often intervened on their behalf with the federal government to make sure they got their benefits. His granddaughter, Gloria Roach, who also lives in Washington State, said he would never talk about the raid or his relationship with Villa because he feared something might happen to his loved ones. "He was very protective of the family," she said.

Fernández became one of the oldest living revolutionary generals in all of Mexico, outliving not only his beloved Pancho Villa, but all the Maderistas, Huertistas, Villistas, and Carrancistas who had fought each other during those turbulent ten years. He died on April 29, 1973, just four months shy of his ninety-ninth birthday.

IN COLUMBUS, the spring windstorms gave way to the summer thunderstorms, which gave way to the bright confetti of migrating birds and finally, the high, vaulted sky of winter. In the dry, shadowed recesses of their stores and homes, the survivors of the raid continued to wrestle with the fears and anxieties that pervaded their dreams and all their waking hours. Susan Moore's pale, lovely face had been reshaped by harrowing trauma. Her mouth was pinched with sadness, her eyebrows stitched together in an anxious, crooked line, and her thick black hair threaded with gray. She hired a young woman named Miss Farrar, who lived with her in the back of the store and helped her run the business. In September of 1918, the bullet lodged in her right leg came to the surface and she went over to the base hospital to have it extracted. An army doctor made two large incisions but was unable to recover the bullet. "So I am now sitting, waiting for the wound to heal, or the bullet to again make its appearance," she said in a letter to New Mexico senator Albert Fall.

Mooreview, the little homestead that she and her husband had built, had become a ruin. The house had been repeatedly vandalized and the windows broken out. She had tried to sell it but no one was interested and whenever she did succeed in renting it out, the tenants never stayed for long. "They said the place was haunted," she told Senator Fall. Periodically rumors wafted across the border about some new raid that Pancho Villa was planning. In March of 1919, the reports had developed such urgency that some residents went out to their garages (still called "auto houses") and turned their cars around so the front ends were facing the street. Mrs. Moore was so frightened that she decided she could not remain in Columbus for another day. She sold off the inventory, leased the store, and moved to the Paso del Norte Hotel in El Paso. Full of despair and anxiety that she seemed unable to shake, she moved from hotel to hotel. She could not sleep, cried easily, and came to the realization that she would never be whole again. From time to time, there was talk in Washington of creating a compensation fund for U.S. citizens who had suffered losses during the Mexican Revolution and Mrs. Moore began writing long letters to Senator Fall, begging for his help:

> *Dear Sir:*
>
> *. . . From the enc. Clipping, you will see I am still suffering from my wounds, and my nerves are all shattered . . . much hard work and suffering are the results of this raid on me — I have broken down my health in the two years and seven months I have come back and endeavored to straighten out the tangles. . . .*
>
> > *Yours Truly,*
> > *(Mrs.) John J. Moore*
> > *(Susan A. Moore)*

> *P.S. Which is the proper way for me to sign my name now?*

Laura Ritchie had also lost everything and did not even have Susan Moore's elegant looks to fall back on. She developed high blood pressure and severe rheumatism and suffered from the same nervous anxiety that Susan Moore had described. But Mrs. Ritchie managed to find happiness again. In 1921, she married a former customs agent named Alvin Ash and moved to El Paso. Her husband got a job on the police force and they built a new life together, going to parties organized by the Masonic Lodge and Eastern Star, playing bingo, and taking short trips.

Rachel Walker also remarried and moved to El Paso. But she and her new husband, Ben Henry, struggled to make ends meet. They resided on an unpaved street in a house that they rented for $12.50 a month. Her husband worked as a part-time street laborer for the city of El Paso, making about $35 to $40 a month. He supplemented his income by mowing lawns and doing other odd jobs and Rachel took in washing and ironing. Her mental health remained fragile, and in the years following the raid, she suffered three more nervous breakdowns.

Milton James also suffered from extreme anxiety. He jumped when he heard noises, couldn't eat or sleep, and complained of overall weakness and numbness in his legs. "In my judgment," wrote one doctor, "the health of Mr. James was materially affected by the nervous shock which he received from seeing his wife shot down and he himself being wounded, and that he suffered intense pain by reason of his wounds; that he will never be a well man, nor restored to his former physical condition." But Milton James defied the glum prediction. Doctors eventually succeeded in extracting the bullet that had been left in his body, and in September of 1922 he married a woman named Merle Corn. Despite his injuries, he was able to have children and largely succeeded in putting the horror behind him.

Ruth Miller, the wife of Charles DeWitt Miller, who was gunned down in front of the Commercial Hotel, also suffered from a "nervous affliction." But she had two small children to support and in the fall of 1916 she secured a teaching job. She then worked as the state's vocational director for a number of years before becoming a district representative for a large insurance company.

Eleanor Dean withdrew from some of the activities she had been involved in, resigning as superintendent of the Methodist church's Sunday school and eventually selling her share of the grocery store to her son, Edwin. On the surface, at least, Eleanor didn't seem to suffer from the anxiety and depression reported by the others. She had already lost two sons and perhaps by the time her husband's death occurred, she had learned to grieve in private.

As for the family members of the young cowboys who were slain on the Palomas ranch, Mamie McKinney was faced with the difficult task of working her homestead claim alone and eventually remarried. The aging father of James O'Neal, the camp cook who was trampled by the horses, was so shocked by his son's murder that his health declined precipitously. "He has suffered and brooded almost constantly," wrote his son. In a terrible oversight, the parents of William Nye Corbett, the other cowboy who was hanged, were never even informed of their son's death and six years later they still had hopes that he might be alive. "Any words would be inadequate to express our appreciation of any information whatever in regards to the whereabouts of our son," wrote Mrs. Edward Corbett in a letter to her congressman.

Beginning in September of 1919 and continuing through March of 1920, Senator Fall held hearings around the country to investigate the losses suffered by U.S. citizens and businesses during the Mexican Revolution. When the Senate panel came to El Paso, many of the Columbus residents were invited to testify. Most believed that Fall would help them. But that hope was cruelly dashed when Fall, who had gone on to serve as secretary of the interior under President Harding, was indicted on felony charges in the Teapot Dome scandal. Fall was accused of secretly leasing out the naval oil reserves in California and Wyoming to two old friends in exchange for "loans" totaling four hundred thousand dollars. He was convicted and served his time in the New Mexico state penitentiary — the same facility that once housed the Villista prisoners.

A special claims commission was established in 1923 to adjudicate claims of U.S. citizens arising from the decade of turmoil during the Mexican Revolution. Many of the Columbus residents who had lost relatives or property during the raid sought compensation.

It was a tedious and time-consuming process in which they had to obtain marriage licenses, birth certificates, diplomas and degrees, and affidavits from numerous witnesses to support their claims. (Rachel Walker suffered yet another nervous collapse and was confined to bed for three days while she was trying to prepare her claim. And the passage of time had not diminished Susan Moore's nervous anxiety and depression. "I am now fifty-three years old and my condition does not improve with age," she wrote.)

In the petitions, attorneys for the U.S. government once again revisited the issue of whether Pancho Villa was a bona fide general or a bandit. A lawyer arguing the case for one of the families came up with a description that was somewhere in between. Pointing to the Mexican government's generous amnesty, he declared that Villa was a true revolutionary who had the "characteristics of a bandit." The claims languished in Washington for nearly fifteen years. Finally in 1938, on the eve of World War II, they were settled and the paltry awards — none higher than fourteen thousand dollars — distributed.

In Columbus, the economy promptly collapsed in 1922 when most of the soldiers were transferred elsewhere. The bank lost its customers, the newspaper closed its doors, and the mayor moved to El Paso. Other residents also departed, abandoning homes and farms and businesses that they had poured their lives into. The Ravel brothers dismantled the new hotel that they had built and shipped the bricks to Albuquerque, where they opened a successful chain of feed stores and nurseries. Other buildings, including the post office, were dismantled and carted off. The electricity stayed on for a few hours every evening and then stopped altogether and the residents returned to their kerosene lamps.

In 1928, much of the town was sold for delinquent taxes and Columbus returned to what it had been in the beginning: a small farming community that once again tried to attract settlers by boasting of its sunshine, fresh underground water, and affordable land. For a time, the trains continued to roll through the town, the clickety-clack of their wheels and their whistles, rising and falling in the night, signaling order and comfort and connection to the greater world. "Oh, those huge, huge steam engines that used to pull the trains through Columbus just seemed like something alive to me," remembered Margaret Perry Epps, who lived in Columbus for many years. "They'd stop there in front of the depot and just kind of chug, chug — just like, just as if they were breathing." The regular passenger service, a train known as the Flying Tortilla, made its last run on March 17, 1958. The population dwindled to roughly 350 residents and the streets grew silent. Some days, it seemed only the wind moved, forever resculpturing the indifferent face of the desert.

Then, in 1959, at the urging of state senator Ike Smalley and others, the state of New Mexico decided to create a fifty-acre park on the west side of the Deming road, which would encompass the ruins of Lieutenant Lucas's shack, the customhouse, and Cootes Hill, behind which the raiders had gathered to finalize plans for their attack. Beautiful cactuses were planted. Campgrounds and walkways were carved out. Relics and photographs of the raid were collected and put on display. When it was finished, state officials named the park after the man who, in the words of Colonel Slocum, had nearly succeeded in wiping the small town of Columbus from the map: Pancho Villa. Several years later, his wife, Luz Corral de Villa, was made an honorary citizen of Columbus — a "Columbusano" — and she donated a field telephone and several other items that had belonged to her late husband to the local museum.

In June of 1960, soon after the park was established, Maud Wright returned to Columbus with her grown son, Johnnie, and several friends. She was seventy-two years old and sun and wind and age had left their marks on her face. Johnnie was now a tall and handsome rancher with a family of his own. Although forty-four years had passed, Maud remembered everything vividly and pointed out where she had held the horses, where she had seen the signal lights, where she had found Susan Moore. Perhaps more than anyone else, Maud had succeeded in putting the past behind her. She had never returned to Mexico to retrieve her husband's body and he is still buried there. In August of 1917, a year and a half after her ordeal, she remarried and moved to the small town of Mountainair, New Mexico, where she grew pinto beans until drought made it almost impossible to grow anything. She had eight more children, five daughters and three sons, one of whom died at birth. Her new husband didn't like her talking about the raid so she rarely mentioned it, and when the claims commission sent out notices to people saying they were eligible for compensation, Maud's notice was returned as undeliverable. But the harrowing experience was always with her and the walled-off darkness somehow illuminated her life. She was never troubled by the craving for material things. It was life itself, the stubborn root of it, always pushing forever upward that she revered and she tried to pass this reverence on to her children. Like Nicolás Fernández, she never lost her passion for horses. She continued to ride, her body swaying like the vanished prairie grass. Perhaps, as her horse picked its way down through a hot arroyo or climbed the crumbling slopes of the Manzano Mountains, she remembered the Mexican soldiers, sitting the choppy trot of their ponies, Mausers slung over their shoulders, and their leader, so different from the others, with his thick neck and heavy shoulders and brilliant eyes, turned inward and focused on the rage that would shape his destiny.

Acknowledgments

A book is often a collaborative effort and I was fortunate to have two wonderful collaborators for this project: Robert Bouilly, a military historian at the U.S. Army Sergeants Major Academy at Fort Bliss, and Richard Dean, the great-grandson of James Dean, one of the Columbus shopkeepers killed in the raid, and the current president of the Columbus Historical Society Museum. We met frequently at Dick and Betty's home in Columbus, New Mexico, poring through records, maps, and old photos. As the ice in our glasses melted and the desert heat filled the office, we invariably adjourned across the border to Palomas for food and entertainment and another look at the towering sculpture of Pancho Villa on horseback. In addition to sharing their knowledge and rare documents and photographs with me, Bob Bouilly and Dick Dean also read the first draft and made many valuable suggestions.

Martha Skinner, the mayor of Columbus, always had encouraging words and room at her beautiful bed and breakfast. Her husband, Javier Lozano, a municipal judge and avid reader of Mexican history, accompanied me on a memorable trip into Chihuahua, where we toured one of the old haciendas belonging to Luis Terrazas, visited several of the still beautiful Mormon towns, and interviewed a grandson of Lem Spilsbury, the flamboyant guide who fought at the battle of Carrizal.

Several descendants of the raid's survivors were also extremely helpful. Johnnie Wright, the little boy left behind when Maud was taken captive, died during the writing of this book. Before he passed away, we spent many afternoons in his Belen, New Mexico, home talking about the heat of that season's green chile crop and his indomitable mother. Among the many things he shared with me were two unpublished accounts of Maud's captivity and photographs of his mother, including one of her on her favorite mount, John the Mule, taken when she was in her eighties. Gloria Roach and Rudy Herrera, the grandchildren of Maud's captor, Nicolás

Fernández, also provided me with photographs, letters, and newspaper clippings about their remarkable grandfather.

I was also fortunate enough to meet several of Herbert Slocum's descendants while researching the book. Lynn Rivard, a lovely woman and great-granddaughter who now lives in California, came to Columbus often, bringing baskets of papers that included letters written by the colonel and newspaper stories that he had clipped and saved. Eileen Slocum, a grand-daughter by marriage, opened her beautiful home in Newport, Rhode Island, to me.

I am indebted to numerous other people as well. Dan Nash reviewed the Spanish portions of the text. Ray Sadler, a professor emeritus at New Mexico State University, read the first draft and offered valuable criticism. Julie Hutchinson, a graphic designer, spent many hours preparing the maps, Adrienne Anderson lent technical assistance, and Loydean Thomas offered encouragement and support. I also received invaluable assistance from librarians and archivists at the New Mexico State Records Center and Archives, the Columbus Historical Society Museum, the Deming Luna Mimbres Museum, the University of Texas at El Paso, the University of New Mexico, the Fray Angélico Chávez Library in Santa Fe, and the Library of Congress and National Archives in Washington, D.C. Espe-cially helpful was the "Gallery of the Open Frontier," the University of Nebraska's online photography collection. The site, which can be found at http://gallery.unl.edu/gallerytour, contains some twenty-three thousand photographs depicting important events in the West and can be searched by key words or names. Hundreds of photos of the Punitive Expedition, scanned in from originals on file at the National Archives, can be viewed at this site.

Jackie Adams, an old family friend in Albuquerque, supplied me with a bed and a hot meal on my long driving trips to and from the border. Lisa Bankoff, my agent, as always, offered encouragement and a sympathetic ear. At Little, Brown, Geoff Shandler did a magnificent job of shaping the manuscript and asking insightful questions. Liz Nagle, who has an extraor-dinary eye for detail, further improved the manuscript, and Melissa Clemence, a copyeditor, did a brilliant job of culling out the errors that remained. As always, my deepest debt of gratitude goes to my husband, Jim, who not only read the book and offered helpful suggestions, but kept our home running while I was away.

CASUALTIES OF THE
COLUMBUS RAID

Military

Private Thomas F. Butler, twenty-eight, was shot five times as he accompanied Lieutenant Castleman's troops into town.

Sergeant Mark A. Dobbs, twenty-four, served under Lieutenant Lucas and was killed while manning one of the machine guns.

Private Fred A. Griffin, nineteen, a young sentry, gave the first warning of the attack.

Private Frank T. Kindvall, twenty-seven, a farrier, was killed while trying to corral the horses.

Sergeant John C. Nievergelt, fifty, a member of the Thirteenth Cavalry band, was shot as he was leading his family to safety.

Corporal Paul Simon, twenty-six, a clarinet player, was killed by a bullet that pierced the walls of his barracks.

Private Jesse P. Taylor, twenty-three, a member of Lieutenant Castleman's troops, died the following day at Fort Bliss.

Corporal Harry Wiswell, thirty-eight, was killed on the international line as the Villistas fled back to Mexico.

Civilians in Columbus

James T. Dean, sixty-one, grocer, was shot and killed when he went downtown to help put out the fires.

Harry A. Davidson, a member of the Texas National Guard, was shot in the head by raiders who circled the town and were attacking from the east.

Harry Hart, thirty-three, a veterinarian, was executed at the Commercial Hotel.

Bessie James, nineteen, was shot twice as she ran from her home with family members toward the Hoover Hotel.

C. C. Miller, druggist, was killed as he exited the Hoover Hotel, keys in hand, to check on his store.

Charles DeWitt Miller, thirty, an engineer and overnight guest at the Commercial Hotel, was killed as he raced toward his car.

John Jay Moore, forty-two, was shot and stabbed at his homestead, Mooreview, as Villistas were fleeing back to Mexico.

William T. Ritchie, fifty-seven, proprietor of the Commercial Hotel, was executed in front of the building.

John Walton Walker, thirty-nine, rancher, was dragged from his wife and executed in front of the Commercial Hotel.

Unidentified hotel guest whose remains were found in the burned rubble of the Commercial Hotel.

Other Civilians

William Nye Corbett, cowboy, was hanged by Villistas on March 7.

Frank Hayden was captured in Mexico with his friend Ed Wright and executed as the Villa column moved north.

Henry Arthur McKinney, ranch foreman of Palomas Land and Cattle Company, was also hanged by Villistas on March 7.

James O'Neal, camp cook, was shot and trampled to death by Mexican soldiers.

Ed Wright, husband of Maud, was captured in Mexico and executed as the Villa column moved north.

Wounded (Military)

Corporal Michael Barmazel suffered a severe neck wound.

Second Lieutenant Clarence C. Benson was shot in the left forearm.

Private Theodore Katzorke was shot in both thighs.

Private James Venner was shot in the right breast and arm.

Captain George Williams's right finger was wounded.

Private John C. Yarborough suffered a severe gunshot wound in the left forearm.

Wounded (Civilians)

Archibald Frost was shot in front of his hardware store and again in his car while he and his wife and child fled toward Deming.

Milton James was shot in both legs and the scrotum as he and his wife ran to the Hoover Hotel.

Susan Moore was shot by raiders who stopped at her homestead.

Susie Parks, telegraph operator, suffered lacerations from flying glass.

CHRONOLOGY

November 20, 1910: The Mexican Revolution begins.

May 10, 1911: Federal forces at Ciudad Juárez surrender, leading to the abdication of Porfirio Díaz.

October 1911: Francisco Madero is elected president.

February 9–22, 1913: Military coup occurs in Mexico City, which results in the assassination of Francisco Madero and the installation of Victoriano Huerta as president.

March 4, 1913: President Woodrow Wilson is sworn into office.

March 6, 1913: Pancho Villa returns to Mexico and rebuilds his army.

April 21, 1914: U.S. troops storm Veracruz.

July 15, 1914: President Huerta resigns and flees to Spain.

August 4, 1914: World War I begins.

September 23, 1914: Villa and Venustiano Carranza split.

April 6–15, 1915: Battles of Celaya.

October 19, 1915: United States recognizes Carranza as de facto Mexican leader.

November 1–3, 1915: Battle of Agua Prieta.

January 10, 1916: Santa Isabel train massacre.

March 1, 1916: Maud Wright captured.

March 9, 1916: Columbus, New Mexico, attacked.

March 15, 1916: Punitive Expedition enters Mexico.

April 12, 1916: Clash at Parral.

April 27, 1916: Scott-Obregón conference begins in El Paso.

June 9, 1916: Juan Sánchez and Francisco Álvarez hung.

June 21, 1916: Battle of Carrizal.

June 30, 1916: Taurino García, Eusevio Rentería, Juan Castillo, and José Rangel hanged.

February 5, 1917: General John Pershing's troops exit Mexico.

April 6, 1917: United States declares war on Germany.

April 10, 1919: Emiliano Zapata assassinated.

May 21, 1920: Carranza assassinated.

April 30, 1921: Acquitted Villistas return to Mexico.

1922: Most troops have departed Columbus.

July 20, 1923: Villa assassinated.

July 17, 1928: President Álvaro Obregón assassinated.

July 15, 1948: Pershing dies.

April 29, 1973: Nicolás Fernández dies.

December 25, 1980: Maud Wright dies.

NOTES

THE NATIONAL ARCHIVES

Many of the people who were in Columbus, New Mexico, at the time of the raid filed claims with a special commission in Washington, D.C., to obtain financial compensation for the loss of property or a loved one. The claim files include sworn affidavits from relatives and eyewitnesses who were in Columbus at the time of the raid and that were written within a few years of when the attack actually occurred. Thus, they appear to be the most reliable source of what happened and I used them extensively to reconstruct the characters and events leading up to and through the raid. The files, which are available at the National Archives and Records Administration in College Park, Maryland, were still wrapped in red ribbon, tied together with string, or clipped with straight pins, and appeared to have been undisturbed for decades. They can be found under the following citation: Record Group (RG) 76, U.S. and Mexican Claims Commissions, Records of the Agency of the United States, Files for U.S. claimants, entry 125. (Hereafter overall collection cited as U.S. and Mexican Claims Commissions, with specific subsets noted.)

Finding these files is a two-step process. First you must go through index cards to find out if someone actually filed a claim. If so, he or she would have been assigned an agency number and that is the number you need in order to have the correct box pulled. Among the claims I looked at were Corbett, No. 5842; Dean, No. 2007; Frost, No. 5995; Griffin, No. 1844; James, No. 2062; Lassiter, No. 1347; Lemmon and Payne, No. 2893; McKinney, No. 1419; Miller, No. 286; Moore, No. 126; O'Neal, No. 2261; Palomas Land and Cattle Company, No. 1850; Ravel, No. 2004; Riggs, No. 3099; Ritchie, No. 1577; Smyser, No. 2277; Walker (filed under name Ben Henry), No. 4094.

Another related and very helpful subset of the U.S. and Mexican Claims Commissions was the Research and Information Section, Information File on Mexican History, which contained a vast quantity of documents on the Mexican Revolution and War Department reports, gathered by commission staffers in preparation for the litigation of the claims. One of these documents was the Punitive Expedition's "Report of Operations of 'General' Francisco Villa since November 1915," which was based in part upon prisoner interrogations and went into great detail about Villa's whereabouts before and after the raid.

At the downtown Washington branch of the National Archives is a third extremely valuable collection, RG 94, Records of the Adjutant General's Office, 1780s–1917, Correspondence Relating to Punitive Expedition, Doc. No. 2377632, which spans a dozen boxes and contains hundreds of military telegrams, letters, and reports related to the raid or expedition. Other record groups that have useful information include:

RG 153, Office of the Judge Advocate General, Mexican Claims Cases Files, 1914–1936, Administrative Correspondence, Entry 48.

RG 159, Inspector General Office, General Correspondence Files, 1914–1917, Entry 25.

RG 165, Records of the War Department General and Special Staffs, Records Relating to History of War Department, 1900–1941, Historical Division Files, Entry 310.

RG 200, Papers of General John J. Pershing, Material Relating to the Punitive Expedition, Entry 17.

RG 395, Records of U.S. Army Overseas Operations and Commands, 1898–1942, WWI, Organizational Records, Punitive Expeditions to Mexico: Entry 1203, War Diaries of Commands and Units of the Mexican Punitive Expedition; Entry 1210, Notebooks and Scrapbooks of Intelligence Officers; Entry 1217, General Correspondence of Intelligence Officer; Entry 1224, Correspondence of Commanding Officer, Camp Dublán; and Entry 1229, Records of Stations in Mexico.

RG 407, Records of the Adjutant General's Office, Mexican Expedition, box 2020.

OTHER ARCHIVES

Robert Bouilly collection, 4021 Esperanza Circle, El Paso, Texas, 79922-1910. Bouilly, a military historian at the U.S. Army Sergeants Major Academy, Fort Bliss, Texas, has a large number of photographs, documents, newspaper clippings, magazine articles, and books relating to the raid, as well as to the Punitive Expedition and the Mexican Revolution. Cited as Bouilly collection.

Columbus Historical Society Museum, Columbus, New Mexico. The museum has numerous photographs and artifacts, as well as some reports about the raid. Cited as Columbus museum.

Richard Dean collection, P.O. Box 203, Columbus, New Mexico 88029-0203. Dean has one of the most complete collections of documents, newspaper clippings, photographs, and other memorabilia related to the raid, as well as bound copies of the *Southwestern* newspaper, which contain many articles on the raid and life on the border. Cited as Dean collection.

Deming Luna Mimbres Museum. Newspaper clippings, photographs, documents related to the prisoners, unpublished academic papers on the raid and Punitive Expedition. Cited as Deming museum.

El Paso Public Library, Border Heritage Center. Vast repository of photographs and books related to the Mexican Revolution, the Columbus raid, and the Punitive Expedition.

Fray Angélico Chávez History Library, Santa Fe, New Mexico. Numerous photos of expedition and raid, as well as letters and diary of Colonel Charles S. Farnsworth, base commander at Columbus.

Library of Congress, Manuscript Division, Washington, D.C. Papers of Hugh Lenox Scott and John Joseph Pershing. Scott's papers are arranged chronologically and by category and most of the material relating to the Mexican Revolution and the Punitive Expedition can be found in his general correspondence, cartons 21 to 27. Pershing's papers are similarly arranged and records relating to the Columbus raid and the Punitive Expedition can be found in his general correspondence, particularly cartons 372 and 373. A card index in the Manuscript Reading Room, arranged alphabetically by the names of correspondents and subjects, is of great assistance to researchers interested in exploring the Pershing papers.

Luna County Clerk's Office. Microfilm records of indictments, arrest warrants, and other miscellaneous information related to the Villista prisoners. Also has bound volumes of *Columbus Courier, Deming Headlight,* and *Deming Graphic.*

New Mexico State Records Center and Archives, Santa Fe, New Mexico. Repository for the only surviving transcript of the trial; photographs and penitentiary information on the prisoners; correspondence of governors; photographs of the raid and of National Guard units stationed on the border.

New Mexico State University, Rio Grande Regional Archives, Las Cruces, New Mexico. Contains photographs of the Mexican Revolution, the Columbus raid, and the Punitive Expedition; papers belonging to Albert Fall and other individuals; and a handwritten map of Columbus prepared by Frank Tompkins.

University of New Mexico, Center for Southwest Research. Contains microfilm copies of Senator Albert Fall's correspondence and other Fall material; papers of Ruth Miller (the wife of Charles DeWitt Miller); clippings and miscellaneous reports on Columbus and the raid itself and on the surrender of Pancho Villa.

University of Texas at El Paso, Special Collections. Contains Haldeen Braddy papers and many other original documents and photographs relating to the Mexican Revolution and early El Paso.

ABBREVIATIONS

AGO: Adjutant General's Office
AMJ: Albuquerque Morning Journal
CC: *Columbus Courier*
DG: *Deming Graphic*
DH: *Deming Headlight*
EPH: *El Paso Herald*
EPMT: *El Paso Morning Times*
EPPL: El Paso Public Library
IGO: Inspector General's Office
JAG: Judge Advocate General
LC: Library of Congress
LCCO: Luna County Clerk's Office
NARA: National Archives and Records Administration
n.d.: no date
NMSRCA: New Mexico State Records Center and Archives
NYT: New York Times
PWW: The Papers of Woodrow Wilson, edited by Arthur Link
RG: Record Group
RMN: Rocky Mountain News
RO: "Report of Operations of 'General' Francisco Villa since November 1915"
SFNM: Santa Fe New Mexican
UNM: University of New Mexico, Center for Southwest Research
UTEP: University of Texas at El Paso

Prologue

1 They were tortured by: The New Mexico State Records Center and Archives has high-quality photographs of the Villistas captured by the U.S. Army, as well as penitentiary records, which contain physical descriptions and background information.

2 Colonel Nicolás Fernández dismounted: Background taken from photographs and author interviews conducted in June and July of 2004 with two grandchildren, Gloria Roach and Rudy Herrera, who both now live in Washington State. There is conflicting information about the last name of the colonel who captured Maud. She gives the name Hernández in her interview with Federal Bureau of

Investigation agent E. B. Stone on March 10, 1916. The *New York Times,* quoting Maud in a March 10, 1916, article, uses the name Servantes. However, I believe that Nicolás Fernández is the correct name for several reasons. First, there was no Nicolás Hernández among the high-ranking Villistas who attacked Columbus. Second, the Punitive Expedition's "Report of Operations of 'General' Francisco Villa since November 1915," which was put together by the army's intelligence officers and is based upon prisoner interviews, notes that Nicolás Fernández was one of Villa's top officers and that he arrived in camp one evening with "the American woman" (p. 7). And finally, Juan Muñoz, one of the highest-ranking prisoners captured by U.S. forces in Mexico, states that he saw Mrs. Wright on the march up to Columbus and that she was "under the escort of Nicolás Fernández" (M. H. Díaz, "Villa Raid on Columbus [Examination of Prisoners]," February 7, 1917, Miller claim).

2 Maud Wright touched: The story of Maud's captivity is taken from multiple interviews conducted by the author between 2002 and 2004 with her son, Johnnie Wright, and two unpublished written reports, which Wright graciously made available to the author. One is an undated account entitled "Maud Wright's Experiences as a Captive of Pancho Villa," as told to Wallace and Verna Crawford, and the second, also undated, is notes in narrative form that were apparently written sometime before 1942 by J. K. Richardson. Articles about her captivity also appeared in numerous newspapers, including the *New York Times,* the *El Paso Herald,* and the *El Paso Morning Times.* E. B. Stone, a federal agent, interviewed her on March 10, 1916, and the following day State Department agent George Carothers interviewed her and sent a report to Secretary of State Robert Lansing. (These latter two documents can be found in the claim of Arthur McKinney.) Some details of Maud's captivity vary, but her basic story, particularly the information surrounding the Columbus attack, is supported in numerous court documents and eyewitness accounts. There have been rumors and speculation that Maud was raped, but there is no evidence whatsoever to suggest that any sort of sexual assault occurred and, in fact, it appears that the soldiers treated her with respect.

3 *Puedo comprar:* I use quotation marks whenever dialogue is taken directly from documents or interviews. Conversations that are not surrounded by quotation marks are an approximation of what was said. While they are also taken from documents or interviews, they are not necessarily the exact words of the individuals.

4 "It was the custom": Affidavit, Martin Lyons, December 12, 1916, NARA, RG 94, AGO, Doc. No. 2377632. This document number is actually a huge collection of documents spanning more than a dozen boxes at the National Archives.

4 Frank Hayden: "Wee Wright Boy Brought Safe and Sound to Pearson," *EPMT,* March 11, 1916.

6 Before the revolution: Friedrich Katz, *The Life and Times of Pancho Villa* (Stanford: Stanford University Press, 1998), 271.

6 "It's not easy": Ibid.

6 "preferred death to": Headquarters Punitive Expedition, Mexico, "Report of Operations of 'General' Francisco Villa since November 1915," July 31, 1916, 23 (hereafter cited as RO). There are several versions of this report in various stages of completion in the National Archives. I am using what appears to be the original and completed version found in U.S. and Mexican Claims Commissions, Research and Information Section, Information File on Mexican History, box 11.

10 "Man of the Hour": Gregory Mason, "The Mexican Man of the Hour," *Outlook,* June 6, 1914, 292.

10 "sinister beauty": Enrique Krauze, *Mexico: Biography of Power, A History of Modern Mexico, 1810–1996* (New York: Harper Perennial, 1997), 318.

1. A Microbe Challenges an Elephant

13 *pan y palo:* Anita Brenner, *The Wind That Swept Mexico* (New York: Harper and Brothers, 1943), 6; Jack Sweetman, *The Landing at Veracruz: 1914* (Annapolis: U.S. Naval Institute, 1968), 9.

13 fifteen million: Krauze, *Mexico,* 31–32.

16 "By 1910": John Mason Hart, *Revolutionary Mexico: The Coming and Process of the Mexican Revolution* (Berkeley and Los Angeles: University of California Press, 1987), 6.

16 90 percent of the Mexican campesino: Ibid., 162.

16 "Practically all of the railways": Senate Committee on Foreign Relations, "Investigation of Mexican Affairs," 2255 (hereafter cited as Fall hearing).

17 torture chamber: Hart, *Revolutionary Mexico,* 64.

17 "I saw this remarkable situation": Fall hearing, 2326.

17 "The attacks were frequently": Hart, *Revolutionary Mexico,* 13, 63–72.

18 "loco Franco": "Mixed Mexico," *Literary Digest,* May 9, 1914, 1133.

18 "microbe's challenge": Alan Knight, *The Mexican Revolution,* vol. 1, *Porfirians, Liberals and Peasants* (Cambridge: Cambridge University Press, 1986), 59.

18 "In a family of clever men": Edith O'Shaughnessy, *A Diplomat's Wife in Mexico* (New York: Harper and Brothers, 1916), 222; John S. D. Eisenhower, *Intervention: The United States and the Mexican Revolution, 1913–1917* (New York: Norton, 1993), 11.

18 "the cream of the enterprising": Knight, *Mexican Revolution,* 1:55.

18 "When Madero first attracted": All of Ambassador Wilson's remarks taken from Fall hearing, 2256–2258.

19 "writing medium": Krauze, *Mexico,* 246.

19 "oppression, slavery and fanaticism": Ibid., 248.

19 "You do not want": Ibid., 255.

20 "His mouth hangs": "Book: Pancho Villa First to Film War," newspaper clipping, *AMJ,* n.d., NMSRCA.

20 "He has the most remarkable": Carlos Husk, "Profile of Pancho Villa," March 5, 1914, Pershing papers, LC.

20 born in 1878: Katz, *Life and Times of Pancho Villa,* 2. At the beginning of his biography, the most definitive to date, Katz points out some of the difficulties in ascertaining what is true and not true about Villa and groups the stories about him into three categories: the white, the black, and epic legends.

20 "My mother wept": Martín Luis Guzmán, *Memoirs of Pancho Villa* (Austin: University of Texas Press, 1965), 3.

21 changed his name: Ibid., 4.

21 hunted coyote: Carlos Husk, "Profile of Pancho Villa," March 5, 1914, Pershing papers, LC.

21 "I believe in God": Mason, "Mexican Man of the Hour," 305.

22 canned asparagus: Jessie Peterson and Thelma Cox Knoles, *Pancho Villa: Intimate Recollections by People Who Knew Him* (New York: Hastings House, 1977), 12.

22 "Yo meuro en": Jim Tuck, *Pancho Villa and John Reed* (Tucson: University of Arizona Press, 1984), 2.

22 "There I learned": Guzmán, *Memoirs of Pancho Villa,* 21.

23 "I thought to myself": Ibid., 38.

23 column of five hundred soldiers: Katz, *Life and Times of Pancho Villa,* 104.

24 "one of the greatest sacrifices": Martín Luis Guzmán, *The Eagle and the Serpent* (New York: Doubleday, 1965), 37, 38.
24 sardines, cookies: Peterson and Knoles, *Pancho Villa*, 30.
24 "It was estimated": Mardee Belding de Wetter, "Revolutionary El Paso: 1910–1917," part 1, *Password*, April 1958, 56.
25 forty men started into Juárez: Paul Hoylen, "The Battle of Juárez: May 8, 1911," *Las Fronteras*, November 1994, 6, EPPL.
25 tin cans and gunpowder: Ibid.
25 drift back to the rear: Herbert Molloy Mason Jr., *The Great Pursuit: Pershing's Expedition to Destroy Pancho Villa* (New York: Konecky, 1970), 30–31; Katz, *Life and Times of Pancho Villa*, 110.
25 "beautiful sight": Leon C. Metz, *Border: The U.S.-Mexico Line* (El Paso: Mangan Books, 1989), 203.
25 Five observers were killed: Hoylen, "Battle of Juárez."
25 reserved seats: Mardee Belding de Wetter, "Revolutionary El Paso: 1910–1917," part 2, *Password*, July 1958, 115.
25 Villa went to a local bakery: Guzmán, *Memoirs of Pancho Villa*, 48.
25 Porfirio Díaz lay suffering: O'Shaughnessy, *Diplomat's Wife*, 222–223.
26 "The revolution never": Fall hearing, 2256.
26 "They were all right until": "Mixed Mexico," 1132.
26 "the Madero government had": Hart, *Revolutionary Mexico*, 260.
27 "bloodthirsty animal": Michael C. Meyer, *Huerta: A Political Portrait* (Lincoln: University of Nebraska Press, 1972), 9.
27 more he drank: O'Shaughnessy, *Diplomat's Wife*, 12.
27 "To even his intimates": "General Huerta Dies at Home in Texas," *NYT*, January 14, 1916.
28 decaying human corpses: Meyer, *Huerta*, 50–51.
28 "My mother had just entered": Brief, Miss Sallie F. Holmes and Percy Griffith, U.S. and Mexican Claims Commissions, Copies of Memorials and Briefs, box 1.
29 "Mr. Wilson, nervous, pale": Meyer, *Huerta*, 53.
29 "*Protestamos lo necessario*": H. R. Rennert, "The Tragic Ten Days from February 9th, 1913, to the Assassination of President Madero, February 22nd, 1913," Monograph No. 12, June 1926, 53, U.S. and Mexican Claims Commissions, Research and Information Section, Information File on Mexican History, box 1.
30 "A wicked despotism": Ibid., 51.
30 deposed leaders: Eisenhower, *Intervention*, 8–9.

2. A Diverting Brute

31 "Puritan of the North": Barbara Tuchman, *The Zimmermann Telegram* (New York: Viking, 1958), 40.
31 Presbyterian minister: The White House, Woodrow Wilson biography, http://www.whitehouse.gov/history/presidents/ww28.htm.
31 "Wicked Puritan with Sorry": O'Shaughnessy, *Diplomat's Wife*, 187.
31 "Our friend Huerta": Sweetman, *Landing at Veracruz*, 15–16; Tuchman, *Zimmermann Telegram*, 40.
32 "I will not recognize": Sweetman, *Landing at Veracruz*, 13.
32 "By hesitating too long": Frank Tompkins, *Chasing Villa: The Last Campaign of the U.S. Cavalry* (Silver City, NM: High-Lonesome Books, 1996), 8.
32 "*Yo soy indio*": "Mixed Mexico," 1136.
33 raw egg and a glass: Ibid.
33 Hennessy and Martell: O'Shaughnessy, *Diplomat's Wife*, 48.
33 "After the bullfight": Ibid., 67.

34 "await the time of their awakening": Sweetman, *Landing at Veracruz,* 21.
34 "watchful waiting": Mason, *Great Pursuit,* 37; Joseph Tumulty, *Woodrow Wilson as I Knew Him* (New York: Doubleday Page, 1921), 144–150.
34 "The present policy of": Tompkins, *Chasing Villa,* 19.
34 150 to 50 million: Ibid., 8.
34 "Settlement by civil war": Ibid., 21.
35 "I think President Wilson": "Letting the Guns into Mexico," *Literary Digest,* February 14, 1914, 303.
35 *el general honorario:* Meyer, *Huerta,* 39.
35 the little drunkard: Tompkins, *Chasing Villa,* 29.
35 "Not once in all the times": Guzmán, *Memoirs of Pancho Villa,* 69.
35 Villa disguised himself: Ibid., 83–84.
35 homing pigeons: Peterson and Knoles, *Pancho Villa,* 186–187.
35 "He had fallen back": James Hopper, "Pancho Villa," *Collier's,* April 29, 1916, 10.
36 two pounds of sugar: Alan Knight, *The Mexican Revolution,* vol. 2, *Counter-Revolution and Reconstruction* (Cambridge: Cambridge University Press, 1986), 35.
36 sign his name: Hopper, "Pancho Villa," 8.
36 *"Mas derecho!":* Gregory Mason, "Campaigning in Coahuila," *Outlook,* June 20, 1914, 394.
37 "Wires cut": John Reed, *Insurgent Mexico* (Westport, CT: Greenwood Press, 1969), 142.
37 "The taking of Juárez": Hugh Scott, "Memorandum for Chief of Staff," May 6, 1914, Scott papers, LC.
38 great sinner: Peterson and Knoles, *Pancho Villa,* xiv.
38 "Civilized people look": Hugh Lenox Scott, *Some Memories of a Soldier* (New York: Century, 1928), 500–501.
38 "It seems to me": Reed, *Insurgent Mexico,* 142–143.
39 "Above all, he is white": V. Blasco Ibanez, "Carranza and the Queer 'Court' He Gathered Around Him in Mexico," *NYT,* May 23, 1920.
39 "Those who have watched": O'Shaughnessy, *Diplomat's Wife,* 19.
39 Hanging on the walls: Reed, *Insurgent Mexico,* 189, 243.
40 "We came fleeing": Guzmán, *Eagle and the Serpent,* 43–44.
41 "By 11 o'clock at night": Fall hearing, 1766.
41 "Whenever war occurs": Tuchman, *Zimmermann Telegram,* 31.

3. Veracruz

43 territory of a sovereign nation: "Our War on Huerta," *Literary Digest,* May 2, 1914, 1030.
43 Mayo demanded: Sweetman, *Landing at Veracruz,* 35–36.
43 "obtain from General Huerta": "Our War on Huerta," 1030; Tompkins, *Chasing Villa,* 23.
43 "it might be construed": "Our War on Huerta," 1031.
43 "impotence, humiliation, and tragedy": Guzmán, *Eagle and the Serpent,* 185.
44 "Veracruz was filthy": Sweetman, *Landing at Veracruz,* 63.
44 "Peering down in the darkness": O'Shaughnessy, *Diplomat's Wife,* 233.
46 Remington Arms Company: Sweetman, *Landing at Veracruz,* 77.
46 126 Mexicans: Ibid., 123.
47 "As far as he was concerned": Tompkins, *Chasing Villa,* 29.
47 "It is Huerta's bull": Clarence Clendenen, *Blood on the Border* (Toronto: Macmillan, 1969), 168.
47 "By precipitating": "Our War on Huerta," 1031.

47 Zapata's rebellion: Krauze, *Mexico,* 274–275.
48 Plan de Ayala: Ibid., 288.
48 "As in the history": Katz, *Life and Times of Pancho Villa,* 433.

4. Downhill

49 private train: Hopper, "Pancho Villa," 45.
49 "Sr. General Zapata, today": Guzmán, *Memoirs of Pancho Villa,* 376–377.
50 "For a half-hour": Katz, *Life and Times of Pancho Villa,* 435.
50 "men who have always slept": Hart, *Revolutionary Mexico,* 302.
51 huge cache of weaponry: Author John Mason Hart argues that this huge weapons cache was extremely important in determining the ultimate victor in the Mexican Revolution and was a deliberate effort by the Wilson administration to ensure that Carranza won.
51 "His ideas, his beliefs": Guzmán, *Eagle and the Serpent,* 70.
51 "I understand you": Ibid., 387.
52 six thousand cavalry: Knight, *Mexican Revolution,* 2:321.
52 "little banty rooster": Mason, *Great Pursuit,* 57.
52 "the prestige of my troops": Knight, *Mexican Revolution,* 2:322.
52 Sitting astride a horse: Description of the two Celaya battles comes mostly from Guzmán, *Memoirs of Pancho Villa,* 453–469.
53 "The city will": Ibid., 455.
53 "We abandoned our dead": Ibid., 459.
53 "Our attacks were thin": Ibid., 466.
53 threw down their guns: Hopper, "Pancho Villa," 45.
54 three thousand of Villa's men: Katz, *Life and Times of Pancho Villa,* 493.
54 captured Villista officers: Ibid.
54 "I feel it to be my duty": "Statement by the President," June 2, 1915, U.S. and Mexican Claims Commissions, Research and Information Section, Information File on Mexican History, box 7.
54 Obregón reached for his pistol: Knight, *Mexican Revolution,* 2:326.
54 "It was a very efficient": George Marvin, "The First Line of Defense in Mexico," *World's Work,* August 1916, 419.
54 "Standing on a rocky": Hopper, "Pancho Villa," 45.
55 "bubbling stew": Knight, *Mexican Revolution,* 2:328.
55 "Oh, yes": Hopper, "Pancho Villa," 45.
55 eighty musicians: Ibid.
55 "And such was the instantaneous": Ibid.
56 "I am thoroughly exhausted": John Middagh, *Frontier Newspaper: The El Paso Times* (El Paso: Texas Western Press, 1958), 176–177.
57 extremely ill from cirrhosis: "General Huerta Slowly Sinking," *EPMT,* January 13, 1916; "To Bury Huerta in Mexico," *NYT,* January 15, 1916; "General Huerta Dies at Home in Texas," *NYT,* January 14, 1916.
57 "The recognition of Carranza": Scott, *Some Memories of a Soldier,* 517.
58 "An enemy weakened": Elías Torres, *Twenty Episodes in the Life and Times of Pancho Villa* (Austin: Encino Press, 1973), 58.
58 "This is the way the United States": "Villa Plans Attack Defying Our Troops," *NYT,* November 1, 1915.
58 "Finally the hour came": Chant Branham, "A Prelude to the Battle of General John J. Pershing vs. General Pancho Villa in the Battle of Douglas, Arizona — Agua Prieta, Mexico — 1916," 6, Dean collection.
58 "Do you expect to take": "Villa's Guns Open on Agua Prieta," *NYT,* November 2, 1915.

59 Villa's artillery pounded: Ibid.; "Villa in Retreat from Agua Prieta," *NYT,* November 4, 1915.
59 "It was horrifying": Branham, "Prelude," 9.
59 376 wounded: Torres, *Twenty Episodes in the Life and Times of Pancho Villa,* 60.
59 emergency medical supplies: "Saddlebag Documents," Braddy papers, UTEP.
59 Villa's army withdrew: "Villa in Retreat from Agua Prieta," *NYT,* November 4, 1915.
60 San Pedro de la Cueva: For a gripping account of Villa's Sonoran campaign and the massacre at San Pedro de la Cueva, see Thomas H. Naylor, "Massacre at San Pedro de la Cueva: The Significance of Pancho Villa's Disastrous Sonora Campaign," *Western Historical Quarterly,* April 1977, 124–150.
60 "they got all the human heaps": Branham, "Prelude," 11.
60 Carranza had cut a deal: For a discussion, see Friedrich Katz's article "Pancho Villa and the Attack on Columbus, New Mexico," *American Historical Review,* February 1978, pp. 101–130.
61 left in a carriage: RO, 5.
61 "We decided not to fire": Letter, Pancho Villa to Emiliano Zapata, January 8, 1916, NARA, RG 94, AGO, Doc. No. 2377632; copy also found in McKinney claim.

5. Tell President Wilson to Save You

62 dwindling cadre of officers: RO, 23–24.
63 *"I hereby order the immediate"*: Ibid., 19.
64 "I want you": Affidavit, Richard Dudley, February 9, 1916, U.S. and Mexican Claims Commissions, Copies of Memorials and Briefs, box 17; "Mining Men Stripped Naked and Ruthlessly Shot Down by Band of Villa Savages," *EPMT,* January 12, 1916. The details of the massacre come from contemporary news reports in the El Paso newspapers or the numerous affidavits relating to the train massacre found in the claim files. Contrary to many reports, there were eighteen — not seventeen — victims. They were: Charles Rea Watson, forty-eight, the general manager; W. D. Pearce, fifty-two, manager of Cusi Mexicana; W. J. Wallace, thirty-two, assistant to the manager; Herman C. Hase, thirty-four, metallurgical engineer and mill superintendent; George Newman, thirty-seven, mining engineer; T. M. Evans, twenty-nine, storekeeper; R. P. McHatton, twenty-four, stenographer; E. L. Robinson, thirty-six, chemist; W. B. Romero, forty-two, bookkeeper; J. P. Coy, thirty-eight, mill shift boss; Charles Wadleigh, about fifty-five, carpenter boss; C. A. Pringle, thirty-eight, another mill shift boss; Maurice Anderson, twenty-five, patio captain; A. H. Couch, forty, mill shift boss and a Canadian resident. Other members of the party included Alec Hall, about fifty-five years old; J. W. Woon, twenty-five and a British citizen; R. H. Simmons, twenty-eight; and Thomas Johnson, a sorting-plant boss who was reported as being between the ages of fifty and sixty-five.
65 "How many others": Affidavit, Thomas B. Holmes, January 22, 1916, U.S. and Mexican Claims Commissions, Copies of Memorials and Briefs, box 17.
65 "He got up, limping,": "The Mexican Murders," *Literary Digest,* January 22, 1916, 157.
66 *"Abajo, gringo!"*: Affidavit, Cesar Sala, January 27, 1916, U.S. and Mexican Claims Commissions, Copies of Memorials and Briefs, box 17.
66 *"Está aqui, traidor?"*: Ibid.
66 "He was cursing": Ibid.
67 "Two soldiers using": Fall hearing, 2759.
67 "The Americans lay": "Mexican Murders," 158.

68 "I lay there perfectly": Affidavit, Thomas Holmes, March 24, 1916, U.S. and Mexican Claims Commissions, Copies of Memorials and Briefs, box 17; "Eyewitnesses Tell of Killing of 18 Americans," *EPH,* January 14, 1916.

68 Villa was far from the scene: RO, 8.

69 several dogs: "Armed Americans Accompany Death Train from Chihuahua," *EPH,* January 14, 1916.

69 "Why did you not send": Affidavit, Frances May Reiser, April 22, 1916, U.S. and Mexican Claims Commissions, Copies of Memorials and Briefs, box 17.

69 riot broke out: "Crowd Starts Riot on Broadway; Officers and Soldiers Stop It," *EPH,* January 14, 1916.

69 Instead of quelling: Paul R. Reyes, "The Santa Isabel Epísode, Jan. 10, 1916: Ethnic Repercussions in El Paso and Ciudad Juárez," *Password,* Summer 1997, 67.

69 "It was estimated that": "Crowd Starts Riot on Broadway," *EPH,* January 14, 1916.

70 Nineteen men were arrested: Ibid.

6. Only One Chance to Die

71 "He intends for you": E. B. Stone, "Villista Activities at Columbus, New Mexico," March 18, 1916, McKinney claim.

71 queen of the Villistas: "Wee Wright Boy Brought Safe and Sound to Pearson," *EPMT,* March 11, 1916.

72 "Untangling the horse": Ibid.

72 "I shall hold none": RO, 11.

73 "I might have let": RO, 11–12.

73 second American hostage: Affidavit, Edward R. Spencer, January 9, 1917, NARA, RG 395, Punitive Expeditions to Mexico, Chief of Staff. Although he is listed as Edward here, Spencer's first name was probably Edwin and appears that way in other official documents and news reports.

73 dreadful fire: By March 17, 1916, the *El Paso Morning Times* was reporting that twenty-five people had died in the blaze.

73 weekly delousing procedure: "Grand Jury Probing Jail Fire; One More Victim Is Identified," *EPH,* March 7, 1916.

74 make "torches": "Woman Held by Villa for Nine Days Tells Her Story," *NYT,* March 10, 1916.

74 five soldiers slipped away: RO, 27.

74 wood stacked on the backs: Katz, *Life and Times of Pancho Villa,* 297.

75 father of two children: RO, Appendix, "Villa's Itinerary from San Geronimo to Columbus and Return," 1.

75 "Cervantes' control over them": RO, 23.

75 investor Edwin Marshall: Hart, *Revolutionary Mexico,* 49.

75 three other bands: D. R. McCormick, an employee of the Palomas ranch, identified José de la Luz Blanco, Inez Salazar, Máximo Castillo, and Pancho Villa as being responsible for the depredations (Fall hearing, 1102–1105).

75 "I know that": Affidavit, Walter P. Birchfield, June 8, 1936, Palomas Land and Cattle Company claim.

76 "To me he was repulsive": Peterson and Knoles, *Pancho Villa,* 210.

76 The McKinneys had deep roots: "McKinney Family in on All History for Last Century," *Southwesterner,* May 1962, 16, Dean collection.

76 letter from General Obregón: Affidavit, Mamie McKinney, April 8, 1916, McKinney claim.

77 "peculiar": Affidavit of Pedro Sotelo, n.d., McKinney claim.

77 "I told him this": Letter, Marcus M. Marshall to Father, March 12, 1916, Scott papers, LC. This letter was also reprinted verbatim in the *New York Times* ("Says Villa Found Border Unguarded," *NYT*, March 19, 1916).

78 "towheaded soldier": Report, E. B. Stone, "Villista Activities," March 19, 1916, McKinney claim.

78 mood in the camp: The description of hangings is taken from Edwin Spencer's account, conveyed in a March 12, 1916, letter from Marcus M. Marshall to his father. Spencer gave numerous interviews to reporters and at least three sworn affidavits. His story changed frequently. One affidavit was given to federal agent E. B. Stone on March 11, 1916; a second on March 20, 1916, to lawyers representing Mamie McKinney; and a third on January 7, 1917, to military authorities. In the March 20, 1916, affidavit, which is found in the microfilm records of Senator Fall at UNM, he states that both men were stripped nude and that he didn't hear McKinney say anything before he was hanged. However, army officials who found McKinney's body stated that he was still wearing most of his clothes. In an interview that appeared on March 15, 1916, in the *El Paso Morning Times,* Spencer says, "McKinney first was pulled off the ground by the rope around his neck, and his hands were left free. After he had been pulled up in the air, the rope was released and quickly pulled again. McKinney threw his hands out and then his body stiffened. Corbett was choked to death before his body was pulled into the air" ("Dramatic Speech by Villa at Palomas Incited His Band of Bandits to Murder Americans," *EPMT,* March 15, 1916).

78 James O'Neal: Affidavit, A. Keeler, June 8, 1916, O'Neal claim.

78 American that Maud saw: J. K. Richardson, interview notes; copy provided to the author by Johnnie Wright.

79 Mexican cowboys: Statement of Sexto Yanez, April 13, 1916, McKinney claim.

80 "A heated discussion": RO, 28–29.

7. Rumors, Warnings, and Telegrams

81 town had been founded: Speech, Richard Dean, "Founder of Columbus: Colonel A. O. Bailey," n.d., Dean collection.

82 James Dean: Dean, "Deans Move to Columbus," 1986–1987, Dean collection.

82 Frost opened a store: Affidavit, Archibald Frost, May 3, 1916, Fall microfilm records, UNM.

83 "He had come": Roy E. Stivison and Della Mavity McDonnell, "When Villa Raided Columbus," *New Mexico Magazine,* December 1950, 37, Dean collection.

83 improve Columbus: Ray Sherdell Page, *Columbus, NM: Queen of the Mimbres Valley,* 1.

83 *Monuments of Egypt:* Ibid., 39.

83 veneer of prosperity: F. Stanley, *The Columbus, New Mexico, Story* (privately printed, 1966), 10–12; available at UNM.

84 home of Captain Rudolph E. Smyser: Craig Smyser, "The Columbus Raid," *Southwest Review,* Winter 1983, 79, Dean collection.

84 "Many an evening": Stivison and McDonnell, "When Villa Raided Columbus," 18.

84 the Commercial Hotel: The information on the hotel, its occupants and guests, comes from statements and exhibits filed by Laura Ritchie; her testimony before the Fall committee; letters and other documents found in the microfilm records of A. B. Fall, UNM; and two accounts of the raid by Blanche Ritchie Dorsey, her youngest daughter. One of Blanche's accounts is an oral-history interview, conducted by Dr. Marinell Ash on May 2, 1981, and available at the NMSRCA. The

other is a firsthand account, "My Personal Story of the 'Pancho Villa' Raid on Columbus, New Mexico, March 9, 1916," *Password,* Fall 1981, 127–131.

84 El Delgado: Antonio R. Garcez, *Ghosts of Las Cruces and Southern New Mexico* (Santa Fe: Red Rabbit Press, 1996), 239.

85 fifty dollars: Affidavit, Sam Ravel, February 10, 1926, Ritchie claim.

85 Curtains framed: "List of Furniture, Household Goods, and Wearing Apparel," May 2, 1916, Ritchie claim.

85 warehouse: Affidavit of Louis Ravel, June 29, 1916, Fall microfilm records, UNM.

85 Rachel and John Walton Walker: Affidavit, Mrs. Ben B. Henry (Rachel Walker), May 6, 1936, Walker claim.

86 attended Ohio State University: Letter, Dr. Thomas Crowl to Richard Dean, August 7, 2000, Dean collection. Crowl did research on Hart and discovered that there was no record of him graduating from Ohio State.

86 "secret agent": "Son of Mr. and Mrs. Maurice Hart of 940 Neil Ave., and Inspector in Employ of U.S. Dept. of Agriculture," *Columbus (Ohio) Evening Dispatch,* March 10, 1916, Bouilly collection; "List of Victims Revised," *NYT,* March 11, 1916.

86 ring: "Colonel's Wife Weeps for the Dead," *EPH,* March 13, 1916.

87 Pereyra had volunteered: "Pereyra Shot Near Columbus," *EPH,* March 16, 1916.

87 Steven Birchfield: Mrs. Ritchie, in her testimony before the Fall committee, identifies the old cattleman as Steven, but Blanche years later refers to him as Billie. He may have been related to Walter Birchfield, who gave a sworn statement in 1936 describing the bandits' depredations on the Palomas ranch.

87 filled with "kibbichers": Arthur Ravel, autobiography, unpublished typescript, July 13, 1966, 3-A, Dean collection.

87 relationship with the Villistas: Historian John Eisenhower, in his book *Intervention,* says on page 50 that Villa had established a business relationship with Ravel early on: "Villa would steal cattle from wealthy landowners in northern Chihuahua and drive them up to Columbus. Ravel would then arrange to sell the stolen livestock in the United States, and Villa would use his share of the proceeds to purchase arms and ammunition." In numerous interviews, however, both Arthur and his brother Louis claimed that Sam did not do business with the Villistas. Nevertheless, the documents make clear that they had some kind of business relationship.

87 "merchandise": Letter, Sam Ravel to A. B. Fall, August 26, 1914, Fall microfilm records, UNM.

88 Figueroa: Statement of Sam Ravel, July 28, 1914, Fall microfilm records, UNM.

88 dashing figure: Dorsey, "My Personal Story," 127.

88 "He still continues": Letter, Sam Ravel to Attorney General, August 26, 1914, Fall microfilm records, UNM.

88 forcibly entering: "Villa Agents Sue Luna County Men for $10,000," *EPH,* October 19, 1914.

89 "Chivalry, courtesy, hospitality": Tompkins, *Chasing Villa,* 191.

89 seventy-five million dollars: Christine Mulhearn, "Women in Philanthropy: Mrs. Russell Sage (Margaret Olivia Slocum), 1828–1918" (case study, John F. Kennedy School of Government, Harvard University, 2000), 3.

89 "improvement of social": "Russell Sage Foundation Records," Rockefeller Archive Center, http://archive.rockefeller.edu/collections/nonrockorgs/sage.php.

89 eight million dollars: "Colonel Slocum Leaves $2,000,000 Estate to Kin and Friends," newspaper clipping, April 8, 1928. Copies of this clipping and numer-

ous other documents and letters involving Herbert Slocum were graciously made available to the author by Slocum's great-granddaughter, Lynn Rivard.

89 gave away more: Letter, Slocum to Son, July 5, 1917, courtesy Lynn Rivard.

89 "Be constant": Letter, Slocum to Teddy, November 8, 1917, courtesy Lynn Rivard.

90 lackluster student: "Official Register of Officers and Cadets," U.S. Military Academy, 1873–1876, courtesy Lynn Rivard.

90 "His rag tail outfit": Letter, H. S. Slocum to Benjamin McAlpin, December 1, 1925, courtesy Lynn Rivard.

90 Slocum participated: "Service in Army," n.d., courtesy Lynn Rivard.

91 "greasers": "Memorandum," in War Department General Staff, "Report of Investigation of Raid on Columbus, New Mexico, by Pancho Francisco Villa and Fellow Bandits," NARA, RG 165, Records of the War Department General Staff, Office of the Chief of Staff, Correspondence, 1907–1917, Report No. 13137, box 138 (hereafter cited as "Investigation of Raid"). Colonel Slocum twice refers to Antonio Múñez as a "half breed" in his interview with Lucien Berry, an inspector with the Punitive Expedition.

91 "The old scoundrel": J. J. Dickinson, "The True Story of the Villa Raid," *Mississippi Valley Magazine*, December 1919, 5, Rivard collection.

91 George Seese: "Seese Is Wedded to Miss Louder," *EPH*, March 18–19, 1916.

91 Zach Cobb: John F. Chalkley, *Zach Lamar Cobb* (El Paso: Texas Western Press, 1998), 12.

92 stumped tirelessly: Ibid., 14–16.

92 second job: Ibid., 8–9.

92 six telegrams: The telegrams can be found in the U.S. Army's "Investigation of Raid," the 1916 volume of *Papers Relating to the Foreign Relations of the United States,* and individual claim files. Only three of the six Cobb telegrams are mentioned in the army report: those sent on March 3, March 6, and March 7. But on March 8, the day before the raid, Cobb sent three more telegrams to the State Department. The noon telegram mentions the fact that Villa had taken the Palomas cowboys hostage (Cobb to Secretary of State, March 8, 1916, McKinney claim). The other two discuss what the Carrancistas were doing to pursue Villa's forces. "If Villa is permitted to remain in the open as at present, without efficient action by the Carranza forces, it will encourage border opposition to Carranza and tend greatly to undermine the de facto government" (*Foreign Relations,* 1916, 479). It's not clear why the army left out Cobb's three March 8 telegrams. The telegrams may not have been received by the War Department, or military officials may have deliberately omitted them because it made them appear even more negligent.

93 "commit some act of violence": Tompkins, *Chasing Villa,* 42.

93 "The General replied": Ibid.

94 received a second report: "Investigation of Raid."

94 "Villa, with 500 men": Ibid.

94 disquieting reports: Ibid.

94 political asylum: Tom Mahoney, "When Villa Raided New Mexico," *American Legion Magazine,* September 20, 1964, 11, EPPL.

94 "supposedly friendly": "Investigation of Raid."

95 "I came on": Affidavit, Juan Favela, June 8, 1916, O'Neal claim.

95 twenty dollars: Tompkins, *Chasing Villa,* 44.

95 sixty-five miles: Ibid.

95 officer's patrol: Ibid.

8. *Villa Is Coming Tonight, for Sure*

97 Milton and Bessie: Affidavit, Myrtle Wright Lassiter, August 14, 1925; affidavit, Fred Gregory, October 31, 1925, James claim.

98 empty the classrooms: Fall hearing, 1606.

98 Susan Moore, a lovely: The background of Susan Moore, the killing of her husband, and the destruction of their home and property come from her affidavit and documents in her claim, as well as her testimony before the Fall committee, and letters, statements, and related documents that she sent to Senator Fall.

100 garter had come loose: Oral-history interview, Blanche Ritchie Dorsey, May 2, 1981, NMSRCA.

100 Charles DeWitt Miller: The details relating to Charles Dewitt Miller's business affairs come from affidavits and background information in the July 3, 1925, claim filed by his wife, Ruth.

101 "That sounds like home": Fall hearing, 1601.

101 "Can they get their": "Army Caught Sleeping in Columbus Raid Despite Numerous Warnings of Villa Attack," *EPT,* May 27, 1956, Braddy papers, UTEP.

102 Ravel's room: Dorsey, "My Personal Story," *Password,* 128.

102 Fonville: Affidavit, J. L. Fonville, March 11, 1916, McKinney claim.

102 "as might be caused": Affidavit, Louis Ravel, June 29, 1916, Fall microfilm records, UNM.

103 spoke Spanish poorly: Tompkins, *Chasing Villa,* 43.

103 "I reported that": Letter, Marcus M. Marshall to Father, March 12, 1916, Scott papers, LC; "Says Villa Found Border Unguarded," *NYT,* March 19, 1916.

103 "too scared": Tompkins, *Chasing Villa,* 44.

103 "I found everyone": "Investigation of Raid."

104 Three sentinels and a watchman: Ibid.

104 Slocum did not increase: Ibid.

104 Carothers had planned: Fall hearing, 1781.

104 Griffin: Affidavit, Ambrose E. Griffin and Leona C. Griffin, July 3, 1926, Griffin claim.

104 Favela: Thelma Cox Knoles and Jessie Peterson, "I Could Have Saved Columbus," *True West,* July–August 1965, 25.

105 "Mr. Moore, being": Affidavit, Susan Moore, December 9, 1925, Moore claim.

105 E. A. Van Camp: Tom Mahoney, "AP Writer Anticipated Villa Raid on Columbus," *Southwesterner,* April 1963, B-10. There is conflicting information about the spelling of the AP correspondent's name. In his book, *Chasing Villa,* Frank Tompkins refers to him as George Seese, but Tom Mahoney uses the last name of Sees and that is also how it's spelled in the congressional report. I am using Seese because a story that appeared in the March 18–19, 1916, edition of the *EPH* also uses that spelling.

106 "were hoping to get in": Letter, Horace Stringfellow Jr. to Haldeen Braddy, August 11, 1966, Braddy papers, UTEP.

106 "A cluster of": Tompkins, *Chasing Villa,* 50.

106 Machine Gun Troop: Ibid., 51.

107 Castleman returned: "The Columbus Raid," *U.S. Cavalry Journal,* April 1917, 490–496.

9. *The Fiddler Plays*

108 Juan Alarconcon: Arthur Jack Evans, the oldest living survivor of the raid, said his house was surrounded by Villistas and that a man next to Villa was playing a violin during the fighting ("March 9: Big Day in history," *DG,* March 8, 1976, 4).

The fiddler is also mentioned in Tom Mahoney's article, "AP Writer Anticipated Villa Raid on Columbus," B9–10.

110   approached her with a rifle: J. K. Richardson, interview notes, courtesy Johnnie Wright.

110   "He told the men": "Dramatic Speech by Villa at Palomas Incited His Band of Bandits to Murder Americans," *EPMT*, March 15, 1916. Spencer's account conflicts with those of a number of prisoners who claimed that they didn't even know they were on U.S. soil.

110   column began marching: RO, 29.

110   Two small groups: "Former Member of Villa's Bodyguard Settles Old Argument; 364 Bandits Raided Columbus," *EPH*, February 21, 1962, Braddy papers, UTEP.

110   deep arroyo: RO, 29. Maud's version of the Villistas' approach differs somewhat from the Punitive Expedition's RO. She maintains that the column, upon reaching the border, turned east, crossed the Deming–Palomas road, and proceeded to cut the fences. Then the soldiers turned west again, making a large half circle that eventually put them on the flat plain behind Cootes Hill. S. H. McCullough, a section foreman for the El Paso and Southwestern Railroad, partially confirmed Maud's version, testifying several years later that the right-of-way fence on both sides of the railroad tracks was cut in three places for a distance of three miles east of Columbus (Fall hearing, 1584–1585).

111   "We were finally": J. K. Richardson, interview notes, courtesy Johnnie Wright.

111   marksmanship training: Mason, "Mexican Man of the Hour," 302.

111   three-pronged assault: RO, 29–30. The Villista attack was tactically more complex than that described by Colonel Slocum in his official report or by Colonel Frank Tompkins, who was in Columbus at the time and later wrote a book about the raid and subsequent expedition. Neither says anything about the raiders descending on the town from the north, but several newspaper accounts published immediately following the raid mention it ("Villa Attacked Columbus by Circling the Town," *EPH*, March 11).

111   dismount and advance: RO, 30–31.

112   "My God, we are": Statement, Mary Slocum, Scott papers, box 22, LC. Although the document is not signed, the contents indicate that it could only be Mrs. Slocum's statement. It is dated February 14, 1916, which is undoubtedly a typographic error, and was probably March 14, 1916.

112   Lucas was awakened: Tompkins, *Chasing Villa*, 51.

112   "Griffin managed to squeeze: "Columbus Raid," 492; James Hopper, "What Happened at Columbus," *Collier's*, April 15, 1916, 11; Tompkins, *Chasing Villa*, 49.

112   killing two: Tompkins, *Chasing Villa*, 49, 51; From the Commanding Officer to the Commanding General, "Border Conditions," March 11, 1916, 1, NARA, RG 159, IGO, General Correspondence Files, 1914–1917, box 17. This is Slocum's official report and is part of the inspector general's investigation into the raid (hereafter cited as IGO Report).

112   poorest shots: Tompkins, *Chasing Villa*, 52.

113   Lucas fed the clip: Letter, John Lucas to Commanding Officer, May 9, 1916, NARA, RG 94, AGO, Doc. No. 2377632.

113   soldiers had recently been drilled: Letter, Horace Stringfellow Jr. to Haldeen Braddy, August 11, 1966, Braddy papers, UTEP.

113   "On account of": Tompkins, *Chasing Villa*, 50.

113   "We made about": Ibid., 50.

114   regiment's officers: Colonel Slocum and his adjutant, Captain Williams, lived in the northeast quadrant. Tompkins, Smyser, and McCain lived in the northwest quadrant on the other side of the dirt road that led into Mexico. A sketch done by

Frank Tompkins after the raid shows the northwest sector to be heavily infiltrated with Villistas (Frank Tompkins, n.d., New Mexico State University, Rio Grande Regional Archives).

114 "The bullets were falling": Statement, Mary Slocum, Scott papers, box 22, LC.

114 "Our greatest fear": Letter, Alice Tompkins to Mother and Father, March 10, 1916, Columbus museum; Tompkins, *Chasing Villa,* 55.

114 outhouse: Frank Tompkins says in his book that the Smysers hid in an outhouse; Mrs. Smyser states in her claim that it was a lean-to, and her son, Craig, maintains it was the stable.

114 "We sat up": "El Pasoan Sees Davidson Shot," *EPH,* March 11, 1916.

115 "When we picked": U.S. Army Sergeants Major Academy, "Staff Ride Walkbook for Pancho Villa's Raid on Columbus, New Mexico, 8–9 March 1916," 2004, 21, Bouilly collection.

115 "brains out": Tompkins, *Chasing Villa,* 21.

115 don the shirts: "Story of Villa Massacre Told in Letter to Gazette Editor," *Wray County Gazette,* Colorado, n.d., Braddy papers, UTEP. This is taken from a letter written by Frank Dow, a passenger-train conductor for the El Paso and Southwestern Railroad, who spent six hours in Columbus on the day of the attack.

115 buggy: Affidavit, Mrs. Rudolph Smyser, October 30, 1925, Smyser claim.

115 "very fine quality" gray trousers: Base Commander to Commanding General Expeditionary Force, "Property Lost in Columbus Raid," May 29, 1916, NARA, RG 395, Punitive Expeditions to Mexico, Correspondence of Commanding Officer.

116 "We did not go": Alberto Calzadíaz Barrera, "El Ataque a Columbus," *Impacto,* January 11, 1961, 34, EPPL. Juan Muñoz, documents show, later served as an informant for the U.S. military authorities and everything he said should be viewed with skepticism.

116 *"No me maten!":* Arthur Ravel, autobiography, unpublished typescript, July 13, 1966, 5, Dean collection.

116 intruders smashed: Affidavit, Louis Ravel, June 29, 1916, Fall microfilm records, UNM.

116 Cervantes: Barrera, "El Ataque a Columbus," 31.

116 *"No molesten":* Affidavit, Arthur Ravel, June 16, 1916, Fall microfilm records, UNM.

116 invaders hammered: The details of the killings at the Commercial Hotel are taken primarily from the congressional testimony and sworn affidavits of Rachel Walker, Laura Ritchie, and Arthur Ravel, as well as those of friends and relatives of Charles DeWitt Miller, and Blanche Ritchie's written account. Their stories differ significantly from the one that several former Villistas gave to Mexican author Alberto Calzadíaz Barrera, which was published in Mexico City's *Impacto* magazine in 1961. According to those interviews, the Villistas went to the hotel to find Sam Ravel. The American men, they insisted, were killed only after they fired upon and killed the Mexican troops. But Mrs. Ritchie testified that, although the men in the hotel considered shooting at the Villistas, they discarded the idea because they were afraid the hotel would be set on fire.

117 Ritchie tried: Fall hearing, 1600.

117 Pereyra stepped: "Mexican Gives His Life for American Women," *RMN,* March 18, 1916.

117 *No disparen:* Ibid.

117 *Cállate!:* Fall hearing, 1600.

117 William Ritchie gave: Affidavit, Laura Ritchie, May 2, 1916, Ritchie claim.

118 pink dress: Dorsey, "My Personal Story," 129.

118   Sam Ravel: Fall hearing, 1601.

118   male guests: The order of the executions is taken from a February 19, 1925, affidavit that Laura Ritchie made in support of Ruth Miller, Miller claim.

118   watch the snow fall: Letters, Ruth Coleman Miller, UNM.

118   *"Éste es gringo"*: Affidavit, Arthur Ravel, February 23, 1925, Miller claim.

119   "They have killed": Affidavit, Mrs. Ben B. Henry, May 6, 1936; affidavit, Mrs. Myrtle Garner, April 30, 1936, Walker claim.

119   Greeley's advice: Dorsey, "My Personal Story," 127.

119   "I cannot go": Fall hearing, 1601.

120   *"No lo matamos"*: Affidavit, Arthur Ravel, February 23, 1925, Miller claim.

120   "He said, 'Humph'": "Boy Won Gamble with Death in Columbus Raid," *Chicago Tribune*, June 13, 1919; Haldeen Braddy, *Cock of the Walk: The Legend of Pancho Villa* (Albuquerque: University of New Mexico Press, 1955), 131.

120   They flung open the door: Affidavit, Milton James, September 12, 1925, James claim.

121   "Why they did not": Letter, Sarah Hoover to E. A. Scammon, March 12, 1916, reprinted in Page, *Columbus, NM*, 47–50.

121   Bessie's skirts: Affidavit, W. C. Hoover, August 4, 1925; affidavit, Dr. T. H. Dabney, August 5, 1925, James claim.

121   "I am safe": Letter, Eleanor Dean to Son, in Richard A. Dean, "Letters to Relatives Written After the Raid, 1986–1987" (privately printed, n.d.), Dean collection. According to some accounts, Bessie James was pregnant at the time of her death. But the claim that Milton James filed several years later makes no mention of that fact even though such a disclosure might have increased the amount of compensation he was seeking. See Richard Dean, "Dean Family Faces Death in 1916 Pancho Villa Raid," *Desert Winds Magazine*, January 1991, 12–13.

121   "They shot him": Sarah Hoover letter reprinted in Page, *Columbus, NM*, 48.

121   "A bugler": "Telephone Central Describes Pancho Villa in Attack," *EPMT*, March 13, 1916.

122   Villa was mounted: Since the day of the raid, Villa's whereabouts and activities have been hotly debated. Maud told newspaper reporters and federal agents that Villa was mounted on a horse and participated in the raid. E. B. Stone, the Federal Bureau of Investigation agent, writes, "Mrs. Wright personally saw Villa's orderly saddle his horse and saw Villa mount with a few of his principal officers and lead the attack in person on the garrison and town of Columbus" (E. B. Stone, "Villista Activities at Columbus, New Mexico," March 18, 1916, McKinney claim). Bunk Spencer, the other hostage, partially confirms Maud's statement in a January 9, 1917, affidavit in which he states that the man who identified himself as Villa "did not remain with the horses while the attack was being made" (affidavit, E. R. Spencer, January 9, 1917, NARA, RG 395, Punitive Expeditions to Mexico, Chief of Staff). In the army's RO, Villa is quoted as saying that he would remain with reserve troops (RO, 30). But an appendix of the same report states, ". . . Villa with bodyguard came up beside us at a distance of thirty yards and waited there until after the fight. He and his guard remained mounted and entered the fight the same way . . ." (RO, Appendix, 8). A Justice Department agent named M. H. Díaz questioned twenty-one prisoners, on February 17, 1917, who had been captured by General Pershing's troops in Mexico and they were specifically asked where Villa was during the Columbus attack. Their answers varied greatly, which is not surprising given the fact that hundreds of men were milling about in the darkness. Some said they saw him in the rear with the horses, some saw him in the front, while others said they saw him only on the retreat, and a few said they didn't see him at all. (M. H. Díaz, "Villa Raid on Columbus [Examination of

Prisoners]," February 7, 1917, Miller claim.) George Carothers, in his testimony before the Fall committee, said that he satisfied himself that Villa had gotten as far as the "gate" (Fall hearing, 1781). And finally, in 1962, a man who was a colonel in Villa's army and participated in the raid said that Villa remained in the rear, in a deep ditch that paralleled the Deming road ("Former Member of Villa's Bodyguard Settles Old Argument; 364 Bandits Raided Columbus," *EPH*, February 21, 1962).

122 Mrs. Parks grabbed: Toby Smith, "A Brave Woman in a Border Town," *Impact Magazine, AJ*, July 28, 1981, 9.

122 Archibald Frost and his wife: The Frost story comes from multiple sources, including Fall hearing, 1614–1616; affidavit of Frost dated May 3, 1916, Fall microfilm records, UNM; an August 10, 1926, affidavit of Frost, Dean collection; and Hopper, "What Happened at Columbus," 12, 32.

122 "We had to pass": Affidavit, Archibald Douglass Frost, August 10, 1926, Dean collection.

123 "I whispered": Fall hearing, 1614–1616.

123 "Usually I give her": Hopper, "What Happened at Columbus," 32.

123 "This Mexican soldier": Affidavit, Archibald Douglass Frost, August 10, 1926, Dean collection.

123 son was catapulted: Author interview, James Dean, September 24, 2002.

123 Multiple bullets: Fall hearing, 1614–1616.

124 mock battle: Interview, Ed Carson, Columbus, NM, May 19, 1983, NMSRCA.

124 "If you have good": Letter, Eleanor to Sons, n.d., in Dean, "Letters to Relatives Written after the Raid," Dean collection. The story of the Dean family comes from the testimony of Edwin Dean, Fall hearing, 1612–1614; the claim and related affidavits filed by Eleanor Dean; letters written by Eleanor and other family members; and numerous author interviews with Richard Dean.

124 "Mr. Dean, you": Interview, Ed Carson, Columbus, NM, May 19, 1983, NMSRCA.

124 "I knew there would": Letter, Eleanor to Sons, n.d., in Dean, "Letters to Relatives Written after the Raid," Dean collection.

124 "I wondered why": Fall hearing, 1603.

124 "The hotel was afire": Fall hearing, 1602.

125 "So it was Edna": Dorsey, "My Personal Story," 130.

125 "remembered a man holding her": Affidavit, Mrs. Ben B. Henry (Rachel Walker), May 6, 1936, Walker claim.

125 "Any more than that": Fall hearing, 1603.

125 Simon: William Adkins, "The Story of Pancho Villa at Columbus, New Mexico," *Family Tree*, n.d., probably sometime in fall of 1969, book 2, 52.

126 Nievergelt: "Mexican Won't Halt, Is Shot by Sentry," *EPH*, March 11, 1916. A band member, William Adkins, however, says that Nievergelt was killed in their quarters along with fellow musician Paul Simon. William Adkins, "The Story of Pancho Villa at Columbus, New Mexico," *Family Tree*, book 2, 52.

126 Dobbs: Tompkins, *Chasing Villa*, 53.

126 skirmish line: Letter, Perrow Moseley to Family, March 13, 1916, reprinted in *Southwesterner*, April 1963, NMSRCA and Dean collection.

126 "about dawn": Robert S. Thomas and Inez V. Allen, "The Mexican Punitive Expedition under Brigadier General John J. Pershing, United States Army, 1916–17" (Washington, DC, 1954), I-15.

126 "that the town": Affidavit, Louis Ravel, June 20, 1916, Fall microfilm records, UNM.

126 "Everything is all": Fall hearing, 1614.

127 "Colonel Slocum had": Letter, Horace Stringfellow Jr. to Haldeen Braddy, August 11, 1966, Braddy papers, UTEP. The *New York Times* also reported that Slocum's gun had been damaged. "Colonel Slocum's revolver was shot out of his hand as he emerged from his quarters. The bullet dented the Colonel's weapon, making it useless" ("Night Attack on Border," *NYT,* March 10, 1916).

127 hold their fire: Letter, Herbert J. Slocum to Adjutant General, "Recommendation for Medal of Honor," May 24, 1916, NARA, RG 200, Papers of General John J. Pershing, Material Relating to the Punitive Expedition, box 1.

127 "Not having field glasses": Letter, Horace Stringfellow Jr. to Haldeen Braddy, August 11, 1966, Braddy papers, UTEP.

127 "They began to bring": Maud's quotes about the retreat of the Villistas are taken from J. K. Richardson's unpublished notes and the unpublished story "Maude Wright's Experiences as a Captive of Pancho Villa," as told to Wallace and Verna Crawford, provided to the author by Johnnie Wright.

127 McCain's party: Robert Bruce Johnson, "The Punitive Expedition: A Military, Diplomatic and Political History of Pershing's Chase after Pancho Villa, 1916–1917" (dissertation, University of Southern California, June 1964); 58; Tompkins, *Chasing Villa,* 59; Hopper, "What Happened at Columbus," 12.

128 bludgeoned the Mexican: Tompkins, *Chasing Villa,* 59.

128 "As I was sitting": "Archbandit López Bares Details of Villista Outrages," *EPMT,* May 27, 1916.

128 *"Por buen rato pelearon":* Calzadíaz Barrera, "El Ataque a Columbus," 32.

129 "Wake up": Susan Moore's account of the murder of her husband and her own injuries taken from her December 9, 1925, claim or her congressional testimony before the Fall committee (Fall hearing, 956–967). Except for some small details, the statements are almost identical.

130 Cervantes and *los namiquipenses:* Calzadíaz Barrera, "El Ataque a Columbus," 34.

131 *Sabe usted dónde:* Ibid. In the article, Juan Muñoz alleges that Mr. Moore fired three shots at Candelario Cervantes. But the allegation is not supported in the myriad accounts that Susan Moore gave to congressional investigators or in her sworn affidavit or letters.

131 "They raised their": In Calzadíaz Barrera's version of the attack, a man named Gabino Sandoval killed Mr. Moore. Sandoval also allegedly helped the Carrancistas capture Villa's beloved and incorruptible general, Felipe Ángeles.

133 man named Gardner: Affidavit, Milton James, September 12, 1925, James claim.

133 Lundy lifted: Affidavit, John E. Lundy, July 15, 1925, James claim.

133 eighteen U.S. civilians and soldiers: There has been a lot of confusion about the number of civilians and soldiers killed in the attack, even among the townspeople themselves. For example, a memorial list of casualties appearing in the *Columbus Courier* on March 9, 1917, includes only seventeen people. Part of the confusion stems from the unidentified body found in the rubble of the Commercial Hotel. Also, many people neglect to count Private Jesse Taylor among the military casualties. He was taken to a hospital at Fort Bliss and died the following day. See appendix for complete list.

133 Tompkins and his men: The details of the chase taken from Tompkins, *Chasing Villa,* 55–57; "The Cavalry Fight at Columbus," *U.S. Cavalry Journal,* July 1916, 183–185; and the official report of the raid written by Colonel Slocum to General Funston, entitled "Border Conditions," found in multiple collections, including the IGO Report.

133 Wiswell: "List of Victims Revised," *NYT,* March 11, 1916. There is a lot of confusion about what the U.S. troops stationed at the Border Gate and at various

points along the border did when the raid occurred. Similarly, there is much confusion about where, exactly, Corporal Wiswell was killed and even the spelling of
his name. The official army casualty list and a 1918 proclamation by the Columbus mayor use the name Wisewell, but I am using the more common spelling and
the one that appears beside his picture in his hometown newspaper. One early
newspaper account has Wiswell killed as he carried a message to the Border Gate
("Mexican Won't Halt; Is Shot by Sentry," *EPH*, March 11, 1916), but Lieutenant Clarence Benson, who was interviewed by the El Paso papers the following
day, said Wiswell was killed when the U.S. soldiers fired upon the Villistas as they
galloped through a hole in the fence ("Cunning of Villa Told by Officer," *EPT*,
March 10, 1916; "Lieutenant Who Helped Corner Villa Is at Post," *EPH*, March
10, 1916, 2, Bouilly collection).

134 five and fifteen miles: Tompkins says he went fifteen miles into Mexico (Tompkins, *Chasing Villa*, 56), but Colonel Slocum, in his early telegrams, noted that
the U.S. soldiers went five miles.
134 seventy-five to one hundred: Tompkins, *Chasing Villa*, 56.
134 sixty-seven Villistas: "Border Conditions," IGO Report.
135 gladiators: Francisco Villa, "Manifesto to the Nation," October 1916, NARA,
RG 94, AGO, Doc. No. 2212358; Mason, *Great Pursuit*, 248–252.
135 two boys: " 'Buck' Chadborn of Deming Recalls Pancho Villa's Raid on Columbus," newspaper clipping, n.d., EPPL.
135 sixty men were missing: Villista casualties at Columbus are tabulated in RO,
Appendix B, "Statement of Casualties among Villistas Who Participated in the
Attack on Columbus, New Mexico, March 9, 1916," 3.
135 "It has come to this": RO, 34.

10. Very Unnatural Deaths

136 Ritchie sleepwalked: Stivison and McDonnell, "When Villa Raided Columbus," 37.
136 "few pitiful remains": Affidavit, Mrs. Ben B. Henry (Rachel Walker), May 6,
1936, Walker claim.
137 "badly perverted": Affidavit, E. C. De Moss, May 2, 1936, Walker claim.
137 father's body: Fall hearing, 1614.
137 "Mama they got Papa": Dean, "Letters to Relatives Written after the Raid,"
Dean collection.
137 "People were crying": Letter, Ozella Stanfield to Lizzie, March 24, 1916, in Dean,
"Letters to Relatives Written after the Raid," Dean collection.
137 "Now I know": "Colonel's Wife Weeps for the Dead," *EPH*, March 13, 1916.
138 crucifixes: Stivison and McDonnell, "When Villa Raided Columbus," 37.
138 "I passed": Letter, Alice Tompkins to Father and Mother, March 10, 1916,
Columbus museum.
138 "When we came": Statement, Mary Slocum, February [actually March] 14, 1916,
Scott papers, box 22, LC.
138 separate investigations: Letter, George Carothers to Secretary of State, March 11,
1916, McKinney claim. In an interview with a *New York Times* reporter at about
the same time, Maud said Villa led the attack on Columbus with fifteen hundred
men and that she was told that he actually had three thousand soldiers in the column. In her interview with Bureau of Investigation agent E. B. Stone, she states
that ". . . on one occasion she counted 3,200 men and another occasion 2,700
men." But the RO puts the number of raiders at 485, a figure that is much lower
than what Maud reported and the number that most historians believe now is
most accurate. The discrepancy is hard to explain; Maud was an experienced
ranchwoman, but she was exhausted and severely traumatized by the experience

and her powers of observation may have been affected. Colonel Slocum uses the large numbers in his early telegrams to the War Department. For example, on March 9, he writes that Villa invaded Columbus with five hundred to one thousand men (telegram, Funston to Adjutant General, March 9, 1916, NARA, RG 94, AGO, Doc. No. 2377632). The following day, he reports, "Am reliably informed it was Villa that made the attack with fifteen hundred men, leaving about one thousand on river east of Boca Grande" (telegram, Funston to Adjutant General, March 10, 1916, NARA, RG 94, AGO, Doc. No. 2377632). Although Slocum doesn't disclose where he got those numbers, the source may well have been Maud. Historian Ray Sadler, in an interview with the author in 2005, maintained that these overinflated numbers had important ramifications; the army felt that it could not pursue Villa until it had amassed an adequate force and the delay led to Villa's ultimate escape.

138 gave her lotion: Wallace and Verna Crawford, "Maud Wright's Experiences"; copy provided to the author by Johnnie Wright.

138 Lemmon: The discovery of the diary and its contents is described in a series of affidavits from Roy Johnson, Leo Lemmon, and S. H. McCullough, and the extract of a report written by E. B. Stone, and found in U.S. and Mexican Claims Commissions, Copies of Memorials and Briefs, box 17. The diary entries are short and consist mainly of brief notations stating where the troops were on various days.

139 portmanteau: The receipts for various expenditures were kept by Villa's secretary and were in the large portmanteau found on the streets of Columbus. They are in the National Archives under RG 94, AGO, Doc. No. 2377632.

139 "I attach importance": Letter, George Carothers to Secretary of State, March 11, 1916, McKinney claim.

140 "He is crazy": Letter, George Carothers to General Scott, March 13, 1916, Scott papers, LC.

140 Seven Villistas: E. B. Stone, "Villista Activities: Attack on Columbus," March 19, 1916, NARA, RG 94, AGO, No. 2377632. This is Stone's most complete report. Portions of the report are found in numerous other places, including many of the claim files of the townspeople. According to this report, the seven captured Villistas were Jesús Paez, Juan Sánchez, Antonio Miranda, Elías Meras, Leno Ruiz, Lieutenant Isabel Chávez, and Captain Pablo García. Of these seven raiders, only Jesús Paez and Juan Sánchez, who had a minor flesh wound, survived. In a later list prepared by the Luna County district attorney's office, Isabel Chávez is deleted from this list and a Y. Saville appears. It's possible that they were one and the same person (memorandum, "Report of Villistas Brought to Deming, New Mexico, March 15th, 1916, after Raid, March 9th, 1916," NARA, RG 395, Punitive Expeditions to Mexico, Chief of Staff, box 2-E).

140 Jesús Paez: Jesús's story varied greatly and should be viewed with caution. One of the captured Villistas, Francisco Solís, for example, years later said that Jesús was actually a resident of Columbus and shot by the Americans as he fled his house (Calzadíaz Barrera, "El Ataque a Columbus," 33). When Jesús testified before Albert Fall's Senate committee, he said that his father had been a boss at the Quintas Carolinas ranch, owned by Luis Terrazas, and that he had joined Villa's men because Carrancista soldiers wanted to kill him. However, when the boy was recuperating from his wound in the hospital, he told his interpreter that Villa and his men appeared at his father's ranch one morning and ordered the older man to accompany them.

140 boy as a witness: Telegram, Stone to Barnes, March 10, 1916, included in Stone's report on Columbus raid.

141 "Only one Mexican store": "Brief Account of the Villa Attack," CC, March 24, 1916.

141 "Local old-timers": William E. Cobb, "An American Woman for Each" (Columbus Historical Society, n.d.), Braddy papers, UTEP.

141 martial law: E. B. Stone, "Villista Activities: Attack on Columbus," March 19, 1916, NARA, RG 94, AGO, Doc. No. 2377632.

142 "have not been heard from": Ibid. According to Stone, those rounded up included Pablo Sánchez; Tomás Gardea; two brothers, José H. and Jesús Casillos; Florencio and Carlo Pacheco, father and son; Victoriano Lloya; Hidado Vavel; Jacinto Flores; Doroteo Acevedo; and José María Rueda.

142 Marcus immediately rounded up: Letter, Marcus M. Marshall to Father, March 12, 1916, Scott papers, LC.

142 "We counted eleven": Letter, Marcus M. Marshall to Father, March 12, 1916, Scott papers, LC.

143 "The past two nights": Ibid.

143 "Most of our Mexicans": Perrow G. Mosely to Sister and All, March 13, 1916, *Southwesterner,* April 1963, B9–10, NMSRCA and Dean collection.

143 "All Mexicans": "Brief Account of the Villa Attack," CC, March 24, 1916.

143 "All peaceful as": This telegram was sent to General Funston at 2:00 p.m. on March 9, but due to a mix-up in the telegraph office, did not reach him until after midnight. The telegrams can be found in NARA, RG 94, AGO, Doc. No. 2377632 and Doc. No. 2212358. Several also reprinted in *PWW,* 37:281.

144 "Just get out": Peterson and Knoles, *Pancho Villa,* 220; Knoles and Peterson, "I Could Have Saved Columbus," 56. In the microfilm records of A. B. Fall at UNM there is also a document entitled "List of Disinterested Witnesses in re the Columbus Raid." Next to Favela's name is the handwritten note: "Juan Favela notified Col. Slocum & his adjutant about the approaching raid and was told to 'mind his business.'"

144 "Down here": Statement, Mary Slocum, February [actually March] 14, 1916, Scott papers, box 22, LC.

144 his son, Ted: Letter, Ted to General Scott, March 10, 1916, Scott papers, LC.

144 "The blame for the": Letter, Marshall Marcus to Father, March 12, 1916, Scott papers, LC.

145 "On the face": Letter, General Funston to General Scott, March 24, 1916, Scott papers, LC.

145 "You have seen from the papers": "Extract from Letter Received by Me," in "Investigation of Raid." A copy also available in Scott papers, LC.

145 fifty-thousand-dollar reward: "Funston Wants to Use Railroad," NYT, March 18, 1916.

146 order an investigation: Scott, *Some Memories of a Soldier,* 521.

146 "Hints of carelessness": "Scandal to Be Aired in Columbus Probe," RMN, March 30, 1916.

146 "nerve specialist": Letter, Laura Ritchie to A. B. Fall, February 9, 1920, Fall microfilm records, UNM.

146 "invasion, insurrection": Affidavit, Laura Holton Ritchie, May 1916, Ritchie claim. Also letter and policy documents from Laura Ritchie to Connecticut Fire Insurance Co., April 4, 1916, in Fall microfilm records, UNM.

146 "I cannot believe": Letter, Laura Ritchie to Connecticut Fire Insurance Co., April 4, 1916, in Fall microfilm records, UNM.

147 "I was badly": Affidavit, Susan Moore, December 9, 1925, Moore claim.

147 "I just lived": Testimony, Susan Moore, December 22, 1919, Fall microfilm records, UNM.

147 "Since his injuries": Affidavit, Milton James, September 12, 1925, James claim.
147 "nervous prostration": Affidavit, Archibald Frost and Mary Alice Frost, April 3, 1916, Fall microfilm records, UNM; affidavit, Archibald Frost, February 9, 1927, Dean collection; affidavit, Archibald Frost, February 9, 1927, Frost claim.
148 "Oh, my baby,": "Little Tot Kidnapped by Villa Band Restored to Mother's Arms," *EPMT,* March 17, 1916.
148 Pereyra: "Pereyra's Body Brought Back," *EPH,* March 18, 1916.
148 his Stetson: "Representative of García Found Dead," *EPMT,* March 17, 1916.
148 Villa and his troops: Movement taken from RO.
148 "alarmingly dangerous": RO, 35.
148 "the Carrancistas need not": Ibid., 36.
148 "they were too damned American": Frank Elser, "Army Hunting Villa Struck by Storm," *NYT,* March 26, 1916; Frank Elser, "Torture Victim Turns on Villa," *NYT,* March 31, 1916; RO, 38.
149 "You may bury": Elser, "Torture Victim Turns on Villa," *NYT,* March 31, 1916.
149 "I am going": Ibid.
150 "Brethren, I have": RO, 38.
150 "War is being": "Villa's Address at El Valle," March 15, 1916, U.S. and Mexican Claims Commissions, Records of Research and Information Section, Information File on Mexican History, box 11.
150 "His custom": "Trying to Force Villa into a Corner," *NYT,* March 28, 1916.
151 Namiquipa: RO, 42.

11. To the End of the Furrow

155 "Are you the new": Frederick Palmer, *Newton D. Baker: America at War* (New York: Dodd, Mead, 1931), 9.
155 "My coming was": Ibid., 13.
157 no knowledge of the army: Ibid., 8.
157 "His friends insisted": Johnson, "Punitive Expedition," 106.
157 "It would be the irony": Tuchman, *Zimmermann Telegram,* 41.
158 "It was the feeling": "Funston to Lead 5,000 Men to Mexico," *NYT,* March 11, 1916.
158 five hundred thousand volunteers: "Republicans Will Demand Army of Half Million Men for Campaign in Mexico," *EPMT,* March 10, 1916.
158 "He has no bonhomie": Johnson, "Punitive Expedition," 167.
158 "who had a great many million:" Fall hearing, 1131.
158 "An adequate force": "Funston to Lead 5,000 Men to Mexico," *NYT,* March 11, 1916. See also *PWW,* 36:283–287, for other telegrams relating to the administration's decision to send troops into Mexico.
159 "We have put": "Funston to Lead 5,000 men to Mexico," *NYT,* March 11, 1916.
159 "You may say": Telegram, Lansing to Special Agents Silliman and Belt, March 9, 1916, in *Foreign Relations,* 1916, 481.
159 "pained to hear": Telegram, Secretary for Foreign Affairs to Special Agent Silliman, March 10, 1916, *Foreign Relations,* 1916, 485.
160 "In both these cases": Ibid.; "Carranza Wants to Cross Border," *NYT,* March 12, 1916.
160 Wilson administration chose: Telegram, Secretary of State to Special Agent Silliman, March 13, 1916, in *Foreign Relations,* 1916, 487–488; "Carranza Wants to Cross Border," *NYT,* March 12, 1916.
160 General Scott urged: Scott, *Some Memories of a Soldier,* 520; Mason, *Great Pursuit,* 70.
161 wanted desperately to head: Johnson, "Punitive Expedition," 132.

161 Funston grew up: Funston's background is taken from Mason, *Great Pursuit*, 65; Dave Young, "Maj. Gen. Frederick Funston: Kansas National Guard's Greatest Soldier," Boyhood Home and Museum of Major General Frederick Funston, http://skyways.lib.ks.us/museums/funston/ksgreat.html; David Haward Bain, "Manifest Destiny's Man of the Hour: Frederick Funston," *Smithsonian*, 1989, 134–155; and Stuart Creighton Miller, "Empire in the Philippines: America's Forgotten War of Colonial Conquest," *True Stories from the American Past*, 2 (1997), 74–92.

161 great-grandniece: Bain, "Manifest Destiny's Man of the Hour," 136.

161 "We roamed the city": Ibid., 137.

162 "and finally, in": Young, "Maj. Gen. Frederick Funston."

162 "Funston, this is": Bain, "Manifest Destiny's Man of the Hour," 148; Young, "Maj. Gen. Frederick Funston."

162 letter of censure: Bain, "Manifest Destiny's Man of the Hour," 155.

163 Pershing it was: Palmer, *Newton D. Baker*, 13; Johnson, "Punitive Expedition," 136.

163 "You will promptly": Memo, McCain to Commanding General, March 10, 1916, Pershing papers, LC; *PWW*, 36:285–286.

163 Pershing seemed: Pershing's background drawn from articles written by George MacAdam and published in the *World's Work* in 1918 and 1919; the extensive obituary that appeared July 16, 1948, in the *New York Times*; and books, dissertations, and thumbnail sketches available through the Internet at the Fort Sam Houston Museum site and the Army Historical Foundation.

164 Pfoerschin: George MacAdam, "The Life of General Pershing," *World's Work*, November 1918, 46.

164 "No, I wouldn't stay": "Leadership, Personal Courage, Devotion to Troops Won for Pershing Affection of Nation," *NYT*, July 16, 1948.

164 lied about his age: Richard Goldhurst, *Pipe, Clay and Drill* (New York: Reader's Digest Press, 1977), 19.

165 "Nigger Jack": George MacAdam, "The Life of General Pershing," *World's Work*, February 1919, 546.

165 "Pershing is the coolest": "Leadership, Personal Courage, Devotion to Troops Won for Pershing Affection of Nation," *NYT*, July 16, 1948; George MacAdam, "The Life of General Pershing," *World's Work*, April 1919, 685.

165 "To promote him": George MacAdam, "The Life of General Pershing," *World's Work*, May 1919, 100; "General of the Armies John J. Pershing," Fort Sam Houston Museum, http://www.ameddregiment.amedd.army.mil/fshmuse/fshmusemain.htm.

166 "Telegram for you": "Leadership, Personal Courage, Devotion to Troops Won for Pershing Affection of Nation," *NYT*, July 16, 1948.

166 led a rescue party: "Fire Kills Family of General Pershing," *NYT*, August 28, 1915.

166 funeral procession: "Honor to the Pershings," *NYT*, September 1, 1916.

166 "From that time on": Johnson, "Punitive Expedition," 141.

167 "Nita" Patton: Frank E. Vandiver, *Black Jack: The Life and Times of John J. Pershing*, vol. 2 (College Station and London: Texas A&M University Press, 1977), 606.

167 "There should be a law": Martin Blumenson, *The Patton Papers* (Boston: Houghton Mifflin, 1972), 318.

167 Patton contacted: Ibid., 319.

167 "Everyone wants": Ibid., 320.

167 "good with correspondents": Ibid., 319.

168   arriving at ten thirty: Ibid., 321.
168   "One sometimes feels": Editorial, CC, July 14, 1916.
168   civilians also pitched: "There Were No Dull Days in Columbus for Army Bride Back in 1916," *Southwesterner,* September 1964, 3, Dean collection.
169   seize the telegraph: "Censorship Bars News of Pershing," NYT, March 15, 1916.
169   "The man who": "Warning to Correspondents," NYT, March 19, 1916.
169   "The desert is support": H. A. Toulmin, "With Pershing in Mexico," 23–24, Deming museum.
169   initial cavalry regiments: "Funston to Lead 5,169 Men to Mexico," NYT, March 11, 1916. In addition to news accounts, information regarding the makeup of the expedition was taken from Tompkins, *Chasing Villa;* Johnson, "Punitive Expedition"; Toulmin, "With Pershing in Mexico," Deming museum; and Mason, *Great Pursuit.*
169   "To transport one": Mason, *Great Pursuit,* 84.
169   Missouri mules: "Funston Wants to Use Railroad," NYT, March 18, 1916.
169   Twenty-seven new trucks: "Four Auto Trucks Rushed to Border," NYT, March 15, 1916; "Arsenal Sends Equipment," NYT, March 14, 1916.
170   emergency legislation: "Add 20,000 Men to the Mobile Army," NYT, March 15, 1916.
170   First Aero Squadron: Roger G. Miller, "A Preliminary to War: The 1st Aero Squadron and the Mexican Punitive Expedition of 1916," Air Force Historical Studies Office, https://www.airforcehistory.hq.af.mil/Publications/Annotations/millerpunitive.htm, p. 15; First Aero Squadron, Signal Corps, "War Diary," March 12–April 23, 1916, Dean collection.
170   larger-than-life officers: Michael D. Hull, "Benny Delahauf Foulois was the Father of Modern American Air Power," *Military Heritage,* February 2003, 10–17.
171   far-fetched statements: Walter J. Boyne, "Maj. Gen. Benjamin D. Foulois Was the Army's First Pilot, a 'One-Man' Air Force, and a Founding Father of Airpower," *Air Force Magazine,* February 2003, http://www.afa.org/magazine/feb2003/02fouloiso3.pdf.
171   coveted seat: Ibid.
171   "correspondence course": Hull, "Benny Delahauf Foulois," 10.
171   "They all believe": Letter, George Carothers to Secretary of State, March 11, 1916, McKinney claim.
172   great, confused body: Tompkins, *Chasing Villa,* 74; "American Cavalry Near Villa's Haunts," NYT, March 17, 1916.
172   Dean Black: "American Troops Chasing Villa," NYT, March 19, 1916.
172   "shone in the sun": "Villa Men Carry Odd Lot of Arms," NYT, March 19, 1916.

12. Sunburn, Frostbite, and Blisters

173   Pershing . . . had apparently "bought off": Vandiver, *Black Jack,* 610.
173   an old couple: John W. Converse, "Report of Observation of Punitive Expedition into Mexico under the Command of General Frederick W. Funston, March 15 to April 19, 1916," May 1916, Bouilly collection.
173   "stockyards, abattoirs": "Pershing Sped Far into Chihuahua," NYT, March 24, 1916.
174   Van Camp: "Correspondent Sent Back," NYT, March 24, 1916.
174   expense booklet: Converse, "Report of Observation of Punitive Expedition," 7.
174   "It looked like": C. Tucker Beckett, "Military Photography in Mexico," *Camera,* November 1916, 607, Bouilly collection.

174 head had been completely severed: Affidavit, Henry T. Cummins, April 25, 1916, McKinney claim.

174 spring wagon: Affidavit, J. L. Fonville, April 14, 1916, McKinney claim.

175 cavalrymen and the infantrymen wore: Converse, "Report of Observation of Punitive Expedition," 21–25.

175 "Most of the fellows": "How They Went into Mexico," *Literary Digest,* April 8, 1916, 1006–1008.

176 "so that caused us": Letter, Henry Huthmacher to Lena Huthmacher, June 1, 1916, Columbus museum.

176 "stood out like": George Brydges Rodney, *As a Cavalryman Remembers* (Caldwell, ID: Caxton Printers, 1944), 255; Johnson, "Punitive Expedition," 222.

176 "kind of a corn cake": Letter, Henry Huthmacher to Lena Huthmacher, June 1, 1916, Columbus museum.

177 "I stole another": Blumenson, *Patton Papers,* 321.

177 packers soon began discarding: James E. Klohr, "Chasing the Greatest Bandido of All," *Old West Magazine,* Spring 1971, 30, Columbus museum.

177 Pershing's column: Tompkins, *Chasing Villa,* 76–77.

177 expedition's combined strength: Thomas and Allen, "Mexican Punitive Expedition," II-18.

177 Dodge touring car: Johnson, "Punitive Expedition," 283.

178 church elders were hesitant: Raymond J. Reed, "The Mormons in Chihuahua, Their Relations with Villa, and the Pershing Punitive Expedition, 1910–1917" (master's thesis, University of New Mexico, 1938), 41, Deming museum.

178 Other scouts: "Assure Pershing of Cooperation," *NYT,* April 14, 1916.

179 main house: Tenth Cavalry, Narrative of Service, Punitive Expedition, NARA, RG 165, Department of the War Department General and Special Staffs, box 284.

179 Foulois and his airplane: The account of the pilots' ill-fated flight into Mexico is taken from Benjamin D. Foulois, "Report of Operations of the First Aero Squadron, Signal Corps, with the Mexican Punitive Expedition, for Period March 15 to August 15, 1916," http://www.earlyaviators.com/esquadro.htm; Tompkins, *Chasing Villa,* 236–245; Mason, *Great Pursuit,* 103–119; Johnson, "Punitive Expedition," 232–243; Marshall Andrews, "Our First Aerial Combat Force," *Washington Post Magazine,* May 26, 1929, 6–7; First Aero Squadron, Signal Corps, "War Diary," March 12–April 23, 1916, Dean collection.

180 "remarkable" event: First Aero Squadron, Signal Corps, "War Diary," March 12–April 23, 1916, 2, Dean collection.

181 "Until daylight": Letter, Henry Huthmacher to Lena Huthmacher, June 1, 1916, Columbus museum.

182 "The pursuit of Villa": Converse, "Report of Observation of Punitive Expedition," 17.

182 "Their tops are always": "Auto Trucks Day and Night," *NYT,* March 27, 1916.

182 drivers used mesquite: "Sidelights on Villa Hike," *NYT,* March 31, 1916.

183 "the last run down": William R. Eastman, "Report," NARA, RG 407, AGO, Mexican Expedition, box 2020.

183 To keep warm: "Messages from Mexico," *World's Work,* August 1916, 433; Converse, "Report of Observation of Punitive Expedition," 14.

183 "In spite of": Converse, "Report of Observation of Punitive Expedition," 14.

184 horses: Information comes from Tompkins, *Chasing Villa,* 116; O. C. Troxel, "The Tenth Cavalry in Mexico," *U.S. Cavalry Journal,* October 1917, 199–208; Colonel Samuel F. Dallam, "The Punitive Expedition of 1916: Some Problems

and Experiences of a Troop Commander," *U.S. Cavalry Journal*, July 1927, 382–398.

185 "Great care was taken": Converse, "Report of Observation of Punitive Expedition," 25.

186 Poor beasts: Tompkins, *Chasing Villa*, 109.

186 Colonel George Dodd: Account of his movements up to and including Guerrero fight is from Commanding Officer to Commanding General, "Narrative of Expeditions and Scouts," July 8, 1916, NARA, RG 395, Punitive Expeditions to Mexico, box 1 (hereafter cited as "Narrative of Expeditions and Scouts"), Headquarters, George Dodd to J. J. Pershing, "Report of Operations of a Portion of the 2nd Cav. Brig. and Seventh Cavalry Column from March 15–April 28, 1916," May 6, 1916, NARA, RG 200, Papers of General John J. Pershing, Material Relating to the Punitive Expedition, box 1.

186 gallant conduct: "Colonel Dodd's Army Career," *NYT*, April 1, 1916.

186 "entered into an agreement": Proclamation, Ignacio Enríquez, March 20, 1916, NARA, RG 395, Expeditions to Mexico, Base Intelligence Office.

187 "I was in doubt": Dodd to Pershing, "Report of Operations," NARA, RG 200, Papers of General John J. Pershing, Material Relating to the Punitive Expedition, box 1.

187 "It cuts like a knife": "Army Hunting Villa Struck by Storm; Aviators Risk Death in 60-Mile Gale," *NYT*, March 26, 1916.

187 "It was bitter cold": "Narrative of Expeditions and Scouts," 6.

188 "The abundant supplies": RO, 44.

188 Guerrero: Ibid., 46.

189 "It was our intention": Modesto Nevárez's account of Villa's wounding and escape from Guerrero appears in several places, including Commanding Officer to Commanding General, "Narrative Report of the Operations of the 11th Cavalry in Mexico," June 8, 1916, 33–35, NARA, RG 165, Records of Historical Section, box 285 (hereafter cited as "Operations of 11th Cavalry"); Tompkins, *Chasing Villa*, 161–164; and "How Villa Eluded the American Troops," *Literary Digest*, July 15, 1916, 138–139.

190 Dargue: Andrews, "Our First Aerial Combat Force," 7.

190 "Words cannot describe": Tompkins, *Chasing Villa*, 109.

191 "strange mounted force": RO, 50.

192 Two collapsed: "Narrative of Expedition and Scouts," 9.

192 "Villa's drug store": "Seized 'Villa's Drug Store,'" *NYT*, April 16, 1916.

192 "Such a mess": Eastman, "Report," NARA, RG 407, AGO, Mexican Expedition, Box 2020.

193 Frenchman: Klohr, "Chasing the Greatest Bandido of All," 35.

193 carriage carrying Villa: Account of Villa's flight from Guerrero taken from RO, 65–69; also "Map of Part of Chihuahua, Mexico," compiled and furnished by Office Intelligence Section, Captain W. O. Reed, Sixth Cavalry, Punitive Expedition, Bouilly collection. This map is actually three large maps, roughly two feet by three feet, showing the movement of the expedition's columns and Villa's troops. Interestingly, it plots Villa's movements down to the hour of his arrival and departure in various towns.

193 "I noticed that after that he": "How Villa Eluded the American Troops," 138–139.

194 Cavazos: RO, 16–17.

194 "They traveled almost": Nevárez account, "Operations of 11th Cavalry," 34.

194 their progress: Tompkins, *Chasing Villa*, 164.

194 Pedrosa: Ibid., 163.
194 "He is a very": Nevárez account, "Operations of 11th Cavalry," 34.
195 "When I last": Ibid.
195 "was concealment for": Ibid., 47.

13. Pershing's Indigestion

199 "on the prowl": Clendenen, *Blood on the Border,* 251.
199 "Little mention is made": Ibid.
199 Pershing traveled: Description of camp from Johnson, "Punitive Expedition,"
     280–284; Frank B. Elser, "Pershing's Lost Cause," *American Legion Monthly,*
     July 1932, 15.
199 "No frost or snow": Blumenson, *Patton Papers,* 325.
200 "On the way to town": Ibid., 324.
200 "On a rock ledge": "Twenty Redskin Scouts Ready to Get Villa," *NYT,* April 7,
     1916; "A Day in Columbus, Base for Army Down in Mexico," *EPH,* April
     29–30, 1916; Mason, *Great Pursuit,* 161–164.
200 The dry climate wreaked: "With Our Airmen in Mexico," *Scientific American,*
     July 8, 1916, 36.
201 "All officer pilots": Details of Aero Squadron from Foulois, "Report of Opera-
     tions of the First Aero Squadron," in Tompkins, *Chasing Villa,* 236–245; Mason,
     Great Pursuit, 103–119; Johnson, "Punitive Expedition," 232–243; First Aero
     Squadron, Signal Corps, "War Diary," March 12–April 23, 1916, Dean collec-
     tion.
201 Bowen: First Aero Squadron, Signal Corps, "War Diary," March 12–April 23,
     1916, 3 Dean collection.
201 two airplanes: Incident described in Tompkins, *Chasing Villa,* 236–245; Andrews,
     "Our First Aerial Combat Force," 6–7; First Aero Squadron, Signal Corps, "War
     Diary," March 12–April 23, 1916, 10–11, Dean collection.
203 Dargue soon found: Andrews, "Our First Aerial Combat Force," 6–7; First Aero
     Squadron, Signal Corps, "War Diary," March 12–April 23, 1916, 10–11, Dean
     collection.
203 "We passed over": Andrews, "Our First Aerial Combat Force," 6–7.
203 "I thought he [Dargue]": "Aviators Burn Biplane Wreck," *EPH,* April 27, 1916.
203 "There was a little town": Andrews, "Our First Aerial Combat Force," 6–7.
204 "The sentiment of the people": Tompkins, *Chasing Villa,* 174.
204 musicians: Elser, "Pershing's Lost Cause," 45.
204 "La Cucaracha": Lyrics from http://elmariachi.com/songs/la_cucaracha.asp.
206 "sanitary village": Klohr, "Chasing the Greatest Bandido of All," 42.
206 Tompkins: Tompkins's activities from his *Chasing Villa,* 110–118, 128–144; and
     Tompkins, Report No. 3, 3rd Squadron, 13th Cavalry, April 13, 1916, NARA,
     RG 407, AGO, Mexican Expedition, box 2020.
206 hand signals: Rodney, *As a Cavalryman Remembers,* 252.
207 "I would esteem": Tompkins, *Chasing Villa,* 131.
208 "I took a good": Ibid.
208 "These head men": Ibid., 114.
209 "I told him we would": Ibid., 135.
209 Howze and his squadron: Activities taken from "Operations of 11th Cavalry";
     Howze to Commanding General, "Report of Operations and Movements, Special
     Column," April 15, 1916, RG 407, AGO, Mexican Expedition, box 2020; Reed,
     "Mormons in Chihuahua," 40–55; and Johnson, "Punitive Expedition," 429–449.
210 "a slender, mean-looking": Reed, "Mormons in Chihuahua," 48.
211 "perpetual smile": Reed, "Mormons in Chihuahua," 50.

211 Villista without a gun: "Pershing Says Hunt Just Beginning," *NYT,* April 8, 1916.

211 private from Tennessee: "Doubt of Villa Death Grows," *NYT,* April 18, 1916.

211 mess kits, forks: Johnson, "Punitive Expedition," 439.

211 Santa Cruz: "Operations of 11th Cavalry"; Howze to Commanding General, "Report of Operations and Movements, Special Column," April 15, 1916, RG 407, AGO, Mexican Expedition, box 2020.

212 "being more or less exhausted": "Operations of 11th Cavalry," 12.

212 "No one of us could": Tompkins, *Chasing Villa,* 161.

212 "Our animals were": "Operations of 11th Cavalry," 12.

213 "Soldiers don't lose": Elser, "Pershing's Lost Cause," 46.

213 "The big moon": Ibid.

213 "We pictured the hot": Tompkins, *Chasing Villa,* 137.

214 "Their entrance into": "Mayor Tells of Parral Attack," *EPH,* April 29–30, 1916.

214 "A big Yank grabbed": Tompkins, *Chasing Villa,* 137.

214 Elisa Griensen: The young woman remains a celebrated figure in Parral. See Armando Comacho Griensen, *Elisa Griensen y la nueva Expedición Punitiva en Parral* (Chihuahua, Mexico: privately printed, July 2001).

214 slop jars: "30 Rioters in Parral Held," *EPH,* April 24, 1916, 2.

215 *"Los hijos de":* Tompkins, "Report No. 3," NARA, RG 407, AGO, Mexican Expedition, box 2020.

215 fruit and stones: "30 Rioters in Parral Held," *EPH,* April 24, 1916.

216 Ord: Affidavit, Gordon R. Dillon, February 15, 1918; affidavit, John Thorsen, February 15, 1918; letter, Frank Tompkins to Adjutant General, March 10, 1917, NARA, RG 200, Papers of General John J. Pershing, box 1.

216 "Ledford begged": Tompkins, *Chasing Villa,* 141.

217 "In a minute or two": Ibid., 141–142.

217 "I supplicate you": Ibid., 142.

218 Major Howze: "Operations of 11th Cavalry."

219 little white dog: Mason, *Great Pursuit,* 140; Tompkins, *Chasing Villa,* 154.

219 six bodies: "Report of Operations of the Quartermaster Corps," NARA, RG 407, Mexican Expedition, box 2020. In addition to Private Herbert Ledford, the remains of the following people were also left in Mexico: Saddler Ralph A. Ray, Seventh Cavalry, buried at Miñaca; Private Herman Kirby, Eleventh, buried at La Joya; Private Oliver Boushee, Seventh, buried at Miñaca; Saddler Hudnell, Tenth, buried at Musica; and civilian scout D. H. Holly, buried at El Rubio.

219 "imprudence": Johnson, "Punitive Expedition," 490.

219 "Uh," he grunted: Elser, "Pershing's Lost Cause," 46.

219 "Nothing should be": Mason, *Great Pursuit,* 140; Johnson, "Punitive Expedition," 473.

219 "We now felt": Tompkins, *Chasing Villa,* 156.

220 "On Saturday, April": Elser, "Pershing's Lost Cause," 47.

220 "Whether the halt": Ibid.

220 was "foolish to chase a single": *PWW,* 36:424; Johnson, "Punitive Expedition," 485–486.

220 "very brilliant way": Letter, Hugh Scott to Wilder, July 22, 1916, Scott papers, LC.

221 "My opinion is general": Telegram, Pershing to Funston, April 16, 1916, Pershing papers, LC.

222 "The tremendous advantage": Telegram, Pershing to Funston, April 18, 1916, Pershing papers, LC.

222 new expedition: Telegram, Funston to War Department, April 10, 1916, Pershing papers, LC.

223 "political difficulties": Telegram, McCain to Funston, April 14, 1916, Pershing papers, LC.
223 *"something, someplace"*: Johnson, "Punitive Expedition," 491.
223 "It is also desirable": Tompkins, *Chasing Villa,* 189–190.
224 "It was the closest": RO, 69.

14. No One to Seek For

225 Villa sympathizers: "Former Villa Officers Arrested by Police; Gen. Banda among Imprisoned," *EPMT,* March 11, 1916; "Ex-Villla Chiefs Seized by Police," *EPMT,* March 13, 1916; "Former Villista Allies Arrested," *EPMT,* March 14, 1916; "Villa Generals Being Detained," *EPH,* March 14, 1916; "Villa Colonels Released on Writ of Habeas Corpus," *EPH,* March 25, 1916.
225 nightly dragnets: "Former Villista Allies Arrested," *EPMT,* March 14, 1916; "Twenty-Five Policemen Released from Duty by Chief of Police Johnson," *EPMT,* March 21, 1916.
226 "We are not always": Sybert-Coronado, "Villismo: Terrorism and Response," seminar paper, UTEP, May 2001, Deming museum. Interestingly, Sybert-Coronado described Villa's raid as an act of terror some five months before the September 11, 2001, airliner attacks on the World Trade Center and the Pentagon.
226 "We all want to": Sybert-Coronado, "Villismo: Terrorism and Response."
226 Spanish-language newspapers: "Mexican Editor Held; Paper Suppressed," *EPMT,* March 15, 1916.
226 chief of detectives had warned: "Former Villista Officers Released; Taken to Juárez," *EPMT,* March 18, 1916.
226 "Young revolutions have": James Hopper, "Browsing on the Border," *Collier's,* May 27, 1916, 32.
226 Terrazas: Victor M. Macias-González, "The Exile of the Chihuahuan Upper Classes in El Paso, 1913–1930," *Password,* Winter 2226, 178–179; Belding de Wetter, "Revolutionary El Paso," part 2, 117–118.
226 "After breakfasting": Macias-González, "Exile of Chihuahuan Upper Classes," 178.
227 Obregón's entourage: "Juárez Happy with the Military Air Everywhere in the Old Town," *EPH,* April 29, 1916.
228 "The drummer was": Ibid.
228 condolences: "Obregón Calls on Scott Here," *EPH,* April 29, 1916.
229 his left hand sideways: Ibid.
229 detailed instructions: Telegram, McCain to General Scott, April 26, 1916, Scott papers, LC.
229 "removing a menace": Ibid.
229 "The government of the United States": Ibid.
229 "so long as the possibility": Ibid.
229 a "very clean cut": "Machine Gun Frowns, Seductive Music Floats in on Conference," *EPH,* May 1, 1916.
229 "The music was": Ibid.
230 "There is no one": Telegram, Scott and Funston to Secretary of War, Secretary of State, April 29, 1916, Scott papers, LC.
230 "It is not a question": "Obregón Is Here to Meet Scott," *EPH,* April 28, 1916.
230 "he allowed his": Scott, *Some Memories of a Soldier,* 525.
230 Paso del Norte Hotel: Hopper, "Browsing on the Border," 6.
230 "A Hearst correspondent": Scott, *Some Memories of a Soldier,* 526.
231 "The closing": "Scott-Obregón Make History in a Twelve-Hour Conference," *EPH,* May 3, 1916.

231 "Without his being assaulted": Scott, *Some Memories of a Soldier,* 526.

231 bellboy walked: "Pancho Villa Is Paged in Hotel While Conference Is in Progress; Not Found," *EPH,* May 3, 1916.

231 "mental struggle": Scott, *Some Memories of a Soldier,* 527.

231 the document: "Memorandum of Conference Between General Álvaro Obregón, Secretary of War of the Republic of Mexico, Major General Hugh L. Scott, Chief of Staff, U.S.A., and Major General Frederick Funston, to Which They All Subscribe and Transmit to Their Respective Governments with Their Recommendations for Approval," May 2, 1916, Scott papers, LC.

231 "So, instead of ending up": Letter, Scott to Lindley M. Garrison, May 19, 1916, Scott papers, LC.

232 was "not equaled": Telegram, Scott to Secretary of War, May 3, 1916, Scott papers, box 23, LC.

232 "I could not afford": Letter, General Scott to R. M. Thomas, August 7, 1916, Scott papers, box 24, LC.

232 "General Obregón": "Scott-Obregón Make History in a Twelve-Hour Conference," *EPH,* May 3, 1916.

232 "Dispose your troops": Telegram, Southern Department, May 1, 1916, Scott papers, LC.

233 "serious loss": Telegram, Funston to War Department, May 3, 1916, Pershing papers, LC.

233 "War with de facto": Telegram, Funston to Pershing, May 9, 1916, Pershing papers, LC.

233 "for ostensible purpose": Telegram, Funston to Pershing, May 19, 1916, Pershing papers, LC.

234 General Luis Herrera: Telegram, Funston to Adjutant General, May 28, 1916, Pershing papers, LC.

234 General José Cavazos: Telegram, Funston to Adjutant General, May 29, 1916, Pershing papers, LC.

234 "We have been": Blumenson, *Patton Papers,* 328–329.

15. Gasoline Baths and Confessions

237 wounded Villistas: Memorandum, "Report of Villistas Brought to Deming, New Mexico, March 15th, 1916, after Raid, March 9th, 1916," NARA, RG 395, Punitive Expeditions to Mexico, Chief of Staff, box 2-E. This memorandum was included in an October 14, 1916, letter written by J. S. Vaught, Luna County assistant district attorney, to Colonel Charles Farnsworth, commander at the Columbus base. According to this document, the first batch of Villistas included Jesús Paez, twelve; Juan Sánchez, sixteen; Elías Miras, twenty-two, an officer who had a gunshot wound over his right ear penetrating his brain; Lino Ruis, twenty-four, from San Luis Potosí, who had a compound fracture of his right hip caused by his gunshot wound; and Y. Saville, also twenty-four, from San Andrés, who had a wound in his left hip and over an eye. Though the names are spelled differently, Elías Miras and Lino Ruis appear to be the same prisoners that E. B. Stone, the federal agent, described in his March 10 report. The Stone report also lists a prisoner named Isabel Chávez, but that name does not appear on the second list. Instead, there is Y. Saville. It's quite possible they are one and the same person but there's no way to be absolutely sure.

238 "Yo soy un": "'Buen Muchacho' Wants New Leg," *EPH,* March 29, 1916; "Villa's 'Baby Bandit' Loses Leg in Raid; Boy, 12, Will Escape Trial for Murder," *RMN,* March 24, 1916.

238 "The Mexican boy": The author of this April 9, 1916, letter is unknown. It is

written to a man named Archie and consists of four handwritten pages. There is no signature page, indicating that at least one and possibly more pages are missing. It is available at the Deming museum in a box containing information on the prisoners and Jesús Paez.

239 Jesús's story: See Fall hearing, 1616–1622; Crelle K. Vickers, "The Villa Raid and Jesús Paez," 1918, Deming museum.

239 *"De una de esas casas"*: Calzadíaz Barrera, "El Ataque a Columbus," 33.

239 second group: "List of Villa Wounded Arrested at El Valle 8 April, 1916," NARA, RG 153, JAG, Mexican Claims Case Files, box 6. In a story that appeared on April 12 ("Villa Spy Was on Ranch Near Columbus Before Raid," *EPH*, April 12, 1916), the *Herald* reported that José Martela was one of the six wounded men, but his name is not on the military list.

240 "The Mexicans knew ": "Little Gibraltars on Pershing's Line," *NYT*, April 22, 1916.

240 parade of citizens: Trial transcript, *State of New Mexico vs. Rentería et al.* The entire transcript is available at the New Mexico State Records Center and Archives. The actual indictments, arrest warrants, death sentences, fees and costs, and other records related to these individuals, as well as to Pancho Villa, are available on microfilm at Luna County Clerk's Office in Deming, New Mexico, under Nos. 651–666.

240 Pablo Sánchez: The alleged spy, slender and of medium height, was taken to the penitentiary with the others. Prison records state that he was being held for "safekeeping" while he was awaiting trial. But no records have surfaced indicating whether he was ever convicted of a crime or when he was released from the state prison.

240 Judge Edward Medler: Medler's statements are taken from his testimony before the Fall committee (Fall hearing, 1624–1627).

241 "boss madam": Letter, Medler to Fall, December 13, 1918, Fall microfilm records, UNM.

241 jail "was unsanitary": The county jail and the "courthouse basement" where the first batch of wounded Villistas were taken are probably the same place. The comment might be a reference to the three men who had died there.

242 contempt of court: Letter, Medler to Fall, December 13, 1918, Fall microfilm records, UNM.

242 Villistas were clad: Description of prisoners taken from photographs and "Seven Villistas Are Convicted of Murder," *DG*, April 21, 1916. Although the ceiling has been lowered, the courtroom where the Villistas were tried looks much the same as it did in 1916. Extensive renovations and additions have been made to the courthouse itself.

242 county physician: Report, P. M. Steed, April 19, 1916, available in trial transcript and LCCO records.

243 Twelve potential jurors: Unless otherwise noted, all quotes and information related to the trial come from the trial transcript. The transcript is missing punctuation and many of the phrases are garbled. It's not clear whether the confused language actually represents what the participants said or whether the court reporter was in error.

247 "The state developed": "Seven Villistas Are Convicted of Murder," *DG*, April 21, 1916.

247 "supported the verdict": "Trying to Save Seven Villistas," *EPH*, May 2, 1916, Bouilly collection.

247 "practically a confession": Fall hearing, 1624–1625.

247 six defendants at once: "Villistas Guilty of Murder, Says Jury in Deming Trial," *EPH*, April 20, 1916, Bouilly collection.

247 "The attention of many": "Six Hanged for Villa Raid," *DH*, January 5, 1978, clipping, Deming museum.

248 clean up the jail: "[Illegible] Arrive at State Prison in Bad Condition; Four Go to Hospital," *SFNM*, April 25, 1916.

248 "It is true that a faint": "Officers Charge Bad Treatment," *DH*, April 28, 1916, Dean collection.

16. Jerked to Jesus

249 The title of this chapter is taken from West Gilbreath's book, *Death on the Gallows: The Story of Legal Hangings in New Mexico, 1847–1923* (Silver City, NM: High-Lonesome Books, 2002), 1.

249 "They are ignorant": Telegram, Edward Charles Wade to President Wilson, April 28, 1916, *PWW*, 36:566–567.

250 "murderous scoundrels," "Those Seven Mexicans," *DG*, May 5, 1916, clipping, Deming museum.

250 Tumulty: "Governor Ready to Furnish All Information That Is Available," *SFNM*, May 4, 1916; also May 5, 1916, telegram from Governor William McDonald to Joseph Tumulty, *PWW*, 36:606.

250 "represented their only": "Governor Visits the Villistas," *SFNM*, May 8, 1916.

250 "Would it not seem": Letter, President Wilson to William McDonald, May 8, 1916, *PWW*, 36:653–654.

251 "I scarcely think": Letter, William McDonald to President Wilson, May 12, 1916, *PWW*, 37:31.

251 reprieve: Executive Order, William C. McDonald, May 13, 1916, NMSRCA.

251 undercover operation: This report is in the microfilm records of A. B. Fall at UNM and also in the claim file of Charles DeWitt Miller. Included with the Fall records is a letter from J. S. Vaught, the prosecutor, to Mr. Ben Williams, asking if he might show the report to Governor McDonald. The report in the Miller claim is incorporated into an affidavit signed by Geck himself.

251 "the plans of their leaders": Affidavit, Samuel Geck, April 25, 1925, Miller claim.

253 paid $250: Order, Judge Edward Medlar, April 22, 1916, LCCO, Criminal nos. 652 and 664.

253 new paying client: Petition, Buel R. Wood to Governor William McDonald, May 15, 1916, NMSRCA; "Trying to Save Seven Villistas," *EPH*, May 2, 1916, Bouilly collection.

253 "I am fully": "Attorney for Columbus Raiders Declares Men Had Fair Trial with Just Judge and Fair, Intelligent Jury," *SFNM*, May 9, 1916.

254 "The report you sent me": Letter, J. S. Vaught to Ben Williams, May 18, 1916, Fall microfilm records, UNM.

254 another telegram: W. C. McDonald to President Wilson, June 3, 1916, *PWW*, 37:159.

254 "I still have": Newton Baker to Joseph Patrick Tumulty, June 6, 1916, *PWW*, 37:171–172.

255 second twenty-one-day reprieve: Executive Order, William C. McDonald, June 7, 1916, NMSRCA.

255 "We are convinced": "Carranza Pact to Take Rope from Necks of Five Bandits," *SFNM*, June 8, 1916.

255 hangings: Descriptions of hangings taken from Gilbreath, *Death on the Gallows*.

256 invitations: "2 Columbus Raiders Pay Extreme Penalty," *DG*, June 9, 1916, clipping, NMSRCA.

257 rope: Oral-history interview, Blanche Ritchie Dorsey, May 2, 1981, NMSRCA.

257 *hombrearse con la muerte:* Krauze, *Mexico*, 362.

257 "He just gurgled": Letter, Edward Schwemler to Haldeen Braddy, August 11, 1975, Braddy papers, UTEP. Schwemler said he interviewed Mr. Hudiburgh in 1967. This story is similar to the event described by Jimmie Hines in a letter to the editor of the *Deming Headlight* in March of 1981, which is available at the Deming museum.

258 Taurino was very: "Bandits March without Tremor up to Scaffold," *AMJ*, July 1, 1916.

258 "I hope you": "Four More Raiders Meet Their Doom, *DG*, June 30, 1916, clipping, NMSRCA.

258 "Don't be afraid": Ibid.

258 "I know I am": Ibid.

258 José Rodríguez: "Rodríguez Set to Work at Making Bricks," *SFNM*, June 30, 1916.

259 Rangel's will: "Bandit Leaves a Will Saying Columbus Raid Was Ordered by Villa," *EPH*, July 10, 1916.

17. A Ripe Pear

260 three dozen or so men: "Record of Prisoners, Mexicans," NARA, RG 395, Punitive Expeditions to Mexico, Headquarters, Historical Data, Intelligence Files, box 1. This document contains lengthy sketches of the prisoners, giving their ages, background, and military history. Approximately twenty-one prisoners were brought back to the United States. The rest were released by military authorities, or escaped or died. Interestingly, all but one of the soldiers who were returned to the United States for trial admitted to having participated in the Columbus raid. The prisoners were:

1. Enrique Adame, eighteen, a private, from San Geronimo Ranch, impressed into service as the column moved north and placed under the command of Nicolás Fernández. Adame became ill en route and never made it across the border, but was captured by Pershing's troops when they entered Mexico. Adame, whose story was substantiated by two other prisoners, later escaped from prison.

2. Pedro Burcíaga, a twenty-four-year-old lieutenant from Namiquipa and member of Cervantes's bodyguard. He joined the revolution in May of 1915 and served under Cervantes. Admitted firing upon expeditionary troops while they were in Mexico but claimed he was intoxicated.

3. Ramón Bustillos, eighteen, a private, from Namiquipa, assigned to Cervantes's detachment. Took up arms in September of 1915 after being told he could make more money as a soldier than as a mill hand. Didn't like soldiering and returned home, and was living quietly when Cervantes ordered him to join up.

4. Tomás Camarena, private, forty-eight, the father of ten children and a native of Cruces, a member of Cervantes's detachment. Said he was forced into column after being threatened with death. He had begun fighting at Villa's side in October of 1913. At some point he was charged with complicity in the murder of a colonel and spent three months in prison. Thereafter he went into concealment but Cervantes

found him and persuaded him to reenlist. When the Villistas fled back to Mexico, he was given the job of guarding a weapons cache.

5. Guadalupe Chávez, private, age twenty-two, a Namiquipa resident, took up arms for Villa in 1914. Served for a while under Cervantes and then was discharged as *pacífico*. Forced to rejoin in late February of 1916.

6. Lorenzo Gutiérrez, a corporal from San Andrés, assigned to General Pedrosa. Took up arms in 1910. Fought with Villa at Torreón, Zacatecas, and Celaya. Admitted going to Columbus. Found with a Winchester rifle and fifty-five rounds of ammunition, a crocheted doily, several yards of blue silk cloth, some black cotton material, a leather money purse, and other items believed to have been taken from Columbus.

7. Francisco Herras, seventeen, private from Namiquipa assigned to Lieutenant Colonel Elijio Hernández. Joined the revolution in 1913. Went to Mexico City and to Monterrey. He was discharged and was planting wheat on his farm on the east bank of the Santa María River when a detail of Cervantes's soldiers arrested him. He was at Guerrero when Dodd's soldiers came through.

8. Mariano Jiménez, a lieutenant, twenty-one years old and a native of San Luis Potosí. He had been a coal passer for Villa in 1915 and accompanied him to Sonora. He was a member of Villa's personal *escolta* until April 4, 1916, when Villa went into hiding.

9. Pedro López, private, twenty-three, orderly to Elijio Hernández, who was killed in the Guerrero fight. A native of Mexico City, López was an experienced soldier who joined Villa in 1913, fought with him at Celaya, Aguas Calientes, and León. Villa himself recruited López for the Columbus raid, saying he was short of men. He participated in the raid and remained with the Villistas until after the Tomóchic fight.

10. Pedro Lujan, forty-eight, a lieutenant colonel and Namiquipa native, admitted helping Cervantes recruit for the Columbus raid and was captured in Mexico by Lieutenant George Patton. He took up arms in favor of Madero and was present at his defeat during the battle of Casas Grandes. He returned home in 1913, cultivated his lands, then took up arms again to "avenge the death of Madero." He was a captain during the Celaya battle and then mustered out. He took up arms for a third time when the Villistas began their trek north and remained with Cervantes until shortly before Cervantes was killed.

11. José de la Luz Márquez, private, twenty, light skinned and blue eyed, from Namiquipa. Fought at Celaya and León. Impressed into service by Cervantes and reported to Nicolás Fernández.

12. Francisco Mejía, a twenty-year-old private from Jalisco, assigned to Elijio Hernández. Took up arms in favor of Villa in 1914 and rose through ranks to become sublieutenant. U.S. Army officials noted that he resembled a "Malay" and had "markedly white teeth." Participated in impromptu attack in which Cervantes and José Bencomo were killed.

13. Juan Mesa, twenty-two, a private from Sonora, assigned to General Beltrán's command during the march to Columbus. Took up arms in 1913 and fought all over Mexico. According to the *New York Times* ("Assure Pershing of Cooperation," *NYT*, April 14, 1916), Mesa was the first prisoner captured. His face was scarred by smallpox and he wore the cotton garb of a peon.

14. Juan Muñoz, a twenty-four-year-old lieutenant, one of the highest-level officers captured by U.S. troops. He helped with the recruiting for the raid. He was college educated, the son of the president of Namiquipa, tall and slender, and "rather light for a Mexican." He fought for Villa for three years, mustered out, but was forced to rejoin in the spring of 1916. After Villa was injured, he attached himself to Cervantes and then deserted him about April 8, 1916. Later he served as an informant for the U.S. Army. "He has been of good service to the United States and should be shown consideration," an intelligence officer wrote. In an interview with a Mexican author years later, he maintained the soldiers went to Columbus only to punish Sam Ravel and killed only people who first shot at them.

15. David Rodríguez, twenty-one, a lieutenant from Ocampo, took up arms in 1914. Spent seven years in the United States. Was forced to join Cervantes or face the "destruction" of his family. He was injured in the raid and left at El Valle with other Villistas.

16. Rafael Rodríguez, forty-two, the father of five and a native of Namiquipa, began fighting for Villa in 1913. Eventually he returned home, but was forced back into service in the spring of 1916. He reported to Elijio Hernández.

17. Francisco Solís, twenty-six, tall and slender, a corporal from Tamaulipas and a member of Brigada Villa in 1913. Eventually he was discharged and relocated to Namiquipa. After Villa's order went out, he said he was forced to rejoin. When he got into an argument with Candelario Cervantes over the forced conscription, he was given ten lashes.

18. Juan Torres, twenty-two, a Namiquipa native, first took up arms in 1914. Left Villa in January of 1916 but was forced by Cervantes to go to Columbus. He deserted him around May 1.

19. Santos Torres, a Namiquipa native, took up arms in 1914, but was discharged because of illness. Persuaded by Cervantes to rejoin in 1915. Received amnesty from Carrancistas in February 1916, but joined Cervantes again, this time under pressure. Served as horse holder during raid. "Has been of service to American troops," an expeditionary intelligence officer wrote.

20. José Tena y Quesada, twenty, Namiquipa resident, was at home when one of Cervantes's men appeared at his house and read Villa's orders. He felt he had no choice but to join and went to the cuartel in Namiquipa and was given a Mauser and one hundred rounds of ammunition.

21. Silvino Vargas, nineteen, a resident of Cruces, short and slender and very dark. Joined Villa in 1913 and returned home a year later because of illness. When he refused to reenlist, the Villistas captured his elderly father, who was released only after the son took up arms.

260 Manquero bolted: "Proceeding of a Board of Officers," April 14, 1916, NARA, RG 153, JAG, Mexican Claims Case Files, box 6.

261 Lieutenant Patton: George Patton, "Report on the Death of Col. Cárdenas," NARA RG 407, AGO, Mexican Expedition, box 2020. Though the ambush was a small event, it was nevertheless widely reported and brought Patton some of the fame he so desired.

261 cowboy's adage: Blumenson, *Patton Papers*, 333.

261 "Bandit": Ibid., 336.

261 "The Gen. has": Ibid.

262 Tomóchic: Account taken from Commanding Officer to Commanding General, "Narrative of Expeditions and Scouts," July 8, 1916, NARA, RG 395, Punitive Expeditions to Mexico, Headquarters; Dodd to Pershing, "Report of Operations," May 6, 1916; NARA, RG 200, Papers of General John J. Pershing, Material Related to the Punitive Expedition, box 1.

262 "Traveled three days": Eastman, "Report," NARA, RG 407, AGO, Mexican Expedition, box 2020.

263 "One case was pulled": Letter, Henry Huthmacher to Lena Huthmacher, June 1, 1916, Columbus museum.

263 "The dead were carried": Eastman, "Report," NARA, RG 407, AGO, Mexican Expedition, box 2020.

264 burned them alive: Dodd to Pershing, "Report of Operations," NARA, RG 200, Papers of General John J. Pershing, Material Related to the Punitive Expedition, box 1.

264 traded the foodstuffs: "Namiquipa Is Old and Big, Yet It Is Primitive City of Mexico," *EPH,* April 24, 1916.

264 "We hope that": RO, 52; "Our Troops Kill Villa's Chief Aide," *NYT,* May 27, 1916.

264 he remained defiant: Killing of Cervantes taken from Commanding Officer to Commanding General, "Report of Engagement with Band of Col. Cervantes," May 27, 1916, NARA, RG 200, Papers of General John J. Pershing, Material Related to the Punitive Expedition, box 1, and Tompkins, *Chasing Villa,* 202–205.

265 two old bullet wounds: Letter, James L. Collins to Captain George E. Adamson, June 29, 1934, Pershing papers, LC.

265 "The death of": Pershing to Commanding Officer, May 26, 1916, NARA, RG 200, Papers of General John J. Pershing, Material Related to the Punitive Expedition, box 1.

265 pine coffins: Telegram, United Press International, May 28, 1916, NARA, RG 153, JAG, Mexican Claims Case Files, box 7.

266 Colonel Henry Allen: Allen's whereabouts and movements taken from Tompkins, *Chasing Villa,* 124–127.

266 gave himself up: "Pablo López Is Held Prisoner," *EPH,* April 24, 1916.

266 Chihuahua City: "Archbandit López Bares Details of Villista Outrages," *EPMT,* May 27, 1916. The story also appears in the Spanish-language edition of the newspaper.

267 López was dozing: All the quotes from Pablo López are taken from the remarkable interview that he gave to an Associated Press reporter on May 25, 1916, at a penitentiary in Chihuahua City.

268 place of execution: Description taken from photos of execution that appeared in *Leslie's Magazine,* July 6, 1916, which was made part of the Punitive Expedition's RO.

269 and smiled: "Pablo López Pays Grim Penalty for Career of Murder," *EPMT,* June 6, 1916.

18. A Terrible Blunder

270 "I have orders from": Thomas and Allen, "Mexican Punitive Expedition," 21.

272 "I shall therefore use": Ibid.

272 "foreign invaders": "Mexicans Trying to Raise Army of 500,000 Men," *NYT,* June 19, 1916.

272 "Cavalry patrols for the safety": "Pershing Calls Situation Tense," *NYT,* June 19, 1916.

272 Charles Boyd: Description taken from photographs and a document entitled "Description of Bodies Recovered at Carrizal," NARA, RG 94, AGO, Doc. No. 2377632.

273 "I've got peace or war": Rodney, *As a Cavalryman Remembers,* 275.

273 Henry Adair: "Description of Bodies Recovered at Carrizal," NARA, RG 94, AGO, Doc. No. 2377632.

273 gored by a bull: Viva Skousen Brown, *The Life and Posterity of Alma Platte Spilsbury* (privately printed, n.d.), 229. Reviewed by the author at Spilsbury home in Mexico.

273 "If the Mexican troops": Statement, Lem Spilsbury, July 4, 1916, NARA, RG 153, JAG, Mexican Claims Case Files, Carrizal investigation, September 20, 1916, box 9. Unless otherwise noted, all quotes and details regarding this battle come from this inch-thick file.

273 occupy the international bridges: *PWW,* 36:284–285.

274 "I only accepted": Funston to Adjutant General, June 25, 1916, NARA, RG 94, AGO, Doc. No. 2377632.

274 hard bread, bacon: Captain Lewis Morey, "The Cavalry Fight at Carrizal," *U.S. Cavalry Journal,* January 1917, 449–456.

276 "I am passing": Note, Boyd to Jefe Político, June 21, 1916, NARA, RG 94, AGO, Doc. No. 2377632.

277 Spilsbury: Spilsbury gave a number of statements to army investigators. Some of the discussion between Boyd and the Mexican general is taken from one of his first statements, which is contained in a telegram from General Bell to General Funston, June 24, 1916, NARA, RG 94, AGO, Doc. No. 2377632.

277 "Tell the son of": Eisenhower, *Intervention,* 295.

277 Adair: Tenth Cavalry, Narrative of Service, Punitive Expedition, NARA, RG 165, Department of the War Department General and Special Staffs.

277 Mexican women: Fall hearing, 1566.

281 facedown in a mud hole: Frank Elser, "Morey Describes Fight and Escape," *NYT,* June 28, 1916.

282 "Who are you": "Surrounded by Enemy and Shot," *EPH,* June 30, 1916.

283 "While we were in": "Five Mexican Officers Killed; Guards Admit Killing Wounded," *EPMT,* June 30, 1916.

283 "The Mexicans got": Ibid.

283 "They wanted to hang": Ibid.

283 "Why in the name of": Telegram, Funston to Pershing, June 22, 1916, Pershing papers, LC.

283 twelve Americans: Telegram, Commanding General to Commanding General, Southern Department, September 2, 1916, NARA, RG 94, AGO, Doc. No. 2377632.

283 "But we are not": *PWW,* 37:301.

284 "Do you think": "War with Mexico Averted," *Literary Digest,* July 15, 1916, 116.

284 twelve troopers: Funston to Adjutant General, July 6, 1916, NARA, RG 94, AGO, Doc. No. 2377632.

285 Arlington National Cemetery: According to a memo from General Pershing, the troopers buried in Arlington were Private Charlie Mathews, Sergeant Will Hines, Lance Corporal William Roberts, Private James E. Day, Private Walter Cleeton, and one unidentified soldier known only as "No. 9." The missing were First Sergeant William Winrow, Horseshoer Lee Talbott, Private Thomas Moses, and

Private William Ware (Pershing to Funston, September 2, 1916, NARA, RG 94, AGO, Doc. No. 2377632).

285 Morey: "Wounded Captain Greets Remnant of His Command," *EPH*, June 30, 1916.

285 "he did not stand forth": Statement, Lem Spilsbury, July 4, 1916, NARA, RG 153, JAG, Mexican Claims Case Files, Carrizal investigation, September 20, 1916, box 9.

285 "No one could": Pershing, Report of Investigation by Lt. Col. George O. Cress, n.d., Pershing Papers, LC.

19. Whore Dust and a Rabid Dog

288 Greeks: Klohr, "Chasing the Greatest Bandido," 42.

288 "woman question": Letter, Pershing to Scott, January 21, 1917, Pershing papers, LC.

288 "As some of the men": Eastman, "Report," NARA, RG 407, AGO, Mexican Expedition, box 2020.

289 bathe "all over": T. S. Bratton, "Sanitary Memorandum for the Commanding Officer," June 6, 1916, NARA, RG 395, Punitive Expeditions to Mexico, Recorded Stations in Mexico.

289 mounted pistol charges: Clendenen, *Blood on the Border*, 336–337.

289 "We are rapidly": Blumenson, *Patton Papers*, 345–346.

289 vacation: Ibid. 349.

289 "We are well advertised": "More People Arriving," *CC*, March 24, 1916.

289 shocking one thousand dollars: James Hopper, "New Columbus and the Expedition," *Collier's*, August 5, 1916, 10–11.

289 "There are dozens": "Many New Business Establishments," *CC*, April 24, 1916.

290 Alfred Everett Wilson: The young boy showed enormous promise as a writer but died on March 16, 1922, four days before his twenty-fourth birthday, from tuberculosis. His unpublished diary can be found in the Columbus museum and the Dean collection.

290 Bool Weevil Wiggle: "Changes from Wet to Dry," *CC*, April 28, 1916.

290 "He's all the time": Blumenson, *Patton Papers*, 350.

290 "No discipline among": "Notes for General Pershing," Pershing papers, LC.

291 secret plot: Charles H. Harris III and Louis Sadler, two professors at New Mexico State University, discovered this plot after they sifted through thousands of declassified documents. The entire story, along with detailed footnotes, can be found in the article entitled "Termination with Extreme Prejudice: The United States versus Pancho Villa," in Charles H. Harris III and Louis Sadler, *The Border and the Revolution* (Las Cruces, NM: Center for Latin-American Studies / Joint Border Research Institute, 1988).

291 Japanese agents: Harris and Sadler, *Border and the Revolution*, 8–12.

291 Dyo and Sato had run: Author interview, Ray Sadler, September 7, 2005.

291 "His long untrimmed": RO, 71.

292 "During the meal": Ibid.

292 "This was my first": Ibid., 71–72.

292 "No one will ever": Ibid., 72.

293 "He took occasion": Ibid., 77.

294 "I see no marked": Ibid., 73.

294 "For that reason": Ibid., 74.

294 "I am here to urge": Ibid., 75.

295 "General Balderio": RO, 76. Harris and Sadler quote the Japanese agent Dyo as saying that Nicolás Fernández did the branding: ". . . those considered physically

unfit were branded in the presence of Villa by General Nicolás Fernández . . . in person, who with dull scissors cut a piece of flesh in one or both ears or tips of nose, and warned that if found again in the Carranza service they would be shot" (Harris and Sadler, *Border and the Revolution,* 15).

295 "They proceeded then": Telegram, British Vice Consulate, July 11, 1916, Scott papers, LC.

296 "He made the usual promises": Ibid.

296 three tubes: Harris and Sadler, *Border and the Revolution,* 15–16. Another alleged attempt to assassinate Villa was described in an October 1962 edition of the *Southwesterner.* Bill McGaw, the editor, published a story in which he quoted a soldier of fortune named Emil Holmdahl as saying that he had been offered a hundred thousand dollars to kill Villa. Holmdahl said, "I asked General Bell who would pay the money, where it was coming from and he told me the $100,000 would be paid by Russell Sage, the millionaire father-in-law of Colonel Slocum. I was informed that Colonel Slocum considered the Villa Raid on Columbus as a reflection on his personal honor and the only way this blot could be removed was by the death of Villa" ("Holmdahl Tells How Colonel Offered Him $100,000 to Kill Villa After His Capture Failed," *Southwesterner,* October 1962, 13, Dean collection).

296 "he might be hungry": Telegram, Funston to Adjutant General, September 20, 1916, NARA, RG 94, AGO, Doc. No. 2377632.

296 "I will give": Ibid.; Eisenhower, *Intervention,* 303–304.

297 "Subordinate failure": RO, "In Camp Near Colonia Dublán, Mexico," January 12, 1917, 10.

297 "Victory will crown": Francisco Villa, "Manifesto to the Nation," October 1916, NARA, RG 94, AGO, Doc. No. 2212358.

297 "You are familiar": Letter, Pershing to Scott, November 18, 1916, Pershing papers, LC.

298 "His career is": Letter, Patrick O'Hea to E. W. P. Thurstan, n.d., NARA, RG 94, AGO, Doc. No. 2212358.

20. An Old Colonel

299 Colonel DeRosey C. Cabell: Interestingly, after Slocum left Mexico for health reasons, Pershing recommended that Cabell take his place (telegram, Funston to Adjutant General, July 27, 1916, NARA, RG 94, AGO, Doc. No. 2377632).

300 Ryan: Letter, James L. Collins to George E. Adamson, June 29, 1934, Pershing papers, LC.

300 "Slocum is in better health": Letter, J. A. Ryan to General Scott, July 6, 1916, Scott papers, LC.

300 infractions: D. C. Cabell to Inspector General, "Delinquencies of the Commanding Officer, 13th Cavalry," July 10, 1916, NARA, RG 395.

300 "To have had scattered": "Border Conditions," IGO Report.

301 "It was an easy matter": Ibid.

301 "I consider that": "Investigation of Raid."

302 "Mrs. Sage in": Letter, H. J. Slocum to General Scott, July 6, 1916, Scott papers, box 24, LC.

302 "God be praised!": Letter, H. J. Slocum to General Scott, July 25, 1916, Scott papers, LC. The July 27, 1916, telegram from General Funston to the adjutant general cited above states that Slocum was "taking leave account poor physical condition, will not again be available for arduous field service."

302 "You have been": Letter, General Scott to H. J. Slocum, July 29, 1916, Scott papers, box 24, LC.

302 "Colonel Slocum seems": IGO Report.

302 "The matter had not": Ibid.

303 "The fact that he": Ibid.

303 "I recommend that": Ibid.

303 "He is old": Letter, Pershing to Bliss, August 18, 1916, Pershing papers, LC. See also letter, Pershing to Funston, August 21, 1916, Pershing papers, box 80, LC.

303 considered Slocum's regiment: Letter, Scott to Slocum, July 29, 1916, Scott papers, LC.

303 "He is too good": Letter, Ryan to Scott, August 1, 1916, Scott papers, LC.

21. A Reborn Town

305 prostitution: Order, Base Commander, July 21, 1916, NARA, RG 395, Punitive Expedition to Mexico, Base Intelligence Office. For sketches of individual prostitutes, see Louis Van Schaick, "Prostitutes in Columbus, New Mexico," n.d., NARA, RG 395, Punitive Expeditions to Mexico, Base Intelligence Office.

305 used only Vaseline: Louis Van Schaick, "Memorandum for Commanding Officer," November 15, 1916, NARA, RG 395, Punitive Expeditions to Mexico, Base Intelligence Office.

305 sale of liquor: Horace Daniel Nash, "Town and Sword: Black Soldiers in Columbus, New Mexico, in the Early Twentieth Century" (dissertation, Mississippi State University, May 1996), 91–93.

305 thirty-three joints: Intelligence Office, Base, Columbus, New Mexico, to Headquarters, Base of Communication, Columbus, New Mexico, January 24, 1917, NARA, RG 395, Punitive Expeditions to Mexico, Base Intelligence Office.

305 "We haven't been able": Louis J. Van Schaick to Headquarters Base of Communication, January 24, 1917, NARA, RG 395, Punitive Expeditions to Mexico, Base Intelligence Office.

305 cocaine and morphine: Memo, K. E. Kern to Adjutant General, "Use of Drugs among Soldiers," November 23, 1916, NARA, RG 94, AGO, Doc. No. 2212358.

306 "notorious saloon keepers": Handwritten note, author's name illegible, July 24, 1916, NARA, RG 395, Base Intelligence Office; Louis Van Schaick, "Memorandum for Commanding Officer," July 23, 1916, NARA, RG 395, Punitive Expeditions to Mexico, Base Intelligence Office.

306 vowed to go to Washington: Captain Van Schaick, handwritten note, July 23, 1916, NARA, RG 395, Punitive Expeditions to Mexico, Base Intelligence Office.

306 bodies of two Mexicans: "Mexicans Murdered on E.P.S.W. Tracks," CC, July 28, 1916; Commanding Officer to Commanding General, "Operations of Intelligence Officer at Base," August 22, 1916, NARA, RG 153, JAG, Mexican Claims Case Files, box 6.

306 "two unknown Mexicans": Louis J. Van Schaick to Commanding Officer Base, "Ten Day Report," July 31, 1916, NARA, RG 153, JAG, Mexican Claims Case Files, box 6; "Findings of Coroner's Jury," July 23, 1916, NARA, RG 395, Punitive Expeditions to Mexico, Base Intelligence Office. Not content with the finding, Colonel Farnsworth had a board of officers conduct its own inquiry. They were able to identify the two murder victims as Eulalio Montes, of San Pedro, Guanajuato, and Louis Silvas of Laguna, Chihuahua. They also succeeded in coming up with the alleged killer: a man named Clifford Trumbel, who had been commissioned a watchman by the Luna County sheriff. Commander Farnsworth recommended to General Pershing that the two murder cases be turned over to the Justice Department, in part to avoid "local prejudices against Mexicans." Pershing immediately agreed but it is not known what became of them. Soon after

this incident, however, the military and civilian authorities decided to rescind the commissions of the watchmen and law-enforcement duties were taken over by two village policemen and the army's provost guard (Base Commander to Commanding General, "Proceedings of Board Investigating Death of Two Mexicans, at Columbus, New Mexico," October 2, 1916, NARA, RG 153, JAG, Mexican Claims Case Files, box 6).

306 Pershing applied for promotion: Vandiver, *Black Jack,* 658–661.
306 "My face looks": Blumenson, *Patton Papers,* 352.
307 "You must remember": Ibid., 354.
307 "If I was sure": Ibid., 367.
307 amended mission: For a succinct discussion on the failure or success of the Punitive Expedition, see Clarence Clendenen, "The Punitive Expedition of 1916: A Reevaluation," *Arizona and the West,* Winter 1961, 311–320.
307 "Going back to the": Letter, General Pershing to General Scott, September 23, 1916, Pershing papers, box 372, LC.
308 "The identity of": Harris and Sadler, *Border and the Revolution,* 16–17.
309 Edison telephone: Details of home taken from letters written by Farnsworth and his wife, which are on file at the Fray Angélico Chávez History Library in Santa Fe, New Mexico.
309 "You know": Dave Young, "Maj. Gen. Frederick Funston."
309 returned to Namiquipa: Katz, *Life and Times of Pancho Villa,* 628, 634.

22. Victims or Bandits?

311 twenty-one Villistas: An enormous amount of confusion exists about how many prisoners were in this second batch and what happened to them as they moved through the criminal-justice system. Historian Robert Bouilly of the U.S. Army Sergeants Major Academy in Fort Bliss and author James Hurst have both made valiant attempts to untangle the issue. Pershing, in a telegram, stated that he sent twenty-one prisoners to Columbus and, as of February 7, 1917, twenty-one prisoners were in the stockade at Columbus (M. H. Díaz, "Villa Raid on Columbus [Examination of Prisoners], February 7, 1917, Miller claim). For unknown reasons, only nineteen of these men were indicted, and only seventeen pleaded guilty and went to the penitentiary. Five men — Guadalupe Chávez, Francisco Herras, Pedro Lujan, Francisco Mejía, and Juan Mesa — are unaccounted for. To complicate matters further, another prisoner, identified as Rafael Bustamante, age twenty-two, from Namiquipa, was indicted and showed up in prison but is not among the men described by the expedition's intelligence officers. Guadalupe Chávez rescinded his plea at the last minute. The prosecutor, J. S. Vaught, intended to try him, but he does not show up in the penitentiary records in Santa Fe. It's not known what happened to the other men. In an article in the February 12, 1921, *Albuquerque Morning Journal,* Silver City Deputy Sheriff Grayson states that two prisoners in the Silver City jail died in a nearby hospital from venereal disease. "They were moved to the hospital shortly after capture and the county jail paid a special guard to watch them." But Mexican author Alberto Calzadíaz Barrera maintains that two prisoners, Juan Mesa and Francisco Herras, died from inadequate food and medical attention during their stay in Silver City jail and a third, Pedro Lujan, was reportedly released for revealing the location of a weapons cache. In 1920, the fifteen Villistas still in prison were pardoned.
312 Villa seemed to be everywhere: M. H. Díaz, "Villa Raid on Columbus [Examination of Prisoners]," February 7, 1917, Miller claim. This is one of the few surviv-

ing documents that delves into Villa's whereabouts during the raid and contains summaries of the twenty-one interviews.

312 Nineteen were indicted: LCCO Indictments Nos. 718–740; James W. Hurst, *The Villista Prisoners of 1916–1917* (Las Cruces, NM: Yucca Tree Press, 2312), 35–40. For an even more concise discussion of all the Villista prisoners, see the article by John O. Baxter entitled "The Villista Murder Trials: Deming, New Mexico, 1916–1921," *La Gaceta* 8, no. 1, 1983.

312 to second-degree murder: "Villistas Go to State Pen," *DH*, August 31, 1917, Dean collection.

312 "most of the witnesses": J. S. Vaught to Gov. W. E. Lindsey, January 7, 1918, NMSRCA.

312 "It seems to us that": "Mexican Convicts," *SFNM*, August 29, 1917.

313 free agents. For an interesting discussion on the question of whether the prisoners were free agents or simply following orders, see Hurst, *Villista Prisoners*, 46–53. Hurst makes a number of correct points about Governor Larrozolo and his executive order. For example, he points out that some of the prisoners were not rank-and-file soldiers, as alleged by Larrozolo, but officers in Villa's army. He also cites evidence that lends support to the idea that some of the Villistas knew they were going to attack a U.S. town. Hurst also notes that under the Hague Convention, the pillaging and assault of a town was an illegal act and that even if the Villistas were acting as soldiers they had no duty to carry out an illegal order. But the rules of the Hague Convention weren't widely known during Mexico's revolution. Villa had been given a pamphlet on the rules of war by General Scott but few of the generals in Mexico adhered to its principles. Towns were routinely pillaged as a reward for soldiers and prisoners on both sides were routinely executed.

313 "... there must be": Executive Order, O. A. Larrazolo, November 22, 1920, NMSRCA. The state archives also have numerous petitions filed with previous governors and letters from friends and relatives of Ramón Bustillos, Pedro Burcíaga, Tomás Camarena, Juan Muñoz, David Rodríquez, and José Tena.

314 American Legion: Resolution, Claud Close Howard Post, American Legion, November 29, 1920, NMSRCA.

314 temporary injunction: Baxter, "Villista Murder Trials," 14.

314 twenty-five thousand dollars: "Fight to Prevent Release of Villistas Enters a New Phase," *SFNM*, November 28, 1920.

314 rearrest the men: LCCO Nos. 1180–1187; "New Mexico Sheriff Arrests 16 Villistas Being Detained in Prison; New Charges Ready," *EPMT*, December 16, 1920, Bouilly collection.

314 state high court: *Ex parte Bustillos et al.*, 26 N.M. 450, *New Mexico Reports: Reported Cases Determined in the Supreme Court of New Mexico, 1920–1921*, 26:449–469; "Pardon of Villa Raiders Legal; So Is Re-Arrest, Says Supreme Court," *SFNM*, December 28, 1920.

314 returned to the Deming jail: "Villistas Are Taken to Deming," *AMJ*, February 12, 1921.

314 trial: "Eyewitnesses to Tell Details of Villa's Murderous Raid at Trial of 16 Followers," *EPH*, April 26, 1921.

315 "Spanish-American" blood: "Woman Would Kill Villa Who Refuses to Aid Men in Trial," *EPH*, April 27, 1921.

315 "Mother of God": "Admirable Señora María Rodríguez," *DH*, April 26, 1921, Dean collection.

315 "Spectators in the court room": "Six Jurors Are Tentatively Selected in Villista Trial Now Being Held at Deming," *AMJ*, April 26, 1921.

315 Laura Ritchie: "'Kill the Gringos' Was War Cry of Men Who Made Raid on Columbus, Witnesses Declare," *AMJ*, April 27, 1921.

316 "I did not see": "Villistas Knew They Were on American Soil during Raid on Columbus, Prosecution Says," *AMJ*, April 28, 1921.

316 thirty-five minutes: "Jury Acquits 16 Mexicans of Columbus Raid Murders," *NYT*, April 29, 1921, Bouilly collection.

316 "Like men drawing back": "Final Chapter in the Columbus Raid," *DG*, May 3, 1921, Dean collection.

316 "Señores, we are": "All Sixteen Men on Trial for Murder in Connection with Columbus Raid Freed," *AMJ*, April 29, 1921.

316 prisoners were delivered: "16 Villistas Cross Line, Going Home," *EPH*, April 30–May 1, 1921.

317 "Perhaps this inability": "Verdict in the Villista Case," *DG*, May 3, 1921, Dean collection.

23. Death Comes for the Horsemen

318 general of the armies: "Overseas Commander in First World War Was Only Officer Ranked as General of the Armies Since Washington," *NYT*, July 16, 1948.

319 Tompkins: Robert Bouilly, "Military Service Chronology of Frank Tompkins," Bouilly collection; also Tompkins, *Chasing Villa*, vii–viii.

319 Castleman: "Brief Account of Columbus Attack," *CC*, March 24, 1916 (the article states, "Lieutenant Castleman has received very little mention for his part in the battle but he was the man who saved the town"); also sketch by Robert Bouilly entitled "Lt. James Pryor Castleman"; "J. P. Castleman, 3-War Vet, Dies," *Louisville Courier-Journal*, April 1950, section 2, Bouilly collection.

320 "They will end up": Martin Blumenson, "General Lucas at Anzio," in *Command Decisions*, Kent Roberts Greenfield, ed. (Washington, DC: Center of Military History, 1990), 335.

320 "I am not worrying": Letter, Father to Son, July 23, 1918, courtesy of Lynn Rivard.

320 Dickinson: Dickinson, "True Story of the Villa Raid," courtesy of Lynn Rivard.

321 shredded by bullets: Author interview, Lynn Rivard, July 15, 2004.

321 three to four million dollars: "Colonel Slocum Willed $3,322,322 to Family," *NYT*, April 8, 1928.

322 Zapata: Eisenhower, *Intervention*, 312–314.

322 *carrancear*: Krauze, *Mexico*, 369.

322 he loaded millions: Eisenhower, *Intervention*, 316–319.

323 "a virgin lost in a crowd": V. Blasco Ibáñez, "Is There a Way Out of Mexican Turmoil?" *NYT*, May 26, 1920.

323 Villa: Details of surrender and amnesty agreement taken from memoranda, Gus T. Jones to Senate Subcommittee Investigating Mexican Affairs, "Recent Surrender of Francisco Villa" and "Text of the Document Drawn Up upon the Surrender of Francisco Villa," Albert Fall papers, Collection No. 131, UNM. Also account by American consul William P. Blocker to Secretary of State, "Conference between Francisco Villa and General Eugenio Martínez, Acting for President de la Huerta," August 2, 1920, McKinney claim.

325 "It would appear from this": Headquarters Southern Department, "Summary of Mexican Intelligence," July 31, 1920–August 2, 1920, Albert Fall papers, Collection No. 131, UNM.

326 "The organization of this": William P. Blocker to Secretary of State, "Conference between Francisco Villa and General Eugenio Martínez, Acting for President de la Huerta," August 2, 1920, McKinney claim.

326 *perfumados:* Peterson and Knoles, *Pancho Villa,* 261.

326 "The peculiarity of the situation": Untitled and undated document that contains intelligence information about Villa's daily activities from September 27, 1920, to July 21, 1923, McKinney claim.

326 "It is said": Ibid.

326 Villa was returning: Eisenhower, *Intervention,* 324–325; Katz, *Life and Times of Pancho Villa,* 765–766.

327 Obregón: Krauze, *Mexico,* 403; Eisenhower, *Intervention,* 326.

328 "He was a very . . . stoic": Author interview, Rudy Herrera, June 22, 2004.

328 "He was very protective": Author interviews, Gloria Roach, June 1 and June 14, 2004.

328 Miss Farrar: The account of Susan Moore is taken from the numerous letters she wrote to A. B. Fall, which are available on microfilm at UNM's Center for Southwest Research, as well as the claim she filed with the federal government and her statements to Congress.

329 "So I am now sitting": Susan Moore to A. B. Fall, September 30, 1918, Fall microfilm records, UNM.

329 Dear Sir: Letter, Susan Moore to A. B. Fall, October 17, 1918, Fall microfilm records, UNM.

330 Laura Ritchie had also lost: Affidavit, T. H. Dabney, January 14, 1926, Ritchie claim; transcript of oral-history interview with Blanche Ritchie Dorsey, May 2, 1981, NMSRCA.

330 washing and ironing: Affidavit, name illegible, June 5, 1936, Walker claim.

330 "the health of Mr. James": Affidavit, Thomas Dabney, August 5, 1925, James claim.

330 "nervous affliction": Affidavit, Ruth Miller, April 21, 1925, Miller claim.

330 she secured a teaching: Affidavit, Ruth Miller, February 17, 1925, Miller claim.

331 resigning as superintendent: Author interview, Richard Dean, May 30, 2004.

331 "He has suffered and brooded": Affidavit of F.A.N. O'Neal, December 1, 1924, O'Neal claim.

331 "Any words would be": Letter, Mrs. Edward Corbett to Carl Hayden, September 21, 1922, Corbett claim.

331 hearings: One of the witnesses was Jesús Paez, the boy whose leg was amputated and who later appeared as a prosecution witness at the Villista murder trials. By then, he was sixteen years old and fluent in English, but his recollection of where he was on the night of the raid was just as confusing and contradictory as ever. Jesús had remained at Ladies Hospital in Deming for nearly a year, becoming a familiar figure to townspeople as he hobbled to and from school on his crutches. He later was turned over to an orphanage in Albuquerque and then went to Gallup. Eventually he returned to Deming, worked in Ladies Hospital for a while, and made his way back to Columbus. At the time of the hearing he was pressing clothes in a tailor shop in Columbus and then disappeared for good ("Villista Sent to Orphanage," *DH,* February 16, 1917; Fall hearing, 1621–1622; and "Jesús Paez Itinerary," Deming museum).

332 "I am now fifty-three": Affidavit, Susan Moore, December 9, 1925, Moore claim.

332 "characteristics of a bandit": Brief, "Dissenting Opinion in Santa Isabel Claims," 209, McKinney claim.

332 paltry awards: According to the National Archives, the Special Claims Commission was established by a convention signed by Mexico and the United States on September 10, 1923, to adjudicate claims for damages sustained by U.S. citizens during the Mexican Revolution, spanning the period from November 20, 1910, until May 31, 1920. The commission functioned from 1924 until 1931, an

eight-year period in which no claims were allowed. Operations were suspended in 1931. In 1934, Mexico agreed to pay a lump sum of roughly $5.5 million to settle all the outstanding claims. A domestic commission, called the Special Mexican Claims Commission, was then established by Congress to review and adjudicate the claims of U.S. citizens. This second panel operated between 1935 and 1938. The commission allowed 1,358 claims and rejected 1,475. The total amount of the initial awards was roughly $9.1 million, but since this was greater than the amount that Mexico had agreed to pay, claimants received 57 percent of the initial award figure. Mrs. Moore received $13,310; Eleanor Dean, $14,000; Archibald and Mary Alice Frost, $6,000; Ambrose and Leona Griffin, the parents of the young sentry, $3,420; James O'Neal, $3,420; and shopkeepers P. K. Lemmon and E. W. Payne, $7,453.21. The amount received by Eleanor Dean comes from records kept by her great-grandson, Richard Dean. The awards for the others come from U.S. and Mexican Claims Commissions, Copies of Awards of Special Mexican Claims Commission, 1935–38, box. 1. I was unable to find the awards for the other people who had lost a relative or property during the raid but a document provided by Richard Dean indicates that they did receive awards. They included the two married daughters of Charles DeWitt Miller; Milton James; his stepsister, Myrtle Wright Lassiter; Rachel Walker; Laura Ritchie; Mrs. Smyser; Sam Ravel; Kathryn Walker (no relation to Rachel and John Walker), and Annie Page. Generally speaking, the relatives who lost loved ones filed claims for $50,000. The claim amounts filed for loss of property varied greatly.

332 soldiers were transferred: Nash, "Town and Sword," 54. Nash writes that as of 1920, 510 white troopers from the Twelfth Cavalry and roughly 3,600 black soldiers of the Twenty-fourth Infantry were stationed in Columbus.

332 dismantled the new hotel: Interview, Margaret Perry Epps, May 19, 1983, NMSRCA.

332 delinquent taxes: Mahoney, "When Villa Raided New Mexico," 44, EPPL.

332 "Oh, those huge": Interview, Margaret Perry Epps, May 19, 1983, NMSRCA.

333 Flying Tortilla: "A Look at Major Moments in Columbus," undated clipping, Deming museum.

333 roughly 350 residents: Mahoney, "When Villa Raided New Mexico," 44, EPPL.

333 fifty-acre park: Ibid.

333 honorary citizen: "Mrs. Villa Donates Museum Items, Becomes Columbusano," *Southwesterner*, May 1963, NMSRCA and Dean collection.

333 Maud: Although a claim exists in the National Archives for Edward Wright, it contains only a note stating that efforts to contact the family had been unsuccessful. Maud died on Christmas Day of 1980. She was ninety-two years old.

SELECTED BIBLIOGRAPHY

BOOKS AND ARTICLES

Adkins, William D. "The Story of Pancho Villa at Columbus, New Mexico." *Family Tree* 1, books 1–3 (July–December 1969).

Andrews, Marshall. "Our First Aerial Combat Force." *Washington Post Magazine,* May 26, 1929, 6–7.

Ash, Marinell. "Columbus: Nostalgia and Community Spirit." *New Mexico Magazine,* March 1986, 58–60.

Bain, David Haward. "Manifest Destiny's Man of the Hour: Frederick Funston." *Smithsonian* 20, no. 3 (1989): 134–156.

Baxter, John O. "The Villista Murder Trials: Deming, New Mexico, 1916–1921." *La Gaceta* 8, no. 1 (1983).

Beckett, C. Tucker. "Military Photography in Mexico." *Camera,* November 1916, 599–616.

Belding de Wetter, Mardee. "Revolutionary El Paso: 1910–1917," part 1. *Password* 3, no. 2 (April 1958): 46–49.

———. "Revolutionary El Paso: 1910–1917," part 2. *Password* 3, no. 3 (July 1958): 107–119.

———. "Revolutionary El Paso: 1910–1917," part 3. *Password* 3, no. 4 (October 1958): 145–148.

Blumenson, Martin. *The Patton Papers.* Boston: Houghton Mifflin Company, 1972.

Boyne, Walter J. "Maj. Gen. Benjamin D. Foulois Was the Army's First Pilot, a 'One-Man' Air Force, and a Founding Father of Airpower." *Air Force Magazine,* February 2003, http://www.afa.org/magazine/feb2003/02fouloiso3.pdf.

Braddy, Haldeen. *Cock of the Walk: The Legend of Pancho Villa.* Albuquerque: University of New Mexico Press, 1955.

———. *Pancho Villa at Columbus: The Raid of 1916.* El Paso: Texas Western College Press, 1965.

———. *The Paradox of Pancho Villa.* El Paso: University of Texas at El Paso Press, 1978.

———. *Pershing's Mission in Mexico.* El Paso: Texas Western Press, 1966.

Brenner, Anita. *The Wind That Swept Mexico.* New York: Harper and Brothers, 1943.

Calzadíaz Barrera, Alberto. "El Ataque a Columbus." *Impacto,* no. 568, January 11, 1961, 30–34.

"The Cavalry Fight at Columbus." *U.S. Cavalry Journal* 27 (July 1916): 183–185.

Chalkley, John F. *Zach Lamar Cobb.* El Paso: Texas Western Press, 1998.

Clendenen, Clarence. *Blood on the Border*. Toronto: Macmillan, 1969.

———. "Mexico: The Comic Opera War." *The Marshall Cavendish Illustrated Encyclopedia of World War I*, vol. 6, 1916–17, 1812–1824. New York: Marshall Cavendish, 1984.

———. "The Punitive Expedition of 1916: A Reevaluation." *Arizona and the West* 3, no. 4 (Winter 1961): 311–320.

———. *The United States and Pancho Villa: A Study in Unconventional Diplomacy*. Port Washington, NY: Kennikat Press, 1961.

"The Columbus Raid." *U.S. Cavalry Journal* 27 (April 1917): 490–496.

Dallam, Samuel F. "The Punitive Expedition of 1916: Some Problems and Experiences of a Troop Commander." *U.S. Cavalry Journal* 36 (July 1927): 382–398.

Dean, Richard. "The Columbus Story." Deming, NM: privately printed, 1994. Available at Columbus Historical Society Museum.

———. "Dean Family Faces Death in 1916 Pancho Villa Raid." *Desert Winds Magazine*, January 1991, 12–13.

D'Este, Carlo. *Patton: A Genius for War*. New York: HarperCollins, 1995.

Dickinson, J. J. "The True Story of the Villa Raid." *Mississippi Valley Magazine*, December 1919, 5, 50.

Dorsey, Blanche Ritchie. "My Personal Story of the 'Pancho Villa' Raid on Columbus, New Mexico, March 9, 1916." *Password* 26, no. 3 (Fall 1981): 127–131.

Eisenhower, John S. D. *Intervention: The United States and the Mexican Revolution, 1913–1917*. New York: Norton, 1993.

Elser, Frank B. "Pershing's Lost Cause." *American Legion Monthly*, July 1932, 14–15, 44–47.

Foster, Lynn. *A Brief History of Mexico*. New York: Facts on File, 1997.

Foulois, Benjamin D. "Report of Operations of the First Aero Squadron, Signal Corps, with the Mexican Punitive Expedition, for Period March 15 to August 15, 1916." http://www.earlyaviators.com/esquadro.htm.

Garcez, Antonio R. *Ghosts of Las Cruces and Southern New Mexico*. Santa Fe: Red Rabbit Press, 1996.

"General of the Armies John J. Pershing." Fort Sam Houston Museum, http://www.ameddregiment.amedd.army.mil/fshmuse/fshmusemain.htm.

Gilbreath, West. *Death on the Gallows: The Story of Legal Hangings in New Mexico, 1847–1923*. Silver City, NM: High-Lonesome Books, 2002.

Glines, C. V. "In Pursuit of Pancho Villa." *Air Force Magazine*, February 1991, 78–81.

Goldhurst, Richard. *Pipe, Clay and Drill*. New York: Reader's Digest Press, 1977.

Greenfield, Kent Roberts, ed. *Command Decisions*. Washington, DC: Center of Military History, 1990.

Griensen, Armando Camacho. *Elisa Griensen y la nueva Expedición Punitiva en Parral*. Chihuahua, Mexico: privately printed, 2001.

Guzmán, Martín Luis. *The Eagle and the Serpent*. New York: Doubleday, 1965.

———. *Memoirs of Pancho Villa*. Austin: University of Texas Press, 1965.

Harris, Charles H., III and Louis R. Sadler. *The Border and the Revolution*. Las Cruces, NM: Center for Latin-American Studies/Joint Border Research Institute, 1988.

———. *The Texas Rangers and the Mexican Revolution: The Bloodiest Decade, 1910–1920*. Albuquerque: University of New Mexico Press, 2004.

Harris, Larry A. *Pancho Villa and the Columbus Raid*. El Paso: McMath Company, 1949.

Hart, John Mason. *Revolutionary Mexico: The Coming and Process of the Mexican Revolution*. Berkeley and Los Angeles: University of California Press, 1987.

Hopper, James. "Browsing on the Border." *Collier's* 57 (May 27, 1916): 1, 6, 27, 30–32.

———. "The Little Mexican Expedition." *Collier's* 57 (July 15, 1916): 5–6, 22–25.

———. "New Columbus and the Expedition." *Collier's* 57 (August 5, 1916): 10–11, 35.

———. "Pancho Villa." *Collier's* 57 (April 29, 1916): 8–10, 43, 45–46.

———. "What Happened at Columbus." *Collier's* 57 (April 15, 1916): 11–12, 32–35.

———. "Wilson and the Border." *Collier's* 57 (July 8, 1916): 7–8, 23–24.

Howard, Michael. *The First World War.* New York: Oxford University Press, 2002.

Howe, Jerome W. "Chasing Villa." *Journal of the Worcester Polytechnic Institute,* July 1916, 380–387.

"How the Gringos Fight." *Literary Digest* 52 (April 15, 1916): 1082–1085.

"How They Went into Mexico." *Literary Digest* 52 (April 8, 1916): 1006–1008.

"How Villa Eluded the American Troops." *Literary Digest* 53 (July 15, 1916): 138–139.

Hoylen, Paul. "The Battle of Juarez: May 8, 1911." *Las Fronteras,* November 1994, 6.

Hull, Michael D. "Benny Delahauf Foulois Was the Father of Modern American Air Power." *Military Heritage,* February 2003, 10–17.

Hurst, James W. *The Villista Prisoners of 1916–1917.* Las Cruces, NM: Yucca Tree Press, 2000.

Hymel, Kevin. "Black Jack in Cuba: General John J. Pershing's Experience in the Spanish-American War." Army Historical Foundation, Army History Research, http://www.armyhistory.org/armyhistorical.aspx?pgID=868&id=96&exCompID=32.

"Invading Mexico to Avert Intervention." *Literary Digest* 52 (March 25, 1916): 799, 802–805.

"Invasion or Intervention." *World's Work* 32 (May 1916): 40–62.

James, Clayton D., and Anne Sharp Wells. *America and the Great War, 1914–1920.* Wheeling, IL: Harlan Davidson, 1998.

Johnson, Benjamin Heber. *Revolution in Texas: How a Forgotten Rebellion and Its Bloody Suppression Turned Mexicans into Americans.* London: Yale University Press, 2003.

Katz, Friedrich. *The Life and Times of Pancho Villa.* Stanford: Stanford University Press, 1998.

———. "Pancho Villa and the Attack on Columbus, New Mexico." *American Historical Review* 83, no. 1 (February 1978): 101–130.

King, Frank M. *Pioneer Western Empire Builders.* Pasadena: Trail's End, 1946.

Kirkwood, Burton. *The History of Mexico.* New York: Palgrave Macmillan, 2000.

Klohr, James E. "Chasing the Greatest Bandido of All." *Old West Magazine,* Spring 1971, 6–15, 30–32, 34–40, 42–46.

Knight, Alan. *The Mexican Revolution.* Vol. 1, *Porfirians, Liberals and Peasants.* Cambridge: Cambridge University Press, 1986.

———. *The Mexican Revolution.* Vol. 2, *Counter-Revolution and Reconstruction.* Cambridge: Cambridge University Press, 1986.

Knoles, Thelma Cox, and Jessie Peterson. "I Could Have Saved Columbus." *True West* 12, no. 6 (July–August 1965): 24–25, 56.

Krauze, Enrique. *Mexico: Biography of Power, A History of Modern Mexico, 1810–1996.* New York: Harper Perennial, 1997.

Larrazolo, Paul F. *Octaviano A. Larrazolo: A Moment in New Mexico History.* New York: Carlton Press, 1986.

"Letting the Guns into Mexico." *Literary Digest* 48 (February 14, 1914): 303–305.

Link, Arthur, ed. *The Papers of Woodrow Wilson,* vols. 39–40. Princeton: Princeton University Press, 1979.

Lodge, Henry Cabot. *War Addresses, 1915–1917.* Boston: Houghton Mifflin, 1917.

London, Jack. "Mexico's Army and Ours." *Collier's* 53 (May 30, 1914): 5–7.

———. "With Funston's Men." *Collier's* 53 (May 23, 1914): 9–10, 26–27.

Machado, Manuel A., Jr. *Centaur of the North.* Austin: Eakin Press, 1988.

Macias-González, Victor M. "The Exile of the Chihuahuan Upper Classes in El Paso, 1913–1930." *Password* 45, no. 4 (Winter 2000): 175–193.

Mahoney, Tom. "When Villa Raided New Mexico." *American Legion Magazine,* September 20, 1964, 10–11, 40–44.

Marvin, George. "Bandits and the Borderland." *World's Work* 32 (October 1916): 656–663.

———. "The First Line of Defense in Mexico." *World's Work* 32 (August 1916): 416–424.

———. "Marking Time with Mexico: Why the National Guard Was Unprepared to Guard the Nation." *World's Work* 32 (September 1916): 526–533.

Mason, Gregory. "Campaigning in Coahuila." *Outlook* 107 (June 20, 1914): 391–397.

———. "The Doughboy and the Truck." *Outlook* 107 (May 31, 1916): 277–283.

———. "The Mexican Man of the Hour." *Outlook* 107 (June 6, 1914): 292, 301–306.

———. "Mexico as Seen in Washington." *Outlook* 107 (July 4, 1914): 524–527.

Mason, Herbert Molloy, Jr. *The Great Pursuit: Pershing's Expedition to Destroy Pancho Villa.* New York: Konecky, 1970.

McCormick, Medill. "The Army in Vera Cruz." *Outlook* 107 (May 30, 1914): 233–234.

"Messages from Mexico." *World's Work* 32 (August 1916): 430–436.

Metz, Leon C. *Border: The U.S.-Mexico Line.* El Paso: Mangan Books, 1989.

"The Mexican Murders." *Literary Digest* 52 (January 22, 1916): 157–159.

Meyer, Michael C. *Huerta: A Political Portrait.* Lincoln: University of Nebraska Press, 1972.

Middagh, John. *Frontier Newspaper: The "El Paso Times."* El Paso: Texas Western Press, 1958.

Miller, Robert Ryal. *Mexico: A History.* Norman: University of Oklahoma Press, 1985.

Miller, Roger G. "A Preliminary to War: The 1st Aero Squadron and the Mexican Punitive Expedition of 1916." Air Force History and Museums Programs, Washington, DC, 2003. Air Force Historical Studies Office, https://www.airforcehistory.hq.af.mil/Publications/Annotations/millerpunitive.htm.

"Mixed Mexico." *Literary Digest* 48 (May 9, 1914): 1131–1133, 1135–1138.

Morey, Captain Lewis S. "The Cavalry Fight at Carrizal." *U.S. Cavalry Journal* 27 (January 1917): 449–456.

Munch, Francis J. "Villa's Columbus Raid: Practical Politics or German Design." *New Mexico Historical Review* 44, no. 31 (July 1969): 189–214.

Naylor, Thomas H. "Massacre at San Pedro de la Cueva: The Significance of Pancho Villa's Disastrous Sonora Campaign." *Western Historical Quarterly* 8, no. 2 (April 1977): 124–150.

"On the Trail of Villa." *Scientific American* 114 (March 25, 1916): 326–327, 335–336.

Orozco vda. de Blanco, Serafina. "My Recollections of the Orozco Family and the Mexican Revolution of 1910." *Password* 25, no. 1 (Spring 1980): 11–16.

O'Shaughnessy, Edith. *A Diplomat's Wife in Mexico.* New York: Harper and Brothers, 1916.

"Our Unpreparedness Revealed by Villa." *Literary Digest* 52 (April 1, 1916): 883–886.

"Our War on Huerta." *Literary Digest* 48 (May 2, 1914): 1029–1032.

"A Pacifist Secretary of War." *Literary Digest* 52 (March 18, 1916): 701.

Page, Ray Sherdell. *Columbus, NM: Queen of the Mimbres Valley.* Silver City, NM: Page One, 2001.

Palmer, Frederick. *Newton D. Baker: America at War.* New York: Dodd, Mead, 1931.
Papers Relating to the Foreign Relations of the United States, 1916. Washington, DC: U.S. Government Printing Office, 1925.
Perkins, Clifford A. "The Revolution Comes to Juárez." *Password* 22, no. 2 (Summer 1977): 61–70.
Pershing, John J. *My Experiences in the World War,* vols. 1 and 2. New York: Frederick A. Stokes, 1931.
Peterson, Jessie, and Thelma Cox Knoles, eds. *Pancho Villa: Intimate Recollections by People Who Knew Him.* New York: Hastings House, 1977.
Quirk, Robert E. *An Affair of Honor.* New York: Norton, 1967.
Rakocy, Bill. *Villa Raids Columbus, New Mexico.* El Paso: Bravo Press, 1981.
Reed, John. *Insurgent Mexico.* Westport, CT: Greenwood Press, 1969.
Reyes, Jesús Trinidad. "Villa as Avenger: The Murder of Claro Reza." *Password* 25, no. 2 (Summer 1980): 76–80.
Reyes, Raúl R. "The Santa Isabel Episode, Jan. 10, 1916: Ethnic Repercussions in El Paso and Ciudad Juárez." *Password* 42, no. 2 (Summer 1997): 55–75.
Rodney, George Brydges. *As a Cavalryman Remembers.* Caldwell, ID: Caxton Printers, 1944.
Ruhl, Arthur. "The Unfinished Drama." *Collier's* 53 (May 30, 1914): 7–8, 22–23.
Sarber, Mary A. "W. H. Horne and the Mexican War Photo Postcard Company." *Password* 31, no. 1 (Spring 1986): 5–15.
Scott, Hugh Lenox. *Some Memories of a Soldier.* New York: Century, 1928.
Smith, Toby. "A Brave Woman in a Border Town." *Impact Magazine, Albuquerque Journal,* July 28, 1981, 9.
Smyser, Craig. "The Columbus Raid." *Southwest Review,* Winter 1983, 78–84.
Stivison, Roy E., and Della Mavity McDonnell. "When Villa Raided Columbus." *New Mexico Magazine,* December 1950, 17–19, 37–45.
Stout, Joseph A. *Border Conflict: Villistas, Carrancistas and the Punitive Expedition, 1915–1920.* Fort Worth: Texas Christian University, 1999.
Stuart, Robert M. "Clash at Columbus." *Frontier Times* 36, no. 2 (Spring 1962): 14–15.
Sweetman, Jack. *The Landing at Veracruz: 1914.* Annapolis: U.S. Naval Institute, 1968.
Tompkins, Frank. *Chasing Villa: The Last Campaign of the U.S. Cavalry.* Silver City, NM: High-Lonesome Books, 1996.
Torres, Elías. *Twenty Episodes in the Life and Times of Pancho Villa.* Austin: Encino Press, 1973.
Toulmin, H. A. *With Pershing in Mexico.* Harrisburg: Military Service Publishing, 1935.
"The Tribute to Those Who Died at Vera Cruz." *Outlook* 107 (May 23, 1914): 139–141.
Troxel, Captain O. C. "The Tenth Cavalry in Mexico." *U.S. Cavalry Journal* 28 (October 1917): 199–208.
Tuchman, Barbara. *The Zimmermann Telegram.* New York: Viking Press, 1958.
Tuck, Jim. *Pancho Villa and John Reed.* Tucson: University of Arizona Press, 1984.
Tumulty, Joseph. *Woodrow Wilson as I Knew Him.* New York: Doubleday Page, 1921.
Vanderwood, Paul J., and Frank N. Samponaro. *Border Fury.* Albuquerque: University of New Mexico Press, 1988.
Vandiver, Frank E. *Black Jack: The Life and Times of John J. Pershing,* vol. 2. College Station and London: Texas A & M University Press, 1977.
"Vera Cruz: A Crusade for Decency." *Outlook* 107 (July 4, 1914): 527–528.
"Villa's 'American Allies.'" *Literary Digest* 52 (April 8, 1916): 951–954.

"Villa's Invasion." *Literary Digest* 52 (March 18, 1916): 700.
Wallace, Andrew. "The Sabre Retires: Pershing's Cavalry Campaign in Mexico, 1916." *Smoke Signal,* no. 9, Spring 1964, 1–24.
"War with Mexico Averted." *Literary Digest* 53 (July 15, 1916): 116–117.
White, E. Bruce. "The Muddied Waters of Columbus, New Mexico." *Americas* 32 (July 1975): 72–98.
"Why Mexico Is Truculent." *Literary Digest* 53 (July 1, 1916): 9–10.
"With Our Airmen in Mexico." *Scientific American* 115 (July 8, 1916): 36.
Yockelson, Mitchell. "The United States Armed Forces and the Mexican Punitive Expedition." Parts 1 and 2, Fall 1997. http://www.archives.gov/publications/prologue/1997/fall/mexican-punitive-expedition-1.html and http://www.archives.gov/publications/prologue/1997/fall/mexican-punitive-expedition-2.html.
Young, Dave. "Major Gen. Frederick Funston, Kansas National Guard's Greatest Soldier." October 1997. Boyhood Home and Museum of Major General Frederick Funston, http://skyways.lib.ks.us/museums/funston/ksgreat.html.
Zornow, William F. "Funston Captures Aguinaldo." *American Heritage Magazine,* February 1958. AmericanHeritage.com/Magazine, http://www.americanheritage.com/articles/magazine/ah/1958/2/1958_2_24.shtml.

MANUSCRIPTS, TRANSCRIPTS, UNPUBLISHED PAPERS

Branham, Chant. "A Prelude to the Battle of General John J. Pershing vs. General Pancho Villa in the Battle of Douglas, Arizona — Agua Prieta, Mexico — 1916." 1977. In Dean collection.
Cobb, William E. "An American Woman for Each." Columbus Historical Society, n.d. In Braddy papers, University of Texas at El Paso.
Converse, John W. "Report of Observation of Punitive Expedition into Mexico under the Command of General Frederick W. Funston, March 15 to April 19, 1916." May 1916. In Bouilly collection.
Crawford, Wallace, and Verna Crawford. "Maud Wright's Experiences as a Captive of Pancho Villa." Provided by Johnnie Wright.
Dean, Richard A. "Deans Move to Columbus, 1986–1987." Privately printed, 1986–1987. In Dean collection.
———. "Founder of Columbus: Colonel A. O. Bailey." Transcript of speech, n.d. In Dean collection.
———. "Letters to Relatives Written after the Raid, 1986–1987." Privately printed, n.d. In Dean collection.
First Aero Squadron, Signal Corps. "War Diary," March 12–April 23, 1916. In Dean collection.
Headquarters Punitive Expedition, Mexico. "Report of Operations of 'General' Francisco Villa since November 1915," July 31, 1916. In NARA, RG 76, U.S. and Mexican Claims Commissions, Research and Information Section, File on Mexican History, Entry 145, box 11.
Johnson, Robert Bruce. "The Punitive Expedition: A Military, Diplomatic and Political History of Pershing's Chase after Pancho Villa, 1916–1917." PhD dissertation, University of Southern California, June 1964.
Mulhearn, Christine. "Women in Philanthropy: Mrs. Russell Sage (Margaret Olivia Slocum), 1828–1918." Case study, John F. Kennedy School of Government, Harvard University, 2000.
Nash, Horace Daniel. "Town and Sword: Black Soldiers in Columbus, New Mexico, in the Early Twentieth Century." PhD dissertation, Mississippi State University, May 1996.

Ravel, Arthur. Autobiography. Unpublished typescript, July 1966. In Dean collection.

Reed, Raymond J. "The Mormons in Chihuahua, Their Relations with Villa, and the Pershing Punitive Expedition, 1910–1917." Master's thesis, University of New Mexico, 1938.

Senate Committee on Foreign Relations, "Investigation of Mexican Affairs," 1919–1920. This is a transcript of the hearings, available in any library that has access to government documents.

Stanley, F. *The Columbus, New Mexico, Story.* Privately printed, University of New Mexico, Center for Southwest Research, February 1966.

"State of New Mexico vs Eusevia [sic] Rentería, et al." Trial transcript, No. 664, April 19, 1916. In New Mexico State Records Center and Archives.

Sybert-Coronado, Juan. "Villismo: Terrorism and Response." Seminar paper, University of Texas at El Paso, May 2001. In Deming museum.

Thomas, Robert S., and Inez V. Allen. "The Mexican Punitive Expedition under Brigadier General John J. Pershing, United States Army 1916–17." Monograph, War Histories Division, Office of the Chief of Military History, Department of the Army, Washington, DC, 1954.

United States Army Sergeants Major Academy. "Pancho Villa's Raid on Columbus, New Mexico, 8–9 March 1916." Fort Leavenworth, KS: Combat Studies Institute, 2004.

Wilson, Alfred Everett. Diary, January 1916–March 1919, Columbus Historical Society Museum, Columbus, NM.

Zontek, Ken. " 'Dammed if They Did, Dammed if They Didn't': The Trial of Six Villistas Following the Columbus, New Mexico Raid, 1916." New Mexico State University, 1993.

Index

Abbott, Col. E. C., 315
Acuña, Jesús, 159
Adair, Lt. Henry, 273, 278–80,
  284–85
Adame, Pvt. Enrique, 312, 374n
Agua Prieta, 55, 56, 57–58; battle of, ix,
  59–60, 91, 110, 251
Aguinaldo, Emilio, 162
airplanes, 170–71, 179–81, 190,
  200–203
Alarconcon, Juan, 108
Albuquerque Morning Journal, 315,
  382n
Allen, Col. Henry, 213, 266; photograph
  of, xi
Álvarez, Francisco, 239–40, 245–46,
  247, 253, 255, 256–57
Anderson, Maurice, 66–67, 68
Ángeles, Gen. Felipe, 10, 29, 40, 47, 51,
  52, 54, 359n
Antireelectionist Party, 19
Aregon, Alfredo, 141–42
Army, U.S., 75, 143, 159, 203, 219,
  376n; and Columbus raid, 144,
  (Slocum's report) 103; Mexican prisoners of, 255, 343n; Southern
  Department, 92, 161, 309; Villa and
  followers as seen by, 6, 37, 58, 68,
  291, 297, 325, 326. *See also* Cavalry,
  U.S.; United States War Department
automobiles, 82, 83, 100–101, 103, 123,
  131, 203, 261; army trucks, 170,
  181, 182; auto accidents, 87, 176;
  Mexican use of, 33, 227; Pershing's
  use of, 176, 177–78, 221

Bailey, Col. Andrew O., 81
Baker, Newton Diehl, 155, 157, 160–61,
  232, 241, 254–55; and Pershing, 163,
  220, 306
Beckett, C. Tucker, 174
Bell, Bill, 178
Belt, John, 159
Beltrán, Gen. Francisco, 63, 224, 293,
  295; at Columbus, 109, 111, 148,
  150; at Guerrero, 188, 191; photo-
  graph of, x
Bencomo, José, 265, 375n
Benson, Lt. Clarence C., 106, 133, 360n
Billy the Kid, 76
Birchfield, "Uncle" Steven, 87, 102, 116,
  117, 125
Birchfield, Walter P., 76, 352n
Black, Pvt. Dean, 172
Blakeslee, H. W., 178
Blasco Ibáñez, Vicente, 38, 323
Bliss, Maj. Gen. Tasker, 90, 160, 163,
  164, 223, 303
Blocker, William P., 325, 384n
Boddington, Rev. C. H., 136
Bonillas, Ignacio, 322
Boone, Daniel, 161
Border Gate, 95, 96, 103, 105, 359–60n
Bouilly, Robert, 382n
Bowen, Lt. Thomas, 201
Boyd, Capt. Charles, 272–81, 284–85
Branham, Chant, 58, 59, 60
Brock, Capt. A. W., 257
Brown, Dave, 209, 210
Brown, Col. William, 181, 206, 213, 218
Buffalo Soldiers. *See* Cavalry, U.S.

Burcíaga, Lt. Pedro, 374n, 383n
Burkhart, Summers, 242
Bustamante, Rafael, 382n
Bustillos, Pvt. Ramón, 374n, 383n
Butler, Pvt. Thomas, 114
Bryan, William Jennings, 22, 32, 34, 43

Cabell, Col. DeRosey C., 299, 300
Call, Bishop A. B., 178
Calles, Gen. Plutarco Elías, 58–59, 228,
    327
Calzadíaz Barrera, Alberto, 356n
Camadurar, Jesús, 260
Camarena, Pvt. Tomás, 374–75n,
    383n
Campanole, Maj. N. W., 315
Camp Furlong, 83, 97, 103–4; attack on,
    111; map of, 109
Carberry, Lt. Joseph, 180, 201–2
Cárdenas, Julio, 261
Carlin, R. L., 114–15
Carnet, Rev. Joseph, 256
Carothers, George, 41, 92, 94, 95, 104,
    139–40, 171; questions Maud
    Wright, 138, 321, 344n
Carrancistas: at Carrizal, 274–75; Cer-
    vantes appeals to, 264; and Colum-
    bus raid, 3, 6, 148; depredations by,
    290; protection of Americans by, 64;
    Punitive Expedition and, 173–74,
    213, (hostility of) 202, 204, 215, 217,
    221–22, 234, 270; Villa feared,
    admired by, 103, 139–40, (professes
    friendship with) 149; Villistas join,
    10, 73; Villistas vs., 3, 49–51, 91, 93,
    159, 194, 211, (at Agua Prieta)
    57–59, 110, (Carrancistas defeated,
    captured, branded) 151, 250,
    294–95, (at Guerrero) 188–89, (and
    López) 150, 266
Carranza, Venustiano: and Columbus
    raid, 102, 159, (Johnnie Wright's
    return) 147–48; followers of, 4 (*see
    also* Carrancistas); gains support, 33,
    86; government of, 65, (protests Par-
    ral incident) 219; greed of, 39, 40,
    322; joins Villa, 38–39, (breaks with,
    fights against) 47–48, 49–51, 218,
    (and deal with U.S.) 60–61, 268,
    (Villa denigrates) 294, 295; Obregón
    as rival of, 225, 322, (killed by
    Obregón's men) 323; and Punitive

Expedition, 169, 220, 221, (demands
    withdrawal of U.S. forces, withdrawal
    refused) 232, 270, 272, (releases pris-
    oners) 283–84; Wilson recognizes,
    56–57, 66, 157, 160, 163, 348n,
    (doubts loyalty) 233, (and train mas-
    sacre) 68
Carrizal, battle at, 274–86, 287, 300;
    map showing route, 271
Casey, Harry, 115
Castillo, Juan, 245, 247, 253, 258
Castillo (Maud Wright's guard), 7, 129
Castleman, Lt. James, 106–7, 113, 126,
    256; as savior of Columbus, 319
Catholic Church, 21–22, 327
Cavalry, U.S., 89, 90, 113, 146, 319; all-
    black units, 165, 176, 272–75, (Buf-
    falo Soldiers) 165, 169, 206, (at
    Carrizal) 276–85, (troops buried at
    Arlington) 285, 378–79n; arrives in
    Columbus, 83, 106, (and Columbus
    raid) 124, 133, 134, 144, 300; horses
    for, 88, 184–86, 207; Pershing in,
    164–65; in Punitive Expedition,
    169–79 *passim*, 187–88, 197,
    206–19, 262–63, 303, (casualties)
    181–82, (at Guerrero) 190–92, (Per-
    shing sends patrols) 272–73; searches
    Mexican households, 141, 211, 261,
    263
Cavazos, Gen. José, 189, 194, 207–8,
    209, 234
Celaya, two battles of, 52–54
censorship. *See* news blackout
Cervantes, Candelario, 63, 74–75, 187,
    189, 191; in Columbus raid, 79, 80,
    109, 111, 116, 130–31, 374–76n,
    (aftermath) 135, 148, 311; photo-
    graph of, x; Punitive Expedition
    against, 224, 262–65
Chacón, Pedro, 64–65, 66
Chávez, Col. Cruz, 135, 148
Chávez, Pvt. Guadalupe, 312, 375n,
    382n
Chicago Tribune, 94, 178
Chinese in Mexico, 21, 287, 308
Clendenen, Clarence, 199
Cobb, William, 141
Cobb, Zach, 91–93
Collier's magazine, 36, 54–55, 230
Collins, James, 168, 300
Columbian Exposition (1893), 81

Columbus, New Mexico: Castleman as savior of, 319; conditions in, 81–88, 97–102, 106, 301, 304–6, 309, 332–33, (accommodations and entertainment) 289–90
Columbus Courier, 141, 143, 289, 359n
Columbus raid, 72, 74, 79–80, 91–96, 97–106 *passim,* 108–35, 211, 380n; aftermath of, 136–51, 237–38, 299–303, 309, 320, (captive Villistas) 361n, (Mexican prisoners brought back to U.S.) 374–76, (prisoners tried) 237–48, 249–59, 260, 268–69, 314–17; casualties of, 338–39; compensation for U.S. survivors of, 329, 331–32, 334, 341, 385–86n; map of, 109; Mexican reaction to, 159, 171; news coverage of raid and trial following, 178, 238, 246–47; number of Villa's troops at, 360–61n; U.S. response, *see* Punitive Expedition; vigilantism following, 143, 255
Columbus Historical Society, 141
Conference of Twenty-seven Generals, 61
Connecticut Fire Insurance Company, 146
conscription, forced, 33, 63, 150–51, 239, 244, 315–16
Constitutionalist troops, 4, 47, 48
Conventionalist army, 48, 63
Converse, Sgt. John, 182, 183, 185
Copp, Ens. Charles, 42
Corbett, William Nye, 77–78, 101, 142, 331
Cortés, Hernán, 14, 43, 44
Covington, Pvt. Melvin C., 279
Cristero Rebellion, 327
Cross, H. M., 74
Cuban revolt against Spain, 161–62, 165
Cummings, Lt. Claude, 216
Custer, Gen. George, 169

Dabney, Dr. Thomas, 305
Daniels, Josephus, 272
Dargue, Lt. Herbert A., 190, 201–3
Davidson, Harry, 114–15
Dean, Edwin, 124, 126, 137, 331
Dean, James and Eleanor, 82, 124; James's death, 137, 146, 175, 240, 312, 331, (compensation) 386n

defensa social, 264
De la Huerta, Adolfo, 322, 323, 324
Deming, New Mexico, 83, 101, 123, 144, 385n; trial of Mexican prisoners held in, 237–48 (*see also* Columbus raid)
Deming Graphic, 250, 316, 317
Deming Headlight, 248, 374n
Deming Vigilantes Committee, 255
De Moss, Dr. E. C., 137
de Wetter, Mardee Belding, 24
Díaz, Porfirio, 13–21 *passim,* 27, 226; forced service under, 63, 244; revolt against, 26, 75; threatened, flees, 25–26
Dickinson, J. J., 320, 321
División del Norte, 6, 40, 49, 63, 108, 139, 311; strength of, 36, 297
Dobbs, Sgt. Mark, 126
Dodd, Col. George, 94, 186–88, 197, 199, 206, 262–63, 303; at Guerrero, 189–93, 375n; photograph of, xi
Dodd, Capt. Townsend, 201, 202
Dolphin, USS, 42
Dorados ("Golden Ones"), 6, 40, 135, 149, 189, 239, 261, 293; photograph of 80 soldiers of, x
Douglas, Arizona, 55, 58, 60, 91, 94, 137
Dow, Frank, 356n
Dublán (Mormon settlement), 177, 179, 181, 182, 219; military camp at, 287–89, 308
Duff, Mrs. Emma, 238–39
Dunn, Robert, 178
Dyo, Tsutomo, 291–94, 295, 296

Eastman, Maj. William, 183, 192, 262, 263, 288
Eisenhower, Lt. Dwight, 309
Elliot, R. W., 124
El Paso, 92, 225–27; jail fire, 73–74; riot, 69–70
El Paso and Southwestern Railroad, 83, 97, 181, 355n, 356n
El Paso del Norte, 226
El Paso Herald, 231, 314, 344n
El Paso Morning Times, 56, 344n
Elser, Frank, 172, 178, 187, 213, 220
Epps, Margaret Perry, 333
Evans, Maj. Ellwood, 181–82

Evans, Arthur Jack, 354n
Evans, T. M. "Tom," 65, 139

Fall, Albert Bacon, 87, 158, 220, 226,
    241, 331; Susan Moore's letters to,
    329, 385n
Farnsworth, Lt. Col. Charles, 305, 309,
    371n, 381n
Favela, Juan, 77–78, 95, 105, 124–25,
    144
federal army, 26, 33, 42, 47, 48; Villistas
    vs., 36–37
Federal Bureau of Investigation, 138,
    140, 241
Fernández, Col. Nicolás, 61, 77, 95, 194,
    293, 310, 324, 334; brands prisoners,
    379–80n; captures Maud Wright,
    2–3, 4–6, 71, 344; and Columbus
    raid, 80, 109–11, 135, 374n, (after-
    math) 148, 150, (Punitive Expedition)
    188, 190, 195, 224, 261; last days of,
    327–28; photograph of, x
Fielder, J. H., and son Forest, 314
Fierro, Rodolfo, 10, 39–40
Figueroa, Capt. Leoncio, 88, 102
Fillmore, Lurid, 240
Fletcher, Rear Adm. Frank F., 44–45, 46
Flores, Father André Abelino, 60
Fody, Michael, 113–14
Fonville, James L., 102, 142, 144
Foulois, Capt. Benjamin, 170–71, 179–80,
    201–2, 204, 219; photograph of, xi
France, 14, 15, 16, 43
Franco, Romualdo, 21
Frost, Archibald and Mary Alice, 82,
    122–23, 147, 386n
fugitive law (*ley fuga*), 30, 263
Funston, Edward Hogue "Foghorn,"
    161
Funston, Gen. Frederick, 145, 161–63,
    171, 273, 309; and Columbus raid,
    92, 241; meets Obregón, 225,
    227–30; Pershing under orders of,
    reports to, 94, 169, 200, 221–22,
    233–34, (angry telegram) 283; and
    Slocum, 302–3, 362n, 380n

Gamiochipi, Fernando, 226
Garcia, Andrés, 69, 228
García, Capt. Pablo, 361n
García, Taurino, 245, 247, 253, 258

Garlington, Inspector Gen. Ernest, 90,
    299, 303
Garret, Pat, 76
Gates, Dr. A. E., 178
Gavira, Gen. Gabriel, 69, 92–95, 228
G. de López, Elena, 64, 66
Geck, Samuel ("Antonio Vásquez"),
    251–53, 254
Germany, 2, 29, 46, 297; interest of, in
    Mexican strife, 41, 52, 56–57, 157,
    220; U.S. declares war on, 309
Geronimo (Indian leader), 164
Gibbons, Floyd, 178
Gibson's Line Ranch, 95, 103, 127
Gómez, Gen. Félix, 277, 280
González, Gen. Abraham, 20, 21, 22, 30,
    69
Gorrell, Lt. Edgar S., 180–81
Grace, Leona, 241
Gray, H. N., 87, 148
Great Britain, 29, 57; British consulate,
    282–83, 295, 296, 298; Mexican
    investments by, 16, (oil from Mexico)
    32, 41
Greeley, Horace, 119
Gregory, Thomas, 220, 241
Griensen, Elisa, 214
Griffin, Ambrose and Leona, 386n
Griffin, Fred, 104, 112
Griffith, Josephine and son Percy, 28–29
Guerrero battle, 188–93, 221–22, 293,
    367n
Guggenheim investments, 14
gun smuggling, 306
Gutiérrez, Corp. Lorenzo, 375n
Gutiérrez, Gen. Luis, 159
Guzmán, Martín Luis, 24, 40, 43, 51

Hague Convention, 383n
Hamilton, R. F., 314
hangings, 78, 142, 174, 253–59
Hapsburg, Ferdinand Maximilian and
    Carlota von, 14
Harding, Warren Gamaliel, 331
Harris, Charles H. III, 308, 379n
Harris, Willie, 282
Harrison, William P., 175
Hart, Dr. Harry, 86, 102, 116, 118, 137
Hart, John Mason, 16, 17, 26, 348n
Hayden, Frank, 3, 4–5, 6, 7–8
Hearst properties, 14, 179, 187, 244

Hernández, Lt. Col. Elijio, 375n
Herras, Pvt. Francisco, 375n, 382n
Herrera, José de la Luz, 213–14, 218
Herrera, Gen. Luis, 234
Herrera, Rudy, 328
Hines, Jimmie, 374n
Hines, Maj. John, 167
Holmes, Minnie, 28–29
Holmes, Thomas, 65–66, 68
Homestead Act, 86
Hoover, Sarah and son William, 120–21
Hoover, Mayor William, 146
Hopper, James, 36, 54, 55, 226, 230
horses, 2, 79, 184–86. See also Cavalry, U.S.; Villa, Francisco (Pancho)
hospital train, Villa's, 39
Howze, Lt. Col. Robert, 206, 209–13; photograph of, xi
Hudiburgh, George Washington Jr., 257
Huerta, Victoriano, 26, 27–28, 31, 57, 63; as president, 29–30, 32–34, (*Dolphin* incident) 42–43, (hold weakens) 41, (recognition by U.S. refused) 32, 43, (resigns) 47; Villa and, 35–36, 38, 40, 47
Huichol Indians, 13, 27
Hulsey, T. A., 88, 244
Hurst, James, 382n
Husk, Carlos, 20
Huthmacher, Henry, 176, 181, 263

Indian tribes, 13–14; attacks by, 159–60, 164; campaigns against, 90; Indian (Apache) scouts, 200
interventionism, 157–58

James, Milton and Bessie, 97–98, 256; Milton wounded, Bessie killed, 120–21, 132–33, 146, 147, 175, 330, 357n, (compensation) 386n
Japan, Japanese agents, 57, 291, 296
Jiménez, Lt. Mariano, 316, 375n
Jiménez (city), Villa takes, 293–96
Johnson, Bruce, 157, 164
Johnson, Roy, 139
Jones, Gus T., 325, 384n
Juárez, Benito, 14, 19, 229
Juárez (city), 40, 56, 69–70, 92, 222, 225; generals meet in, 229; Villa attacks (1911), 23–25, (spectators of battle) 25; Villa captures (1913), 37

Katz, Friedrich, 48, 297, 345n
Keeler, A. A., 78
Kindvall, Frank T., 115
Knight, Alan, 18

"La Cucaracha" (song), 108, 112, 204–5
land reform, 48
Lane, Franklin, 220
Lansing, Robert, 139, 159, 171, 219, 220, 272, 344n
"La Paloma" (song), 205
Larrazolo, Gov. Octaviano, 312–13
Lassiter, Myrtle Wright, 97–98, 120, 132, 386n
Ledford, Pvt. Hobart, 216–17, 218–19
Lemmon, Leo, 138–39
Lerdo de Tejada, Sebastián, 14
Letcher, Marion, 201
Lind, John, 33
Lindsley, Maj. Elmer, 95, 105
Lininger, Lt. Clarence, 215, 216, 219
Little Bighorn, battle of, 90
López, Martín, 63, 135, 188, 191, 224
López, Col. Pablo: and Columbus raid, 109, 111, (wounded) 128, 135, 148–49, 150; photograph of, x; and train massacre, 66–67, 128; U.S. hunt for, 63, 213, 224, (AP interview with) 267–68, (death of) 268–69
López, Pvt. Pedro, 375n
López Negrete, Agustín, 20–21
Lowry, George, 46
Lozano, Gen. Ismael, 213–15, 217
Lucas, Lt. John P., 106–7, 109, 112–13, 126, 333; in World Wars I and II, 319–20
Lucero, Antonio, 250
Lujan, Lt. Col. Pedro, 375n, 382n
Lundy, John, 133
Lyons, Martin, 4

Maass, Gen. Gustavo, 45
MacArthur, Gen. Arthur, 162
MacArthur, Gen. Douglas, 162, 309
McCabe, W. P., 274–76, 281–82, 285
McCain, Lt. William, 114, 117–18
McCullough, S. H., 355n
McDonald, William, 250–51, 254, 255, 258, 312
McGaw, Bill, 380n
McGhee, Corp. Benjamin, 216, 218

McKinney, Henry Arthur and Mamie and McKinney family, 76–78, 93, 101, 142, 174, 331, 344n

Macias-González, Victor, 227

Madero, Francisco "Maderito": heads revolt, 18–20, 23, 26, 178, 193, 267, (cease-fire) 24–25; joins forces with Villa, 23–25, 35, 61; as president, 26–27, 28, 33, 35, 231, (arrested, assassinated) 29–30, 31, 35, 36, 39, 40, 283

Madero, Gustavo, 18, 29

Maisel, George, 315

Manifest Destiny, 157

Manquero, Adolfo, 260

Márquez, Pvt. José de la Luz, 375n

Marshall, Edwin, 75, 142, 143

Marshall, Marcus, 103, 142–43, 144

Martínez, Gen. Eugenio, 324

Mason, Herbert Malloy, 170

Mayo, Adm. Henry T., 42–43

Medler, Judge Edward, 240–43, 245–46, 247–48, 249, 253, 313

Mejía, Pvt. Francisco, 375n, 382n

Mesa, Capt. Antonio, 213, 214

Mesa, Pvt. Juan, 375n, 382n

Mexican-American relations. *See* United States–Mexico relations

Mexican revolution (1876), 13, 14

Mexican Revolution (1910–11), 348n; begins, 3, 16–20, 23, 87, 267, (continues) 26; deaths of leaders of, 322–23; federal army surrenders, 25; reportage of, 36; revolutionary convention following, 47–48; U.S. Army view of, 37. *See also* Columbus raid

Mexican War (1846–48), 14

Mexico: civil war (1910–20), 3–4, 16, 34, 48, 50–51, 64, 86; Constitution, 48, 322, (dissolved) 34; economic conditions, 14–18; foreign investment in, 14–15, 16, 32, 64, (during revolution) 18, (by U.S., *see* United States); foreign relations with, 41; gains, loses independence, republic restored, 14; Indians invade, 159–60; population, 13–14; U.S. relations with, *see* United States–Mexico relations

Mexico City, 14, 43, 49; during Revolution, 25, 26, (Tragic Ten Days) 28; social life in, 15, 16, 18, 33, 37

Miles, Gen. Nelson, 164

Miller, Charles DeWitt, 100–101, 116, 118, 132, 137–38, 330; trial for murder of, 240, 243–44, 255, 312

Miller, Mrs. Charles DeWitt (Ruth) and daughters, 101, 118, 330, 386n

Miller, Charlie, 83, 121, 289

Mississippi Valley Magazine, 320

Moody's Ranch, 96

Moore, Earl, 100

Moore, John and Susan, 82, 98–100, 105, 108, 128; John killed, Susan wounded, 129, 131–32, 146–47, 240, 250, 312, 328–29, 332, 333, (compensation) 386n

Moreno, Col. Aristides, 308

Morey, Capt. Lewis, 273, 274–76, 278–81, 285

Morgan, Commo. E. D., 148

Mormon scouts, 178, 209, 273

Mormon settlement (Colonia Dublán), 177, 179, 181, 182, 219, 287

Mosely, Perrow, 143

Múñez, Antonio, 77–78, 95, 102–3, 142, 144, 353n

Muñoz, Lt. Juan, 116, 128, 315, 344, 359n, 376n, 383n

Napoleon III, 14

National Guard, 114, 233, 255, 315

National Railroad of Mexico, 169

Nevárez, Modesto, 189, 193, 194–95

news blackout, 169, 226

news correspondents, 36, 178, 213, 219, 230–31, 238, 246–47, 267, 284; and El Paso fire, 73–74; at hangings, 256

New York Herald Tribune, 94, 178

New York Times, 27, 94, 143, 145, 151, 158, 172, 178, 213

New York Tribune, 94

Nievergelt, John C., 126

Norwich University, 319

Obregón, Gen. Álvaro, 51–55, 64, 272, 322, 323, 325; assassinated, 327; safe-conduct letters from, 76, 186–87; U.S. generals meet with, 225, 227–32

O'Hea, Patrick, 298

O'Neal, James, 78–79, 174, 331, 386n

Ord, Lt. James, 207, 208, 216

Ornelas, Porfirio, 73

Orozco, Pascual, 23, 25

Ortiz, Carmen, 80
O'Shaughnessy, Edith, 33, 39, 44, 322

Paez, Jesús, 140, 237–39, 246, 247,
    385n
Page, Annie, compensation to, 386n
Page, W. R., 115
Palomas Land and Cattle Company,
    75–79, 93–94, 103, 142–43, 301, 331
Panama Canal, 157
Parks, G. E. and Susan and daughter
    Gwen, 121–22, 168, 256
Parral Skirmish, 206–8, 212–19, 222–23,
    225, 266, 307–8; map illustrating
    route of, 198
Patton, Anne "Nita," 167, 168, 289, 290
Patton, Lt. George, 167–68, 176–77,
    185, 199–200, 234, 261–62, 290,
    306–7; photograph of, xi; Wilson as
    viewed by, 289; in World Wars I and
    II, 318–19
Patton, Mrs. George (Beatrice), 168,
    262, 289, 290, 306–7
Peak, John, 136
Pedrosa, Gen. Juan, x, 63, 148, 189–90,
    194–95, 224, 375n
peons, treatment of, 16–17
Pereyra, José, 87, 102, 116–17, 120, 148
Pershing, Gen. John "Black Jack,"
    163–68, 171, 290, 300; and camp
    conditions, 289, ("woman question")
    288, 305; and Carrizal, 273, 275,
    285–86, 287, (reprimand) 283; and
    hunt for Villa, 297, (assassination
    plot) 291, 308, ("dead or alive") 307,
    (whereabouts of) 93–94; obituary,
    364n; photograph of, xi; promoted,
    165, 306; and Punitive Expedition,
    167–90 passim, 196, 197, 199–200,
    204–6, 212–13, 219–24, 231, 241,
    249, (assumes command) 163–64,
    (deaths of Cervantes and López)
    264–66, 270, (news blackout, news
    dispatches) 69, 219, (prisoners)
    260–61, (public disbelief in success)
    172, (refuses to withdraw) 233–34,
    (sends cavalry patrols) 272–74;
    returns from Mexico, 308–9; and
    Slocum, 299, 302–3; wife and daugh-
    ters killed in fire, 166–67; in World
    War I, 309, (returns from) 318
Pershing, Warren, 166, 167

Pfoerschin, Frederick, 164
Phelps Dodge Corporation, 15
Pino Suárez, José María, 28, 29, 30, 31,
    40
Plan de Ayala, 48
Polanco, Mucio and Gregorio Jr., 149
Porfiriato, the, 14. *See also* Díaz, Porfirio
Prado, Capt. Francisco, 139
prostitution, 288, 304–5
Punitive Expedition, 158–61, 167–72,
    173–96, 197–224; Carrizal battle,
    274–86, 287, 300, (map) 271; com-
    munication during, 200; and danger
    of war, 157–58, 233, 273–74, 302;
    last fight of, 287; map showing route
    of, 195, (illustration) 156; Mexican
    prisoners from, 311–14, (trials of)
    239–49, 314–17; mission of, 291;
    negotiations following, 225, 227–33;
    newsmen with, 178, 213, 219; Per-
    shing commands, 163–64, 308 (*see
    also* Pershing, Gen. John); provisions
    for, 182–83, 190, 220, 264; smaller
    version organized, 233; troop with-
    drawal demanded, refused, 232, 270,
    272; weapons cache, 266

racism, 90–91
Ramsay, Hugh, 316
Rangel, José, 239, 245, 247–48, 252,
    258, 259
Ravel, Arthur, 116, 118, 120
Ravel, Louis, 102, 104, 116, 126
Ravel, Sam, 85, 116, 118, 124, 131, 289,
    386n; arrested, 87–88, 306
Reed, John, 20, 38
Remington Arms Company, 46
Rentería, Eusevio, 244–45, 247, 253, 258
Richley, Sgt. Jay, 215, 218, 219
Ritchie, William, 84–85, 100–101,
    116–17, 119–20, 125, 146, 250
Ritchie, Mrs. William (Laura) and
    daughters (Edna, Blanche, Myrtle),
    84–88, 100–101, 116–19, 124–25,
    136, 138, 146, 244, 256–57, 330,
    351n; compensation to, 386n; at
    trials, 315
Rivas Guillén, Lt. Col. Genovevo,
    276–77
Roach, Gloria, 328
Rockefeller investments, 15, 17
Rocky Mountain News, 145

Rodríguez, Lt. David, 316, 376n, 383n
Rodríguez, Dolores, 211, 223
Rodríguez, José, 244, 247, 253, 258–59, 312
Rodríguez, María, 315
Rodríguez, Rafael, 376n
Romero, Rev. Alfonso, 256
Roosevelt, Theodore, 32, 157, 162, 165
Rucker, Pvt. DeWitt, 285
Ruiz, Juan Ramón, 7
rules of war, 38
Ryan, Capt. James, 300, 303
Ryan, Judge Raymond, 312, 313–14, 316

Sadler, Louis, 308, 379n
Sage, Russell and Margaret Olivia, 89, 302, 321, 380n
Sala, Cesar, 65, 66–67
Salas, Col. Jorge, 186–87
Sample, Maj. W. R., 169
Sánchez, José María, 65–66, 67
Sánchez, Juan, 140, 239–40, 246–47, 251–52, 255, 256–57, 371n
Sánchez, Pablo, 142, 240, 246–47
San Pedro de la Cueva massacre, 60
Santa Fe New Mexican, 312
Santa Fe Railroad, 248
Santa Isabel. *See* train massacre
Sato, A., 291
Scott, Brig. Gen. Hugh L., 57, 90, 92, 140; acquainted with Villa, 37–38, 94, (gives him pamphlet on rules of war) 38; meets Obregón, 225, 227–32; Pershing's letters to, 288, 297, 307; and Punitive Expedition, 160–61, 163–64, 220, 291; and Slocum (Columbus affair), 299–300, 301–3
Scott, Gen. Winfield, 43
Seese, George, 91, 106, 174, 178, 320–21, 354n
Shallenberger, Martin C., 167
Sherman, Gen. William Tecumseh, 92, 164
Silvas, Louis, 381n
Silvas, Capt. Manuel, 211
Simon, Corp. Paul, 125–26, 240, 311
Simpson, (Deming sheriff), 256
Sitting Bull, 90
Slocum, Col. Herbert, 88–92, 186, 319, 321–22; and Columbus raid, 92, 94–96, 102–5, 112, 114, 124, 126–27, 133–34, 138, 333, 355n,

380n, (aftermath) 141–46, 299–303, 320, (Punitive Expedition) 172, 176; Villa's plot against, 320–21
Slocum, Mrs. Herbert (Mary), 114, 138, 144, 320–21, 355n
Slocum, Joseph Jermain, 89, 302
Slocum, Ted, 144
Smalley, Ike, 333
Smyser, Capt. Rudolph E., 84, 114, 127, 132
Smyser, Mrs. Rudolph and son Craig, 356n, 386n
Solís, Corp. Francisco, 316, 361n, 376n
Southwesterner (periodical), 380n
Spain, 14, 15, 21, 29; Cuban revolt against, 161–62
Spanish-American War, 90, 157, 162, 165, 186
Spencer, Edwin "Bunk," 138, 142, 174, 244; as hostage, 73, 110, 176, 241, 350n, (escapes) 127
Spilsbury, Lem, 178, 273–74, 275, 277, 278, 282, 284, 285
Spiritualism, 19
Standard Oil Company, 14–15
Standish, Myles, 89
Stanfield, Ozella, 137
Stedje, Capt. Jens. E., 95
Stivison, Roy E., 83, 84, 136
Stone, E. B., 138, 140, 142, 241–42, 291, 321, 344n
Stringfellow, Lt. Horace Jr., 106, 126, 127
Sweetman, Jack, 44

Taft, William Howard, 29, 34
Tarahumara Indians, 13, 211, 262, 264
Taylor, Pvt. Jesse P., 113, 359n
Teapot Dome scandal, 158, 331
Tena y Quesada, José, 376n, 383n
Terrazas, Luis, 6, 179, 226–27, 294, 361n
terrorism, 370n
Texas, 72; lost to U.S., 14, (loss resented) 38
Texas Declaration of Independence, 76
Tolstoy, Leo, 15
Tompkins, Maj. Frank, 272, 319; and Columbus raid, 93, 114, 127, 133–34, 145, 355n, (Punitive Expedition) 172, 190, 234; and Parral skirmish, 198, 206–9, 213–18, 219, 266; photograph of, xi

Tompkins, Mrs. Frank (Alice), 114, 138
Torreón, Villistas take, 36, 41
Torres, Frank, 315
Torres, Juan and Santos, 376n
Toulman, Col. H. A., 169
Tragic Ten Days, 28
train massacre, 64–70, 93, 128, 267;
 U.S. reaction to, 157–58; victims of,
 349n; Villa linked to, 91, 139, 174,
 251–52, 266
Treviño, Gen. Jacinto, 270, 272, 277,
 285, 296
Tuchman, Barbara, 41
Tumulty, Joseph, 250, 254

United States: Mexican investments by,
 14–18 *passim,* 32, 40, 61, 64, 75,
 284, 295, (as incentive to free elections) 33–34, (during revolution) 18,
 (suspected) 61; and World War I, 57,
 157. *See also* Wilson, Woodrow
United States–Mexico relations: Carranza
 and, 60–61, 208, 270; Columbus raid
 and, 157–58, 171 (*see also* Columbus
 raid); *Dolphin* incident, 42–43; El
 Paso riot, 69–70; reciprocity agreement, 160; tension, 56–57, 270, 272,
 (war feared) 157–58, 220, 223, 241,
 273–74, 283–84, 285–86, 302; train
 massacre and, 66–69; trial of Mexicans and, 241–42, 246, 250–51; U.S.
 aggressiveness: (arms embargo) 34,
 46, (invasion of Veracruz) 45–47, 51,
 57, 161, 166, (invasion plans)
 273–74, (march on Mexico City) 43,
 (territory seized) 14, (violence against
 Mexicans in U.S.) 306, (warships
 sent) 34, 272 (*see also* Punitive Expedition); Villa and, 35, 41, 58–59,
 60–61, 139–40, (his curiosity about)
 292
United States Department of State, 26,
 86, 104, 321, 326; policy, 34, 41, 92,
 94, 159
United States Justice Department, 321,
 357n
United States War Department, 37, 57,
 90, 134, 161; orders violated, 134;
 and Punitive Expedition, 160, 200,
 (invasion plans) 273–74, (new expedition denied) 222–23, (negotiations
 following) 229, 232; and Slocum,

143, 320, 321; warned about Villa,
 92, 94, 140, (offers reward for capture) 145. *See also* Army, U.S.
Urbina, Tomás, 325
Uribe, Gen. Baudelio, 295

Van Camp, E. A., 105, 174
Vargas, Silvino, 312, 376n
Vaughn, Henry, 178
Vaught, J. S., 242–44, 246, 254, 312,
 371n, 382n
Vavel, Hidado, 142
Veracruz, 26, 43–44, 51; labor strike
 suppressed in, 19; U.S. invades,
 45–47, 57, 166, (pulls out) 51, 161
vigilantism, 143, 255
Villa, Francisco "Pancho": Americans
 acquainted with, 38, 86, 91, 321;
 baptismal name, 20, (changes) 21;
 captures Juárez, 36–37; Carranza
 joins, 38–39, (breaks with, fights
 against) 47–48, 49–51, 61, 110, (deal
 with U.S. suspected) 60–61; in
 Columbus raid, 72, 79–80, 91–96,
 97, 99–100, 102–6, 110–35, (aftermath) 148–51, 300, (indicted for
 murder) 240, 241, (position shown
 on map of) 109, (in thick of) 122,
 127, 128, (whereabouts known)
 144–46; comrades of, 39–40, (loyalty
 of) 6, 62–63, 69, (loyalty betrayed,
 pretended) 10, 189; defeated, 6, 61,
 (at Agua Prieta) 59–60, 91, 110, (at
 Chihuahua) 37, (by Obregón) 52–56,
 64; education of, 36, 51; executions/
 atrocities by, 38, 41, 60, 73, 149,
 178, 244–45, 297, 310 (*see also* train
 massacre); final days and death of,
 324–27; followers of, *see* División del
 Norte; Dorados; Villistas; fortunes
 rebound, 296–98; gathers support,
 33, 36; horses of, 9–10, 39, 209; and
 Huerta, 35–36, 38, 47; "invincibility"
 of, 49, 51, 53, 73, 140, 172, (imprisoned, escapes) 35–36; as "jaguar,"
 10, 40; Madero ("Maderito") joins,
 23–25, (assassinated) 30, 35, 36; personal appearance, 20, 21, 291,
 (photograph of) x; popularity of, 63,
 68, 171, (as idol) 21, 22, 67, (song
 celebrating victories) 204–5; protects
 Americans, 41; "Punitive Expedition"

against, *see* Punitive Expedition; quoted, ix, 21, 22–23, 35, 56, 58, 63; and U.S. investments, 40, 61, 64, 295; U.S. policy and, 60–61, (Baker) 155, (Villa as "Man of the Hour") 10, (Wilson) 35, 56–59, 68; wanted dead or alive, 160, 307, (fears assassination) 62, 296, (U.S. plans assassination) 291, 296, 308; whereabouts of, 91, 93–95, 121–22, 144–46, 311–12; wounded, in hiding, 189–90, 193–96, 197, 208, 209–12, 261, 286, 291–96, (close to capture) 223–24, 303, 323; Zapata meets with, 49–51, (Villa suggests alliance) 61, 64, 139

Villa, Sra. Luz Corral de, 291–92, 294

Villistas, 47, 50, 174; attack foreign-owned property, 17, 73; Carrancistas against, *see* Carrancistas; in Columbus raid, 76, 78–79, 110–31, 133–35, (aftermath) 140–42, 148–51, (local aid to) 141; desertions by, 6, 10, 63, 73, 74, 91; vs. federal army, 36–37; imprisoned, 69, 225–26; looting by, 4, 65, 73, 115–16, 117–18, 142, 192, 281, 291, 295, 375n, (loot discarded) 135, (Villa stops) 41, 297; Maud Wright as "queen" of, 72; against Obregón, 52–56; Punitive Expedition against, 197, 199, (prisoners on trial, executed) 239–48, 249–59, 260, (wounded) 263–64 (*see also* Punitive Expedition); released by Villa, 66; troops split up, 209

Wade, Edward C. Jr., 249
Walker, J. L., 115
Walker, John Walton and Rachel, 85–86, 101–2, 116, 118–19, 124, 244, 330, 332; John's death, 119, 125, 136, (compensation) 386n
Walker, Kathryn, compensation, 386n
Warren, Francis E., 165
Washington, George, 318
Washington Post, 94, 202, 203
Walton, Charles Rea, 64–66, 67, 68, 174
White, William Allen, 161
Wilhelm II, kaiser of Germany, 41
Williams, Ben, 251, 253
Williams, Capt. George, 102, 103, 114, 128

Williams, Lt. Summer, 212
Willis, Lt. Robert, 180, 203
Wilson, Alfred Everett, 290
Wilson, Henry Lane, 16, 18–19, 26, 29–30; recalled, 32
Wilson, Woodrow, 17, 22, 35, 46–47; appeals to revolutionaries, 54; and Baker as Secretary of War, 155, 157; calls up troops, 233, 272; election campaigns, 92, 307, 308; hatred of, 289, 307; and Huerta, 31–34, 43; promotes Pershing, 306; reaction to Columbus raid, 157–60, 170, 171, 220, 231, 233, (promotes Dodd) 193, (and reprieve for prisoners) 249, 250–51, 254–55; recognizes Carranza as leader, 56, 57, 68, 157, 160, 163, 348n, (and Americans killed in ambush) 66, 68, (and Carrizal) 283–84, (refuses Carranza's demands) 272; term ends, 323, 325; and Villa, 68, 94, ("dead or alive") 160, (Villa admires) 35, (Villa betrayed by) 56, 59

Wiswell, Harry, 133
Wood, Buel, 242–46, 247, 253–54, 255, 313
World War I, 47, 57, 157, 297, 308; U.S. in, 309, 312, 319, 320; war ends, 318
World War II, 318–19, 320
Wounded Knee, massacre at, 164
Wright, Edward, 3, 4–5, 6, 7–8, 386n
Wright, Johnnie, 3, 5, 147–48, 333
Wright, Maud, 2–5, 333–34; as captive, 5–10, 62, 71–73, 110–11, 122, 127, 128, 343–44, (as "queen of the Villistas") 72; freed by Villa, 129, 132; Johnnie returned to, 147–48; as witness to Columbus raid, 244, (questioned about) 138, 241, 321
Wright, Orville, 171

Yaqui Indians, 13, 17, 53, 212, 223, 244
Young, Dave, 162
Ypiranga (munitions ship), 43, 46

Zapata, Emiliano, 26, 32, 47–48; assassinated, 322; Villa meets, 49–51, (suggests alliance) 61, 64, 139
Zapatistas, 17, 50, 61

ABOUT THE AUTHOR

Eileen Welsome is the winner of the 1994 Pulitzer Prize in national reporting and numerous other awards for her journalism. Her first book, *The Plutonium Files,* was the recipient of two PEN awards in 2000.